Finding Hot Horses

Finding Hot Horses

Vincent M. Reo

Bonus Books, Inc., Chicago

97 96 95 94 93   5 4 3 2 1

Library of Congress Catalog Card Number: 92-075930

International Standard Book Number: 0-929387-96-1

Bonus Books, Inc.
160 East Illinois Street
Chicago, Illinois 60611

Composition by Point West Inc., Carol Stream, IL
Cover photo courtesy of the Breeders' Cup
Printed in the United States of America

Contents

Class Level

1

The horse with the most money won is the classiest, right?

Wrong.

This *could* be true if we were evaluating the horse's performance throughout his career, but we are only interested in **current class**. When determined in the right fashion, class level is a great tool that pays high dividends. It can also stop you from making a betting mistake.

Obvious class is usually recognized by the betting public. When spotted, such a horse more than likely carries odds of being the favorite, but in more cases than not this horse is not the classiest. Many times drop downs will appear to be better than they are. Horses that take suspicious drops in class are usually sore, hurt, or just not the horse they were at one time.

One way of determining class level is knowing the conditions of the races that a horse has been running in. Conditions are the parameters that a horse must meet to be entered. (This subject will be covered later in this chapter.)

How do we analyze a horse to find his true class level? Frozen Dew is a good example.

Frozen Dew — Gr. g. 5, by Zoot Alors—Sweet Jenny, by Aloha Mood

$13,000 Br.—Winchell Verne H (Ky)

Tr.—Garcia Efrain T (310 71 39 40 .23)

Own.—Lojeski Shirley A

115

Lifetime								
46 16 7 4	1992	13	3	1	2	$28,614
$196,621	1991	12	4	4	0	$69,135
	Wet	6	1	0	1	$9,639

27Oct92- 4Pha	fst	6f	:222	:46	1:111	3↑Clm 16000	80	1	4	31½	52¼	21	31	Cruz C	L	115	*1.70	84-19	Jill's Prospect116½ Alsway117½ Frozen Dew115	Hung	7
17Oct92- 7Pha	fst	6½f	:222	:453	1:18	3↑Clm 16000	87	1	8	52¼	53¼	2½	11¼	Cruz C	L	112	4.30	88-20	FrozenDew1121¼FestivColony1151¼MnilHmp116	Driving	9
3Oct92- 5Pha	fst	7f	:221	:45	1:23	3↑Clm 20000	77	6	3	43	43½	25	38½	Cruz C	L	112	2.80	83-16	InMsrdBt1198HollywodZs114½FrznDw112	Outside, tired	6
16Aug92- 5Pha	sly	6f	:222	:454	1:103	3↑Clm 15000	80	3	4	1½	1½	11½	12¼	Cruz C	L	116	*1.00	88-19	FroznDw1162¼ArgntnEmpror122¾ImplsvPrnc116	Driving	5
6Aug92- 6Pha	fst	6f	:214	:444	1:101	3↑Clm 15000	86	3	8	74¼	75¼	33	2nk	Cruz C	L	116	13.20	90-18	FestiveColony115nkFrozenDw1166RomnStrt113	Fin fast	10
27Jly92- 6Pha	fst	6½f	:222	:452	1:164	3↑Clm 15000	70	5	6	67½	66½	57½	410½	Cruz C	L	116	4.70	83-17	ChrlYouKnow1163VslSgnl1224½PromsdLd122	No threat	8
1Jly92- 6Mth	fst	6f	:212	:444	1:111	3↑Clm 25000	56	3	8	811	812	89¼	810¼	Black A S	L	116	3.90	75-17	RinbowQurtz1161ClnndBold116¾ExcutvBd116	No threat	8
5Apr92- 8Pha	fst	6f	:221	:453	1:102	Batty	77	3	4	53¼	54½	56½	56	Cruz C	L	120	10.30	83-19	RockbyeJoshu1221Jwlr'sChoic1162½Pstn'Ps118	No rally	8
29Feb92- 8Pha	fst	6f	:223	:463	1:121	Alw 23833	63	4	1	11½	2½	35	610¾	Madrigal R Jr	L	119	8.30	69-28	Jy'sFrstJv1197MyOthrBrthr116noHtthMhgn119	Stopped	7

LATEST WORKOUTS Nov 7 Pha 3f fst :37 B Oct 11 Pha 4f fst :503 B Sep 25 Pha 4f fst :491 B Sep 19 Pha 5f fst 1:021 B

Frozen Dew has been victorious sixteen times out of forty-six and has earned $196,621. The first step in determining class level is looking back at the horse's most recent five starts. These starts have to be at today's distance, or a closely related distance. These starts cannot reach back in time more than three months.

If we go back five starts on Frozen Dew, this takes us to July 27, 1992. On that day, Frozen Dew finished fourth. At this point Frozen Dew's class level is under claiming $15,000, since he did not win. His performance by finishing second on August 6th moved him closer to the class level of $15,000 claimings, but he's not quite there yet. On August 16, 1992, a victory put him on that level and he looked to go further up on October 3rd. On October 3rd, Frozen Dew finished third in a claiming $20,000 event. This performance raised his class level from the established $15,000 to somewhere between $15,000 and $20,000. We now know that Frozen Dew has the class to win at $15,000 and not enough to win at $20,000. This would make his class level approximately $17,500. Frozen Dew's victory on October 17th reconfirmed our class level analysis of $17,500.

Horses must win to establish a base class level. If a horse runs consistently second and third then this particular horse has not reached the class level at which he is currently running.

A horse who has never won anything but a maiden race has only its maiden win as a class level base. This can lead to underlays when these horses are dropped down. Take the example of Mount Titan.

Mount Titan accomplished virtually nothing in his first seven starts, but he was regularly bet down below 6-1 on five of those occasions. On September 26, Mount Titan was dropped from maiden claiming $30,000 where he finished last, beaten by twenty-five

Mount Titan

B. g. 2(Feb), by Titanic—Mountmessene, by Mount Hagen

$11,000 Br.—Elphand George Partnership (Fla)

Tr.—Lotti Gene A Jr (15 3 2 2 .20)

Own.—Elphand George

115

Lifetime 7 0 0 1 $1,685 | 1992 7 M 0 1 $1,685 | Wet 1 0 0 0 $70

7Oct92- 3Med	fst	6f	:23	$:46^{4}$	$1:12^{2}$	Md 14000	16	7	5	$5^{2\frac{1}{2}}$	$7^{6\frac{1}{4}}$	$6^{8\frac{3}{4}}$	$6^{14\frac{1}{4}}$	Vega A	L	114	3.30	67-12	Half Cat114$^{2\frac{1}{2}}$ TonyRay118^{nk}ElGuillermo118	Wide, tired	9
26Sep92- 1Med	sly	6f	$:22^{3}$	$:46^{2}$	$1:12^{4}$	Md 14000	30	8	2	7^{3}	7^{7}	$7^{8\frac{1}{2}}$	$6^{7\frac{1}{4}}$	Vega A	L	114	4.70	72-11	WldMstng118^{1}ExltdDstny118$^{\frac{3}{4}}$PrsnSrgon114	Wide, lane	10
25Aug92- 5Mth	fst	6f	$:21^{4}$	$:45^{1}$	$1:11^{4}$	Md 30000	6	2	5	$4^{2\frac{1}{4}}$	6^{9}	8^{16}	$8^{25\frac{3}{4}}$	Ramos A	b	115	26.90	56-17	Jade Carving118^{6}Timeforathrill115$^{3\frac{3}{4}}$Entroski118	Faded	8
22Jly92- 6Bel	fst	$5\frac{1}{2}$f	$:22^{2}$	$:45^{4}$	$1:05^{1}$	Md 45000	31	1	1	3^{3}	5^{5}	$6^{6\frac{1}{4}}$	8^{13}	Krone J A	b	114	9.10e	76-14	CrclTrck118$^{7\frac{1}{4}}$MstrBomBm118$^{\frac{1}{2}}$JHrtwck118	Brief speed	10
9Jly92- 4Bel	fst	$5\frac{1}{2}$f	$:22^{3}$	$:45^{3}$	$1:04^{3}$	Md 45000	39	10	4	3^{3}	5^{8}	$7^{9\frac{1}{2}}$	$8^{11\frac{3}{4}}$	Bailey J D		114	3.40e	80-14	ThrillCourier114$^{2\frac{1}{2}}$MrSledg114^{4}CirclTrick118	Thru early	10
1Jly92- 4Bel	gd	$5\frac{1}{2}$f	$:22^{2}$	$:46^{2}$	$1:05^{2}$	Md 35000	59	5	1	$1^{\frac{1}{2}}$	$1^{\frac{1}{2}}$	$3^{\frac{1}{2}}$	$3^{3\frac{1}{2}}$	Krone J A		118	4.60	84-11	DstnctvDn118^{no}JHrtwck114$^{3\frac{1}{2}}$MntTtn118	Dueled inside	7
27May92- 4Bel	fst	5f	$:22^{3}$	$:46^{2}$	$:58^{4}$	Md 70000	26	7	7	$5^{2\frac{1}{4}}$	$6^{2\frac{1}{2}}$	$6^{4\frac{3}{4}}$	$6^{11\frac{1}{4}}$	Krone J A		114	5.90	76-13	UntdPrspct114$^{1\frac{1}{2}}$LcFvrt118$^{1\frac{3}{4}}$OnThBrdl114	Broke slowly	7

LATEST WORKOUTS ●Sep 16 Mth 4f fst $:48^{3}$ H Sep 10 Mth 5f fst $1:02^{1}$ B

Courtesy of Daily Racing Form ©

lengths. On this night the public bet Mount Titan down to 5-1. Why? Did Mount Titan improve in his last start? No! The reason for this betting was because of his drop in class. Just because Mount Titan is dropped in class does not mean he is going to win. Mount Titan's class level might be maiden claiming $5,000. Until he reaches a level where he can win, obviously he will never win. If Mount Titan was consistently running third and fourth in maiden claiming $30,000 then the drop would warrant his chance to do better. But there is still a risk because he does not have a winning base level.

Now let's examine Dr. Fountainstein's form.

Dr Fountainstein

B. g. 3(Apr), by Fountain Of Gold—Malani, by Battleamal

$5,000 Br.—Wiltse Georganne J (Fla)

Tr.—Dowd John F (10 0 0 0 .00)

Own.—Tombs K & W

116

Lifetime 7 2 0 2 $55,430 | 1992 3 0 0 0 $930 | 1991 4 2 0 2 $54,500 | Wet 1 0 0 0 $125

24Oct92- 7Med	sly	6f	$:22^{1}$	:45	$1:10^{2}$	Clm 25000	30	5	4	$4^{4\frac{1}{2}}$	7^{10}	7^{12}	$7^{22\frac{1}{4}}$	Sousonis S		116	11.10	69-09	Contarito113^{no} Blazing Cat117^{nk} Sacre Bleu116	Outrun	7
2Oct92- 5Med	fst	6f	:22	$:44^{3}$	$1:09^{4}$	Clm 25000	75	7	3	$3^{3\frac{1}{2}}$	3^{3}	$3^{4\frac{1}{2}}$	$4^{3\frac{1}{2}}$	Sousonis S		116	7.60	90-11	WildDnte114$^{\frac{1}{2}}$ScrBlu116$^{\frac{3}{4}}$Dvil'sDoom116	Lacked fin bid	8
6Sep92- 8Mth	fst	6f	$:21^{3}$	$:44^{3}$	$1:10^{1}$	3↑Alw 18000	50	4	3	$4^{2\frac{1}{4}}$	$5^{5\frac{1}{2}}$	7^{10}	$7^{15\frac{3}{4}}$	Gryder A T	b	112	2.30	74-12	JtFrth113$^{1\frac{3}{4}}$FrtNnSmls112$^{1\frac{1}{2}}$Dvl'sDm112	Wide, gave way	7
13Sep91- 8Med	fst	6f	:22	$:44^{4}$	$1:11^{3}$	Jonthn Daytn	78	1	3	1^{hd}	1^{hd}	1^{1}	$1^{\frac{1}{2}}$	Gryder A T	b	112	*1.10	84-14	DrFtst112$^{\frac{1}{2}}$EstblshdL114$^{3\frac{1}{4}}$ThrtEtCrt121	Drifted out,lstd	5
10Aug91- 9Mth	fst	6f	:22	$:45^{1}$	$1:10^{4}$	Sapling	77	1	7	$1^{1\frac{1}{2}}$	1^{hd}	2^{hd}	3^{5}	Ferrer J C	b	122	8.30	82-18	BigSur122^{2}NvrWvring122^{3}Dr.Fountinstin122	Weakened	8
10Aug91-Grade II																					
28Jly91- 9Mth	fst	$5\frac{1}{2}$f	:22	$:44^{4}$	$1:03^{4}$	Tyro	78	2	4	2^{hd}	$2^{2\frac{1}{2}}$	3^{4}	3^{3}	Ramos W S		116	7.20	97-10	ThnsTRnd118$^{\frac{1}{2}}$GldmnrsDrm116$^{2\frac{1}{2}}$DrFntnstn116	Good try	6
10Jly91-10Mth	fst	$5\frac{1}{2}$f	$:22^{4}$	$:46^{1}$	$1:05^{1}$	Md 30000	77	11	2	$2^{\frac{1}{2}}$	1^{hd}	1^{1}	1^{9}	Toscano P R		118	*2.30	93-11	Dr.Fountnstn118^{9}Clrwy118^{4}SlpngFox118	Much the best	12

LATEST WORKOUTS Oct 15 Med 3f fst $:36^{1}$ Bg ●Sep 20 Med 5f fst $1:01^{3}$ B

Courtesy of Daily Racing Form ©

An equation to remember:

DROP DOWNS = LOW ODDS = NEVER WINNING

Dr. Fountainstein was supposed to be a very good horse and was on that path until he got hurt. Dr. Fountainstein made his first start of 1992 at Monmouth Park. He ran seventh in an Allowance $18,000 event. He then ran fourth and seventh in claiming races for $25,000.

Apparently, Dr. Fountainstein is not the horse he was last year. On November 6, 1992, Dr. Fountainstein was entered in a claiming $5,000 event. His owner and trainer had obviously given up on him. Sore and not having any class left are good words to describe this three-year-old gelding. Still, as a result of the drop in class, the public sent him off at 4-1. In return Dr. Fountainstein ran a dismal fourth.

Don't get sucked into suspicious droppers.

As we've mentioned, conditions are the parameters of any given horse race. If the conditions state that all horses have to be non-winners of three races lifetime, obviously, if a horse has won five races, he could not be allowed to enter. What does this have to do with class level? When determining a horse's class level, knowing who and what kind of competition a particular horse is running against is quite advantageous. A good example of this is Silent Wizard.

Silent Wizard — **Ro. f. 3(Jun), by Westheimer—Reel Sterling, by Silent Screen**
$5,000 **Br.—Wisniewski Mary F (Mo)**
Own.—Barbuto Vincent — **Tr.—Sofio Peter (2 0 0 0 .00)** — **112**

Lifetime	1992	13	4	0	0	$11,375
18 4 2 2	1991	5	M	2	2	$3,455
$14,830	Turf	1	0	0	0	
	Wet	2	0	1	0	$992

24Sep92-	8Med	fst	6f	:22	:45^2	1:11^2		ⒻClm 18000	2	3	6	4^6	6^{8½}	7^{18}	7^{26½}	Sousonis S	Lb	114	29.60	59-13	AngelTop108^{5}DressdtoGo113^{1}Hvn'sADrm113	Gave way	7
20Sep92-	7Mth	fst	6f	:21^4	:45^2	1:12^2		ⒻClm 10500	3	2	7	4^{2½}	7^{12}	8^{21}	8^{26½}	Barbazon D S	Lb	114	10.10	52-16	OnfrDrthy115^{nk}CrftyGyps115^{4½}HlfMnHtl110	Thru early	8
17Sep92-	7Med	fst	6f	:22^1	:45^1	1:10^2	3↑	ⒻClm 20000	43	4	8	6^{2¾}	6^{5¾}	6^9	6^{12½}	Chavis S T	Lb	112	43.10	78-12	MrnflMsc114^{no}MnrNrth119^{nk}Flrfrlxndr116	Bmpd break	8
11Aug92-	8Atl	sly	1$\frac{1}{16}$	:47	1.12^3	1:40	3↑	ⒻAlw 8200	26	7	4	2^{1½}	2^4	6^{12}	6^{20½}	Rodriguez R B	Lb	114	*2.80	49-28	Yieldtonone113½TwoElvir's115^{4½}PrincessShng116	Tired	7
11Aug92-Originally scheduled on turf																							
6Aug92-	8Atl	fst	5½f	:21^4	:46^3	1:05	3↑	ⒻAlw 12500s	64	1	7	7^{7¾}	7^9	6^{6¾}	4^3	Rodriguez RB^5	Lb	109	12.60e	89-17	Rchl'sTurn117^{2¼}HorrblGft122¾FourPnch114	Some gain	7
21Jly92-	5Atl	fst	5½f	:22	:45^4	1:04^4		ⒻClm c-5500	68	4	4	2^{hd}	2½	1^{2½}	1^{2¼}	Umana J L^5	Lb	116	*.60	93-10	SilntWzrd116^{2¼}Pupp114^{1½}DmondsOnmyMnd118	Driving	6
21Jly92-Claimed from King Julie A, King Julie A Trainer																							
10Jly92-	9Atl	fst	6f	:22	:45^3	1:11^4	3↑	ⒻClm 5000	68	1	6	2^1	1^{hd}	1^{hd}	1^2	Azeff Y	Lb	115	*1.40	87-14	SilentWizard115^{2}SweetSide119^{2¾}Lulu'sDnce112	Driving	7
24Jun92-	11Del	fst	6f	:22	:45^4	1:11^3		ⒻClm 6500	72	4	3	1½	1^5	1^9	1^{8½}	Umana J L^5	Lb	111	*1.10	89-25	SilentWizrd111^{8½}Sol'sGirl122^{4½}SfuzziExpress116	Sharp	5
17Jun92-	4Del	fst	5½f	:22	:46	1:04^4	3↑	Clm 7500	43	2	7	6^{5¼}	6^7	6^8	6^{10}	Muino D R	Lb	108	5.70	81-18	JstApprsl114^{3}Snh'sStr116^{1¼}Yrsnfrt114	Brk in air,chckd	7
7Jun92-	10Del	fm	5f	Ⓣ:22	:46^2	:59^2		ⒻAlw 9000	52	2	10	10^{9¾}	10^{11}	9^{10}	9^{7¾}	Muino D R	Lb	119	12.10	79-12	I Do Dazzel114^1 Clever Slote119^{nk}Carol'sEcho114	Wide	10

LATEST WORKOUTS **Oct 7 Pen 3f fst :36^1 B** **Sep 14 Med 4f fst :49 B**

Courtesy of Daily Racing Form ©

Silent Wizard was entered on June 17, 1992, at the claiming $7,500 level. This race's conditions were non-winners of three in the last thirty days. This means if a horse won two races in the last thirty days, that horse would be able to run in these conditions. Such a horse would be a monster compared to a horse with only a maiden win to her credit. Silent Wizard was in over her head. She beat only one horse. The misadvised public sent the filly off at 6-1 because of her drop down in class. This race was also against boys. This is signified by the absence of a filly mark in front of the claiming amount.

She was badly outrun and finished sixth, beaten by ten lengths. Silent Wizard was then dropped into a claiming $6,500 race for three year old fillies that had not won two races lifetime. This race was much easier and it showed in her eight and one-half length victory. On July 10, 1992, at Atlantic City she met three-year-olds and up, fillies and mares at a claiming tag of $5,000. This race consisted of non-winners of three races lifetime. She responded by winning by two lengths. Her next race was against non-winners of four lifetime. She was victorious there, too.

After that start Silent Wizard faced open company. There are no more non-winners conditions after a horse has won four races. It appears to the naked eye that the wins in claiming $6,500, $5,000, $5,000 are in the same company as her race on October 26, 1992. There Silent Wizard went off as the 5-2 co-favorite. She tired to seventh and was beaten by fourteen lengths.

In our first example, the $50,000 added Moccasin Stakes at Belmont Park on June 3, 1992, the field consisted of three maidens, three maiden winners and one stakes winner.

D'Accordress	B. f. 2(Mar), by D'Accord—Quick Results, by Icecapade		Lifetime	1992 3 2 0 1	$32,240
PERRET C (23 5 1 4 .22)	Br.—Bright View Farm Inc (NJ)		3 2 0 1		
Own.—Boiko John	Tr.—Dowd John F (1 0 0 0 .00)	**121**	$32,240		
				Wet 1 1 0 0	$15,240
16May92-10Suf fst 5f :22³ :46³ :59³	Paul Revere	64 7 1 1¹ 1½ 3½ 31½ Sousonis S	119 *1.10	99-16 DncsWthFr116½ErthnsFn114½DAccrdrss119	Alt crse str 10
3May92-10Suf my 5f :22³ :47⁴ 1:01¹	ⓟPriscilla	58 1 2 1³ 1⁴ 1⁹ 18½ Sousonis S	119 *.50	92-14 D'Accordress119⁸½ RailroadLady119¹⁵Anzarro112	Easily 4
14Apr92- 4Aqu fst 4½f :22³ :46³ :53	ⓕMd Sp Wt	54 2 1 2½ 11½ 1⁵ Sousonis S	117 *1.20	95-12 D'Accordrss117⁵ScrtBundl117⁴Infrstructur117	Drew off 7
LATEST WORKOUTS	May 30 Mth 5f fst 1:01 B	May 23 Mth 5f fst 1:02² B	Apr 25 Suf 5f sly 1:02² B	Apr 9 GS 3f fst :37 B	

Courtesy of Daily Racing Form ©

Icy Warning, Turcomedy, and Anquilla Holiday were all maidens when entered in the Moccasin Stakes. Icy Warning and Anquilla Holiday both made their second starts against Tropico Cielo. Since there are no excuses for either of them, Tropico Cielo must be given the class edge over Icy Warning and Anquilla Holiday because she has beaten them both easily before.

Turcomedy raced in three maiden races, finishing second every time. She could be a factor in a maiden special weight contest but should not be in stakes competition.

The three maiden special weight winners consisted of High Berger, Tropico Cielo, and Artful Pleasure.

High Berger and Artful Pleasure both graduated at Philadelphia Park. Both of them beat much lesser horses in their graduating races. High Berger would have more class than Artful Pleasure for the simple reason that High Berger ran against and beat the boys.

Tropico Cielo has beaten two competitors in this stakes race and should be chasing the top choice.

D'Accordress is that top choice. D'Accordress began her career with a five length victory at four and one-half furlongs. She was shipped to Suffolk Downs and came up with an impressive victory in the Priscilla Stakes for fillies in the mud.

Then, D'Accordress took on the boys in the Paul Revere Stakes. If it wasn't for some traffic in the stretch she would have been battling to the end in that contest.

D'Accordress was the class horse in the Moccasin Stakes because of her proven ability in stakes company. D'Accordress would not have been the class horse just because she was entered in these stakes races. Her ability shown in these races put her at the top. Another factor: the competition in the those stakes races that D'Accordress participated in have gone on to win against better.

5 ½ FURLONGS. (1.03) 1st Running THE MOCCASIN STAKE Purse $50,000 Added. Fillies, 2–year–olds. By subscription of $100 each, which should accompany the nominations; $100 to pass the entry box. $200 to start, with $50,000 added. The added money and all fees to be divided 60% to the winner, 22% to second, 12% to the third and 6% to fourth. 121 lbs. Non–winners of a race other than Maiden or Claiming allowed 3 lbs.; other than claiming, 5 lbs. Maiden, 7 lbs. A trophy will be presented to the owner of the winner. Closed Sunday, May 24 with 17 nominations.

High Berger
COLTON R E (—)
Own.—Green Leonard C
Dk. b. or br. f. 2(May), by High Brite—Wild Beat, by Iron Ruler
Br.—Crompton Kathleen (Pa)
Tr.—Contessa Gary C (6 0 0 0 .00)
Lifetime 1992 1 1 0 0 $8,100
1 1 0 0
$8,100
118
22May92- 5Pha fst 4½f :22² :46 :52² Md Sp Wt 63 2 2 13 15 14 Lloyd J S 115 2.30 99–15 HighBergr115⁴CountOnPrinc118²¼Sl'snw118 Ridden out 5
LATEST WORKOUTS May 31 Mth 4f gd :48² H May 20 Mth 3f fst :37 B Apr 24 Bel 4f fst :49³ Bg Apr 9 Bel tr.t 3f fst :38 B

Icy Warning
CHAVEZ J F (18 12 13 7 .14)
Own.—Ryehill Farm
Ro. f. 2(Apr), by Caveat—Northern Sting, by Northern Jove
Br.—Ryehill Farm (Md)
Tr.—Boniface J William (2 0 0 1 .00)
Lifetime 1992 2 M 1 1 $8,160
2 0 1 1
$8,160
114
24May92- 4Bel fst 5f :21⁴ :45² :58¹ ⓜMd Sp Wt 72 7 6 78¼ 75¼ 66¼ 33 Chavez J F 117 3.20 87–11 TropcoClo117²AnguilHoldy117¹IcyWrnng117 Fin strong 8
23Apr92- 4Aqu gd 4½f :23 :46² :52³ ⓜMd Sp Wt 57 7 7 21 2¼ 2¹ Reynolds R L 117 4.10e 96–12 SecretBundl117¹IcyWrning117²EgrEcdysist117 Greenly 7
LATEST WORKOUTS Apr 11 Del 4f fst :49⁴ Hg ●Apr 5 Del 4f fst :48¹ Hg

Panama Jane
MADRID A JR (18 5 11 7 .87)
Own.—Rice Linda
B. f. 2(Feb), by Perrault—Goodness Sakes, by The Real McCoy
Br.—Forbush Richard J (Ky)
Tr.—Rice Linda (9 1 1 1 .11)
Lifetime 1992 1 M 1 0 $5,280
1 0 1 0
$5,280
114
14May92- 4Bel fst 5f :22 :45 :57² ⓜMd Sp Wt 67 2 3 2¹ 2¹ 2³ 23¼ Madrid A Jr 117 22.00 90–08 DistinctHbit117³¼PnmJn117¹¼BtthWorld117 In tight tn 8
LATEST WORKOUTS May 6 Bel 4f fst :48⁴ Hg Apr 29 Bel 4f fst :48 Hg Apr 22 Bel tr.t 3f my :37⁴ B Apr 16 Bel tr.t 3f fst :40 B

Tropico Cielo
BAILEY J D (77 14 18 8 .18)
Own.—Canonie Anthony Jr
B. f. 2(Jan), by Secreto—Distant Rose, by Distant Day
Br.—Berger Bob & Calumet Farm (NC)
Tr.—Hough Stanley M (13 3 2 4 .23)
Lifetime 1992 1 1 0 0 $14,400
1 1 0 0
$14,400
118
24May92- 4Bel fst 5f :21⁴ :45² :58¹ ⓜMd Sp Wt 81 2 2 21¼ 2¼ 12 1² Bailey J D 117 *1.10 90–11 TropicoCilo117²AnguillHoldy117¹IcyWrning117 Driving 8
LATEST WORKOUTS May 31 Bel 3f fst :36¹ B May 18 Bel 5f fst 1:00¹ Hg May 13 Bel 4f fst :47 Hg

Real Zeal B. f. 2(Apr), by Unreal Zeal—Here's to Reality, by Sunny Clime
VELAZQUEZ J R (92 9 17 13 .10) Br.—Jan Siegel, Mace Siegel & Samantha (Fla) **114**
Own.—Siegel Jan Tr.—Mayberry Brian A (1 0 0 0 .00)
Lifetime 2 0 1 1 $4,830 | 1992 2 M 1 1 $4,830 | Wet 1 0 1 0 $3,530
9May92- 1CD sly 5f :23^2 :48 1:01^2 ⒻMd Sp Wt 49 4 1 2½ 1^1 3^{1½} 2^1 Peck B D LB 118 4.00 85-22 Hono'sHoney118^{1}RelZel118^{1}ShdedHert118 Second best 8
8Apr92- 2Kee fst 4½f :23^1 :47 :53 ⒻMd Sp Wt 24 1 2 2^{1½} 3^{4½} 3^{8½} Perret C 117 *.80e 85-09 ZelousndTrue117^{2½}Turcomdy117^{6}RIZI117 Used up early 5
LATEST WORKOUTS May 29 Bel 4f fst :47^2 H

Turcomedy Ch. f. 2(Apr), by Turkoman—Grecian Comedy, by Fast Hilarious
KRONE J A (119 22 26 13 .18) Br.—Lindh Henry C B & Humphrey R Watts (Ky) **114**
Own.—Mowat David A Tr.—Pierce Joseph H Jr (3 0 0 2 .00)
Lifetime 3 0 3 0 $11,520 | 1992 3 M 3 0 $11,520
4May92- 5Aqu fst 4½f :22^3 :46^3 :53 ⒻMd Sp Wt 65 2 1 3^{1½} 2^2 2^{1½} Krone J A 117 2.30 93-11 EgrEcdysst117^{1½}Trcomdy117^{1½}SprBowlGold117 Gamely 8
22Apr92- 4Kee fst 4½f :22^4 :46^2 :52^1 ⒻMd Sp Wt 48 3 6 7^{4½} 4^{6½} 2^8 Day P 117 *.70 90-11 Clarwithaflare117^{8}Turcomedy117½Fanciflir117 Mild bid 11
8Apr92- 2Kee fst 4½f :23^1 :47 :53 ⒻMd Sp Wt 45 2 3 4^{4½} 2^3 2^{2½} Day P 117 1.40 91-09 ZelousndTru117^{2½}Turcomdy117^{6}RIZI117 St'd'd, gamely 5
LATEST WORKOUTS May 30 Mth 4f fst :49 B May 25 Mth 4f fst :49 B Apr 18 Kee 4f fst :51^2 B

D'Accordress B. f. 2(Mar), by D'Accord—Quick Results, by Icecapade
PERRET C (23 5 1 4 .22) Br.—Bright View Farm Inc (NJ) **121**
Own.—Boiko John Tr.—Dowd John F (1 0 0 0 .00)
Lifetime 3 2 0 1 $32,240 | 1992 3 2 0 1 $32,240 | Wet 1 1 0 0 $15,240
16May92-10Suf fst 5f :22^3 :46^3 :59^3 Paul Revere 64 7 1 1^1 1½ 3½ 3^{1¼} Sousonis S 119 *1.10 99-16 DncsWthFr116½ErthnsFn114¾DAccrdrss119 Alt crse str 10
3May92-10Suf my 5f :22^3 :47^4 1:01^1 ⒻPriscilla 58 1 2 1^3 1^4 1^9 1^{8½} Sousonis S 119 *.50 92-14 D'Accordress119^{8½} RailroadLady119^{15}Anzarro112 Easily 4
14Apr92- 4Aqu fst 4½f :22^3 :46^3 :53 ⒻMd Sp Wt 54 2 1 2½ 1^{1½} 1^5 Sousonis S 117 *1.20 95-12 D'Accordrss117^{5}ScrtBundl117^{4}Infrstructur117 Drew off 7
LATEST WORKOUTS May 30 Mth 5f fst 1:01 B May 23 Mth 5f fst 1:02^2 B Apr 25 Suf 5f sly 1:02^2 B Apr 9 GS 3f fst :37 B

Artful Pleasure Ch. f. 2(Apr), by Nasty and Bold—Clever But Costly, by Clever Trick
ANTLEY C W (112 21 5 13 .19) Br.—Conway James D (Ky) **118**
Own.—Williams Arthur Tr.—Reid Mark J (14 5 0 4 .36)
Lifetime 1 1 0 0 $8,100 | 1992 1 1 0 0 $8,100
18May92- 4Pha fst 4½f :22^3 :46^2 :52^2 ⒻMd Sp Wt 60 4 2 2^1 2^{1½} 1^{1¾} Lloyd J S 118 4.60 99-15 ArtfulPlesure118^{1¾}MedievlAnne118^{12}Vivenci118 Driving 10
LATEST WORKOUTS Jun 1 Pha 3f sly :38^4 B May 13 Pha 5f fst 1:02 Bg May 6 Pha 4f fst :48^4 B Apr 29 Pha 4f fst :49^4 B

Anguilla Holiday B. f. 2(Mar), by Lear Fan—Angalia, by Damascus
ROJAS R I (59 5 4 9 .08) Br.—Thompson Roland E (Ky) **114**
Own.—Sweedler Joseph Tr.—Figueroa Carlos R Jr (7 1 4 0 .14)
Lifetime 2 0 1 0 $5,280 | 1992 2 M 1 0 $5,280
24May92- 4Bel fst 5f :21^4 :45^2 :58^1 ⒻMd Sp Wt 75 5 4 3^3 4^{1½} 2^2 2^2 Rojas R I 117 16.50 88-11 TropcoClo117^{2}AngllHldy117^{1}IcyWrnng117 Rallied wide 8
4May92- 5Aqu fst 4½f :22^3 :46^3 :53 ⒻMd Sp Wt 50 4 6 7^9 5^{7½} 5^6 Rojas R I 117 30.40 89-11 EgrEcdysst117^{1½}Trcmdy117^{1½}SprBlGld117 Took up brk 8
LATEST WORKOUTS ●May 13 Aqu 5f fst 1:00^4 H May 1 Aqu 4f fst :51^1 Bg

SIXTH RACE
Belmont
JUNE 3, 1992

5 ½ FURLONGS. (1.03) 1st Running THE MOCCASIN STAKE. Purse $50,000 Added. Fillies, 2-year-olds. By subscription of $100 each, which should accompany the nominations; $100 to pass the entry box. $200 to start, with $50,000 added. The added money and all fees to be divided 60% to the winner, 22% to second, 12% to the third and 6% to fourth. 121 lbs. Non-winners of a race other than Maiden or Claiming allowed 3 lbs.; other than claiming, 5 lbs. Maiden, 7 lbs. A trophy will be presented to the owner of the winner. Closed Sunday, May 24 with 17 nominations.

Value of race $54,000; value to winner $32,400; second $11,880; third $6,480; fourth $3,240. Mutuel pool $197,424. Exacta Pool $433,508

Last Raced	Horse	M/Eqt.A.Wt	PP	St	¼	⅜	Str	Fin	Jockey	Odds $1
16May92 10Suf^3	D'Accordress	2 121	5	5	3^1	3½	2^{1½}	1^{2¾}	Perret C	2.60
4May92 5Aqu^2	Turcomedy	2 114	4	2	6^{hd}	5½	3^{1½}	2½	Krone J A	16.00
24May92 4Bel^1	Tropico Cielo	2 118	3	3	2^3	2^1	1½	3^1	Bailey J D	.90
18May92 4Pha^1	Artful Pleasure	2 118	6	6	7	6^{hd}	4^{hd}	4^{hd}	Antley C W	19.00
24May92 4Bel^2	Anguilla Holiday	2 114	7	7	4^1	4^1	5½	5no	Rojas R I	15.80
24May92 4Bel^3	Icy Warning	2 114	2	4	5½	7	6^2	6^{11}	Chavez J F	5.00
22May92 5Pha^1	High Berger	2 118	1	1	1^{hd}	1^{hd}	7	7	Colton R	11.50

OFF AT 3:31 Start good. Won driving. Time, :22 , :46 , 1:05^2 Track fast.

$2 Mutuel Prices:

7-(G)-D'ACCORDRESS	7.20	4.00	3.00
6-(F)-TURCOMEDY		7.80	3.20
4-(D)-TROPICO CIELO			2.20

$2 EXACTA 7-6 PAID $83.80

B. f, (Mar), by D'Accord—Quick Results, by Icecapade. Trainer Dowd John F. Bred by Bright View Farm Inc (NJ).
D'ACCORDRESS, settled just behind the early leaders, circled four wide rallying into the stretch, accelerated to the front inside the furlong marker then drew clear under brisk uring. TURCOMEDY, unhurried for a half, closed well between horses to gain the place. TROPICO CIELO forced the pace from outside fo ra half, surged to the front in upper stretch then weakened under pressure in the final eighth. ARTFUL PLEASURE outrun for a half, advanced five wide into the stretch then rallied mildly in the middle of the track. ANGUILLA HOLIDAY raced within striking distance while four wide for a half then tired. ICY WARNING never reached contention. HIGH BERGER dueled along the rail into upper stretch and gave way.
Owners— 1, Boiko John; 2, Mowat David A; 3, Canonie Anthony Jr; 4, Williams Arthur; 5, Double S Stable; 6, Ryehill Farm; 7, Green Leonard C.
Trainers— 1, Dowd John F; 2, Pierce Joseph H Jr; 3, Hough Stanley M; 4, Reid Mark J; 5, Figueroa Carlos R Jr; 6, Boniface J William; 7, Contessa Gary C.
Scratched—Panama Jane (14May92 4Bel2); Real Zeal (9May92 1CD2).

Smart bettors who watch silly bettors bet foolish money. The forty-first running of the Miss Woodford Breeders Cup Handicap is a perfect example of ignoring the obvious. In a six horse field one horse stood out and could not be ignored.

Debra's Victory was shipping in from Woodbine. First of all, **Woodbine horses are generally better than the horses on the East Coast.** Her track record would run circles around her competition today. Debra's Victory has compiled a record of 10-7-2-0 and earnings of over $340,000. Debra's Victory has carried significant amounts of weight. Even though she is top weight here, she is still dropping five pounds. Also, as we handicap Debra's Victory we see that she made the very difficult transition from two to three very easy by winning her first three starts as a three-year-old. She ran second in her last start, losing by a neck. Debra's Victory had been racing mostly in state-bred competition in 1991. When she started racing in 1992 she successfully tackled open company with ease. That's what I call a difficult transition.

Not To Be Outdone might have been the main competition if this race was at this time last year. Not To Be Outdone had a semi-successful campaign in 1991, but she is a changed horse in 1992, so we must reevaluate her new class level. In her first start of the year Not To Be Outdone faded after leading against three-year-olds in Allowance $20,000 company. In this start, she ran a slow first half in :47 and if she had what she had last year, she would have pulled away and won for fun. After this performance, Not To Be Outdone's class level is below the $20,000 allowance level. She is in way over her head in the race we are studying.

Marilyn's Magic is a hard-hitting three-year-old filly coming off a victory at the claiming $75,000 level at Belmont. This victory might have been enhanced by the sloppy track conditions. Marilyn's Magic

8 6 FURLONGS MONMOUTH PARK START FINISH

6 FURLONGS. **(1.08) 41st Running. MISS WOODFORD BREEDERS' CUP HANDICAP Purse $60,000 added. (Includes $25,000 from Breeders' Cup Fund). Fillies, 3-year-olds. By subscription of $50 each which should accompany the nomination, $200 to pass the entry box, $150 to start with $35,000 added and an additional $25,000 from the Breeders Cup Fund for Cup nominees only. The host association's added money and all fees to be divided 60% to winner, 20% to second, 11% to third, 6% to fourth and 3% to fifth. Breeders' Cup Fund money also correspondingly divided providing a Breeders' Cup nominee has finished in an awarded position. Any Breeders' Cup Fund money not awarded reverts to the fund. Field will be limited to 15 starters. If more than 15 entries pass the entry box, preference will be given in the following order. Breeders' Cup nominated highweights, (including scale of weights); Breeders' Cup nominees. Non-Breeders' Cup nominated highweights (including scale of weights) Weights, 5:00 p.m. Monday, June 1. Starters to be named through the entry box by the usual time of closing. The owner of the winner to receive a trophy. Closed May 26, 1992 with 26 nominations.**

LASIX—Debra's Victory, Marilyn's Magic, Toots La Mae.

Not To Be Outdone — B. f. 3(Mar), by Smile—Jane Arnold, by Damascus
Br.—Miller Mr-Mrs M & West Mr-Mrs R S (Ky)
Tr.—Perkins Ben W Jr (8 2 2 2 .25)
113
Lifetime 5 2 1 0 $41,500 | 1992 1 0 0 0 | 1991 4 2 1 0 $41,500
Own.—Hesse Charles J
16May92- 4Pim gd 6f :232 :47 1:123 ⒻAlw 20000 63 6 4 2hd 1hd 1hd 54¼ Wilson R 114 *1.70 78-13 StrlghtSrprs1171½PrctclSsn1131¾RllcngDll114 Gave way 7
3Aug91- 9Mth fst 6f :211 :442 1:103 ⒻSorority 65 9 1 51¾ 31 45½ 47¾ Gryder A T 119 3.50 80-11 FluttryDnsur119¾MssLglty1191½CpturThCrown114 Tired 9
3Aug91-Grade III
21Jly91-10Mth fst 5½f :221 :442 1:024 ⒻColleen 72 4 6 21½ 25 28 210¾ Wilson R 117 1.50 94-13 AmrcnRoyl11510¾NotToBOtdon1175GlorHl115 2nd best 6
26Jun91- 8Mth fst 5½f :222 :454 1:044 ⒻAlw 16500 72 7 2 1hd 1½ 14 18½ Wilson R 117 *.20 95-14 NotToBeOutdon1178½GloriHlo1174Ayspcilgirl113 Easily 7
5Jun91- 5Mth fst 5f :223 :461 :583 ⒻMd Sp Wt 75 6 7 21½ 2½ 14½ 19 Wilson R 117 *.70 90-14 NtTBOtd1179CrstlCscc1171¾Sttclctrct1[illegible]kSlwly,rddnOut 7
LATEST WORKOUTS May 30 Mth 4f fst :483 B ●May 12 GS 5f fst 1:002 H May 7 GS 4f fst :482 B Apr 30 GS 3f fst :384 Bg

Ms. Copelan — B. f. 3(Apr), by Copelan—Effigy, by Valid Appeal
Br.—Shaw Jay (Fla)
Tr.—Fisher John R S (2 0 1 1 .00)
114
Lifetime 5 3 0 0 $30,251 | 1992 2 1 0 0 $12,851 | 1991 3 2 0 0 $17,400
Own.—Kligman Joel
Entered 4Jun92- 8 ATL
3May92-10Pim fst 6f :231 :462 1:114 ⒻMsPrekness 56 6 2 31 2½ 32½ 47½ Luzzi M J 118 6.20 78-17 TtsLM1133¾MssyWhtOk1181½JzzyOn121 Fractious gate 6
31Mar92- 8Pim fst 6f :234 :473 1:122 ⒻAlw 17000 70 7 1 11 2hd 12 1¾ Wilson R 114 1.80 83-19 Ms.Copln114¾MssyWhtOk112noStrlghtSrprs114 Driving 7
24Jly91- 8Sar fst 6f :214 :453 1:12 ⒻSchuylrvle 51 13 1 42 5¾ 32 511½ Bailey J D 116 21.30 72-14 TrbcThAlr1141½SpdDlr1192½TddsTpT114 Fractious gate 13
24Jly91-Grade II
9Jly91- 5Mth fst 5½f :223 :47 1:07 ⒻAlw 16500 51 3 5 1½ 11½ 14 15 Gryder A T 117 *.80 84-20 Ms.Cpln1175PrctclSsn1143Dr'sMssn113 Botherd str clr 6
26Jun91- 1Pha fst 4½f :222 :462 :523 ⒻMd Sp Wt 65 1 1 1hd 13 18½ Colton R E 118 *1.40 98-10 Ms.Copeln1188½UFirst1181½WhentoSyWhen118 Handily 8
LATEST WORKOUTS ●May 27 Fai wc 5f gd 1:01 B May 21 Fai wc 4f fm :51 B Apr 24 Fai tr.t 5f gd 1:022 B

Debra's Victory — Dk. b. or br. f. 3(Apr), by Cool Victor—Bold Debra, by Dom Alaric
Br.—Knob Hill Stables (Ont-C)
Tr.—England Phillip (—)
120
Lifetime 10 7 2 0 $340,766 | 1992 4 3 1 0 $128,170 | 1991 6 4 1 0 $212,596 | Wet 4 3 1 0 $168,850
Own.—Knob Hill Stables
2May92- 9WO sly 6f :22 :453 1:13 ⒻStar Shoot 78 4 3 43 42 2hd 2nk Walls M K L 125 *.35e 80-20 MainTopic114nkDebr'sVictory1256Apeli114 Just missed 4
2May92-Grade II-C
25Apr92- 9Grd sly 7f :224 :474 1:273 ⒻLady Angela 76 6 1 1½ 11½ 12 1¾ Walls M K L 125 *.35 70-29 Dbr'sVictory125¾VillgDncr1206½VictoriousL1115 Driving 6
11Apr92- 8Grd sly 6½f :234 :483 1:201 ⒻHandicap 87 1 2 11½ 11 12½ 13½ Walls M K L 124 *.50 80-22 DbrsVctr1243½SngAndSn1142VllDncr113 Ducked in, out 6
28Mar92- 7Grd fst 4½f :22 :46 :521 ⒻHandicap 86 4 3 2hd 1½ 13 Walls M K L 121 *.50 91-13 Dbr'sVctry1213SngAndSng1141½CntssStff116 Authority 5
16Nov91- 9Grd fst 7f :233 :472 1:253 ⒻⓇGlorosSng 76 3 2 11½ 11½ 12½ 11½ Walls M K Lb 125 7.00 80-22 Dbr'sVctr1251½Prsnthsprng114hdBcsSltn128 Ridden out 10
27Oct91- 4WO sly 6f :222 :461 1:13 ⒻⓈFnfreluche 75 6 2 11 11 14 12 Hawley S Lb 122 5.65 80-17 Dbr'sVctry1222SngAndSwng1161VctrsL1115 Ridden out 6
14Oct91- 8WO fst 5½f :223 :464 1:062 ⒻAlw 24400 49 4 4 3½ 2hd 32½ 68¾ Walls M K Lb 116 *1.55 79-21 ContssStff1164MssCls119¾GttngArndtt116 Early speed 9
13Jly91- 9WO fst 6f :22 :452 1:13 ⒻⓇNandi 69 5 1 12 15 13½ 1hd Seymour D J b 116 *.50 80-18 Dbr'sVctory116hdMplLk1219HlburtonRuckus116 Driving 8
29Jun91- 9WO fst 5½f :222 :461 1:063 ⒻⓈShadyWell 65 4 3 1½ 14 12 2hd Ramsammy E b 116 *.40 87-20 MpleLke114hdDbr'sVictory1164½SttlMoon114 Lost whip 7
29Jun91-Grade III-C
15Jun91- 7WO fst 5f :222 :454 :59 ⒻⓈMd Sp Wt 72 7 2 12 15 112 19¾ Ramsammy E b 117 8.35 94-10 Debr'sVictory1179¾SettleMoon117¾Goodle117 Authority 9
LATEST WORKOUTS ●Jun 2 WO 4f fst :472 B ●May 27 WO 4f fst :472 B May 23 WO 4f fst :48 B May 19 WO tr.t 3f fst :363 B

Marilyn's Magic — Ch. f. 3(Apr), by Shananie—Vincesca, by Darby Creek Road
Br.—Campbell Gilbert G (Fla)
Tr.—Allard Edward T (2 0 2 0 .00)
114
Lifetime 11 5 0 3 $47,344 | 1992 6 4 0 1 $37,404 | 1991 5 1 0 2 $9,940 | Turf 2 0 0 0 $400 | Wet 2 2 0 0 $21,600
Own.—Campbell Alexander G Jr
16May92- 6Bel sly 6f :22 :45 1:104 ⒻClm 75000 87 7 4 32 2½ 21 11½ Maple E 116 3.90 86-15 Mrlyn'sMgc1161½NorthrnDstr112nkVDPortc112 Driving 8
3May92- 8Pha fst 6f :22 :45 1:094 ⒻChocolateEg 44 5 1 43 47½ 410 313½ Lloyd J S L 120 2.90 78-10 StrMnstr1221FstFngrs11812½MrlnsMc120 Dropped back 5
13Apr92- 8Suf fst 6f :223 :47 1:133 3↑ⒻAlw 11000 71 5 2 12½ 13½ 15 13½ Vargas J L B 114 *.90 79-21 Marilyn's Magic1143½AvieReigns116½BarWays116 Easily 9
4Apr92-10Pha fst 170 :454 1:112 1:43 ⒻBryn Mawr 33 9 1 13 69½ 927 929½ Lloyd J S 115 3.30 51-17 TrnnNrth1154½Alphbls117¾LnsMst117 Hard used, stppd 9
25Mar92- 3Suf fst 6f :23 :464 1:133 3↑ⒻAlw 10500 67 2 1 12½ 14 15 15¼ Vargas J L B 114 *.60 79-25 Mrilyn'sMgc1145½Ann'sScrt1192¾PromsMHop111 Easily 7
7Mar92- 3Suf my 6f :223 :47 1:131 ⒻAlw 10000 73 7 1 11 12 14½ 17¼ Vargas J L B 116 *1.50e 81-27 Mrilyn'sMgic1167¼MggiesProspect116hdBittrs122 Easily 7
30Sep91- 9Med gd 170 Ⓣ:471 1:124 1:44 ⒻAlw 16000 54 4 4 53 1hd 34 59 Vargas J L 113 18.90 64-23 Froze1131½MissValidFund1171½LovelyFlier113 Bid, tired 9
15Sep91-10Rkm gd 6f :22 :454 1:122 ⒻConcord 65 3 7 73¾ 45 45½ 34½ Vargas J L 116 4.80 79-15 Cncrd'sInf116½OhDnn1164Mrlyn'sMgc116 Tgt qtrs early 12
31Aug91- 9Atl fm 5½f Ⓣ:22 :461 1:043 ⒻMermaid 52 9 2 1hd 22½ 66 810 Vargas J L 114 3.30 76-14 Casa Barasita118¾ Froze1141 Cherokee Mist115 Tired 12
22Aug91- 3Atl fst 5½f :22 :453 1:043 ⒻMd Sp Wt 75 2 4 12½ 12 15 16¾ Vargas J L 117 *.70 93-15 Mrlyn'sMgc1176¾Ambr'sJt1173½RckMrsh117 Ridden out 9
LATEST WORKOUTS Jun 3 Suf 4f fst :483 B

Little Gray Wolf Ro. f. 3(Feb), by Wolf Power-SA—Recycled, by Replant
Br.—Clark Sandra D (Ky)
Own.—Maple Leaf Farm Tr.—Murray Carol Ann (1 0 0 1 .00) **112**
Lifetime 6 3 1 0 $25,967 | 1992 4 2 0 0 $15,867 | 1991 2 1 1 0 $10,100 | Wet 1 1 0 0 $6,000

26May92- 9Pha fst 6f :214 :443 1:103 3+ ⒻAlw 15000 78 7 2 2hd 1½ 12 14 Pennisi F A 114 7.90 88-14 LttlGryWolf1144HlfofAfrc116hdLdySmtr113 Drew clear 9
4Apr92-10Pha fst 170 :454 1:112 1:43 ⒻBryn Mawr 64 4 5 33 35½ 69½ 511½ Pennisi F A 115 50.40 69-17 TurnngNorth1154½Alphblos117¾Logn'sMst117 Steadied 9
19Mar92- 6GS sly 6f :222 :462 1:132 3+ ⒻAlw 10000 67 1 6 2hd 12 1½ 1hd Pennisi F A 111 *.80 75-23 LttlGrWlf111hdSmldrngEmbrs1162½GlngBldl116 Driving 7
21Feb92- 7Aqu fst 6f ⊡:224 :471 1:13 ⒻAlw 27000 46 1 7 56 55 610 613¼ Bravo J 116 3.30 65-24 NrtrDstr1166½AsCtss116noPrttNc116 Attmptd to wheel 7
15Nov91- 6Pha fst 6f :221 :451 1:103 ⒻAlw 13000 54 5 4 2½ 2hd 25 28¼ Pennisi F A 121 *.50 82-12 TrnngNorth1108½LttlGryWlf1212OvrlyRyl115 No match 5
3Nov91- 7Pha fst 6f :222 :453 1:113 ⒻMd Sp Wt 62 10 5 31 1½ 12 13¼ Pennisi F A 121 5.90 86-12 LttlGryWlf1213¼Cntr'sSgr12110CStr121 Speed to spare 12
LATEST WORKOUTS ●Jun 3 Atl 4f fst :473 H ●May 20 GS 5f fst 1:00 H ●May 14 GS 5f fst 1:01 H ●Apr 29 GS 4f fst :472 H

Toots La Mae B. f. 3(Apr), by Danzig Connection—Fortuante Bid, by Lucky Debonair
Br.—Tilly Foster Farms (NY)
Own.—Someday Farm Tr.—Reid Mark J (7 1 1 4 .14) **115**
Lifetime 6 3 2 0 $58,125 | 1992 5 3 2 0 $58,125 | 1991 1 M 0 0

3May92-10Pim fst 6f :231 :462 1:114 ⒻMsPrekness 75 5 5 62½ 1½ 12½ 13¾ Bravo J Lb 113 *1.60 86-17 TtsLM1133¾MssyWhtOk1181½JzyOn121 Wide drftd drvg 6
25Apr92- 5GS fst 6f :223 :463 1:114 ⒻAlw 10000 92 5 1 1hd 12½ 16 110½ Wilson R Lb 118 *.30 83-27 TootsLM11810½DisyBuck1211¾MgickTop115 Ridden out 6
27Feb92- 7Aqu fst 6f ⊡:23 :464 1:122 ⒻAlw 27000 79 7 6 62¼ 2hd 21½ 22¼ Bravo J b 121 *.60 78-18 JointhRnks1162¼TootsLM1216AnglTop116 Rallied wide 9
13Feb92- 7Aqu fst 6f ⊡:231 :463 1:12 ⒻMd Sp Wt 92 8 4 1½ 12½ 15 17 Bravo J b 121 *1.50 83-22 TootsLMe1217Lizelity1213DshingWv121 Stead rddn out 9
23Jan92- 6Aqu fst 6f ⊡:232 :471 1:134 ⒻMd Sp Wt 64 5 — — — — 21½ Bravo J 121 4.90 72-28 Super Charmer1211½ TootsLaMae1212DashingWave121 7
23Jan92-Broke in tangle, attempted to wheel
26Dec91- 9GS fst 6f :223 :461 1:13 ⒻMd Sp Wt — 4 12 — — — — — Jocson G J 120 *.80 — — Saucy Sioux1202¾ Jumping toJoy121nkCallMeAngel115 12
26Dec91-Ducked out start, lost rider
LATEST WORKOUTS May 28 GS Ⓣ 5f fm 1:033 B (d) May 20 GS 4f fst :482 B Apr 18 GS 4f fst :471 H Apr 12 GS 4f fst :51 B

Star Minister B. f. 3(Feb), by Deputy Minister—Dynamic Star, by Silent Screen
Br.—Meyerhoff Robert E (Md)
Own.—Meyerhoff Robert E Tr.—Small Richard W (—) **116**
Lifetime 8 4 2 1 $135,750 | 1992 2 1 1 0 $21,160 | 1991 6 3 1 1 $114,590 | Turf 1 0 0 0

3May92- 8Pha fst 6f :22 :45 1:094 ⒻChocolateEg 79 1 2 12½ 11½ 12 11 Seefeldt A J L 122 *.70 92-10 StrMinistr1221FstFingrs11812½Mrilyn'sMgic120 Driving 5
28Mar92- 8Pha fst 6f :221 :461 1:122 ⒻⓇDaffodil 76 1 7 2hd 1hd 11 2nk Seefeldt A J L 122 *.90 79-23 Lynn's A Dream120nk Star Minister1222¼ Willed120 7
28Mar92-Flipped in paddock, off slow, drifted in, just failed
23Nov91- 9Lrl fst 1$\frac{1}{16}$:483 1:131 1:452 ⒻⓈJuv'nlFilly 81 9 2 21 1½ 11½ 1¾ Prado E S 119 14.10 86-14 StrMinistr119¾GoodLookingTrri1193Dputton119 Driving 9
3Nov91- 8Lrl fst 6½f :223 :461 1:193 ⒻAlw 16500 74 7 6 2hd 12 11½ 12½ Saumell L 116 3.90 79-20 StrMnstr1162½NrthrnSnctn1191¾RmntcSmr113 Driving 9
3Oct91- 9Pim fst 6f :231 :461 1:124 ⒻAlw 16500 60 2 4 2½ 2hd 1½ 31¼ Seefeldt A J 116 *1.50 80-18 DmondDo119½RomntcSmmr113¾StrMnstr116 Weakened 10
22Sep91-10Pim fm 1 Ⓣ:472 1:124 1:40 ⒻQuenEmprss 62 6 2 2½ 21½ 43 68¾ Prado E S 112 3.10 70-21 SndLdy1114¾PntSprd111nkCrrtwn'sMrgrt113 Gave way 11
7Sep91- 1Pim fst 6f :232 :472 1:13 ⒻMd Sp Wt 74 5 1 11 12 13½ 16¾ Seefeldt A J 119 *.70 80-20 StrMnstr1196¾DmondD1192¾EskmEscpd119 Ridden out 7
18Aug91- 7Lrl fst 6f :223 :471 1:13 ⒻMd Sp Wt 56 4 9 85¼ 53¼ 31 22 Seefeldt A J 119 6.70 74-25 OnsNtEngh1192StrMnstr1193MssWht0114 Wide, rallied 10
LATEST WORKOUTS ●Jun 1 Pim 5f fst 1:004 H May 26 Pim 6f gd 1:142 H May 18 Pim 7f my 1:271 B May 12 Pim 5f fst 1:01 H

Reissaurus Ro. f. 3(Apr), by Country Pine—Gorgeously Divine, by Al Hattab
Br.—Hidden Point Farm Inc (Fla)
Own.—Schweiger Stable Inc Tr.—Richards Robert J Jr (1 0 0 0 .00) **113**
Lifetime 12 3 3 3 $49,085 | 1992 5 1 1 1 $25,660 | 1991 7 2 2 2 $23,425
Entered 4Jun92- 8 ATL

3May92-10LaD fst 6f :221 :453 1:112 ⒻDixie Miss 75 6 2 12 1½ 21 32¾ Romero S P L 115 7.50 88-11 ExplosivSilnc1132¾ChrokVil115nkRissurus115 Weakened 6
4Apr92- 6Aqu fst 6f :214 :45 1:094 ⒻBlueNorther 64 5 3 32 3½ 36½ 814¾ McCauley W H 118 9.50 77-11 AmricnRoyl1189½AlpnMusc116½MssCovrGrl116 Used up 8
13Mar92-10GP fst 6f :213 :452 1:114 ⒻAlw 38400 82 5 1 21 22 23 48 Fires E 114 1.90 76-23 Rvnsmoor1153½MysticObsssion1122MssVldPch113 Tired 5
25Feb92- 7GP fst 6½f :22 :443 1:17 ⒻAlw 23800 85 7 1 12½ 12½ 12½ 11 Fires E 115 3.40 94-15 Reissurus1151TrickyCinderell1171½Roy'sGirl115 Driving 7
29Jan92- 5GP fst 6½f :221 :451 1:172 ⒻAlw 18000 78 1 5 12½ 1½ 11½ 2no Fires E 115 5.30 92-09 RunforBby114noReissurus115noSilfishLdy115 Just failed 6
9Nov91- 7Crc fst 6f :221 :461 1:123 ⒻAlw 17400 70 7 1 12 11 12½ 1¾ Valles E S 112 4.50 87-12 Reissurus112¾SpinDrem1131½Copeln'sCchet113 Driving 7
19Oct91- 5Crc fst 6f :22 :46 1:131 ⒻClm 50000 59 3 2 1hd 2hd 1½ 2hd Valles E S 114 4.00 84-15 VldMssZnd118hdRssrs1142½Cpln'sCcht114 Failed to last 8
26Sep91- 4Crc fst 6f :221 :462 1:133 ⒻClm 40000 65 4 2 1½ 1hd 1hd 31 Valles E S 116 5.40 81-16 SpnnnOut116½SngulrlySunny118½Rssurs116 Grudgingly 8
2Sep91- 5Crc fst 6f :213 :454 1:131 ⒻClm 30000 55 4 2 2hd 2hd 13½ 22¾ Valles E S 114 13.00 81-12 ChngetheShow1162¾Rissurus1141½SwissMrk114 Gamely 7
21Aug91- 3Crc fst 6f :223 :471 1:142 ⒻMd 20000 49 5 4 43½ 2hd 12 12 Valles E S 116 5.80 78-18 Reissaurus1162 RomanyRoad1121½RoyalMed116 Driving 12
LATEST WORKOUTS ●May 30 Mth 4f fst :47 B May 23 Mth 5f fst 1:012 H ●Apr 25 Crc 4f fst :462 H ●Apr 19 Crc 5f fst 1:003 H

C. C.'s Return
Br.—Seahorse 86 (Ky)
Own.—Break Away Racing Stable Tr.—Reid Robert E Jr (4 1 1 0 .25) **115**
7 4 1 0 $59,470 | 1991 1 1 0 0 $7,500

23May92-10Crc fst 7f :22 :444 1:251 ⒻAzalea H 88 2 6 3½ 2hd 14 15½ Thibeau R J Jr 113 25.40 89-13 C.C.'sRtrn1135½FortnFortyFor1142½SbtlDncr113 Driving 7
8May92- 9Crc fst 7f :223 :46 1:253 3+ ⒻAlw 15000 86 1 3 11½ 11½ 15 1hd Douglas R R 113 4.60 92-15 CC'sRtrn113hdWhBNrml1184½LIScrtr109 Fully extended 8
19Apr92- 9Crc fst 7f :221 :444 1:241 ⒻTa Wee 70 6 2 3½ 32 58½ 714 Lee M A 112 13.10 85-05 Rvnsmoor1145½NovmbrSnow1161LylScrtry112 Faltered 8
28Mar92- 7Crc fst 6½f :22 :45 1:182 ⒻAlw 15000 85 6 1 1hd 12 13 15½ Ramos W S 112 *.60 — — C.C.'sRturn1125½MggsPstol1175½AllOurBst112 Drew off 6
8Mar92- 7GP fst 6f :22 :45 1:104 ⒻAlw 24300 81 4 4 42¼ 31 22 23 Krone J A 112 9.80 86-12 WinnieD.1133C.C.'sReturn112½Copeln'sCchet113 Faded 8
13Feb92- 5GP fst 6f :214 :443 1:104 ⒻAlw 20600 42 7 4 53¾ 43½ 712 715¾ Bailey J D 113 4.50 73-12 EnjoyTheSilnc112nkWinniD.1131PiPhiHiD113 4 wide trn 8
17Nov91- 3Pha fst 6f :223 :463 1:113 ⒻMd Sp Wt 66 8 1 11 11 12½ 13 Jocson G J 121 *1.00 86-14 CC'sRtrn1213ThsOn'sFrUs12110MtlAmss121 Ridden out 9
LATEST WORKOUTS May 2 Crc 4f fst :49 B Apr 13 Crc 4f fst :483 H

is now two for two on this surface, but in her second to last start on a fast track against Star Minister she showed her true self. She could not keep up in that contest and should have the same problem here.

Toots La Mae did not get off to a great career. She lost her rider in her first start but has rebounded since and will be chasing a tiger in this contest. Toots La Mae has some questions, though, that prohibit her from being a contender. First, who did she run against? All of the horses that Toots La Mae beat in her past two races have not even come close to winning since. Second, the rider switch is not normal, even though Rick Wilson did ride her once. Third, why would you work this horse on grass unless you were looking to a different race or thought the horse was a better horse on turf? Fourth, if this horse was pressured, would she produce or quit? Too many questions and too much risk for the price of 2-1.

Star Minister is a Deputy Minister daughter who had a successful two-year-old campaign and looks like she has picked up right where she left off. She has been drilling for this race by working out on May 26 and June 1, both in quick fractions. The last race on May 3, 1992, showed her acceleration and newly acquired high speed as she completed the six furlongs in 1:09⁴/₅. As you will see in the upcoming chapter on Time Analysis, Philadelphia Park has a fast surface when compared to Monmouth Park. A performance like that should be good enough to use this facility in the gimmicks.

C.C.'s Return is a Kentucky bred who has faced tougher horses. When she has, she has performed miserably. A top performance should have her there early, but she does not look to be a threat at the end.

You should be able to predict what happened.

Debra's Victory led all the way and drew off at the end in record time for this filly. Her class was too much for this field and it showed from the outset. The public eventually sent Debra's Victory off the

---

EIGHTH RACE
Monmouth
JUNE 6, 1992

6 FURLONGS. (1.08) 41st Running MISS WOODFORD BREEDERS' CUP HANDICAP. Purse $60,000 added. (Includes $25,000 from Breeders' Cup Fund). Fillies, 3-year-olds. By subscription of $50 each which should accompany the nomination, $200 to pass the entry box, $150 to start with $35,000 added and an additional $25,000 from the Breeders' Cup Fund for Cup nominees only. The host association's added money and all fees to be divided 60% to winner, 20% to second, 11% to third, 6% to fourth and 3% to fifth. Breeders' Cup Fund money also correspondingly divided providing a Breeders' Cup nominee has finished in an awarded position. Any Breeders' Cup Fund money not awarded reverts to the fund. Field will be limited to 15 starters. If more than 15 entries pass the entry

box, preference will be given in the following order. Breeders' Cup nominated highweights, (including scale of weights); Breeders' Cup nominees. Non–Breeders' Cup nominated highweights (including scale of weights) Weights, 5:00 p.m. Monday, June 1. Starters to be named through the entry box by the usual time of closing. The owner of the winner to receive a trophy. Closed May 26, 1992 with 26 nominations.
Value of race $64,000; value to winner $38,400; second $12,800; third $7,040; fourth $3,840; fifth $1,920. Mutuel pool $142,638. Exacta Pool $197,861

Last Raced	Horse	M/Eqt.	A.	Wt	PP	St	¼	½	Str	Fin	Jockey	Odds $1
2May92 9WO2	Debra's Victory	Lb	3	120	2	5	1hd	12½	16	18	Walls M K	1.80
3May92 8Pha1	Star Minister	L	3	115	5	1	4hd	42	21½	21¼	Seefeldt A J	4.10
23May92 10Crc1	C. C.'s Return		3	115	6	2	6	5½	53	3no	Thibeau R J Jr	4.40
3May92 10Pim1	Toots La Mae	Lb	3	115	4	3	31½	3½	3hd	45	Wilson R	2.10
16May92 6Bel1	Marilyn's Magic	L	3	114	3	4	52	6	6	5hd	Rivera L Jr	9.90
16May92 4Pim5	Not To Be Outdone		3	113	1	6	22	22	4½	6	Bravo J	13.10

OFF AT 4:18. Start good. Won ridden out. Time, :21¹, :44 , :56¹, 1:09² Track muddy.

$2 Mutuel Prices:				
	2–DEBRA'S VICTORY	5.60	3.00	2.60
	6–STAR MINISTER		4.40	3.00
	7–C. C.'S RETURN			3.40
	$2 EXACTA 2–6 PAID $24.00			

Dk. b. or br. f, (Apr), by Cool Victor—Bold Debra, by Dom Alaric. Trainer England Phillip. Bred by Knob Hill Stables (Ont–C).

DEBRA'S VICTORY reached the front soon after the opening sixteenth, drew clear on the turn and was rated on the lead into the lead while removed from the rail then drew off while being ridden out. STAR MINISTER towards the inside turning for home, advanced into upper stretch and was second best. C. C.'S RETURN along the rail into the lane, lacked a solid stretch bid. TOOTS LE MAE lodged a bid outside midway on the turn and offered little in the drive. MARILYN'S MAGIC retired early. NOT TO BE OUTDONE saved groiund while pressing the early issue and tired through the lane.

Courtesy of Daily Racing Form ©

slight favorite over Toots La Mae who was nine and a quarter lengths behind the winner. Debra's Victory paid $5.60, but she was worth a bet at $2.60.

Can a horse that is entered in a claiming $4,000 race have class? Such a horse may not have class, but it has a class level. When we figure who has the highest class level, we will have the winner, even in a claiming $4,000 race. The following race will show what we mean.

3 START 5½ FURLONGS PHILADELPHIA FINISH

5 ½ FURLONGS. **(1.02⁴) CLAIMING. Purse $4,500. Fillies and mares, 3–year–olds and upward which have not won two races since January 10, 1992. Weight: 3–year–olds 115 lbs., older 122 lbs. Non–winners of two races since December 10 allowed 3 lbs.; a race since then, 6 lbs. Claiming price $4,000.**

LASIX—Nashua's Evening, Betula, Evidence, Paint Me, Roodle, Frannie Britches.

Nashua's Evening — **B. m. 6, by Noble Nashua—Evening Romp, by Silent Screen**

$4,000 **Br.—High Ride Stables (NY)**

Own.—Ruberto Louis V Jr — **Tr.—Ruberto Louis V Jr (55 1 3 3 .02)** — **112**10

Lifetime						
47 7 0 4	1992	8	1	0	1	$2,965
$23,312	1991	11	3	0	2	$6,612
	Turf	1	0	0	0	
	Wet	9	1	0	1	$4,849

19Jun92- 7Del	my	6f	:22	:45⁴	1:12²	3↑ⒻClm 4000	54	7	6	68½	68¾	54½	43	Smith C L5	L	117	5.60	82–21	CtchHerImge116½BlondeGirl110½Ironsville116	Late run	7
27May92- 6Del	fst	6f	:22³	:47²	1:13³	3↑ⒻClm 4000	53	2	5	44	32½	11	14¾	Smith C L5	L	117	2.70	79–22	Nsh'sEnng1174¾BbIslnd1224EdstNBrt118	Lugged in 1/8	7
8May92-10Del	sly	5½f	:22²	:47²	1:07¹	3↑ⒻClm 3500	52	1	7	88¼	88¼	54¾	31½	Smith C L5	L	113	14.10	77–22	KytoRun113¾GlfstrmJt118¾Nsh'sEvnng113	Mild, bid ins	10
8Apr92- 7Del	fst	6f	:22¹	:46²	1:14	3↑ⒻClm 3500	39	8	7	108¾	77¾	66¼	66¼	Smith C L5	L	113	7.00	71–23	MoonOn1131¾ImptosLs1181½DshofElgnc118	No menace	12
22Mar92-11Del	fst	6f	:22¹	:46³	1:13¹	3↑ⒻClm 3500	45	4	2	45½	45½	44	46½	Luzzi J B Jr	L	118	13.20	74–25	CttleAnnie1184¾Islnd'sEnd1221¼HdyImp118	No menace	6

29Jan92-10Pen fst 5½f :223 :47 1:062 ⒻClm 2500 27 7 6 82½ 74¾ 65 66¼ Hastie R M L 115 16.50 83-17 BreezyHuld119²½ScrletO'Rerr115¾QuiElite118 No threat 9
24Jan92- 4Pha my 6f :222 :464 1:133 ⒻClm 4000 27 1 3 32½ 44½ 811 813 Giglio D Jr L 116 47.60 60-28 KolcttMny122²½Gs'Nghtmr116⁶½FlynCtfsh116 Stopped 8
13Jan92- 3Pha fst 170 :473 1:142 1:474 ⒻClm 4000 7 6 2 710 912 921 925 Lopez C C L 116 22.40 32-32 DncngLgs116³½NoDoblDts111nkGlorosPrsnt116 Stopped 9
22Dec91- 4Pha fst 6f :224 :464 1:123 3↑ⒻClm 4000 30 4 2 42½ 66 613 611¾ Matz N L 116 15.90 69-21 SunshinRcitl119³¾Logn'sBlush116½Bt'sBigMm116 Tired 12
15Nov91- 2Pha fst 6f :22 :451 1:112 3↑ⒻClm 4000 50 3 8 34½ 34 33 55½ Lopez C C L 119 18.80 81-12 Kpn'Thoughts1141½[DH]ArtTmpo109[DH]SuzQt119 No rally 10

Betula B. m. 5, by Sauce Boat—Ode to Romeo, by Mr Leader
$4,000 Br.—Doe Run Inc (Pa)
Own.—Solano Rafael Tr.—Solano Rafael (42 5 5 4 .12)
109¹⁰
Lifetime 36 4 7 2 $40,100
1992 6 1 0 0 $3,975
1991 14 2 2 0 $11,055
Turf 7 1 0 0 $4,860
Wet 10 1 3 1 $10,355

25Jun92- 4Pha fst 5½f :221 :452 1:051 3↑ⒻClm 5000 47 4 9 108 88¾ 611 56½ Ortiz R10 Lb 106 10.10 81-12 HitThHights112hdPtti'sSstr116noSomrstrod116 Off slow 10
12Jun92- 8Pha fm 1 1/16 Ⓣ:472 1:143 1:454 3↑Ⓕ[S]Alw 15500 45 2 2 34 51¾ 69¾ 720¾ Ortiz R10 Lb 106 28.60 61-22 Irish Reach115³½ Regallino116¹½ Miss McCann116 Tired 9
6Jun92- 3Pha gd 5½f :221 :454 1:053 3↑ⒻClm 5000 49 1 5 1½ 11½ 11½ 42½ Bisono C10 Lb 106 *2.20 83-11 LwofLel116nkJustAboutNow116½Licin119 Off sl, weak'd 6
24May92- 4GS fm 5f Ⓣ:22 :45 :571 3↑ⒻAlw ---s 61 8 4 52½ 44 47½ 58¾ Lovato F Jr Lb 117 36.30 86-06 PrncssFddld117⁵¾RglBll119¹½AuntSgourny117 Even trip 11
15May92-11GS fm 5f Ⓣ:213 :453 :581 3↑ⒻClm 14000 — 2 10 — — — — Bisono J 113 4.50 — — Islnd'sEnd113¾JustAired113²¾FlmingLibrl117 Lost rider 10
8May92- 2Pha sly 6f :221 :461 1:131 3↑ⒻClm 4000 52 5 1 31½ 21 11½ 13½ Bisono J Lb 116 7.20 75-20 Btul116³½NoDoublDts119nkBoundlssBou116 Drew clear 8

22Nov91- 9Pha sly 6f :221 :452 1:112 3↑ⒻClm 4000 42 9 9 41½ 31 33 611½ Capanas S Lb 119 5.10 75-17 NoDoubleDtes119¹CouldBVrs122⁶¾WigsDlight110 Tired 11
6Nov91- 5Pha fst 6f :22 :452 1:104 3↑ⒻClm 6500 48 4 4 33½ 54½ 45 68¼ Somsanith N5 Lb 111 3.70 82-12 DoubletimeMiss116³½ShoalBay116¾ShrpCircle112 Tired 7
15Oct91- 9Pha sly 7f :222 :452 1:242 3↑Ⓕ[S]Alw 18225 47 1 8 64¾ 66 99¾ 911¼ Capanas S Lb 116 7.30 74-17 Calskey114³¾ Grey Salve112¹ Brusis115 Tired 10
2Oct91- 7Pha fst 6½f :221 :453 1:18 3↑ⒻClm 5000 70 9 1 55½ 3½ 15 18 Capanas S Lb 119 7.00 88-15 Betul119⁸ArtTempo108¾MorningStrshin122 Ridden out 11
LATEST WORKOUTS Jly 7 Pha 3f fst :384 B

Evidence B. f. 4, by Lord Carlos—Silver Memory, by Silver Badge
$4,000 Br.—Cuprill Charles A (Pa)
Own.—Broome Edwin T Tr.—Broome Edwin T (189 31 32 32 .16)
116
Lifetime 33 4 4 8 $45,792
1992 2 0 0 0 $270
1991 22 4 3 6 $39,996
Wet 3 1 0 0 $9,675

25Jun92- 2Pha fst 5½f :223 :462 1:062 3↑ⒻClm 4000 27 5 4 21½ 21 34½ 48½ Matz N L 116 2.40 73-12 BoldRedWing116nkQukrLdy116³¾HiddnMistrss116 Tired 7
18Jun92- 6Pha fst 5½f :214 :451 1:052 3↑ⒻClm 7500 45 5 1 42½ 33½ 33½ 911 Matz N L 116 13.50 76-16 Tender Georgia122⁶ Sharp Circle122¹¼ Profile122 Tired 11

27Dec91- 3Pha fst 5½f :224 :463 1:061 3↑ⒻClm 4000 40 6 1 2½ 2hd 22 58¼ Ryan K L 114 *2.40 75-21 ModlAForbs116²FstyDchss111nkLwfLl116 Dueled, tired 7
11Dec91- 4Pha fst 6f :221 :46 1:122 ⒻClm 6000 46 3 4 2½ 2hd 34½ 38½ Ryan K L 112⁴ 17.30 73-17 GreatValley111⁵½TitiKak119³[DH]Evidence112 Weakened 12
11Dec91-Dead heat
28Nov91- 7Pha fst 6f :221 :454 1:13 ⒻClm 6000 49 9 1 3nk 1hd 11 52¾ Ryan K L 112 16.40 76-18 DontAct119nkRareDoll116½MedowMouse116 Weakened 10
19Nov91- 3Pha fst 6f :221 :46 1:121 ⒻClm 6000 38 4 5 31½ 31½ 53¾ 77½ Ryan K L 112 7.60 75-14 CleverRear116¹½RreDoll116²½SweetAvtr119 Steadied st 12
20Oct91- 4Pha fst 6f :223 :464 1:122 ⒻClm 10000 19 9 3 1hd 1hd 913 916½ Colton R E L 114 10.40 65-18 ProudGlori116⁴½GoldenFizzle112noLepinLuren116 Tired 10
8Oct91- 5Pha fst 5½f :223 :463 1:061 ⒻClm 8500 51 4 1 1hd 2½ 2hd 46 Colton R E L 119 *1.70 77-22 MissShawnee116²½LeapinLauren115¹½RareDoll115 Tired 7
8Sep91- 9Pha fst 6f :222 :454 1:114 ⒻClm 10000 52 8 2 1hd 1½ 22 36 Jocson G J5 L 112 3.40 79-17 PrincessAlberta110³½Yang'sLst116²½Evidence112 Tired 9
28Aug91- 2Pha fst 6f :224 :46 1:13 ⒻClm 10000 60 5 1 1½ 2hd 2hd 2nk Colton R E L 117 2.50 79-19 Rare Doll114nkEvidence117nkMissShawnee116 Good try 8
LATEST WORKOUTS ●Jun 13 Pha 5f fst 1:00 B ●Jun 9 Pha 5f fst 1:002 B ●Jun 2 Pha 4f fst :473 B

Quaker Lady Ch. f. 4, by Tim Tam Aly—Whisky Dad, by Tumiga
$4,000 Br.—Kennon Lyle (Fla)
Own.—Miller Nancy Tr.—Lopez Daniel J (35 4 7 3 .11)
116
Lifetime 21 2 2 5 $24,800
1992 4 0 2 1 $2,240
1991 13 1 0 3 $11,035
Wet 3 1 0 0 $9,300

2Jly92- 3Pha fst 6f :222 :461 1:134 3↑ⒻClm 4000 44 1 2 1hd 13 13 2nk Jocson G J b 116 *1.60 72-17 It'sLlyTm109nkQkrLdy116²JstAbotNw119 Couldn't last 8
25Jun92- 2Pha fst 5½f :223 :462 1:062 3↑ⒻClm 4000 49 3 3 31½ 31 21½ 2nk Jocson G J b 116 4.10 82-12 BoldRdWng116nkQkrLdy116³¾HddnMstrss116 Game try 7
28May92- 1GS fst 6f :23 :47 1:131 3↑ⒻClm 4000 42 4 3 2hd 21 32½ 34 Underwood S b 117 3.10 72-13 Ls'sIslnd117¾Prncssofthrss117³½QkrLdy117 No final bid 7
19May92- 3Pha fst 6f :214 :444 1:114 3↑ⒻClm 4000 36 5 2 36 49 815 89¾ Underwood S 116 4.20 72-15 Lilyane'sDevil109½PintMe116noClires World116 Stopped 8

22Oct91- 6Med fst 6f :223 :46 1:114 ⒻClm 9000 41 10 1 1½ 42 710 89½ Gryder A T b 113 4.90e 73-15 PorclnGddss115½IrshLmrck111¹½Intnwththtms115 Tired 10
28Sep91- 7Med fst 6f :221 :451 1:104 ⒻClm 10000 36 9 3 104¼ 1013 913 917¼ Wilson R b 115 *2.50 71-15 PunchlinePtty113³¾Shbrr115nkSwnniesFinle114 Outrun 12
11Sep91- 7Med fst 6f :223 :461 1:121 ⒻClm 14000 63 2 10 4nk 42 51½ 32¼ Ortiz F L5 b 108 6.70 79-17 Southbound115²Brd'sTrbut113nkQkrLdy108 Came again 11
21Aug91- 3Mth gd 6f :214 :451 1:104 ⒻClm 16000 65 4 5 2hd 2hd 21 43 Pagano S R b 115 3.60 84-14 RnforLov115¾ColrMTrly111¹½Mnnst'sWy112 Weakened 8
10Aug91- 3Mth gd 6f :221 :453 1:114 ⒻClm 12500 78 7 1 1hd 12 13 12¾ Pagano S R b 115 30.80 82-18 QkrLdy115²¾Mnnst'sWy115²½IrshLmrck115 Ridden out 8
28Jly91-10Mth fst 6f :22 :452 1:112 ⒻClm 10000 50 4 8 43 5¾ 34½ 46½ MacMillan JR5 b 110 21.60 77-10 BrfootAv114noMrryMony115²¾NoholmsScrtry113 Tired 11

Paint Me B. m. 6, by Habitony—Cheerful Bidder, by Bold Bidder
$4,000 Br.—Fountainebleau Farm Inc (Ky)
Own.—Scetta Robert T Tr.—Scetta Robert T (112 9 12 13 .08)
119
Lifetime 27 2 4 6 $22,685
1992 23 1 4 4 $14,545
1990 4 1 0 2 $8,140
Wet 4 0 0 2 $2,490

29Jun92- 9Pha fst 170 :48 1:124 1:443 3↑ⒻClm 5000 47 7 11 108¼ 811 515 412 Anderson A M L 122 8.30 61-23 SclnSunshn122½ClodyWntrs116⁷½T.V.Crct107 No threat 11
20Jun92- 4Pha fst 6f :223 :454 1:114 3↑ⒻClm 13000 44 3 8 814 716 715 711¼ Anderson A M L 118 16.50 71-15 R'sRondzvos114hdShr'sGlory116hdIslfBchs115 Off slow 8
8Jun92- 7Pha fst 5½f :221 :454 1:06 3↑ⒻClm 5000 48 2 9 1011 109½ 57 21¾ Anderson A M L 122 6.90 82-16 WdsdDnn119¹¾PntM122½Mr'sBrwnEys116 Finished fast 10
1Jun92- 8Pha my 1 1/16 :49 1:132 1:47 3↑ⒻAlw 21096 54 1 6 611 615 511 512¼ Anderson A M L 116 18.70 62-28 JvRey119³½PrincessCouldBe113²¼Imllkeydup113 Outrun 6
26May92- 6Pha fst 6½f :222 :46 1:183 3↑ⒻClm 4000 61 5 6 715 69½ 43 1½ Anderson A M L 116 2.90 85-14 PintMe116½HiddenMistrss116noGrciLighting120 Driving 7
19May92- 3Pha fst 6f :214 :444 1:114 3↑ⒻClm 4000 59 1 8 811 712 48 2½ Anderson A M L 116 14.00 81-15 Lilyne'sDvil109½PintM116noClirsWorld116 Gained place 8
12May92- 2Pha fst 6½f :222 :453 1:182 3↑ⒻClm 4000 52 5 8 714 716 612 47¾ Rodriguez J G7 L 110 5.70 78-13 Tahaha116³BilliesLdy119³½GrecieLighting120 No threat 8
1May92- 2Pha fst 6f :222 :451 1:102 3↑ⒻClm 5000 42 5 6 714 713 614 39¼ Rodriguez J G7 L 110 3.80 80-08 FstBrekfst122⁸½ChngeTheFilter113¾PintM110 Off slow 7
25Apr92- 1Pha fst 6f :224 :461 1:111 3↑ⒻClm 5000 49 1 6 65½ 67 612 28 Rodriguez J G7 L 110 6.70 77-12 Samarcrd116⁸PintMe110nkRollingWve122 Gained place 7
19Apr92-11Pha fst 1 1/16 :472 1:13 1:472 ⒻClm 5000 40 2 9 912 711 612 310¾ Rodriguez J G7 L 110 15.70 61-25 NiteRiderLibels122¾BlzingBth116¹⁰PintM110 No threat 9

Roodle Dk. b. or br. f. 4, by On to Glory—Rooh El Hara, by Novarullah
$4,000 Br.—Colson Enterprises (Fla)
Own.—Fallon Martin L Tr.—Fallon Martin L (132 23 24 18 .17)
113³
Lifetime 27 5 2 1 $22,483
1992 4 0 0 0
1991 13 5 0 1 $19,955
Turf 2 0 0 0 $540
Wet 1 1 0 0 $3,720

22Jun92 5Pha fst 6½f :224 :464 1:191 3↑ⒻClm 6000 12 7 1 3nk 56 713 723¼ Somsanith N3 Lb 109 12.50 59-21 BtsBgMm113⁴½DnsLtDrln114¹¾Chlsnt119 Wide, stopped 7
11Jun92- 2Pha fst 1 1/16 :472 1:123 1:463 3↑ⒻClm 7500 0 6 3 34½ 618 827 841¾ Somsanith N3 Lb 113 2.70 34-23 OverLightly116½LovelyVlvt122⁵¾MyHighnss116 Stopped 8

27Apr92- 7Pha fst 7f :23 :462 1:242 ⒻClm 10000 22 1 4 21 42½ 714 716¾ Somsanith N3 Lb 113 7.30 88-16 Intnthtmc116³½NnGrnd114⁵WhtTrph112 Faded inside 9
10Apr92- 5Pha fst 6f :221 :451 1:103 ⒻClm 11000 39 2 3 33 59½ 516 616 Somsanith N3 Lb 113 8.70 72-15 DixiCrd116³HlfofAfric116⁶Rock'nRollMdm112 Stopped 8

7Sep91- 4Pha fst 170 :474 1:131 1:453 ⒻClm c-10000 50 5 2 31 44 44 46½ Vigliotti M J Lb 122 7.40 61-26 Ima Pip116hd Puggy117⁴½ Wajadama112 No rally 10
24Aug91-10Pha yl 1 1/16 Ⓣ:473 1:132 1:464 3↑ⒻAlw 14500 19 6 2 26 615 829 842 Vigliotti M J Lb 110 18.30 31-31 AntSgrny116¹⁶½PrncssRl116⁷½NgrnNghtmr114 Stopped 9
9Aug91- 3Atl sly 1⅛ :482 1:13 1:53 ⒻClm 10000 68 5 1 11½ 11 13 16½ Vigliotti M J Lb 116 *1.40 84-19 Roodle116⁶½ Nine Grand115⁷½Celebreath116 Ridden out 5
2Aug91- 8Pha fst 1 1/16 :464 1:122 1:461 ⒻClm 14000 58 2 2 21 41¾ 45 49½ Lopez C C Lb 113 5.90 68-20 Pgg107³¾I'mAClssBrd116⁴½Gnn'sSlp116 Fractious gate 7
11Jly91- 3Atl fst 1 1/16 :481 1:133 1:48 ⒻClm 10000 50 8 3 31 1½ 12½ 12¼ Vigliotti M J Lb 114 4.00 67-29 Roodle114²½ Randette110¹½ Ange116 Driving 8
4Jly91-12Pha fm 1⅛ Ⓣ:492 1:152 1:554 ⒻClm 13000 50 9 1 11 1hd 34 411½ Vigliotti M J Lb 112 3.80 53-27 TwoThirtyTea112⁵½MegOMyHert116½PenArgyl112 Tired 9
LATEST WORKOUTS Jun 5 Pha 6f my 1:172 B May 30 Pha 6f fst 1:171 B May 23 Pha 5f fst 1:031 B May 16 Pha 5f sly 1:05 B

Frannie Britches | Dk. b. or br. f. 4, by Explosive Bid—Pokey Britches, by Poker | Lifetime 38 6 4 4 $38,325

$4,000 Br.—Belk & Pou Mmes (Fla)

Own.—R M L Stable | Tr.—Menarde Frank J (76 6 6 5 .08) | **116**

1992	11	0	3	0	$4,885
1991	19	4	1	3	$23,240
Turf	2	0	0	0	
Wet	6	2	0	1	$9,720

25Jun92-	4Pha fst	5½f	:22^{1}	:45^{2}	1:05^{1}	3↑ⒻClm 5000	38	1	10	$8^{6\frac12}$	9^{11}	9^{15}	$9^{9\frac34}$	Bisono C^{10}	Lb	106	25.70	78-12	HtThHghts112^{hd}Ptt'sSstr116^{no}Somrstrd116	Off slowest	10
15Jun92-	3Pha fst	1$\frac{1}{16}$	:47^{3}	1:14^{1}	1:48^{4}	3↑ⒻClm 4000	—	4	1	$3^{3\frac12}$	$6^{8\frac12}$	7^{22}	—	Lafler B M	Lb	116	18.30	— —	MyAnglJlln116$^{8\frac12}$NoDoblDts116^{11}BbyPrcs112	Distanced	7
5Jun92-	1Pha sly	6f	:21^{4}	:46	1:12	3↑ⒻClm 4000	26	1	4	1^{2}	1^{1}	$5^{8\frac12}$	$5^{15\frac14}$	Lafler B M	Lb	122	*1.80	66-16	Voodoo'sSister116$^{1\frac12}$Imakieb116$^{6\frac12}$Disclimer119	Stopped	6
23May92-	7Pha fst	5½f	:21^{4}	:45^{2}	1:05	3↑ⒻClm 6500	45	10	1	3^{1}	$3^{2\frac12}$	4^{5}	7^{9}	Lafler B M	Lb	116	26.40	80-10	AnitaLass116^{nk}KolucttheMoney117$^{3\frac12}$Chalsant119	Tired	10
19May92-	7Pha fst	6½f	:21^{4}	:45	1:17^{4}	3↑ⒻClm 7500	26	4	3	1^{2}	2^{hd}	10^{15}	$10^{17\frac12}$	Lafler B M	Lb	116	11.20	71-15	CrftyRen116^{6}ShrpCircle116^{hd}Citlin'sWrrior109	Stopped	12
2May92-	3Pha fst	6f	:21^{2}	:44^{3}	1:10^{3}	3↑ⒻClm 9000	53	2	3	1^{hd}	3^{nk}	6^{8}	$7^{7\frac12}$	Bisono J	Lb	112	21.10	80-05	Rock'nRollMdm116$^{\frac34}$DixiCrd119$^{\frac12}$RoylCinch119	Used up	7
10Apr92-	7Pha fst	7f	:22	:45^{1}	1:26	ⒻClm 7000	49	5	1	$1^{2\frac12}$	1^{3}	$1^{1\frac12}$	$2^{2\frac12}$	Bisono J	Lb	112	3.80	74-15	PgnRtl116$^{2\frac12}$FrnnBrtchs112^{nk}RlCmmnctr116	Just mis'd	9
23Mar92-	5Pha my	5½f	:22	:45^{4}	1:04^{4}	ⒻClm 5000	51	3	3	$4^{2\frac12}$	$4^{3\frac12}$	4^{6}	$5^{5\frac34}$	Pagan N	Lb	116	*2.30	84-19	Natacular116^{3}Beat'sBigMm116^{1}WolfLuck116	Drftd out	6
17Mar92-	5Pha fst	5½f	:21^{4}	:46	1:06	ⒻAlw 8500s	53	4	3	2^{4}	$2^{3\frac12}$	5^{5}	5^{7}	Pagan N	Lb	116	8.20	77-22	SaucyBird116^{nk}LinesofLdy116$^{3\frac14}$AnitLss116	Drifted out	6
2Mar92-	2Pha fst	6f	:22^{2}	:45^{3}	1:12^{2}	ⒻClm 7500	65	8	2	$2^{\frac12}$	$2^{\frac12}$	2^{3}	$2^{1\frac34}$	Mendez J P^{7}	Lb	109	4.10	77-24	SecrtBlnd116$^{1\frac34}$FrnniBritchs109^{no}QuitPro112	Held place	8

LATEST WORKOUTS ●Jly 5 Pha 3f fst :35^{2} H

All of Nashua's Evening's last five starts were at Delaware Park. If we dissect this mare's past starts we see that she was victorious two starts back at the claiming $4,000 level at Delaware. She then came back in the same class on a muddy track to finish fourth, three lengths behind. Nashua's Evening's class level would be claiming $4,000 at Delaware Park and we have to adjust this to fit Philadelphia Park's class level. Since Philadelphia Park has a slightly better grade of horses than Delaware, Nashau's Evening's class level would be slightly lower than claiming $4,000.

Betula is a five-year-old out of Sauce Boat. This mare has started six times this year and has made three of those starts on the turf course. We eliminate these starts on the turf and dissect the three starts on the dirt. In Betula's first start of the year she was entered in a claiming $4,000 event at six furlongs. She won by three-and-a-half lengths, establishing her class level at $4,000. Her second encounter on dirt was June 6, 1992, in a claiming $5,000 event. Betula led and came up a little short. In her next start on dirt, Betula broke slow. If she does not get the lead or come very close, she eliminates all her chances of winning the race. Entering this claiming $4,000 contest, Betula's class level is above $4,000 because of her victory on May 22. It is under $5,000 because she could not win when put at that level.

Evidence is a four-year-old filly making only her third start of the year. In her first start, she ran a dismal ninth, beaten by eleven lengths. Then she was dropped to claiming $4,000 and finished fourth, beaten by eight lengths. Evidence was obviously a better horse last year but her current class level is below $4,000 and she would have to be dropped farther down to achieve her class level.

Quaker Lady: This Tim Tam progeny has four races under her belt and has not won any of them. Even though she keeps coming close she has not established a class level. Coming into this race Quaker Lady's class level would be close to claiming $4,000, but not quite there until she wins.

Paint Me established a class level on May 26, 1992, by winning at the claiming $4,000 level. Her next race was at a distance of a mile and a sixteenth, so we would not use this race because of the distance. She was then dropped back down to the $5,000 level and finished a fast closing second. Paint Me then shot up to claiming $13,000 and was outrun. Her last start would not matter because of the distance. Paint Me's class level would be above $4,000 because of her win and not quite $5,000.

Roodle has run four times this year and has been outrun in every start. She has no class level base and we don't know how far she must be dropped until she improves. But dropping her to $4,000 is not going to do it.

Frannie Britches is another four-year-old filly that has not won this year and has no established class level.

Two horses in this race have established class levels; Betula and Paint Me. They both have virtually the same class level so we are going to have to look at other factors to determine between the two. Betula has a distinct edge in races, weight, and times. Betula is making only her 7th start compared to Paint Me's 24th. Twenty-four starts is too many for this time of the year and it will start to take its toll. Also, Betula will be racing with 109 pounds and Paint Me, 119. Betula has advantage in times; 1:06 compared to 1:06³/₅. Three-fifths does not sound like much, but it is equivalent to three lengths. For these reasons Betula has a slight advantage, with Paint Me close behind.

THIRD RACE 5 ½ FURLONGS. (1.02⁴) CLAIMING. Purse $4,500. Fillies and mares, 3–year–olds and

Phila Park upward which have not won two races since January 10, 1992. Weight: 3–year–olds 115 lbs., older 122 lbs. Non–winners of two races since December 10 allowed 3 lbs.; a race

JULY 10, 1992 since then, 6 lbs. Claiming price $4,000.

Value of race $4,500; value to winner $2,700; second $900; third $495; fourth $270; fifth $135. Mutuel pool $32,077. Exacta Pool $42,148 Trifecta Pool $25,059

Last Raced	Horse	M/Eqt.A.Wt	PP	St	¼	¾	Str	Fin	Jockey	Cl'g Pr	Odds $1
25Jun92 4Pha5	Betula	Lb 5 109	2	2	2hd	2hd	13½	12	Ortiz R10	4000	6.50
29Jun92 9Pha4	Paint Me	L 6 119	5	7	7	7	53	22	Cruz C	4000	5.60
19Jun92 7Del4	Nashua's Evening	L 6 110	1	3	5hd	52	42½	3½	Smith C L10	4000	8.40
2Jly92 3Pha2	Quaker Lady	b 4 116	4	4	3hd	34	21½	45½	Jocson G J	4000	.90
22Jun92 5Pha7	Roodle	Lb 4 113	6	6	612	66	65	5nk	Somsanith N3	4000	11.00
25Jun92 2Pha4	Evidence	L 4 116	3	1	1hd	1hd	3½	68½	Colton R E	4000	5.10
25Jun92 4Pha9	Frannie Britches	Lb 4 116	7	5	45	4hd	7	7	Fiorentino CT	4000	13.60

OFF AT 1:50 Start Good. Won Driving. Time, :22³, :46³, 1:06³ Track fast.

$2 Mutuel Prices:

2–BETULA	—————————————	15.00	7.60	4.20
5–PAINT ME	—————————————		5.80	4.20
1–NASHUA'S EVENING	—————————————			4.00

$2 EXACTA 2–5 PAID $95.20 $2 TRIFECTA 2–5–1 PAID $487.20

B. m, by Sauce Boat—Ode to Romeo, by Mr Leader. Trainer Solano Rafael. Bred by Doe Run Inc (Pa).

BETULA dueled for command inside, opened a clear lead in midstretch and held off PAINT ME under strong handling. PAINT ME was badly outrun early, rallied outside and finished fast. NASHUA'S EVENING saved ground, moved to challenge in deep stretch but flattened out. QUAKER LADY dueled for the lead three wide and tired. ROODLE was two wide and failed to threaten. EVIDENCE vied for command between foes and tired. FRANNIE BRITCHES raced wide and bore out wider into stretch.

Owners— 1, Solano Rafael; 2, Scetta Robert T; 3, Ruberto Louis V Jr; 4, Miller Nancy; 5, Fallon Martin L; 6, Broome Edwin T; 7, R M L Stable.

Trainers— 1, Solano Rafael; 2, Scetta Robert T; 3, Ruberto Louis V Jr; 4, Lopez Daniel J; 5, Fallon Martin L; 6, Broome Edwin T; 7, Menarde Frank J.

Corrected weight: Nashua's Evening 109 pounds. **Overweight:** Nashua's Evening 1 pound.

Courtesy of Daily Racing Form ©

Betula held off Paint Me to complete one of the easiest $95.20 exactas. **Always remember the public makes the favorite in every race and 67% of the time they are wrong.** So, when you are handicapping, do not give in to favorites automatically. In this example eliminating the favorite proved very profitable.

So far, we've discussed the "ins and outs" of class level. D'Accordress had a stakes class level base when no one else had anything but a maiden win. Betula, a $4,000 claimer, had a class level edge over the mis-handicapped 4-5 shot. This 4-5 shot had no class level base. Debra's Victory had an outstanding class level edge on the rest of the field and was the favorite despite hesitations by the betting public. **Remember: knowledge is the number one weapon for a handicapper**.

Shipping Horses

2

Horses that ship in from other tracks (shippers) are usually mis-handicapped and deliver huge payouts. Shippers take more time to handicap because they require more knowledge from the handicapper. The average horseplayer cannot determine why a horse is shipping from one place to another. This creates an opportunity for you. It occurs every day at all tracks. A horse ships in from a well known track to a track that is not as competitive and is also dropping in class. This horse is usually the favorite, and usually loses. Learning this angle can be very profitable. It can move the handicapper to more value plays with less risk. In the upcoming example you will see how this angle can be played.

As we've mentioned, knowledge is the key to figuring out if the shipper we are handicapping is worth our bet. Diamonds Galore was the obvious pick to the handicapper with no knowledge, even though he was not the favorite. It did not take an expert to notice that Diamonds Galore held the track record on the Monmouth Park Turf Course.

10

TURF COURSE — START — 5 FURLONGS — MONMOUTH PARK — FINISH

5 FURLONGS. **(Turf). (.544) 5th Running OCEAN HOTEL STAKES. Purse $35,000. 3-year-olds and upward. Free nominations close Saturday, July 4. $100 supplementary nominations close Friday, July 10. $300 to start. Weight, 3-year-olds, 116 lbs. Older, 122 lbs. Non-winners of $16,000 twice in 1992 allowed 3 lbs.; $13,500 twice since April 1, 5 lbs.; $12,000 twice in 1992, 7 lbs.; $9,600 twice since May 1, 9 lbs. (Maiden, claiming and starter races not considered.) The owner of the winner to receive a trophy. Closed with 30 Nominations July 4, 1992.**

LASIX—Camden Harbor, Slewfoot Seven, Junk Bond King, L. J.'s Terminator, Nucleon, Roger Jon–Nz.

BUTAZOLIDIN—Devil On Ice, Valamont.

Devil On Ice

B. c. 3(Mar), by Devil's Bag—Ivy Road, by Dr Fager
Br.—Costelloe John (Ky)
Own.—Due Process Stable **Tr.—Gleaves Philip A (—)** **107**

Lifetime 6 2 0 1 $63,680 — 1992 1 0 0 0 $200 — 1991 5 2 0 1 $63,480 — Wet 1 1 0 0 $16,200

29Feb92- 7GP fst 6½f :221 :444 1:152 Alw 23800 57 3 3 32½ 54½ 512 523½ Krone J A 117 1.80 78-10 D.J.Cat117¾Binlong1172½ToughndRugged112 Gave way 5

2Nov91- 6CD fst 1¹⁄₁₆ :463 1:12 1:443 Br Cp Juv 59 11 5 54½ 88¼ 1123 1024½ Santos J A B 122 18.50f 67-09 Arazi1225Bertrndo1223½SnppyLnding122 5-W, gave way 14
2Nov91-Grade I; 5-wide, gave way

12Oct91- 8Bel fst 1 :45 1:102 1:363 Champagne 74 13 1 21 52½ 47½ 411 Santos J A 122 8.00 76-16 TrtoWtch1227½SnppyLndng1223½PnBlff122 Wide, tired 15
12Oct91-Grade I

25Sep91- 1Bel sly 7f :221 :451 1:232 Alw 27000 93 5 1 11 11½ 11½ 11¼ Santos J A 122 4.40 87-14 Devil On Ice1221¼ Lure11714CraftyCoventry119 Driving 5

8Sep91- 3Bel fst 6f :221 :452 1:102 Md Sp Wt 84 2 1 1½ 13 13 13¾ Santos J A 118 *.90 88-11 DevilOnIce1183¾SnppyLnding1133¼Onlooker118 Driving 9

28Jly91- 4Sar fst 6f :22 :451 1:11 Md Sp Wt 74 12 4 31 32 32½ 32¼ Antley C W 118 *1.80 87-13 Big Sur1182¼ TritoWatch118hdDevilOnIce118 Weakened 12

LATEST WORKOUTS ●Jly 9 Sar tr.t 4f sly :483 H — Jly 5 Sar tr.t 5f sly 1:024 H — ●Jun 30 Sar tr.t 3f fst :353 H — Jun 24 Sar Ⓣ 5f fm 1:04 B (d)

Valamont

B. c. 4, by Prince Valid—Brief Moment, by Timeless Moment
Br.—Hughes Fred (Md)
Own.—Krems Elliott **Tr.—Garcia Efrain T (4 0 0 0 .00)** **117**

Lifetime 27 11 2 3 $127,536 — 1992 12 4 1 0 $47,693 — 1991 15 7 1 3 $79,843 — Turf 2 1 0 0 $3,900 — Wet 2 1 0 0 $10,113

4Jly92- 5Pha gd 5f :214 :451 :574 3↑Alw 21500 77 6 4 32½ 32 53 4¾ Black A S L 119 *1.00 92-11 ImSrtn116½BndllOdds116nkShllMstr116 Squzd,sted late 6
4Jly92-Originally Scheduled on Turf

25Jun92- 4Atl fm *5½f Ⓣ:22 :462 1:042 3↑Alw 7500s 90 3 3 1½ 11½ 1½ 1hd Black A S L 119 1.80 96-07 Vlmont119hdSlewfootSevn1173½FirmnFiv117 Stiff drive 5

11Jun92- 8Pha fst 6f :213 :444 1:101 3↑Alw 23005 99 3 4 2hd 1hd 1hd 11¾ Black A S L 116 4.00 90-15 Vlmont1161¾DukeofSxony1191¾BornToShop119 Driving 6

16May92-10Pha sly 6f :211 :434 1:083 3↑Musket H 76 4 2 32 34 39 414½ Aguila G E L 114 2.60 83-16 EgleAve.1149½Miner'sDrem1163RockbyeJoshu119 Tired 5

18Apr92- 1Pha gd 6f :22 :45 1:092 Alw 8500s 97 1 3 11½ 1½ 11½ 11½ Black A S L 116 *.90 94-11 Vlmnt1161½TrffcPcr1191¾EthrlMnt122 Drifted, driving 7

4Apr92- 8GS fst 6f :221 :451 1:102 3↑Equus Bc H 84 4 3 1hd 33½ 68¼ 68¾ Black A S L 115 7.70 81-20 Joy'sFrstJov1164½Fftysvnvtt1222Ncln114 Thru after 1/2 6

14Mar92- 8Pha fst 7f :22 :442 1:224 The Hemlock 88 6 2 11½ 1½ 57½ 74½ Madrigal R Jr L 122 *1.50 89-17 VldNy1161½ThClMyrrh1221¾RckbyJsh122 Came in, tired 8

4Mar92- 8Aqu fst 6f ⊡:223 :46 1:114 Alw 41000 78 7 2 2½ 2½ 37½ 511 Velazquez J R 119 3.40 73-24 Rppl1152½Sl'nAvngr1195ACrkngLmrck115 Dueled, tired 7

17Feb92-11Lrl fst 7f :221 :444 1:214 3↑Gen George 17 7 6 55¾ 1218 1234 1241¼ Madrigal R Jr L 118 28.30 57-16 SnorSpdy1262SunnySnrs1232½FormlDnnr123 Thru early 12
17Feb92-Grade II

25Jan92-10Pha fst 7f :221 :444 1:212 3↑Fairview H 104 6 1 1½ 12 15 15¼ Molina V H L 117 *2.10e 100-09 Valmont1175¼Arborcrest1184BidToRomeo111 Drew off 9

LATEST WORKOUTS ●Jly 10 Pha 3f fst :352 B — Jun 19 Pha 5f fst 1:013 B — Jun 9 Pha 4f fst :472 B — Jun 4 Pha 4f fst :491 B

Camden Harbor

B. g. 5, by Distinctive Pro—Hatchet Baby, by Hatchet Man
Br.—Aisco Stable (Fla)
Own.—Minassian Harry **Tr.—Serpe Philip M (43 6 7 6 .14)** **113**

Lifetime 33 7 4 3 $153,405 — 1992 3 0 0 0 $495 — 1991 15 5 1 1 $92,168 — Turf 1 0 0 0 — Wet 5 1 0 0 $15,745

24Jun92- 7Mth my 6f :212 :442 1:104 3↑Clm 35000 84 8 1 12 12 2½ 52½ Ferrer J C L 116 4.70 84-17 Brave Adventure116nkDaddyRex1161½BigJewel119 Tired 8

7Jun92-10Mth fst 5f :213 :442 :564 3↑Wolf Hill 48 3 4 3½ 42½ 58½ 615¼ Ferrer J C b 113 4.30 82-09 JunkBondKing1131SltLk111noFrindlyLovr117 Gave way 7
7Jun92-Originally scheduled on turf

16May92- 9GS sly 6f :22 :451 1:092 3↑Alw 15000 66 4 5 1½ 63¾ 811 914½ Ferrer J C 117 3.20 81-17 HtthMhgony1175BrnTShp1172½DstyScrn117 Brief speed 10

1Nov91- 9Med fst 6f :213 :442 1:09 3↑Chf Pn'kck H 27 2 1 11 42½ 814 828¼ Migliore R b 113 13.70 69-15 J.R.'sFortn113nkTddyDron1161½GllntStp116 Brief speed 8

4Oct91- 7Bel fst 6f :22 :45 1:094 3↑Alw 41000 33 6 1 1hd 31 713 725¼ Smith M E 119 3.30e 66-19 Wondrlof1151¾DrummondLn115¾KingofWll115 Used up 7

14Sep91-10Pha fst 6f :212 :442 1:092 3↑Bud Bdrs' H 51 1 2 1½ 41 716 721 Ramos W S 112 3.40 76-13 KeySpirit1183¼Hdif1152Pulvrizing113 Tired badly, easd 7
14Sep91-Grade III

28Aug91- 7Bel fst 6f :22 :45 1:091 3↑Alw 41000 86 2 1 11 1hd 31½ 44¼ Ramos W S 115 3.40 90-10 SunnyBlossom1222½SixSpeed1151½TomCobbly115 Tired 5

3Aug91- 8Mth fst 6f :21 :432 1:083 3↑Sneakbox 103 5 5 11½ 1½ 11 1¾ Ramos W S 117 *2.10 98-11 CmdenHrbor117¾CndinSilvr1141½DHGllntStp113 Driving 12

14Jly91- 8Mth gd 5f :211 :441 :564 3↑Alw 26000 103 1 2 1½ 11½ 13½ 14 Ramos W S 122 *1.40 99-08 CmdenHrbor1224BigTedK.1153Millersvill115 Ridden out 8
14Jly91-Originally scheduled on turf

4Jly91- 6Mth fm 5f Ⓣ:213 :443 :564 3↑Ocean Hotel 81 8 2 2hd 1hd 3½ 64¾ Pezua J M 119 2.80 88-07 MFrnchmn117nkJ'sFrstJ1153¼PlPrnc113 Bad step bkstr. 8

LATEST WORKOUTS ●May 30 Mth 3f fst :343 H

My Frenchman

Dk. b. or br. g. 7, by Superbity—French and Bold, by L'Aiglon
Br.—Falls Ridge Stable (Md)
Own.—Torsney Philip J **Tr.—Murphy James W (1 1 0 0 1.00)** **113**

Lifetime 46 17 6 4 $427,535 — 1992 2 1 1 0 $24,585 — 1991 10 5 1 1 $137,750 — Turf 23 13 2 4 $358,135 — Wet 3 1 0 0 $6,360

3Jly92- 7Mth fm 5f Ⓣ:212 :441 :561 3↑Alw 26000 89 6 4 52¼ 21 2½ 11¾ Bravo J b 115 *.70 93-07 MyFrnchmn1151¾Shll'sChrmr115noBlWlf115 Drew clear 9

25May92- 9Pim fm 5f Ⓣ:223 :46 :574 3↑Roman H 90 8 1 31½ 22 21 2¾ Prado E S Lb 122 *.90e 92-07 GreenWyCourt114¾MyFrenchmn1221D'Prrot113 Gamely 8

20Oct91- 9Lrl sf 6f Ⓣ:23 :463 1:112 3↑Laurel Dash 88 3 3 42 34½ 49 410½ Prado E S b 120 5.60 74-15 Forest Glow1246 Robinski-NZ1202 Hadif120 Weakened 6
20Oct91-Grade III

6Sep91- 6Med fm 5f Ⓣ:212 :442 :554 3↑Mercer Cty 97 4 2 2½ 21 2hd 11 McCauley W H b 122 *2.30 98-02 My Frenchman1221 D'Parrot114nkPurrmont113 Driving 11

24Aug91- 8Mth yl 5f Ⓣ:22 :451 :573 3↑Wolf Hill 95 8 1 72½ 63¼ 43½ 31¼ Bravo J b 122 *2.10 88-11 DmndsGlr1131¼Jy'sFrstJv113noMyFrnchmn122 Good try 10

11Aug91-11Lrl fm 6f Ⓣ:224 :46 1:093 3↑Groovy H 93 4 3 22½ 21 22 23 Prado E S b 123 *.90 91-06 Woodsy1093MyFrenchman1231½Murmurtion113 Gamely 7

21Jly91- 6Atl fm 5½f Ⓣ:213 :441 1:022 3↑Atl Sprint 95 6 2 31½ 31½ 3½ 11¼ Day P b 122 *1.40 97-03 MyFrnchmn1221¼EtolDF111nkDontclosyorys113 Driving 8

4Jly91- 6Mth fm 5f Ⓣ:213 :443 :564 3↑Ocean Hotel 96 7 1 4¾ 3nk 1½ 1nk Bravo J b 117 *1.30 93-07 MyFrnchmn117nkJoy'sFirstJov1153¼PlyPrnc113 Driving 8

18Jun91- 9Mth my 5f :213 :44 :561 3↑Alw 26000 59 1 4 52 78 611 613½ Santagata N b 119 4.30 88-06 CmdnHrbor1224VidoMgc1193½ArForsGun119 Thru early 7
18Jun91-Originally scheduled on turf

2Jun91-10Mth fm 1 Ⓣ:452 1:082 1:331 3↑Red Bank H 93 6 2 21½ 32½ 47 58¾ Santagata N b 115 23.60 98 — DoubleBooked1221GretNormnd118¾NowListen112 Tired 10
2Jun91-Grade III

LATEST WORKOUTS ●Jly 10 Lrl 3f fst :35 H — Jun 29 Lrl 4f fst :484 H — Jun 23 Lrl Ⓣ 5f fm 1:01 H (d) — ●Jun 16 Lrl Ⓣ 5f fm 1:011 H (d)

Slewfoot Seven

B. g. 4, by Lines of Power—Table Vice, by Round Table
Br.—Farish W S & Hancock A (Ky)
Tr.—Reid Mark J (59 6 6 14 .10)
Own.—Someday Farm

113

Lifetime						
19 7 5 2	1992	2	0	2	0	$4,300
$68,615	1991	14	7	2	1	$62,145
	Turf	9	5	3	1	$55,245
	Wet	1	0	0	0	

25Jun92- 4Atl	fm	*5½f	(T):22 :462 1:042	3↑Alw 7500s	90	4	1	31	21½	2½	2hd	Colton R E	L 117	*.40	96-07 Valmont119hdSlewfootSeven1173¼FiremnFive117	Hung	5
24May92- 8GS	fm	5f	(T):221 :453 :573	3↑Handicap	81	1	3	21½	22	21	2no	Ferrer J C	L 116	*1.40	93-06 BlueWolf116noSlwfootSvn1161NustFlsh113	Just missed	6
7Nov91- 7Med	fm	5f	(T):22 :443 :561	3↑Alw 12500s	91	5	1	2½	2hd	1½	11½	Bravo J	L 115	1.50	96-03 SlewfootSvn1151½Purrmont1122St.Pt'sMircl115	Driving	10
7Oct91- 8Med	fst	5f	:214 :451 :572	3↑Alw 12500s	92	6	1	31	21½	2hd	13¾	Bravo J	L 114	*1.70	96-13 SlewfootSeven1143¾SugarGuy1112VlidNtion117	Driving	7
7Oct91-Originally Scheduled on turf																	
4Sep91- 6Med	fm	5f	(T):214 :444 :562	Susex County	92	8	2	2½	3½	2½	1nk	Bravo J	L 113	9.80	95-05 SlewfootSvn113nkFrindlyLovr1173OlGrumby115	Driving	1[illegible]
11Aug91- 8Del	yl	5f	(T):221 :463 :593	3↑Alw 7700	82	5	1	41½	42	41½	1nk	Molina V H	L 116	*.80	86-14 SlwfootSvn116nkLdPowr1161½ContrryContr113	Driving	8
12Jly91- 7Pha	fm	5f	(T):224 :454 :58	3↑Alw 14500	87	12	2	2hd	11	12	13¼	Castillo R E	L 114	3.20	92-08 SlewfootSvn1143¼FirmnFiv116nkTonyCool116	Drew out	12
17Jun91- 9Pha	fm	*5f	(T) :583	3↑Alw 13500	82	1	1	1hd	1½	12½	17	Jocson G J5	L 103	*.70	91-09 SlewfootSvn1037DrtoExcl1161KyToNobility116	Driving	8
9Jun91- 8Del	fm	5f	(T):214 :453 :574	Alw 7800	84	4	3	2½	3½	21	2no	Jones S R	L 116	4.10	95-05 ContrryContre116noSlwfootSvn1161¾WizJim116	Gamely	12
24May91- 7GS	fm	5f	(T):22 :454 :582	Alw 11500	81	2	3	62¼	53¼	54½	32	Jocson G J5	L 111	37.90	87-11 Algrm116noDelphinusStr1112SlwfootSvn111	Belated bid	8

LATEST WORKOUTS Jly 8 Pha 4f fst :483 Bg Jun 17 Pha 4f fst :53 B Jun 9 Pha 4f fst :503 B Jun 2 Pha 4f fst :514 B

Junk Bond King

Dk. b. or br. h. 5, by Baldski—Shesurecandance, by Winged T
Br.—Farnsworth Farm & Marcochio (Fla)
Tr.—Jennings Lawrence Jr (25 6 3 2 .24)
Own.—Fox Four Stable

122

Lifetime						
19 5 5 2	1992	4	2	1	1	$49,750
$93,595	1991	9	2	2	1	$27,205
	Turf	2	0	1	0	$3,600
	Wet	2	2	0	0	$17,700

27Jun92- 8Mth	fst	6f	:214 :442 1:094	3↑Decathlon	99	4	3	1½	12½	12	11	Rivera L Jr	Lb 115	9.40	92-15 JunkBondKing1151SunnySrv1151½Hoolgnsm114	Driving	7
7Jun92-10Mth	fst	5f	:213 :442 :564	3↑Wolf Hill	96	2	3	1½	11	11½	11	Rivera L Jr	Lb 113	11.70	97-09 JunkBondKing1131SltLke111noFriendlyLovr117	Driving	7
7Jun92-Originally scheduled on turf																	
15Apr92- 7Crc	fst	6f	:213 :442 1:11	3↑Clm 50000	93	5	1	2hd	1hd	2hd	2nk	Ramos W S	Lb 119	2.10	97-09 FrnklnM119nkJnkBndKng1193½EtrnlOrg119	Grudgingly	6
26Mar92- 7Crc	fst	6f	:22 :452 1:103	Clm 55000	90	5	6	62¾	41¾	32½	35¾	Penna D	Lb 114	15.00	— — DrndLn118¾PrChp1165JnBndKn114	Improved position	7
14Aug91- 9Mth	fst	6f	:213 :441 1:094	3↑Alw 19000	82	8	1	2hd	1hd	2½	62½	Rivera L Jr	Lb 116	3.00	89-13 SurSensitive116hdColdDiggr116noRglKris116	Weakened	8
3Aug91- 9Lrl	fst	6f	:22 :451 1:11	3↑Alw 18000	88	4	3	2½	1hd	12	12	Pino M G	Lb 117	7.60	86-18 JunkBondKing1172BlueWolf114nkOnTheOne117	Driving	10
23Jly91- 9Mth	gd	*5f	(T):212 :451 :573	3↑Alw 18000	84	2	4	1½	11½	11½	2½	Rivera L Jr	Lb 116	9.90	91-08 Murmrton116½JnkBondKng116¾I'mWld110	Yielded late	8
9Jun91- 5Mth	fst	1	:474 1:12 1:372	3↑Alw 19000	67	3	1	11	1½	32	49¼	Ramos W S	Lb 119	6.80	73-21 IslndEdition1171½SirSlim1176Drby'sNotic117	Gave way	5
1Jun91- 3Mth	gd	6f	:214 :451 1:103	3↑Alw 18000	59	5	3	2½	21½	44½	710¼	Gryder A T	Lb 118	4.30	77-15 Fiftysvnvtt1162¾IslndEdition1161SlfEvdnt113	Gave way	7
6May91- 8Pha	sly	6f	:214 :443 1:094	3↑Alw 13500	89	2	1	11½	11½	13	15½	Bisono J7	Lb 109	3.00	95-13 JunkBondKing1095½Honor'sCll1112TrythStg122	Driving	6

LATEST WORKOUTS May 12 Mth 5f fst 1:05 B

L. J.'s Terminator

Dk. b. or br. c. 4, by Slewpy—Bridge Table, by Riva Ridge
Br.—Lin-Drake Farm (Fla)
Tr.—Reid Mark J (59 6 6 14 .10)
Own.—T-Bird Stable

113

Lifetime						
17 5 2 2	1992	6	1	1	0	$21,934
$72,999	1991	11	4	1	2	$51,065
	Wet	2	0	1	0	$7,720

11Jun92- 8Pha	fst	6f	:213 :444 1:101	3↑Alw 23005	73	6	5	63¾	67¼	68½	610¼	Lloyd J S	L 116	5.20	80-15 Valamont1161¾DukeofSaxony1191¾BornToShop119	Dull	6
16May92- 9GS	sly	6f	:22 :451 1:092	3↑Alw 15000	75	5	4	2½	32	37	711	Lovato F Jr	L 119	7.20	84-17 HitthMhgony1175BornToShop1172½DustyScrn117	Tired	10
21Feb92- 8Pha	fst	1	:47 1:121 1:383	Alw 22500	93	5	1	1hd	2½	25	26¾	Lloyd J S	L 119	*.60	81-29 BoldBlzr1166¾L.J.'sTrmntor1191¾Drn'tDbt113	No match	7
26Jan92- 9Pha	fst	1 1/16	:464 1:112 1:431	[R]Ivy	78	4	2	27	25	512	49	Jocson G J	L 120	2.30	84-15 Riflery122½RedPine1221½ReputedTestmony116	No rally	6
11Jan92- 8GS	fst	1	:462 1:12 1:384	3↑C Bradley	95	5	2	1hd	1½	2½	41½	Capanas S	L 112	*3.00	86-23 RdPn114nkThCoolMyrrh114½Dontclsyrys116	Grudgingly	9
1Jan92- 9Pha	fst	1	:462 1:102 1:353	Alw 22500	105	2	1	1½	11½	13	16½	Lloyd J S	L 116	5.10	103-10 L.J.'sTermintor1166½Riflery119¾Findr'sChoic116	Driving	6
14Dec91- 9Pha	my	170	:454 1:104 1:422	Flintlock	78	3	1	1½	2hd	24	210	Jocson G J	L 115	6.10	74-30 Riflery11510L.J.'sTrmintor1151½Arrowtown117	Held 2nd	8
16Nov91- 8Med	fst	170	:46 1:113 1:412	Stockton	64	1	1	2½	46½	38½	317	Jocson G J	L 115	4.60	74-21 Arrwtwn1141½VchfrM11415½L.J.'sTrmntr115	Used early	6
25Oct91- 9Pha	fst	1 1/16	:471 1:11 1:422	3↑Alw 17500	101	3	1	1hd	11	1½	1nk	Jocson G J	L 111	*1.50	97-20 L.J.'sTrmintor111nkBltvo1167ColdByDy116	Dckd in,drvg	8
7Oct91- 9Med	fst	6f	:22 :451 1:102	3↑Alw 18000	72	4	3	2½	21	32½	46¼	Jocson G J	L 115	*1.80	84-13 Hualapai1163¾FabulousFee116nkClenndBold113	No rally	6

LATEST WORKOUTS Jly 8 Mth 4f fst :473 H Jly 2 Mth 4f fst :50 B May 29 Pha 5f fst :593 H ●May 13 Pha 4f fst :474 B

Beyond all Odds

B. g. 7, by What Luck—Beyond Reasoning, by Hurry to Market
Br.—Mihovich Matt (NY)
Tr.—Picou James E (—)
Own.—Miho Stable

113

Lifetime						
72 9 11 7	1992	10	2	2	1	$20,775
$112,948	1991	23	5	8	3	$41,030
	Turf	9	1	1	2	$12,565
	Wet	7	1	2	0	$6,030

4Jly92- 5Pha	gd	5f	:214 :451 :574	3↑Alw 21500	77	3	6	57½	44½	31½	2½	Molina V H	Lb 116	13.10	92-11 ImSrtn116½BndllOdds116nkShllMstr116	Wide drifted in	6
4Jly92-Originally Scheduled on Turf																	
23May92- 9FL	fst	6f	:214 :45 1:101	3↑[S]GeoWBarker	55	5	5	67½	58	68	615¾	Messina R	b 115	5.90	79-19 SHuntr113¾Lordofthmountin11511SwtRgmn113	Outrun	6
26Apr92- 8GS	fst	5f	:221 :453 :582	3↑Handicap	79	3	5	55	58	56½	43¼	Picon J	Lb 115	8.60	93-24 Jesuit118nk Blue Wolf1162½ KingShamong113	Even trip	6
11Apr92- 8FL	fst	5f	:223 :463 :581	3↑[S]Alw 11700	84	5	2	41½	31	3nk	16½	Messina R	b 116	*1.20	95-09 BeyondllOdds1166½SlutIt1162CobyEscpd116	Ridden out	6
26Mar92- 8GS	sly	5½f	:22 :46 1:051	3↑Alw 11000	85	6	7	56	44	42½	52¼	Colton R E	Lb 119	*1.30	84-28 IrsBlEs116¾ArctcDcr1161½RcrdMcQN116	Flattened out	7
19Mar92- 8GS	sly	5½f	:221 :46 1:044	3↑Alw 12000	89	5	3	33½	33	2hd	2¾	Picon J	Lb 119	7.10	87-23 VideoMgic116¾ByondllOdds1192½FbulousF116	2nd best	7
7Mar92- 8GS	sly	6f	:221 :451 1:094	3↑J Kilmer H	76	2	5	53½	76¼	79¾	713½	Dentici A	Lb 109	40.30	79-15 Fftysvnvtt1203HtthMhgony1142½Arbrcrst116	No factor	7
18Feb92- 9Pha	gd	5½f	:22 :451 1:032	Alw 17500	62	5	4	56½	45	36½	38¾	Lloyd J S	Lb 118	2.60	88-14 RDWldWrl1187VdMc1161¾BdllOdds118	Wide, crrd wider	5
24Jan92- 4GS	gd	5f	:222 :463 :593	Alw 6500s	76	2	6	64½	31½	12½	13¼	Colton R E	Lb 117	*.60	90-25 ByondllOdds1173¼CldBVrs1122ShrpScty119	Ridden out	6
9Jan92- 8Aqu	gd	6f	⊡:223 :46 1:111	Alw 28000	68	2	7	85¾	76	79¾	712	Carr D	b 117	18.90	75-16 TrnChrmng1171BombStppr1193½AlwysAshly117	Outrun	8

LATEST WORKOUTS Jun 16 Bel 3f fst :361 B Jun 11 Bel 3f fst :39 B

Nucleon

Ch. h. 6, by Mr Prospector—Nonoalca, by Nonoalco
Br.—Societe Aland (Ky)
Tr.—Hennig Mark (1 0 0 0 .00)
Own.—Clover Racing Stable

113

Lifetime						
30 4 3 6	1992	6	1	0	1	$26,903
$95,822	1991	9	1	1	3	$44,175
	Turf	15	0	3	2	$22,986

18May92- 7Bel	gd	1 1/16	:45 1:09 1:402	3↑Alw 47000	70	4	3	33½	44	57	518½	Smith M E	117	8.60	82-13 ModlDncr117½Pcktt'sLndng1171¾WndhnConty117	Tired	5
25Apr92- 6Aqu	fst	6f	:222 :452 1:092	3↑Alw 41000	91	1	4	32½	32½	41½	44¼	Flores D R	117	10.40	90-15 Arrowtown1171¾Arugul117½SoldSnny117	Saved ground	5
4Apr92- 8GS	fst	6f	:221 :451 1:102	3↑Equus Bc H	90	2	6	54¼	54	45¼	36¼	Lovato F Jr	L 114	15.00	84-20 Joy'sFrstJov1164¼Fftysvnvtt1222Ncln114	Finished well	6
4Mar92- 8Aqu	fst	6f	⊡:223 :46 1:114	Alw 41000	76	4	4	65	54½	610	712	Smith M E	115	2.90	72-24 Rppl1152½Sizzl'nAvngr1195ACorkingLimrick115	Outrun	7
17Feb92-11Lrl	fst	7f	:221 :444 1:214	3↑Gen George	79	1	7	67¼	66	88½	813¼	Prado E S	L 118	54.50	85-16 SenorSpedy1262SunnySunris1232½FormlDinnr123	Tired	12

17Feb92-Grade II
20Jan92- 8Aqu fst 6f [•]:223 :46 1:114 Alw 30000 97 1 4 43 42½ 21 1hd Smith M E 117 2.20 84-23 Nucleon117hdGaz1173FightingAffir117 Altered crs drvg 4
27Dec91- 7Aqu fst 6f [•]:23 :46 1:10 3↑Alw 30000 86 3 5 66½ 46½ 38 310 Migliore R 117 21.80 83-22 BoomTownr1208YllowMtl1172Nuclon117 Saved ground 7
23Nov91- 8Lrl fst 6f :221 :454 1:101 3↑Alw 20500 62 6 7 66 77 68¾ 612 Rocco J L 117 7.60 78-19 WinAGm115¾MightyMlody1172½Philosophicl117 Outrun 7
12Oct91- 6Lrl fst 6f :22 :45 1:10 3↑Alw 20500 75 3 6 45 57 58 56¼ Juarez C L 117 7.10 85-15 BlWolf1162H'sHotShot1193¼ForryCowHw114 No factor 6
24Aug91- 8Mth yl 5f Ⓣ:22 :451 :573 3↑Wolf Hill 65 10 2 94¼ 97 109 1010¾ Colton R E L 113 3.90 78-11 DmndsGlr1131¼J'sFrstJv113noMFrnchmn122 Shwd little 10
LATEST WORKOUTS ●Jly 2 Bel 5f fst :59 H Jun 24 Bel 4f gd :482 B Jun 18 Bel 5f fst 1:013 B ●Jun 4 Bel 5f fst :584 H

D'Parrot

B. g. 5, by D'Accord—Ornately, by Val De L'orne
Br.—Forest Retreat Farms Inc (NY)
Own.—Heatherwood Farm
Tr.—Schosberg Richard (—)
113
Lifetime 31 6 4 4 $257,996
1992 5 0 0 1 $4,942
1991 11 2 2 1 $94,290
Turf 12 2 2 2 $80,542
Wet 2 0 0 0

26Jun92- 8Pim fm 1 1/16 Ⓣ:494 1:144 1:444 3↑Alw 23000 88 4 2 1hd 1hd 1½ 52 Luzzi M J Lb 118 10.20 75-26 Rebuff118noCubCper-NZ118noSocilRetire118 Weakened 7
13Jun92-11Pim fm 1 1/16 Ⓣ:46 1:104 1:423 3↑Chieftain H 78 7 4 43 33 66¾ 612 Luzzi M J Lb 112 13.80 76-25 BarondeVaux1132¼Rebuff113hdEternalOrge112 Steadied 10
25May92- 9Pim fm 5f Ⓣ:223 :46 :574 3↑Roman H 87 4 6 64 66 54½ 31¾ Luzzi M J Lb 113 4.40 91-07 GrnWyCourt114¾MyFrnchmn1221D'Prrot113 Very wide 8
26Apr92- 9Pim sly 6f :231 :462 1:12 Alw 23000 72 3 5 55½ 58½ 58½ 510½ Luzzi M J Lb 114 2.70 74-25 Root Boy1141¾ Kelly's Class114¾ Big Jewel119 Trailed 5
13Apr92- 5Aqu gd 6f :224 :452 1:091 Clm 85000 77 2 2 1½ 2hd 3½ 57½ Santos J A b 116 3.20 87-08 ArgyleLke113hdJo'sDollr116nkTrundBlu114 Dueled,tired 5
22Dec91- 7Aqu fst 6f [•]:224 :454 1:102 3↑Alw 41000 78 6 2 41½ 32 46 512¼ Santos J A b 115 9.60 79-16 Collegian1156¾ TokenDance1191ScottishMonk115 Tired 6
15Dec91- 8Aqu fst 6f [•]:22 :452 1:104 3↑[S]Joe Palmer 61 9 1 2hd 2½ 99¼ 915 Santos J A b 122 5.00 74-19 Shine Please119nkZeeBest1191½Jesuit117 Thru after 1/2 9
1Nov91- 8Aqu fst 6f :22 :45 1:101 3↑Handicap 78 1 3 1½ 1hd 42 59 Smith M E b 114 *2.00 81-17 HertofHero112¾Collegin1141½SnorCilo117 Dueled, tired 6
10Oct91- 8Bel fm 6f Ⓣ:214 :443 1:082 3↑Handicap 86 3 5 51¾ 61¾ 5¾ 85 Santos J A b 114 *1.30 — — ClubChmp1122¼Hdif114¾Kt'sVlntin115 Blocked,steadied 9
29Sep91- 8Bel fst 7f :23 :453 1:22 3↑[S]Hudson H 106 2 2 11½ 12½ 14½ 14 Santos J A b 114 4.00 94-13 D'Prrot1144ShnPls110noHrrVnKnnchn118 Kept to drive 8
LATEST WORKOUTS Jly 9 Bel tr.t 3f sly :383 B Jun 6 Bow 1 my 1:38 H ●May 19 Bow 5f fst :59 H

Roger Jon-NZ

B. g. 4, by Indian Ore—Pot of Gold, by Barcas
Br.—Conway F A (NZ)
Own.—Gold-N-Oats Stable
Tr.—Klesaris Robert P (—)
113
Lifetime 38 10 10 5 $94,142
1992 4 0 1 2 $26,763
1991 27 9 5 2 $60,659
Turf 38 10 10 5 $94,142

Entered 11Jly92- 9 MTH
13Jun92-11Rkm fm *1⅛ Ⓣ 1:464 3↑N Hmpshr H 98 10 8 87 93¾ 62¾ 52 McCauley W H LB 112 12.80 99-08 RinbowsforLf119nkNowLstn112noBuckhr118 Sted nr str 12
13Jun92-Grade III
8May92- 5Hol fm 1 Ⓣ:461 1:094 1:331 Clm c-80000 95 8 8 86 63¾ 42½ 31½ Nakatani C S L 116 *2.00 97-07 OldAllinc116hdC.SmMggio1171½RogrJon-NZ116 Rallied 8
8May92-Claimed from Cottrell & Neuberger, Roberts Donald Trainer
19Apr92 2SA fm *6½f Ⓣ:211 :431 1:122 Alw 41000 101 5 5 66¼ 65¼ 33½ 2½ Delahoussaye E L 116 5.40 96-03 Gogrty-Ir114½RogrJn-NZ116hdNnCrt116 5-wide stretch 6
3Apr92- 5SA fm *6½f Ⓣ:212 :431 1:123 Alw 41000 97 5 6 68½ 710 65 32¼ Delahoussaye E LB 116 17.30 94-04 RlGrm117nkGrt-Ir1142[DH]UmBrn-GB120 5-wide stretch 7
3Apr92-Dead heat
30Dec91 ♦7Ellerslie(NZ) fm*7½f 1:30 Ⓣ Harrison Grierson Hcp 82¾ Williamson M J 125 — — — — Force Fillee 112no Pure Lust 1121 Herculanea 112 11
23Nov91 ♦6Ellerslie(NZ) fm*1¼ 2:074 Ⓣ BlandfordLodgeDerby Trial 89½ Cropp L K 121 — — — — Te Akau Nick 1213½ Sir Winston121½ PrinceAlibhai121 14
16Nov91 ♦6TeRapa(NZ) sf*1 1:401 Ⓣ Waikato Guineas(Gr3) 41¾ Cropp L K 122 — — — — Solvit 122nk Call On Me 122nk Mr. Trevino 122 15
9Nov91 ♦5TeRapa(NZ) yl*7f 1:293 Ⓣ Citidancer Guineas Trial 22 Wilkinson M J 122 — — — — Call On Me 1182 Roger Jon 1224 Lance McCarthy 118 9
19Oct91 ♦5Ellerslie(NZ) fm*1 1:341 Ⓣ Lindauer Guineas(Gr2) 97¼ Cropp L K 123 — — — — Lodore Lady1171½ Overwhelmed1231¼ CaptainCook124 15
12Oct91 ♦4Caulfield(Aus) gd*1 1:363 Ⓣ Caulfield Guineas(Gr1) 7 Cropp L K 122 — — — — Chortle 122½ Naturalism 122¾ Ready to Explode 122 16
LATEST WORKOUTS Jun 26 Bel tr.t 6f fst 1:143 H ●Jun 3 Bel tr.t 1 fst 1:402 H (d)

Diamonds Galore

B. g. 7, by Diamond Shoal—Sirona, by Irish Stronghold
Br.—Beechwood Farm Ltd (Ont-C)
Own.—Stronach Frank
Tr.—Vella Daniel J (—)
113
Lifetime 41 13 8 2 $269,554
1992 1 1 0 0 $18,540
1991 13 4 1 1 $88,396
Turf 27 11 3 1 $218,684
Wet 4 0 1 1 $9,250

21Jun92- 7WO fm 7f Ⓣ:221 :45 1:231 3↑Alw 30900 92 2 2 1hd 11 12 12 Attard L 121 4.00 85-15 DimondsGlore1212KeyTwentyTwo114¾Dnsil113 In hand 8
7Nov91- 8Grd fst 6½f :23 :46 1:182 3↑Alw 27200 82 1 1 11½ 1½ 2hd 63 Landry R C 121 10.65 89-19 VictoryArch113nkICn'tBelieve119noMemorized111 Tired 7
27Oct91- 7WO my 7f :231 :461 1:234 3↑Alw 27200 79 7 1 22 33 511 611¾ David D J 121 10.00 82-17 TwistTheSnow1242ICn'tBeliv1176½Tjbo119 Not keep up 7
13Oct91- 7WO fm 7f Ⓣ:222 :45 1:214 3↑[R]Alw 33600 99 7 1 3½ 2hd 11½ 3hd Walls M K 119 8.65 96-04 SlfAnls119hdDsAndDnts116noDmndsGlr119 Just missed 9
25Sep91- 9WO fm 6½f Ⓣ:22 :45 1:162 3↑Alw 27200 81 1 1 1½ 1hd 34 67½ Hawley S 124 *1.25 82-10 SlwofAngls1192½StormyGlditor119hdAmd'sRul113 Tired 7
8Sep91- 9WO fm 1⅛ Ⓣ:45 1:09 1:463 3↑Jky Clb H 94 8 1 12 12½ 1½ 73 Platts R 115 15.65 88-09 TotofRum1142Cozzene'sPrince117noMarribunt108 Tired 9
8Sep91-Grade II-C
24Aug91- 8Mth yl 5f Ⓣ:22 :451 :573 3↑Wolf Hill 99 1 7 3½ 1hd 12 11¼ Gryder A T 113 2.80 89-11 DmondsGlr1131¼Jy'sFrstJv113noMyFrnchmn122 Driving 10
10Aug91-10WO fm 1 Ⓣ:462 1:114 1:371 3↑Alw 29900 96 7 1 11½ 13 1hd 23 Attard L 113 *.75 78-19 TotofRum1143DiamondsGalore1133½BriarBush119 Tired 7
26Jly91- 7WO fm 6½f Ⓣ:222 :451 1:154 3↑Clm 100000 94 1 2 11½ 12 17 13½ Attard L 121 *.45 93-07 DmondsGlor1213½Lordhyxctonr1153½GMssn118 In hand 5
7Jly91- 3WO sf 1 [T]:46 1:11 1:38 3↑Handicap 97 8 4 31½ 2hd 2hd 42 Attard L 119 7.20 62-16 Asturino-Ch115½PltDncr1171StormyGlditor122 No rally 10
LATEST WORKOUTS Jly 9 WO tr.t 3f sly :373 B ●Jly 4 WO tr.t 5f gd 1:013 B ●Jun 18 WO tr.t 3f fst :352 B ●Jun 13 WO tr.t 5f fst :593 H

Camden Harbour made only one appearance on the turf course and tired while taking a bad step on the back stretch. He has improved since that start. Since he will go right to the lead because of his inside post, he will be a good play in the gimmicks, but not a serious threat to Diamonds Galore.

My Frenchman is a seven-year-old gelding like Diamonds Galore. My Frenchman is making his third start of this year and if we look back to the Wolf Hill Stakes on August 24, 1991, My Frenchman could not make up enough ground as Diamonds Galore led all the way. That was the last time these two met. He still puts up good speed figures and should be used in the gimmicks.

Slewfoot Seven is a four-year-old gelding who is consistently close but has no class and should not be close against these horses.

Junk Bond King is a Baldski offspring that can run with these on the dirt, but has not proven itself on the turf. If this was an allowance race, Junk Bond King would probably be effective on the turf, but not against this competition.

L.J.'s Terminator has never run on turf and cannot even keep up with this kind on dirt. How is he going to on turf?

Beyond All Odds is another seven-year-old gelding who has run fairly well on the turf in the past, but he doesn't have enough class to compete with these.

Nucleon was beaten by ten lengths against this kind of competition on August 24, 1991, so why should he improve? Also, he has never won on the turf.

D'Parrot did have a good run on May 25, 1992, but that was all. He does not appear to be the horse he once was. His post from the outside will hurt his chances considerably.

The fact that Diamonds Galore is a gelding from Woodbine is an advantage in itself. As we noted earlier, Woodbine horses are always better than the East Coast competition. Diamonds Galore makes it a habit to come to Monmouth Park, as he has for the last three years, winning in every trip. The last trip to the East Coast was on August 24, 1991, where Diamonds Galore met many of the horses that are in this race. He led from the start, cutting fractions of 22 flat, 45$\frac{1}{5}$, and 57$\frac{3}{5}$. This horse seemed too obvious until I realized that 90 percent of the handicappers at Monmouth Park could not pick a winner to save their lives. His workouts are better than any of these. He is the outstanding selection.

10

THE OCEAN HOTEL STAKES
$35,000

FOR THREE-YEAR-OLDS AND UPWARD. Free nomination fee, $300 to pass the entry box and an additional $300 to start. Three-Year-Olds: 116 lbs.; Older: 122 lbs.. Non-winners of $16,000 twice in 1992 allowed 3 lbs.; $13,500 twice since April 1, 5 lbs.; $12,000 twice in 1992, 7 lbs.; $9,600 twice since May 1, 9 lbs. (Maiden, claiming and starter races not considered.) The owner of the winner to receive a trophy. Closed Saturday, July 4, 1992 with 30 nominations. $100 supplemental nominations were made at time of entry Friday, July 10, 1992. (If deemed inadvisable by management to run this race over the turf course, this race will be run on the main track.)

↓ MAKE SELECTION BY PROGRAM NUMBER	MORNING LINE
OWNER / TRAINER	JOCKEY

1 DUE PROCESS STABLES — P. A. GLEAVES Green, Green Shamrock on White Ball, Orange Band on Sleeves, Green Cap **DEVIL ON ICE (S)** 107 B. c.'89, Devil's Bag-Ivy Road, by Dr. Fager	**15** RICHARD YBARRA
2 HARRY MINASSIAN — P. M. SERPE Blue, Yellow Sash, Orange "M", Blue Bars on Orange Sleeves, Blue Cap **CAMDEN HARBOR** (L) 113 B. g.'87, Distinctive Pro-Hatchet Baby, by Hatchet Man	**15** ROSEMARY HOMEISTER
3 PHILIP J. TORSNEY — J. W. MURPHY Green, Orange Hoops, Orange Bars on Sleeves, Green Cap **MY FRENCHMAN** 113 Dk.b/br. g.'85, Superbity-French and Bold, by L' Aiglon	**2** JOE BRAVO
4 SOMEDAY FARM — M. J. REID Blue, Blue "C" on Grey Ball, Grey Dots on Sleeves, Blue Cap **SLEWFOOT SEVEN** (L) 113 B. g.'88, Lines Of Power-Table Vice, by Round Table	**8** JOHN GRABOWSKI
5 FOX FOUR STABLE — L. W. JENNINGS, JR. Fluorescent Pink, White Sash and "F", White Chevrons on Sleeves, Pink Cap **JUNK BOND KING** (L) 122 Dk.b/br. g.'87, Baldski-Shesurecandance, by Winged T.	**4** LUIS RIVERA, JR.
6 T-BIRD STABLE — M. J. REID Yellow, Black Sash and Circled Emblem, Black Bars on Sleeves, Yellow Cap **L J.'S TERMINATOR** (L) 113 Dk.b/br. g.'88, Slewpy-Bridge Table, by Riva Ridge	**20** FRANK LOVATO, JR.
7 MI-HO STABLE — J. E. PICOU Purple, Orange Diamond Frame, Orange Chevrons on Sleeves, Purple Cap **BEYOND ALL ODDS** (L) 113 B. g.'85, What Luck-Beyond Reasoning, by Hurry To Market	**20** JUAN PICON
8 CLOVER RACING STABLES — M. HENNIG Black, Green Four Leaf Clovers, Black Cap **NUCLEON** (L) 113 Ch. h.'86, Mr. Prospector-Nonoalca, by Nonoalco	**20** NICK SANTAGATA
9 HEATHERWOOD FARM — R. SCHOSBERG Black, Black Dots on Blue Sleeves, Black Cap **D'PARROT** (L) 113 B. g.'87, D'Accord-Ornately, by Val De L' Orne	**15** DAVID W. LIDBERG

	GOLD-N-OATS STABLE	R. P. KLESARIS	**5**
	Yellow, Turquoise Diamonds, Turquoise Bars on Sleeves, Turquoise Cap		
10	**ROGER JON (NZ) (S)** (L) 113	JOSE ROMERO	
	B. g.'88, Indian Ore-Pot Of Gold, by Barcas		
	FRANK H. STRONACH	D. J. VELLA	**5**
	Light Blue, Black Diamond Frame, Black Band on Sleeves, Blue and Black Cap		
11	**DIAMONDS GALORE** 113	AARON T. GRYDER	
	B. g.'85, Diamond Shoal-Sirona, by Irish Stronghold		

(L) Treated with Lasix - (S) Supplementary Nomination
Equipment Change: (BLINKERS ON) SLEWFOOT SEVEN
Scratched: VALAMONT

In course record time, Diamonds Galore drew off in the stretch to win easily over the favored My Frenchman. He beat the East Coast challengers for the third time. Not every shipper is as consistent as Diamonds Galore, but this angle can be very profitable on a day to day basis.

TENTH RACE

Monmouth

JULY 12, 1992

5 FURLONGS.(Turf). (.544) 5th Running OCEAN HOTEL STAKES. Purse $35,000. 3-year-olds and upward. Free nominations close Saturday, July 4. $100 supplementary nominations to start Friday, July 10. $300 to start. Weight, 3-year-olds, 116 lbs. Older, 122 lbs. Non-winners of $16,000 twice in 1992 allowed 3 lbs.; $13,500 twice since April 1, 5 lbs.; $12,000 twice in 1992, 7 lbs.; $9,600 twice since May 1, 9 lbs. (Maiden, claiming and starter races not considered.) The owner of the winner to receive a trophy. Closed with 30 Nominations July 4, 1992.

Value of race $35,000; value to winner $21,000; second $6,650; third $3,850; fourth $1,750; balance of starters $350 each.
Mutuel pool $97,327. Exacta Pool $143,529

Last Raced	Horse	M/Eqt.A.Wt	PP	St	¼	½	Str	Fin	Jockey	Odds $1
21Jun92 7WO1	Diamonds Galore	7 113	9	1	3½	1hd	11½	1½	Gryder A T	3.40
3Jly92 7Mth1	My Frenchman	b 7 113	2	5	4½	31	35½	22½	Bravo J	1.10
24Jun92 7Mth5	Camden Harbor	L 5 113	1	4	1hd	21	2hd	34	Homeister R B Jr	16.90
25Jun92 4Atl2	Slewfoot Seven	Lb 4 115	3	3	6½	7hd	51½	42	Grabowski J A	6.90
18May92 7Bel5	Nucleon	L 6 113	7	8	71	6½	7½	5no	Santagata N	54.90
4Jly92 5Pha2	Beyond all Odds	Lb 7 115	6	9	8½	85	85	6no	Picon J	39.40
27Jun92 8Mth1	Junk Bond King	Lb 5 122	4	2	2½	4½	4hd	7no	Rivera L Jr	4.00
26Jun92 8Pim5	D'Parrot	Lb 5 114	8	6	53	52½	6½	84	Lidberg D W	11.60
11Jun92 8Pha6	L. J.'s Terminator	L 4 114	5	7	9	9	9	9	Lovato F Jr	76.90

OFF AT 5:16 Start good. Won driving. Time, :21², :43⁴, :55⁴ Course firm.

$2 Mutuel Prices:

11-DIAMONDS GALORE	8.80	4.00	3.60
3-MY FRENCHMAN		2.80	2.60
2-CAMDEN HARBOR			5.60

$2 EXACTA 11-3 PAID $19.40

B. g, by Diamond Shoal—Sirona, by Irish Stronghold. Trainer Vella Daniel J. Bred by Beechwood Farm Ltd, (Ont-C).
DIAMONDS GALORE broke alertly, moved to the front soon after entering the turn, drew clear in upper stretch then held off MY FRENCHMAN. The latter saved ground until nearing the lane, moved out for the drive and finished gamely. CAMDEN HARBOR saves ground while vying for the lead into the lane and weakened in the drive. SLEWFOOT SEVEN, in tight soon after the start, lacked the needed bid. JUNK BOND KING pressed the early issue, came out nearing the top of the lane, was quickly straightened then gave way. D'PARROT was forced to steadily briefly and forced wide nearing the top of the lane then gave way.
Owners— 1, Stronach Frank; 2, Torsney Philip J; 3, Minassian Harry; 4, Someday Farm; 5, Clover Racing Stable; 6, Milio Stable; 7, Fox Four Stable; 8, Heatherwood Farm; 9, T-Bird Stable.
Trainers— 1, Vella Daniel J; 2, Murphy James W; 3, Serpe Philip M; 4, Reid Mark J; 5, Hennig Mark; 6, Picou James E; 7, Jennings Lawrence Jr; 8, Schosberg Richard; 9, Reid Mark J.
Overweight: Slewfoot Seven 2 pounds; Beyond all Odds 2; D'Parrot 2; L. J.'s Terminator 1.
Scratched—Devil On Ice (29Feb92 7GP5); Valamont (4Jly92 5Pha4); Roger Jon-NZ (11Jly92 9Mth8).

Many times when horses ship from one track to another it is because the horse cannot compete and is brought to a new, less competitive track. That is often the case with maidens.

The sixth race at Monmouth Park on July 2, 1992, featured eight horses from different tracks, and one first time starter. Four of these horses were from Garden State, which was closed at the time. It is normal for these horses to transfer to Monmouth Park. The four true shippers were Rahesa-Mx, shipping in from Mexico, Basket Leave from Calder in Florida, Made For Rain from Belmont Park in New York, and Malefactor from Keeneland in Kentucky.

TURF COURSE

6 START 1 1/16 MILES MONMOUTH PARK FINISH

ABOUT 1 $\frac{1}{16}$ MILES. **(Turf, Chute). (1.41^3) MAIDEN SPECIAL WEIGHT. Purse $15,500. 3–year–olds and upward. Weight, 3–year–olds, 114 lbs. Older, 123 lbs.**

Coupled—Malefactor and Basque's Ad.
LASIX—Petit Parisien, Basket Leave, Kinsalee.

Made for Rain — Dk. b. or br. c. 3(Mar), by Sovereign Dancer—Please Answer, by Be My Guest
Br.—Mrs. Horatio Luro (Ky)
Own.—Wright William W — Tr.—Wright William W (—) — **114**
Lifetime 2 0 0 0 $960 — 1992 2 M 0 0 $960 — 1991 0 M 0 0 — Wet 1 0 0 0 $960
13May92- 4Bel fst 7f :22^2 :45 1:23 Md Sp Wt 22 1 10 3^1 4^4 9^{14} 9^{23} Cruguet J 122 23.60 66–07 Spancil Hill122$^{3\frac{3}{4}}$ Emerald Fable122^{nk} Croon122 Faded 10
16Apr92- 3Kee my 6f :22^3 :47 1:12 Md Sp Wt 42 6 8 5^4 5$^{2\frac{1}{4}}$ 4$^{5\frac{1}{2}}$ 4$^{11\frac{3}{4}}$ Hernandez R B 121 9.70 71–14 SkyTrckr121^{2}SucyLtin121^{9}Mr.PrimRt121 Flattened out 11
LATEST WORKOUTS May 24 Bel 4f fst :49^3 Hg — May 10 Bel tr.t 5f my 1:04^1 B — May 4 Bel 4f fst :48^4 H — Apr 14 Kee 4f fst :51 B

Justabonus — Dk. b. or br. c. 3(Apr), by Dallasite—Nimbra, by Alhambra
Br.—Ted J. Mims (Ky)
Own.—Mims Sandra — Tr.—Mims Ted J (—) — **114**
Lifetime 5 0 2 1 $10,470 — 1992 5 M 2 1 $10,470 — 1991 0 M 0 0 — Turf 1 0 1 0 $5,090 — Wet 1 0 0 0
17May92- 7CD fm 1⅛ Ⓣ:47^3 1:12 1:49^3 3↑Md Sp Wt 68 5 5 3^2 2^1 2^2 2^5 Peck B D LB 111 20.50 83–08 GalleyLd111^{5}Justbonus111^{2}MidwyHeir123 Second best 10
3Apr92- 4Kee fst 1$\frac{1}{16}$:49 1:14^1 1:46^3 Md Sp Wt 38 11 7 8$^{2\frac{3}{4}}$ 8$^{8\frac{1}{4}}$ 9^{17} 9$^{23\frac{1}{2}}$ Mella S A LB 117 20.30 47–28 Chourve117$^{\frac{3}{4}}$HloNorthern110^{3}Westring117 Bore in start 11
21Mar92- 6TP fst 1$\frac{1}{16}$:48^2 1:14 1:48 Md Sp Wt 73 7 2 1^{hd} 1$^{1\frac{1}{2}}$ 1^2 2no Bruin J E LB 121 5.60 67–34 Untmyfr121^{no}Jstbns121^{6}HstrcMdwy121 Failed 2nd best 8
16Feb92- 6TP my 6$\frac{1}{2}$f :23 :46^4 1:20^2 Md Sp Wt 39 6 5 5$^{3\frac{1}{4}}$ 8$^{8\frac{1}{2}}$ 7$^{8\frac{3}{4}}$ 8^{11} Puckett H B 122 9.20 67–24 RstcOtlw122$^{1\frac{1}{2}}$SorOnWngs122^{4}ToPncht122 Brief speed 12
1Feb92- 7TP fst 1$\frac{1}{16}$:49 1:14^4 1:47^1 Md Sp Wt 66 3 3 3^3 4$^{1\frac{3}{4}}$ 4$^{6\frac{1}{2}}$ 3^{12} Peck B D B 121 16.10 59–36 ReturnVoyg121^{5}Skylin121^{7}Justbonus121 Saved ground 7

Majestic Pirate — B. c. 3(Feb), by Majestic Light—Ambo, by Olden Times
Br.—Miss Barbara Hunter (Ky)
Own.—Due Process Stable — Tr.—Nobles Reynaldo H (—) — **114**
Lifetime 2 0 1 0 $3,420 — 1992 2 M 1 0 $3,420 — 1991 0 M 0 0 — Wet 1 0 0 0 $180
27Feb92- 4GP fst 1⅛ :49 1:15^2 1:56^2 Md Sp Wt 51 6 3 2^2 2^{hd} 2$^{1\frac{1}{2}}$ 2^3 Douglas R R 120 34.30 52–35 King'sBech120^{3}MjesticPirte120^{2}Woodlord120 2nd best 9
27Feb92-Originally scheduled on turf
21Feb92- 5GP sly 1$\frac{1}{16}$:47^4 1:12^4 1:45^1 Md Sp Wt 45 5 9 9^{21} 9^{23} 8^{24} 8$^{25\frac{1}{4}}$ Douglas R R 120 61.60 61–23 ImprilGold120^{7}Unscurd120^{4}RblDoctor120 Showed little 9
LATEST WORKOUTS May 30 Mth 4f fst :48 H — May 25 Mth 5f fst 1:03 B — Apr 25 GP 3f fst :38 B — Apr 21 GP 3f fst :36^3 H

Malefactor — Ch. c. 3(Apr), by Secretariat—Captive Spirit, by Affirmed
Br.—Carolyn T. Groves (Ky)
Own.—Dogwood Stable — Tr.—Raines Virgil W (—) — **114**
Lifetime 5 0 0 0 $660 — 1992 5 M 0 0 $660 — 1991 0 M 0 0 — Turf 1 0 0 0 $190
14Apr92- 3Kee fst 1⅛ :49^3 1:15^4 1:53^4 Md Sp Wt 43 6 4 5$^{2\frac{1}{4}}$ 2^1 4$^{2\frac{1}{2}}$ 5$^{16\frac{3}{4}}$ Razo E Jr Bb 116 8.40 49–26 MrHl116^{3}DlStrm116$^{2\frac{1}{2}}$NtnlJdgmnt116 Bid falttened out 8
10Mar92- 4GP fm *1⅛ Ⓣ 1:50^3 + Md Sp Wt 70 1 7 6^8 6^{12} 6^{12} 5^{11} Martin C W b 120 73.60 — — WhtAboutMchl120^{1}QurtrTon120$^{\frac{1}{2}}$Rowng120 No menace 10
27Feb92- 4GP fst 1⅛ :49 1:15^2 1:56^2 Md Sp Wt 43 7 5 3^3 4$^{1\frac{1}{2}}$ 5$^{6\frac{1}{2}}$ 6$^{8\frac{1}{2}}$ Martin C W b 120 12.90 46–35 King's Beach120^3 Majestic Pirate120^2 Woodlord120 9
27Feb92-Originally scheduled on turf
19Jan92- 4GP fst 1$\frac{1}{16}$:47^3 1:12^2 1:46^2 Md Sp Wt 48 3 8 8^{10} 9^{16} 11^{18} 11$^{17\frac{1}{4}}$ Bailey J D b 120 21.00 63–23 PeerlessPerformer120^{1}Chourave120$^{1\frac{1}{2}}$Skywy120 Outrun 12
4Jan92- 3Hia fst 7f :23^2 :46^3 1:25 Md Sp Wt 42 8 7 8$^{7\frac{3}{4}}$ 10^{15} 8^{13} 5^{18} Penna D 122 10.50 60–17 DtchPlns122$^{\frac{1}{2}}$TrExplodng122^{9}GldnHt122 5 wide stretch 10
LATEST WORKOUTS May 23 Mth 4f fst :48 H — May 14 Mth 7f fst 1:31^2 B

Rahesa-Mx Ro. c. 3(Mar), by Found—Martha G., by Proud Birdie
Br.—Ramon Toca Narro (Mex)
Own.—Rahesa Farm Tr.—Romero Jorge E (4 0 1 0 .00) 114
Lifetime 1 0 0 0 $123 1992 0 M 0 0 1991 1 M 0 0 $123
24Nov91- 1Mex fst 6½f :224 :462 1:203 Md Sp Wt — 2 6 620 618 511 45¾ Vergara J 111 10.60 — — ChrmntDncur1111½NturlAglty114nkChtDLor111 Slow st 6
LATEST WORKOUTS May 26 Mth 4f fst :484 B May 23 Mth 3f fst :374 B May 16 Mth 4f my :481 H Apr 14 Crc 3f fst :373 Bg

Jail House Lawyer Dk. b. or br. g. 3(Apr), by Val de l'Orne-Fr—Glamosa, by Gallant Man
Br.—Koerner John H (NY)
Own.—Morris Thomas F Tr.—Tammaro John J III (2 0 0 0 .00) 114
Lifetime 2 0 0 0 $1,980 1992 1 M 0 0 $540 1991 1 M 0 0 $1,440
23May92- 5GS fst 6f :224 :462 1:11 3+Md Sp Wt 33 2 4 69 613 512 415¼ Black A S 115 2.40 72-15 Portage Path1154½DancingChas1153FlingFlam122 Rank 6
27Sep91- 6Bel gd 7f :23 :463 1:251 ⓈMd Sp Wt 40 1 7 1hd 31½ 48¼ 414 Sarvis D A 118 2.10 64-17 RealCielo11810LoclProblem1182WinningRiver118 Tired 8
LATEST WORKOUTS May 13 Mth 3f fst :361 Bg

Kinsalee Ch. g. 4, by Transworld—Am a Treasure, by Princely Pleasure
Br.—Gorman John (Ky)
Own.—Mountie Stable Tr.—Gorman John R (1 1 0 0 1.00) 123
Lifetime 7 0 1 2 $4,430 1992 5 M 1 2 $4,430 1991 2 M 0 0 Turf 2 0 0 0 Wet 2 0 1 1 $3,450
22May92- 7GS fm 1 Ⓣ:48 1:124 1:373 3+Md Sp Wt 49 11 11 11121013 916 916 Eldridge P K L 122 9.00 88-03 LovThtMtt1152½Qudrigminl1122½Monopolizr112 Outrun 11
27Mar92- 3GS my 1 1/16 :473 1:133 1:481 3+Md Sp Wt 65 5 6 612 55½ 22½ 2½ Eldridge P K L 122 5.10 72-27 UltimteWrrior122½Kinslee1222½RorWithKlss122 Gamely 6
20Mar92- 7Pha my 170 :46 1:111 1:421 Md Sp Wt 58 7 6 618 614 512 314½ Eldridge P K L 122 21.30 70-22 Mjesty'sScrt12210HollywoodJo1224½Kinsl122 No factor 7
12Mar92- 1GS fst 5½f :224 :462 1:052 Md Sp Wt 59 4 4 66 610 511 48½ Eldridge P K L 122 2.80 76-21 Slpy'sStyl1223FlngFlm1223½JstPlnChckn122 No factor 7
7Feb92- 9GS fst 6f :23 :48 1:144 Md 7500 57 6 3 78 64½ 51½ 31½ Woods J A 122 11.40 66-27 Cntmplt-En1221½DyTmSpcl122nkKnsl122 Saved ground 8
29Aug91- 5Mth fm 1 1/16 Ⓣ:472 1:113 1:441 + 3+Md Sp Wt 27 6 10 918 921 9211032½ Yang C C 115 42.70 47-20 FitforRoylty1152½Howrd'sHlo115¾PrreLooss115 Outrun 10
10Aug91- 1Mth gd 6f :221 :46 1:113 3+Md Sp Wt 37 8 2 88½ 811 815 817¼ Rivera L Jr 117 56.20 66-18 Dr. Zoom1172 Impropriety1174 OutintheRain117 Outrun 8
LATEST WORKOUTS May 30 Mth 5f fst 1:024 B May 20 Mth 4f fst :504 B May 16 Mth 4f gd :522 B May 6 GS 4f fst :492 B

Petit Parisien B. g. 4, by Double Sonic—Amouret, by All Hands
Br.—Gasadell Farm (Fla)
Own.—Sandoval Gaston D Tr.—Sandoval Gaston D (—) 123
Lifetime 11 0 0 3 $4,626 1992 2 M 0 2 $1,980 1991 9 M 0 1 $2,646 Turf 2 0 0 2 $1,980 Wet 2 0 0 1 $1,485
21May92- 4GS fm 1 Ⓣ:474 1:121 1:373 3+Md Sp Wt 65 6 9 64¾ 55½ 45 35½ Aguila G E L 122 5.90 98 — Bondi1224½AgentCooper1121½PetitParisien122 Mild bid 11
7May92- 4GS yl 1 1/16 Ⓣ:474 1:131 1:45 3+Md Sp Wt 65 7 6 53 53 31 33 Aguila G E L 122 37.00 86-10 SudiSe1151¾MidnightStge1221½PtitPrisin122 Lost irons 11
15Nov91- 9Pha fst 170 :471 1:13 1:442 3+Md 8000 43 4 8 67½ 76½ 68 810 Aguila G E L 118 5.60 64-17 Buckshooter1207½ Oslek111nk Spellsinger122 Outrun 12
8Nov91- 9Pha fst 1 1/16 :48 1:143 1:484 3+Md 8000 42 8 7 83¾ 66 45½ 46 Martinez J R Jr L 118 *2.80 59-34 MnlghtRmntc1184DbltDbl118hdHndcm116 Fanned wide 12
25Oct91- 1Pha fst 1 1/16 :481 1:132 1:483 3+Md 8000 37 8 5 64½ 67½ 68½ 43 Ayarza I 117 *2.70 63-20 Mxy'sKds110½SrPssng1102½Brookstn115 Raced outside 12
14Oct91- 7Pha fst 1 1/16 :481 1:134 1:48 3+Md Sp Wt 14 9 6 75½ 811 820 830 Ayarza I 117 74.70 39-36 Rajestic1173½ Sulawesi1222 Tara's Dream117 Outrun 9
20Oct91- 3Pha fst 170 :471 1:134 1:45 3+Md Sp Wt 38 3 8 76¾ 75½ 68½ 515½ Ayarza I 117 75.70 56-23 Cn'tTrickthefox1176Rjestic1175½Tony'sTowr117 Outrun 10
22Sep91- 6Del fst 1 :474 1:14 1:41 Md Sp Wt 34 1 8 813 610 59 59 Torso M A 122 26.90 67-20 CrptcQt1221½FrFlsh119½DHIntnsn'Sprm122 No menace 9
31Aug91- 5Pha fst 1 1/16 :482 1:124 1:461 3+Md Sp Wt 39 1 2 36 412 720 717 Jocson G J5 110 15.30 61-22 MimiHet115½Cn'tTrickthefox1157Rjestic115 Tired badly 8
20Aug91- 6Pha sly 1 :474 1:124 1:393 3+Md Sp Wt 26 4 5 59½ 512 318 323 Martinez J R Jr 115 38.40 60-18 Popsgotago1221Rajestic11522PetitPrisien115 No threat 7
LATEST WORKOUTS ●May 18 Pha 3f my :352 B May 3 Pha 1 fst 1:414 B Apr 28 Pha 4f fst :481 B

Irish Deputy Gr. c. 3(Apr), by Deputy Minister—Mira Irish Key, by Irish Castle
Br.—Ledyard Lewis C (Pa)
Own.—Ledyard Lewis Tr.—Clark Sharon B (—) 114
Lifetime 0 0 0 0 1992 0 M 0 0 1991 0 M 0 0
LATEST WORKOUTS May 28 Fai tr.t 4f fst :51 B

Running Double Ch. g. 3(Apr), by Hello Gorgeous—Ere Dawn, by Cloudy Dawn
Br.—Mottola Gary F (NJ)
Own.—Daisy Stable Tr.—Cash Russell J (—) 114
Lifetime 4 0 0 1 $1,568 1992 4 M 0 1 $1,568 1991 0 M 0 0 Turf 1 0 0 0
7May92- 4GS yl 1 1/16 Ⓣ:474 1:131 1:45 3+Md Sp Wt 45 2 11 11151011 711 714½ Marquez C H Jr 113 31.10 74-10 SaudiSe1151¾MidnightStge1221½PetitPrisien122 Outrun 11
24Apr92- 3GS fst 1 :48 1:134 1:402 3+Md Sp Wt 30 2 7 510 512 517 626¼ Bravo J 111 4.70 53-30 Pewter'sBill11315LtstIssu1144ChifExcutiv122 No factor 10
4Apr92-11GS fst 170 :49 1:162 1:492 3+Md Sp Wt 32 1 8 814 52¾ 34 37½ Olea R E 111 4.60 48-34 Disho114¾SilentPtrol1226½RunningDoubl111 Some gain 8
13Mar92- 7GS fst 6f :222 :46 1:12 ⓈMd Sp Wt 42 9 9 814 816 614 512½ Olea R E5 117 94.70 69-19 OlympicPrk1225¾TwoUnderPr122nkLivelyOk122 Outrun 11
LATEST WORKOUTS May 29 Mth 4f fst :494 B May 19 Mth 5f fst 1:043 B May 3 GS 4f fst :503 B Apr 11 GS 3f fst :382 B

Basket Leave
Br.—Appleton Arthur I (Fla)
Own.—Appleton Arthur I Tr.—Jennings Lawrence W (1 0 0 0 .00) 114
4 0 0 1 $2,590 1991 0 M 0 0 Turf 1 0 0 0 $750 Wet 1 0 0 0 $150
10Apr92- 5Crc fm *1 1/16 Ⓣ 1:444 3+Md Sp Wt 67 3 3 32 32½ 33½ 48½ Ramos W S Lb 112 *1.80 81-07 JohnHyes1122½AllegdVlntin1256IAmthMn112 Weakened 8
25Mar92-10Crc my 1 1/16 :491 1:141 1:48 Md Sp Wt 61 1 8 84½ 66¼ 56½ 510½ Ferrer J C Lb 120 4.10 — — Ponch1202SlvrConqust120½Dnzg'sDnc120 Passed faders 8
5Mar92- 3GP fst 6f :221 :452 1:11 Md 70000 60 7 9 65 67 67 39½ Ferrer J C b 116 3.50 78-16 Connecticut1164RpidoSol1165½BsketLev116 Up for 3rd 10
9Feb92- 4GP fst 6f :22 :452 1:101 Md Sp Wt 55 3 8 75½ 68 811 714 Rivera L Jr 120 6.90 78-09 DlHsD120noDntSllthFrm1202AbssdrS120 Steadied early 11
LATEST WORKOUTS May 24 Mth 5f fst 1:011 H May 18 Mth 5f my 1:03 B Apr 22 GP 4f fst :501 B Apr 16 GP 4f fst :48 H

Rahesa-Mx had not run in seven months and had very good workouts coming into his second race. Most handicappers would look at Rahesa's past form and figure he broke bad and made a run at the end. This is all true, but if you break down his past performance a little further it will become clear why he won this race.

First, there was not much competition in this race. Next, Rahesa broke dead last in his debut and made up 12¼ lengths in the last three furlongs. This would not have been an achievement if the race came home in 36 or 37 seconds, but this race come home in 34⅕, giving Rahesa less time to make up this ground. The fact that he made up 12 lengths meant he was flying. The added distance will not hurt him, as it will with the rest of the competition. The winner in Rahesa's first start went on to win $87,897 in 1991, and everyone in that race has broken their maiden. This means that Rahesa was running with above average horses in his debut. His workouts are consistent and very good. All of these positive angles point toward Rahesa, and everyone else is eliminated on the two-to-three start theory (which will be covered in the Maiden/Workout chapter) except for Irish Deputy, who is making his first start with an unimpressive workout.

SIXTH RACE
Monmouth
JUNE 2, 1992

$1\frac{1}{16}$ MILES. (1.41) MAIDEN SPECIAL WEIGHT. Purse $15,500. 3-year-olds and upward. Weight, 3-year-olds, 114 lbs. Older, 123 lbs. (ORIGINALLY SCHEDULED TO BE RUN AT ABOUT 1 1/16 MILES TURF COURSE.)

Value of race $15,500; value to winner $9,300; second $2,945; third $1,705; fourth $775; balance of starters $155 each. Mutuel pool $71,896. Exacta Pool $96,868

Last Raced	Horse	M/Eqt.	A.Wt	PP	St	¼	½	¾	Str	Fin	Jockey	Odds $1
24Nov91 ^{1}Mex^{4}	Rahesa-Mx		3 114	9	8	$6^{1\frac{1}{2}}$	5^{hd}	3^{3}	$1^{\frac{1}{2}}$	1^{nk}	Rivera M A	9.40
10Apr92 ^{5}Crc^{4}	Basket Leave	Lb	3 114	6	4	$2^{3\frac{1}{2}}$	2^{5}	2^{1}	2^{hd}	$2^{1\frac{1}{4}}$	Marquez C H Jr	2.80
22May92 ^{7}GS^{9}	Kinsalee	L	4 123	7	5	9	9	8^{6}	$5^{\frac{1}{2}}$	3no	Eldridge P K	4.10
13May92 ^{4}Bel^{9}	Made for Rain		3 114	1	3	$1^{\frac{1}{2}}$	1^{hd}	1^{hd}	3^{3}	4^{1}	Cruguet J	2.90
	Irish Deputy		3 114	4	9	5^{hd}	$6^{1\frac{1}{2}}$	4^{hd}	4^{hd}	$5^{2\frac{1}{2}}$	Colton R E	9.60
7May92 ^{4}GS^{7}	Running Double		3 114	5	6	8^{3}	8^{4}	$5^{1\frac{1}{2}}$	6^{2}	$6^{1\frac{1}{4}}$	Tejeira J	58.60
21May92 ^{4}GS^{3}	Petit Parisien	L	4 123	3	2	$7^{2\frac{1}{2}}$	7^{1}	7^{1}	$7^{\frac{1}{2}}$	$7^{\frac{3}{4}}$	Aguila G E	14.60
14Apr92 ^{3}Kee^{5}	Malefactor	b	3 114	2	1	3^{hd}	$3^{1\frac{1}{2}}$	6^{2}	8^{18}	8^{23}	King E L Jr	13.50
23May92 ^{5}GS^{4}	Jail House Lawyer	b	3 116	8	7	4^{2}	4^{1}	9	9	9	Black A S	5.20

OFF AT 3:15 Start Good, Won driving. Time, :23^{2}, :47^{4}, 1:13^{2}, 1:40^{3}, 1:47^{3} Track muddy.

$2 Mutuel Prices:

11-RAHESA-MX	20.80	9.20	5.20
8-BASKET LEAVE		4.20	3.60
9-KINSALEE			3.00

$2 EXACTA 11-8 PAID $129.20

Ro. c, (Mar), by Found—Martha G., by Proud Birdie. Trainer Romero Jorge E. Bred by Ramon Toca Narro (Mex).

RAHESA, hung wide into the first turn, angled over and joined the leaders approaching the top of the lane, bumped with MADE FOR RAIN at intervals through the stretch and finished steadily to prevail. BASKET LEAVE reached the front briefly on the backstretch then pressed the pace to the lane outside of MADE FOR RAIN and finished gamely. KINSALEE, outrun early, closed well late. MADE FOR RAIN alternated for the early lead, raced removed from the rail was bumped in the stretch run and weakened late. IRISH DEPUTY offered a late gain from the outside. RUNNING DOUBLE advanced inside into the far turn then tired in the drive. MALEFACTOR gave way on the final turn. JAIL HOUSE LAWYER raced wide and was through after a half. JUSTABONUS WAS AN EARLY AFTERNOON SCRATCH WITH ALL WAGERS ON HIM BEING ORDERED REFUNDED.

We know that shippers are dangerous from state to state, but how do we handicap when a horse comes from overseas? Raven Runner is a filly coming off a maiden victory in England. In Raven Runner's debut in the United States she catches a bad field of allowance horses.

In Irish Intern's last start she was way back as usual and received fast fractions to fancy her stretch run. The fractions were 45³/₅, 1:09²/₅, and 1:42 flat. With these fractions Irish Intern could not make up enough ground in time, losing by ½ of a length. She will not get any faster today.

Lady of Mann made her first start of the year by leading and then stopping by the three quarter pole and backing up. The competition is just too much for this filly. She will not be able to keep up.

Salsflower could not win in claiming company and has not improved. She has only her maiden win to her credit and in her last race was off slow, recovered, and then tired, losing by six lengths. Salsflower should be coming on late with Irish Intern but does not have the same kick and will come up short.

Raven Runner is a three-year-old filly that was obviously respected a great deal by her connections, as she was entered in stakes races for her first two starts. She performed well in these two races and did not make her next start until 1992. In her fifth start, Raven Runner was placed against the boys. It was obvious that someone knew she had made tremendous improvements as she went off at 4-5. In that start, Raven Runner completed the six furlongs in a quick 1:10 flat. Obvious adjustments were made as she trounced the boys by seven lengths. The time of 1:10 flat is good in the United States. When this is performed overseas, it is a tremendous achievement. Today, Raven Runner will be piloted by top jockey Jerry Bailey and is also shedding ten pounds. As I stated earlier about the confidence shown by her connections with her debut in a stakes race, her quality becomes evident again by running her right back on thirteen days rest. This is not much time for a horse coming from overseas, meaning she is razor sharp and her connections want to take advantage of it.

Kris' Dear Deby is a filly that seems to wake up when placed on the turf. It is obvious in her last start that she did not like the inner turf course and she takes better to the Widener course, as she did in her second to last start. If she can control her speed she should be in the lead coming home. Use in the gimmicks.

Five Dreams woke up with blinkers last time out and should improve off of that effort. This race has a lot of speed and Five Dreams is on the cheap side.

Miss Garland is another one with speed but she is also on the cheap side and should come up a little short.

Via Del Portici will take money for her apparent speed, but compare her speed figures with the speed figures from the last race. This filly will be nowhere to be found. In this contest the fractions should be close to 22 3/5, 46, 1:10 3/5, and final time around 1:36. The fractions that Via Del Portici set in her last race were three seconds slower than what they will be running today. She can not run as fast as these horses.

Top Kiss was outrun in her only turf start with slow fractions. She will never keep up unless there is a tremendous improvement.

Windedawler made a nice showing in her first start on the turf at Monmouth Park, but this is another filly that should back up when pressure is applied, as she did on August 11, 1991 and June 16, 1992.

7

WIDENER TURF COURSE

1 MILE. **(Turf). (1.32^2) ALLOWANCE. Purse $29,000. Fillies and mares, 3–year–olds and upward which have never won a race other than Maiden, Claiming or Starter. Weights: 3–year–olds, 116 lbs.; older, 122 lbs. Non–winners of a race other than claiming at a mile or over since June 15, allowed 3 lbs.; of such a race since June 1, allowed 5 lbs.**

Irish Intern — B. f. 3(Apr), by Dr Blum—Erin's Slew, by Seattle Slew

SAMYN J L (141 12 16 21 .09) — Br.—Fried Albert Jr (NY)

Own.—Fried Albert Jr — Tr.—Destasio Richard A (47 2 4 4 .04) — **111**

Lifetime: 10 1 2 3 — $40,340

1992	4	1	0	1	$22,560
1991	6	M	2	2	$17,780
Turf	1	0	0	0	$1,740
Wet	2	0	1	1	$8,840

30May92- 5Bel	fm	1 1/16	Ⓣ:45^3	1:09^2	1:42	3↑ⒻⓈAlw 29000	77	5	9	107 1/2	107 1/4	7^4	4 1/2	Smith M E	b	112	7.90e	85-13	DH Thtfdnslf110^{nk} DH ShrMDrs110^{nk}DRb115	Bmpd, stead	12
21Feb92- 2Aqu	fst	1 1/8	⊡:49^1	1:14^3	1:54^4	ⒻⓈAlw 29000	59	9	7	7^{12}	78 1/2	4^{11}	4$^{14\frac{3}{4}}$	Smith M E	b	118	3.90	54-31	LdJF116$^{13\frac{1}{4}}$FlhtVsblt116^{nk}EsttsPrcss116	Passed faders	9
2Feb92- 5Aqu	fst	1 1/16	⊡:50^4	1:16^2	1:50	ⒻⓈAlw 29000	53	5	7	5^2	41 1/2	41 1/2	33 3/4	Smith M E	b	121	1.50	54-25	Untlthmscstps116$^{2\frac{3}{4}}$EsttsPrncss118^{3}IrshIntrn121	4-wide	7
18Jan92- 9Aqu	fst	170	⊡:50^1	1:16^2	1:47^2	ⒻⓈMd Sp Wt	63	6	6	5^4	43 1/2	11 1/2	17 1/2	Smith M E	b	121	*.70	68-29	Irish Intern121$^{7\frac{1}{2}}$DarlingLydia121^{no}R.E.Darla121	Driving	8
30Dec91- 4Aqu	sly	1 1/8	⊡:48^3	1:15	1:54^1	ⒻMd Sp Wt	62	2	6	68 1/2	52 1/2	3^4	38 1/4	Smith M E	b	117	5.20	63-18	D RomntcDnnr117^{6}ShrdMgc117$^{2\frac{1}{4}}$IrshIntrn117	Bothered	6
30Dec91-Placed second through disqualification																					
13Dec91- 6Aqu	sly	1 1/16	⊡:48^3	1:13^3	1:45^4	ⒻMd Sp Wt	59	9	9	98 1/4	6^9	5^{12}	3^{15}	Smith M E	b	117	6.60	64-19	CityDnce117^{8}CoolJudgment117^{7}IrishIntrn117	Mild rally	10
21Nov91- 1Aqu	fst	1	:47	1:12^2	1:39^2	ⒻMd 72500	69	5	6	6^3	52 1/4	42 1/2	3^{hd}	Smith M E	b	115	2.70	65-30	Zingdoon113^{no}ShrdMgic113^{no}IrishIntrn115	Rallied wide	7
27Oct91- 6Aqu	fst	6f	:22^2	:46	1:11^4	ⒻⓇNyStallion	44	4	—	—	—	7^{11}	79 1/4	Santos J A	b	114	9.50	73-14	QunofTriumph112$^{2\frac{1}{2}}$FinlCrossing112^{hd}Kt'sCollg112	Fog	10
27Oct91-Filly Division																					
11Oct91- 9Bel	fst	6 1/2f	:23	:46^2	1:18	ⒻⓈMd Sp Wt	58	10	11	96 1/2	54 1/2	2^6	28 1/2	Santos J A		117	2.60	78-19	FnlCrossng117$^{8\frac{1}{2}}$IrshIntrn117^{4}RbccLrn117	Rallied wide	13
19Sep91- 5Bel	fst	6f	:22^4	:46^3	1:12^1	ⒻⓈMd Sp Wt	47	3	9	12^{19}	128 1/2	96 3/4	4^4	Smith M E		117	11.00	75-18	QnofTrmph117^{3}SndThnkng117^{1}R.E.Drl117	Rallied wide	12

LATEST WORKOUTS Jly 7 Bel tr.t 4f fst :48^3 B — Jly 1 Bel tr.t 4f fst :50^2 B — Jun 25 Bel Ⓣ 4f sf :50^1 B (d) — Jun 18 Bel Ⓣ 6f fm 1:15 B (d)

Lady of Mann

Ch. f. 3(May), by Great Above—Dessi O'Day, by Cutlass
DAVIS R G (147 17 19 9 .12)
Own.—Reynolds William G Jr
Br.—Jacobsen William L (Fla)
Tr.—Howe Peter M (5 0 1 0 .00)
111
Lifetime 6 1 0 2 $7,767
1992 1 0 0 0
1991 5 1 0 2 $7,767
Turf 3 0 0 2 $4,036

4Jun92- 2Bel fm 1⅛ Ⓣ:45 1:10 1:421 3+ⒻAlw 29000 42 12 1 12½ 31½ 1214 1224½ Carr D 109 75.90 60-13 FrenchStl1111½HombyTn1111½HrFvorit119 Used in pace 12
18Nov91- 7Aqu fst 6f :221 :454 1:113 ⒻAlw 27000 32 10 11 127½ 128½ 1211 1217½ Pezua J M 116 61.10 65-18 GvNotc116¾BlssOrHom1161MssClvrAppl116 Brk slowly 12
24Oct91- 8Aqu fst 7f :224 :454 1:224 ⒻAstarita 31 4 6 53½ 69½ 620 628¾ Chavez J F 112 28.50 59-12 EsyNow112¾StolnButy112¾ClstClo112 Stumbled start 6
24Oct91-Grade II
5Jun91♦3Beverley(Eng) gd 5f 1:034 ⓉⒻHilaryNeedlerTrophyStks 32¾ Eddery Paul 122 4.50 — — Herora122¾ TwoShoes1222 LadyofMann122 Bid, evenly 8
28May91♦4Sandown(Eng) gd 5f 1:012 Ⓣ ChHeidsieckNationalStk 312 Eddery Pat 119 10.00 — — Mrlng123nk MssBlbrd11612 LdyfMnn119 Flattened out 4
18May91♦1Southwell(Eng) fst 5f 1:004 DesignCntrctrsStks(Mdn) 1nk McKeown D 121 *1.80 — — LdyofMnn121nk TshbCmtStr1265 HnySngft121 In tight 9
18May91-Raced on all-weather track
LATEST WORKOUTS Jly 8 Bel 4f fst :471 H Jly 3 Bel 4f fst :512 B May 27 Bel 6f fst 1:14 Hg May 19 Bel 6f fst 1:132 H

Salsflower

B. m. 5, by Diamond Shoal—Albany Girl, by Alydar
MAPLE E (159 25 25 19 .16)
Own.—Jackson Evan S
Br.—Court R H A (Pa)
Tr.—Jackson Evan S (1 0 0 0 .00)
117
Lifetime 17 1 1 0 $23,430
1992 5 0 0 0 $370
1991 11 1 1 0 $23,060
Turf 14 1 1 0 $23,340

14Jun92- 7Bel fm 1⅛ Ⓣ:464 1:113 1:42 3+ⒻAlw 29000 73 5 10 1011 82½ 83¼ 66 Maple E 117 62.90 82-13 Heed1091½ Home by Ten1092¼ Turkolady111 4 wide 10
3Apr92- 4Aqu fst 1 :483 1:141 1:40 ⒻClm 20000 49 5 7 64¾ 65 67½ 711½ McMahon H I7 106 17.10 51-36 NotAScrtch1134¼ComeOnCindy110¾JonneW.115 Outrun 7
5Mar92- 4GP fst 6f :222 :46 1:113 ⒻClm 14000 47 2 9 117 118¼ 1112 1111¾ Frost G C10 106 109.30 73-16 TcAMrnng1141½ImHrrt1161½PrsntfrGr116 Showed little 11
29Jan92-10GP fm *1⅛ Ⓣ 1:531 + ⒻClm 35000 62 10 6 613 69½ 913 913½ Thibeau R J Jr 112 34.40 — — FlshyColrs1162½Cdydnt1161MrflsMm116 Dropped back 10
17Jan92-10GP fm *1⅛ Ⓣ 1:45 + ⒻClm 37500 61 8 6 612 1011 1041 1112¼ Frost G C10 104 33.20 — — TrplConncton1121Wondrlnd114noHdwnHny114 Faltered 11
24Oct91- 7Aqu fm 1⅛ Ⓣ:492 1:14 1:452 3+ⒻAlw 29000 82 6 10 107½ 84¾ 64 41½ McMahon H I10 107 42.20 84-17 RightWngHot114½FvDrms118nkRdJourny114 Brk slowly 10
11Oct91- 7Bel fm 1⅛ Ⓣ:504 1:141 1:441 3+ⒻAlw 29000 77 4 7 41½ 41 43 65 McMahon H I10 107 33.20 72-19 PrimeVlue1141½TirMiss114¾SpyLdrLdy114 Lacked rally 10
9Sep91- 6Bel fm 1 Ⓣ:451 1:093 1:35 3+ⒻAlw 29000 72 3 7 69 76½ 75¾ 66¾ Thibeau R J Jr 122 25.30 80-09 Sh'sAcdmic1131¾AShkyQun118hdMutSwn117 No threat 7
1Sep91- 7Bel fm 1⅛ Ⓣ:48 1:114 1:432 3+ⒻMd Sp Wt 76 1 8 83¾ 65½ 42 1hd Thibeau R J Jr 122 4.70 79-21 Salsflower122hd Bates Gal1182½ Miss Fapp118 Driving 9
25Aug91- 2Sar fm 1⅛ Ⓣ:481 1:122 1:424 3+ⒻMd Sp Wt 57 11 5 31½ 21 89½ 814½ Nelson D 122 12.40 67-13 AShkyQun1171½Strk'sProms117noChrlottAgst122 Tired 11
LATEST WORKOUTS Jun 12 Bel 4f fst :49 B

Raven Runner

B. f. 3(Jan), by Storm Bird—Simple Taste, by Sharpen Up
BAILEY J D (190 37 38 20 .19)
Own.—Kirk Ronald K
Br.—Ronald K. Kirk (Ky)
Tr.—O'Connell Richard (30 4 4 1 .13)
111
Lifetime 5 1 1 1 $7,579
1992 3 1 0 0 $2,367
1991 2 M 1 1 $5,212
Turf 5 1 1 1 $7,579

27Jun92♦3Lingfield(Eng) fm 6f 1:10 Ⓣ Manston Stks(Mdn) 17 Reid J 121 *.80 — — RnRnnr1217 Shrptn1231½ WndrngStrnr118 Led thruout 8
10Jun92♦2Kempton(Eng) gd 7f 1:271 ⓉⒻFairclough Stks(Mdn) 43¾ Cochrane R 123 *3.00 — — StrGoddss1232 Goodntout123nk LndryMd123 Bid, hung 15
23May92♦2Kempton(Eng) gd 1 1:383 ⓉⒻCalifornian Stks(Mdn) 510 Cochrane R 123 8.00 — — Mahasin1233½ QueenWarrior1231½ Cchou123 Bid, wknd 14
27Sep91♦7Ascot(Eng) gd 7f 1:331 ⓉⒻKensingtonPalaceGradStk 36¾ Reid J 120 4.50 — — RdSlpprs1206 GlclMon120½ RvnRnnr120 Prom thruout 7
6Sep91♦5Kempton(Eng) gd 7f 1:27 ⓉⒻMilcars Stks 25 Cochrane R 120 25.00 — — PrfctCrcl1205 RvnRnnr120½ Goodntot120 Bid, in close 14

Kris' Dear Deby

B. f. 3(Mar), by Kris S—Our Dear Deby, by In Reality
MCCAULEY W H (88 14 10 12 .16)
Own.—Bauld James R
Br.—Meadowbrook Farm Inc (Fla)
Tr.—Klesaris Robert P (76 7 17 8 .09)
111
Lifetime 9 1 3 2 $19,655
1992 7 0 2 2 $10,730
1991 2 1 1 0 $8,925
Turf 4 0 2 1 $8,880
Wet 2 1 0 1 $8,785

14Jun92- 7Bel fm 1⅛ Ⓣ:464 1:113 1:42 3+ⒻAlw 29000 58 10 3 31½ 3nk 95¾ 915 Nelson D 110 3.50 73-13 Heed1091½ Home by Ten1092¼ Turkolady111 Gave way 10
15May92- 2Bel fm 1⅛ Ⓣ:451 1:093 1:41 3+ⒻAlw 29000 81 1 3 44½ 2½ 3½ 36¾ Velazquez J R 111 6.60 84-14 GnRntc1191½FITThMn1195½KrsDrDb111 Bid, weakened 10
16Apr92-10Crc fm *1⅛ Ⓣ 1:442 ⒻClm c-40000 77 5 3 31½ 3½ 1½ 22 Ferrer J C L 116 3.10 90-06 SmokeyGry1162Kris'DerDby1161½MiBirdToo116 Rallied 10
16Apr92-Claimed from Three G Stable, Reid Robert E Jr Trainer
2Apr92- 8Crc fm *1⅛ Ⓣ 1:482 ⒻAlw 16000 76 5 6 54½ 42 1hd 22½ Ferrer J C L 112 13.40 90-08 InViw1122½Kris'DrDby112nkTimlyKris112 4-wide fnl trn 11
25Mar92- 2Crc my 7f :231 :463 1:263 ⒻClm 35000 57 6 1 32½ 42½ 33 34½ Douglas R R L 116 4.00 — — KnghtEncntr1051½TmStll1163Krs'DrDb116 4 wide, drftd 7
28Feb92- 5GP fst 6f :223 :463 1:122 ⒻClm c-27500 57 6 6 86 86½ 87¾ 66 Bailey J D 116 13.90 75-14 GoldenBimmr116¾TrsFinss1141½FortuntGin120 Faltered 8
8Jan92- 5GP fst 6f :222 :464 1:122 ⒻAlw 17000 50 7 4 85¾ 1012 1014 812½ Santos J A 114 13.80 69-16 Roy'sGirl1153PersianAffir1151½Zingdoon115 5-Wide str 10
29Nov91- 6Hia sly 6f :22 :46 1:122 ⒻMd 35000 58 7 6 64½ 64¾ 12 11½ Vasquez J 119 3.10 80-17 Kris'DerDby1191½TrsDulc1191½Cpot'sPrincss119 Driving 12
6Nov91- 3Crc fst 7f :231 :473 1:264 ⒻMd 25000 54 3 3 2hd 1hd 2½ 21½ Vasquez J 119 4.60 79-14 April'sLuci1191½Kris'DerDeby1192CrolinHop119 Gamely 6
LATEST WORKOUTS Jly 1 Bel tr.t 4f fst :502 B Jun 12 Bel tr.t 3f fst :40 B

Five Dreams

Dk. b. or br. f. 4, by Palace Music—Fleet Arada, by Fleet Nasrullah
SANTOS J A (215 31 23 36 .14)
Own.—Ju Ju Gen Stable
Br.—Runnymede Farm Inc (Ky)
Tr.—Carroll Henry L (10 0 0 3 .00)
117
Lifetime 15 1 3 2 $41,805
1992 7 0 1 1 $8,465
1991 8 1 2 1 $33,340
Turf 10 1 2 2 $35,225
Wet 1 0 1 0 $6,380

29Jun92- 8Bel fm 1⅛ Ⓣ:463 1:10 1:413 3+ⒻAlw 29000 81 3 2 12½ 11½ 11 31½ Santos J A b 117 7.20 87-14 Turkoldy112¾MissGrlnd109½FiveDrms117 Bid,weakened 10
16Jun92- 7Mth fm 1⅛ Ⓣ:474 1:111 1:414 + 3+ⒻAlw 16500 65 5 6 54½ 43½ 44½ 55½ Verge M E L 117 4.30 87-10 MdmDhr108¾Wnddlr1081¾TrPrncss117 Bothered slightly 10
30May92- 5Mth fm 1⅛ Ⓣ:472 1:111 1:421 + 3+ⒻAlw 17000 69 7 2 2½ 2hd 21 42 Velazquez J R L 118 2.80 88-06 WeedItOut1041½MdmeDhr108¾TrioPrincss118 Tired late 9
4May92- 2Aqu fm 1⅛ Ⓣ:483 1:132 1:441 3+ⒻAlw 29000 46 4 2 21½ 31½ 711 721¾ Santos J A 119 2.90 68-07 SnowTitle110¾Tremonett1124½HombyTn110 Wide early 8
26Mar92- 7Aqu fst 1 :473 1:124 1:374 ⒻAlw 29000 20 4 2 32 43 611 631¼ Santos J A 117 1.80 42-21 SpphireSkies1173SteedofBold1174¾CherokButy110 Bled 6
3Mar92- 8GP fm *1⅛ Ⓣ 1:451 + ⒻAlw 24500 75 9 3 34 21 2½ 24½ Ramos W S L 113 2.50 — — PrncingBllrin1154½FvDrms113½Frforbnd113 Saved place 10
23Feb92- 6GP fst 1⅛ :473 1:124 1:471 ⒻAlw 20000 51 10 2 11 21½ 36 514 Ramos W S L 115 *2.00 62-19 Hro'sLov112¾DiplomticCovr113¾BguBlu-Ir114 Faltered 11
23Feb92-Originally scheduled on turf
14Dec91- 9Hia fm *1⅛ Ⓣ 1:432 ⒻBal Harbour 71 7 3 33½ 32½ 69 69 Vega A 112 14.30 80-14 SthrnMrnng112nkPrvtTrsr114hdDncO'MyLf114 Faltered 10
14Dec91-Run in Divisions
10Nov91- 7Aqu fm 1⅛ Ⓣ:481 1:134 1:514 3+ⒻAlw 31000 86 1 1 15 12 11 42½ Verge M E 115 6.60 84-16 HhlndCrstl115noShsAcdc1152½AdsAppl107 Speed, tired 9
LATEST WORKOUTS May 26 Bel tr.t 4f fst :48 H

Miss Garland

Ch. f. 3(Mar), by Palace Music—Miss Actress, by Mr Cockatoo
CHAVEZ J F (220 28 23 26 .13)
Own.—Speigel Robert
Br.—Palace Music Syndicate & Spiegel (Ky)
Tr.—Schaeffer Stephen W (36 2 6 6 .06)
111
Lifetime 13 1 4 4 $45,150
1992 2 0 1 1 $9,380
1991 11 1 3 3 $35,770
Turf 7 1 2 2 $35,380

29Jun92- 8Bel fm 1⅛ Ⓣ:463 1:10 1:413 3+ⒻAlw 29000 82 8 5 55 43½ 42½ 2¾ Chavez J F b 109 4.50 87-14 Turkoldy112¾MissGrlnd109½FiveDrems117 Up for place 10
29May92- 2Bel fm 1⅛ Ⓣ:464 1:104 1:414 ⒻClm 50000 78 2 3 32 31 31½ 34¾ Pezua J M b 116 4.10 84-14 Mckymckenn1132½KyChnc1122½MissGrlnd116 Stead str 7
28Nov91- 6Aqu fst 1 :463 1:12 1:381 ⒻAlw 29000 39 4 5 74½ 75 79¾ 720¼ Migliore R b 118 9.60 50-26 Contrdiction116½SnowTitle1162½AplchSunst116 Outrun 7
9Nov91- 6Aqu fm 1⅛ Ⓣ:484 1:142 1:454 ⒻMd Sp Wt 70 4 3 33 1½ 1½ 1½ Cordero A Jr b 117 *2.10 83-10 MissGarland117½FrenchSteal117nkIrishRech117 Driving 10
28Oct91- 7Aqu fm 1⅛ Ⓣ:481 1:14 1:453 ⒻMd Sp Wt 72 8 8 65 74½ 45½ 46½ Cordero A Jr 117 *.70 77-19 ChineseEmprss1175½LLup117½FrnchStl117 Lacked rally 10
3Oct91- 8Bel fm 1⅛ Ⓣ:451 1:092 1:423 ⒻMiss Grillo 78 5 8 76 75 45½ 53½ Cordero A Jr 114 17.30 79-20 GoodMod1142¾PntSprd114nkGldfAtmn114 Lacked rally 14

Top Kiss B. f. 3(Mar), by Topsider—Kissapotamus, by Illustrious
MCMAHON H I (134 9 13 18 .07) Br.—LeBus Clarence L (Ky)
Own.—Stroud Murray Tr.—Combs Don (10 1 2 3 .10) 1047
Lifetime 10 1 4 1 $34,260 | 1992 5 0 0 1 $4,860 | 1991 5 1 4 0 $29,400 | Turf 1 0 0 0 | Wet 2 0 0 1 $3,240

21Jun92- 7Bel fst 6f :22 :444 1:102 3↑ⒻAlw 27000 61 7 8 96½ 106¾ 85¾ 79 Maple E b 111 34.10 79-10 Tarq114½ Epic Villa117hd West Virginia111 Wide trip 10
5Jun92- 7Bel sly 6f :22 :451 1:101 ⒻAlw 27000 70 1 5 68½ 66 57 311¾ McMahon H I7 b 109 34.10 77-13 StrtgcRwrd11610½OnDmplng1161½TopKss109 No threat 6
29May92- 6Bel fst 6f :222 :452 1:101 3↑ⒻAlw 27000 71 3 2 43 41¾ 33½ 45½ McMahon H I7 b 107 21.20 83-13 MyNecessity1101¾Bob'sLittlGl1103SpicyScrt110 Outrun 5
17May92- 5Bel my 7f :223 :454 1:23 3↑ⒻAlw 27000 55 1 5 41½ 66 57 515 McMahon H I7 b 109 14.60 74-13 Aquilegia1102½ Epic Villa1198¼LadyofIron112 Sv'd grnd 6
4May92- 2Aqu fm 1 1/16 Ⓣ:483 1:132 1:441 3↑ⒻAlw 29000 30 3 1 53 88 821 830¾ Maple E b 112 8.40 59-07 Snow Title110¾Tremonetta1124¼HomebyTen110 Drifted 8
3Dec91- 6Grd fst 4½f :221 :461 :524 ⒻMd Sp Wt 69 1 2 12 15 13 Hawley S b 119 *.55 92-18 TopKss1193MdwRgn119hdSh'sAnrtcGrl117 Wrapped up 6
16Nov91- 7Grd fst 4½f :221 :464 :532 ⒻMd Sp Wt 55 1 4 43 3½ 2½ Hawley S b 119 *.50 88-22 DremReglly114½TopKiss1191½AffirSoGrt119 Closed well 9
2Nov91- 8Grd fst 4½f :214 :461 :524 ⒻMd Sp Wt 69 4 4 22 21½ 2hd Hawley S b 119 *.75e 92-23 Veruschk114hdTopKiss1194½AffirSoGret119 Closed well 6
13Oct91- 3WO fst 6f :223 :463 1:121 ⒻMd Sp Wt 71 7 2 12 3½ 22½ 23½ Hawley S b 119 *.30e 80-21 VidKid1143½TopKiss1194½ShwnhollrRos119 Early speed 7
2Oct91- 7WO fst 5½f :221 :461 1:061 ⒻMd Sp Wt 61 8 3 41 42½ 33 22¼ Hawley S b 119 *1.60e 87-15 GttngArndtt1192¼TpKss1192½ShwnhllrRs119 Wide turn 8
LATEST WORKOUTS Jun 18 Bel [T] 4f fm :50 B (d) May 14 Bel [T] 4f gd :493 B

Windedawler B. f. 3(Feb), by Sovereign Dancer—Syrian Dancer, by Damascus
KRONE J A (280 55 48 33 .20) Br.—Farish W S (Ky)
Own.—Mijal Stables Tr.—Penna Angel Jr (16 2 1 2 .13) 111
Lifetime 8 1 2 0 $16,395 | 1992 2 0 1 0 $3,135 | 1991 6 1 1 0 $13,260 | Turf 1 0 1 0 $3,135 | Wet 1 0 0 0

16Jun92- 7Mth fm 1 1/16 Ⓣ:474 1:111 1:414 + 3↑ⒻAlw 16500 73 1 1 1hd 2hd 11½ 2½ Krone J A L 108 5.40 91-10 MdmeDhr108½Windedwler1081¾TrioPrincss117 Good try 10
23May92- 6Bel fst 7f :223 :453 1:234 ⒻAlw 27000 36 2 8 63½ 83¾ 1110 1120¼ Krone J A 116 46.00 65-15 EndlessDesire1212½StrtegicRwrd116noLizlity116 Outrun 11
20Nov91- 7Hia fst 7f :224 :453 1:233 ⒻAlw 14000 68 11 3 52¼ 41½ 43½ 55¼ Nunez E O L 114 35.10 80-16 RunforBby114½Sttclctrcty114nkGoldnBmmr114 Faltered 11
18Oct91- 8Crc fst 7f :223 :461 1:264 ⒻAlw 17000 37 3 5 31 21½ 79 713½ Castillo H Jr L 116 3.10 67-18 BlncheBeMine1161½HiSki1091Bobby'sSweti116 Faltered 8
13Sep91- 5Crc fst 6f :222 :463 1:134 ⒻMd Sp Wt 59 1 4 11 11 15 11½ Castillo H Jr L 117 *.90 81-12 Windedwler1171½FriskyDonn1172½Toscnurse117 Driving 7
31Aug91-10Crc sly 7f :222 :462 1:264 ⒻRiviera 40 6 6 31 21½ 610 1011¾ Valles E S L 112 17.70 69-15 MissVldPch112noPtty'sPrncss1143WhtlyWy116 Stopped 11
11Aug91- 3Crc fst 6f :22 :454 1:123 ⒻMd Sp Wt 72 3 5 1hd 11 12 21½ Gonzalez M A L 116 2.70 85-13 Frn'sFolly1161½Wnddwlr1165Sndbrod116 Best of others 9
6Jly91- 2Crc fst 5½f :223 :462 1:07 ⒻMd Sp Wt 55 11 2 21½ 21 22½ 45½ Alferez J O 116 4.60 85-08 WhetlyWy1161RunforBby116hdApchGlory116 Weakened 11
LATEST WORKOUTS Jly 7 Bel 4f fst :502 B Jly 2 Bel [T] 7f fm 1:284 B (d) Jun 26 Bel 5f fst 1:023 B Jun 11 Bel [T] 7f fm 1:274 B (d)

3Oct91-Grade III
22Sep91- 6Bel fm 1 1/16 Ⓣ:472 1:121 1:434 ⒻMd Sp Wt 69 10 2 21 1½ 11½ 2nk Migliore R b 117 *2.00 77-16 Artful Tri117nk Miss Garland1175 Wild Ten117 Gamely 10
12Sep91- 3Bel fm 1 Ⓣ:46 1:103 1:351 ⒻMd Sp Wt 66 5 4 61¾ 62½ 42½ 32½ Samyn J L b 117 5.70 83-17 Tremonett1171½AplchSunst1171MissGrlnd117 Willingly 11
5Sep91- 4Bel fst 6f :23 :463 1:112 ⒻMd 45000 62 7 2 31 2½ 2½ 2no Migliore R b 114 2.60 83-13 LngfrWn117noMssGrlnd114¾QnfTrmph113 Game effort 13
22Aug91- 4Mth fst 6f :214 :453 1:114 ⒻMd 45000 49 7 2 64¾ 67¼ 59 38¼ Olea R E5 b 110 6.00 74-15 WinnieD.1177Helen'sIdea1171¼MissGarlnd110 Late gain 8
LATEST WORKOUTS Jly 8 Bel tr.t 3f fst :351 H Jun 22 Bel tr.t 4f fst :482 H Jun 15 Bel tr.t 4f fst :48 H May 21 Bel 6f fst 1:16 B

Via Dei Portici Ch. f. 3(Mar), by It's Freezing—Via Appia, by Proudest Roman
VELAZQUEZ J R (179 12 25 25 .07) Br.—Happy Hill Farm Inc (Ky)
Own.—Happy Hill Farm Tr.—Preger Mitchell C (17 3 3 2 .18) 111
Lifetime 3 1 1 1 $16,700 | 1992 2 0 1 1 $9,500 | 1991 1 1 0 0 $7,200 | Turf 1 0 1 0 $6,380 | Wet 1 0 0 1 $3,120

14Jun92- 4Bel fm 1 1/16 [T]:49 1:124 1:422 3↑ⒻAlw 29000 77 2 1 1½ 11 11½ 21 Velazquez J R 110 7.30 85-13 ForestKey1131ViDiPortici1101¾EniMniMiny109 Gamely 9
16May92- 6Bel sly 6f :22 :45 1:104 ⒻClm 70000 83 3 3 44½ 31 31½ 31¾ Velazquez J R 112 14.90 84-15 MrlnsMc1161½NrthrDstr112nkVDPrtc112 Bid, weakened 8
9Nov91- 2Aqu fst 6f :232 :48 1:132 ⒻMd 35000 64 13 11 33 2½ 11½ 1nk Carr D 117 3.60 74-26 ViDeiPortici117nkBstilleBell1178SwtCountry117 Driving 14
LATEST WORKOUTS Jly 7 Bel 4f fst :493 B Jly 2 Bel 4f fst :473 H ●Jun 24 Bel 3f gd :35 H Jun 4 Bel 4f fst :473 H

Raven Runner chased down the early pacesetter and edged clear in a late stretch run under a hand ride. Kris' Dear Deby set most of the pace and hung on to earn the place spot. The mediocre fractions of 22 3/5, 45 3/5, 1:10 3/5, and 1:35 1/5 hurt all the horses that were too far back. Irish Intern could not come back at 1:09—how was she going to make it today? Via Del Portici attracted money as expected and could not keep up. Raven Runner showed too much in her last start. Combined with other factors, she was just too good for these horses. Raven Runner rewarded her conscientious handicappers a return of $10.60.

SEVENTH RACE
Belmont
JULY 10, 1992

1 MILE.(Turf). (1.322) ALLOWANCE. Purse $29,000. Fillies and mares, 3-year-olds and upward which have never won a race other than Maiden, Claiming or Starter. Weights: 3-year-olds, 116 lbs.; older, 122 lbs. Non-winners of a race other than claiming at a mile or over since June 15, allowed 3 lbs.; of such a race since June 1, allowed 5 lbs.

Value of race $29,000; value to winner $17,400; second $6,380; third $3,480; fourth $1,740. Mutuel pool $221,073. Exacta Pool $490,688

Last Raced	Horse	M/Eqt.A.Wt	PP	St	¼	½	¾	Str	Fin	Jockey	Odds $1
27Jun92 3Eng1	Raven Runner	3 111	4	10	82	7hd	4hd	28	11	Bailey J D	4.30
14Jun92 7Bel9	Kris' Dear Deby	3 113	5	4	62	6½	11	11	26½	McCauley W H	12.60
29Jun92 8Bel2	Miss Garland	b 3 114	7	6	71	8hd	6hd	31	33½	Antley C W	2.70

30May92	5Bel4	Irish Intern	b	3 111	1	9	10	10	9³	4¹	4¾	Samyn J L	5.20
14Jun92	7Bel6	Salsflower		5 117	3	8	9⁴	9½	7ʰᵈ	6¹⁰	5¹	Maple E	17.20
29Jun92	8Bel3	Five Dreams	b	4 117	6	5	5½	5ʰᵈ	5½	5ʰᵈ	6¹²	Santos J A	5.60
16Jun92	7Mth2	Windedawler		3 112	10	3	1ʰᵈ	3ʰᵈ	3½	7²	7¹¼	Smith M E	8.50
14Jun92	4Bel2	Via Dei Portici		3 111	8	1	3¹	2ʰᵈ	8¹½	9¹⁰	8²	Velazquez J R	4.70
4Jun92	2Bel12	Lady of Mann		3 111	2	7	4½	1ʰᵈ	2ʰᵈ	8ʰᵈ	9¹⁴	Davis R G	61.50
21Jun92	7Bel7	Top Kiss	b	3 106	9	2	2½	4½	10	10	10	McMahon H I⁷	72.20

OFF AT 3:58 Start good. Won driving. Time, :22³, :45³, 1:10³, 1:35¹ Course good.

$2 Mutuel Prices:		
4-(D)-RAVEN RUNNER	10.60 8.80 4.00	
5-(E)-KRIS' DEAR DEBY	12.60 5.00	
7-(G)-MISS GARLAND	2.80	

$2 EXACTA 4-5 PAID $133.20

B. f, (Jan), by Storm Bird—Simple Taste, by Sharpen Up. Trainer O'Connell Richard. Bred by Ronald K. Kirk (Ky).

RAVEN RUNNER was off a bit slowly, advanced between foes on the turn, steadied briefly, regained best stride to challenge outside KRIS' DEAR DEBY in midstretch and edged clear late. KRIS DEAR BABY moved up quickly along the rail on the turn, took command in upper stretch but couldn't hold the winner safe while easily best of the others. MISS GARLAND advanced four wide on the turn and lacked the needed closing response. IRISH INTERN trailed for a half mile, rallied widest in the stretch but was no factor. SALSFLOWER passed tired foes. FIVE DREAM steadied early, loomed a factor while outside rivals on the turn and tired thereafter. WINDEDAWLER set or vied for command while widest and gave way in the lane. VIA DEI PORTICI vied for the early lead and tired. LADY OF MANN moved through the inside to take command after a half mile and was finished soon after TOP KISS had brief foot and stopped.

Owners— 1, Kirk Ronald K; 2, Bauld James R; 3, Speigel Robert; 4, Fried Albert Jr; 5, Jackson Evan S; 6, Ju Ju Gen Stable; 7, Mijal Stables; 8, Happy Hill Farm; 9, Reynolds William G Jr; 10, Stroud Murray.

Trainers— 1, O'Connell Richard; 2, Klesaris Robert P; 3, Schaeffer Stephen W; 4, Destasio Richard A; 5, Jackson Evan S; 6, Carroll Henry L; 7, Penna Angel Jr; 8, Preger Mitchell C; 9, Howe Peter M; 10, Combs Don.

Overweight: Kris' Dear Deby 2 pounds; Miss Garland 3; Windedawler 1; Top Kiss 2.

Scratched—Noholmes Secretary (1Jly92 3Bel3); Dashing Baroness (24Jun92 4Bel1); Tiffany Hall (26Jun92 1Bel4); Fashion Ridge (8May92 7Bel2); Sabal Way (4Jly92 8Bel3); Lace Up (2Jly92 7Bel8); Larceny (26Jun92 6Bel5); Tango Dip (22Oct91 8FL7).

Courtesy of Daily Racing Form ©

Every handicapper has to be very careful not to mis-handicap horses that ship from different tracks. It is easy to get sucked into these horses if the knowledge is not there. Knowing who the leading owners, trainers, and jockeys are at the tracks in your area will definitely come in handy. We will evaluate some of the top jockeys and trainers later on in the book.

Mini-Angles

CHAPTER 3 When do we watch certain jockeys? When do we not play a horse because he is running at night? Which maidens are ready? These are just some of the mini-angles that can help you win by a nose or make you decide to throw out a losing favorite. All of these angles are minor but important additions to your handicapping.

Give "Certain Jockey" Angles Special Attention

Jockeys work together with their agents to select certain horses to ride. You want to watch for significant occasions when certain jockeys return to certain horses that they have ridden in the past, but not necessarily to horses that they have been assigned to consistently.

This sort of assignment can come about because a particular trainer explicitly wants a certain rider back on his horse. When a certain jockey returns to a mount which he has not ridden in the horse's past few starts, this can be a very profitable angle. This is especially so if the player knows that the jockey in question has won with this horse before.

Example I

Memories of Spring is a three-year-old filly that had been racing in Canada. She had been ridden by several jockeys in her first thirteen starts while compiling a record of 13-2-3-0. One Canadian jockey, Daniel David, had been aboard for five of those 13 starts. In the first of those starts, a $20,000 maiden claimer on September 7, David piloted Memories of Spring to a second place finish. This same combination scored two more second place finishes on September 21 and October 4.

When David was replaced with the leading jockey at Woodbine on October 19, the filly ran a dismal fifth. In her next two starts, with David back up, Memories of Spring visited the winner's circle both times, first in a $25,000 maiden claimer and then in a $40,000 claiming event. For her first 13 starts, Memories of Spring was 5-2-3-0 with David aboard, and 8-0-0-0 with all of her other jockeys.

Example II

Upon My Soul, a three year old colt on the East Coast circuit, began to reflect this "certain jockey" trend after only six lifetime starts. In his first two starts, Upon My Soul was ridden by Eddie Maple. For his third start, Richard Migliore was given command. On that day he was seven wide while tiring late to the eventual winner Lost Mountain.

In the colt's fourth career start, Migliore took this horse back and decided not to challenge the early speed as he had previously. Instead, he waited until the top of the stretch to challenge King Mutesa and put him away, driving to a three length victory. Next, with Jerry Bailey aboard, Upon My Soul finished eighth by 8½ lengths in a Gulfstream Park $17,000 Allowance race. But when Migliore was reassigned, Upon My Soul drew off to a seven length triumph in a Belmont Park $27,000 Allowance, paying $24.80.

Pay attention. Some jockeys ride for certain trainers, other for certain owners and still others for certain horses. Horses that have particular jockeys on a consistent basis do have an advantage. Such riders have gained experience with the horse's running style and have an advantage over a new jockey. **Special attention should be given when a previously successful jockey returns to a particular horse.**

Consider Day-Night Factor for Sudden Profit

As soon as Race 5 became "Official" during Garden State Park's opening night in 1991, two gentlemen became involved in a rather vigorous conversation. When Gentleman-A exclaimed that he could not understand how his horse ran out of the money, Gentleman-B offered that maybe the horse had run poorly "because he was running at night." By his reaction, Gentleman-A obviously was not buying that explanation.

In that race, Gentleman-A had played the favorite, a shipper from Tampa Bay Downs (Day Racing). The winner, which had most recently raced at the Meadowlands (night racing), returned $24.00 for a $2-win ticket. Is this "day-night angle" something that an astute handicapper should consider?

Over the first weekend (not including Sunday's day card) at Garden State, these two horses had run their most recent races during the day. The six other favorites were "night shippers." Of those 23 "day favorites," nine won (39.1 Wpct.). By contrast, four of the six night-shipper favorites won (66.7 Wpct.).

Horses who are taken abruptly from a day race regimen into a night race regimen are faced with some serious adjustment problems. For example, they must change their feeding schedules and adapt to a different post-time temperature. A horse shipping in from Miami's Calder Race Course, where it has been experiencing day-card racing temperatures of 80 degrees, can show adverse effects from racing in Garden State's 20-degree night cards.

There are a number of examples of excellent horses who consistently raced during the day and then couldn't adjust successfully to an illuminated night race course.

Example I

Allen E. Paulson's Blushing John arrived at the Meadowlands about three days prior to his scheduled appearance in the 1989 Meadowlands Cup (night). Over the next two days, so reported, Blushing John "didn't sleep a wink." Too much crowd noise was believed to be the reason. Blushing John finished poorly in the Meadowlands Cup, but then bounced back to run a strong third to Sunday Silence and Easy Goer in the 1989 Breeder's Cup Classic at Churchill Downs (day).

Example II

Voodoo Lily, a filly trained by D. Wayne Lukas, was entered in Monmouth Park's $35,000 Dearly Precious Stakes on Saturday, August 25, 1990 (day). As in past starts, Voodoo Lily went right to the front, never looking back, and won by five lengths in a final time of 1:09⁴/₅ for the 6 furlongs. Next, in the $35,000 Half Moon Stakes at the Meadowlands (night), Voodoo Lily never sustained a legitimate challenge and finished sixth (last) by 23 lengths.

Just as suddenly, on Saturday, September 29, 1990, Voodoo Lily regained top form, taking command from the outset in Laurel Race Course's $100,000 Columbia Stakes (day). While winning in 1:10³/₅, the Maryland crowd sent her off at odds of 4-1. And, if Voodoo Lily hadn't had superstars Kent Desormeaux and Lukas as her jockey-trainer combo, he would have went off at least 8-1.

While handicapping, throw out night races of horses who are back to running during the day only if they have run consistently in the daytime, as was indicated by Voodoo Lily. Then, horses who have gained experience racing "under the lights" have a distinct advantage over recent "day shippers."

Example III

During October 1990, 91% of the horses that won races at the Meadowlands were those who had at least one start under the lights (for many, their most recent start had been at night). Victor Resk's Great Normand, a 5-year-old gelding usually considered a turf horse, had actually run three of his last four starts on the dirt coming into the 1990 Meadowlands Cup. Great Normand had shipped over to the Meadowlands following a victory in Monmouth Park's Longfellow Handicap.

On September 14, the gelding finished a tiring fourth in the $100,000 New Jersey Classic, with usual rider Carlos Lopez aboard. Then, Great Normand rebounded in her second start at night in the Grade 1 $500,000 Meadowlands Cup. He returned an unimaginable $364.80-$91.40-$15.40 across the-board! Moreover, three starters in that nine-horse field had run their last race under the lights—and they finished first, second (Norquestor) and fifth (Silver Survivor). The exacta returned $1,206.60!

While handicapping races at Garden State, Charles Town, Turfway Park or the Meadowlands, this day-night angle might not only reveal an obvious loser, but also pinpoint a potential winner.

Don't Eliminate Maidens Off One Bad Race

Next time you are handicapping a maiden race don't immediately throw out those horses who haven't performed well. With young, inexperienced horses, many unique factors can play a significant role in their early races. Breaking awkwardly, an "off" track, being bumped, racing greenly, and racing wide are some of the more familiar factors that affect the outcomes of such races.

Example I

Siblings Brother's past two starts certainly hadn't indicated the promise of a good 3-year-old gelding. During his first career start, February 9, this gelding broke badly and then didn't sustain much of anything. Turning for home, Siblings Brother went four wide and finished sixth.

In his second start, February 17, Siblings Brother rushed up to second and, after dropping back to sixth, was once again forced six-wide before finishing a well-run fourth, beaten by 3¾ lengths. Next, on March 7, Siblings Brother rushed to the front immediately, avoiding all traffic problems, and went wire-to-wire—$28.00.

Example II

Rapid Speed, a 3-year-old colt, showed good early speed in his first start. However, he also tired, finishing seventh by 9½ lengths. The factor that apparently influenced the colt's performance the most was the "sloppy" track. His pedigree didn't indicate any potential for handling "off" tracks, and he performed terribly.

As such, next time out, treat this horse as a first-time starter. Ignore that previous race altogether and look directly to his workouts. On February 14, he had galloped 3 furlongs in :38-flat (breezing) and then, on February 27, logged an impressive bullet work for 1:15¾ for 6 furlongs. That workout, with the addition of veteran jockey Earlie Fires in the irons, provided a winning handicapping combination. In his next start, Rapid Speed completed 6 furlongs in a 1:12-flat, paying $21.80 to win.

Example III

Court Scandal, a 3-year-old colt trained by Richard Schosberg, was sent off at 8-1 in his first start, January 31. This is an indication that he was somewhat well-thought-of by the public. Court Scandal rushed up behind the leader on the rail and dropped back. He was then forced to circle the field, going four wide, and finished fifth. His second start, February 7, at 1¹/₁₆ miles on a muddy track did not agree with this colt. He tired badly, finally beaten by 55 lengths!

With a "fast" track for his third start, as well as dropping back to 6 furlongs, Court Scandal was sent off at odds of 35-1. Steadied along the backstretch, when he hit the stretch, he was ready. Not encountering any traffic, he finished a well-run third beaten by only a length.

Conclusion

By reputation, maiden races might be the worst races to handicap. Yet, spending some special time in reviewing past performances of maidens, while carefully considering the particular characteristics of such horses, can pay off. In the preceding examples, "off" tracks and poor racing positions were the key factors linked to poor initial performances.

Some of these points will be repeated in the "trouble comments" of a horse's past-performance lines and in the chartcaller's comments accompanying the results chart of any race. Additionally, reviews of race replays also point toward horses who might be better than their previous finishing positions.

Which Morning Glory Leads to Profit Tree?

Any horse—even a maiden or a mediocre claimer—might log great workouts. Does this necessarily mean that this horse is ready for an upcoming race?

For first-time starters or for horses coming off layoffs, handicappers must depend upon workouts as a primary source of information. On one hand, great workouts are a signal that a horse is in top form. On the other hand, the effectiveness of these performances depends heavily on *when* the workouts were performed.

If a horse works out impressively too close to his next start, there is every chance that he "ran his race in his workout" and his workout will be followed by a poor showing in the race.

Example I

Emperor of Love became a tremendous underlay in his first career start. Obviously, the public sent the colt off as the 3-5 favorite based upon a series of eyecatching workouts. However, he was clocked in :47²/₅ handily on the previous Thursday, January 24, and in :49²/₅ (breezing) on Tuesday, January 29. Older, more experienced horses might handle this schedule, but it is probably too rigorous for most first-time starters.

Emperor of Love went right to the front, going a slow :23-flat for the first quarter and hitting the half in :48¹/₅ with a comfortable 1¹/₂ length lead. Emperor of Love's backers were heading to cash their tickets. The slow pace, plus a two length advantage, seemed to ensure that he would draw off in the stretch. Yet Emperor of Love finished a dismal fourth after being moved up a place on a disqualification. Had the recent workouts taken too much out of this colt?

Example II

Kelly's Kris, a Florida-bred gelding, worked a very quick :34⁴/₅ at Philadelphia Park on Friday, January 18, and was then allowed to rest and recover for 12 days. On Wednesday, January 30, Kelly's Kris took the lead at the outset of Philadelphia Park's fifth race and won by a neck, paying $7.60.

Example III

Frame, a Howard Tesher-trained filly, was sent off as the second choice in Gulfstream Park's Race-5 on Sunday, February 10, an $18,000 allowance sprint. The filly had worked a quick :35⁴/₅ (breezing) on Thursday, February 7, three days before her racing date. Jockey Pat Day had the filly close to the front, but when it was time to kick it in, there was nothing left. She finished a tiring fifth, beaten by eight lengths. In that race, another filly, Sunlight Royalty, worked three furlongs in :35³/₅ (breezing) one day before her race. She had also been close to the pace but she flattened out, finishing fifth, beaten by 14 lengths.

Conclusion

Horses with demanding workouts very close to their next start (1-3 days) appear to be at a disadvantage, due to lack of recovery time. Moreover, be aware of (1) false workouts on speed-oriented tracks and (2) workouts by horses coming from other tracks. In such situations, give the horses an opportunity to indicate how they will perform on the new surface.

"Slop Sires" Pedigrees Pass on Fast Profits

Every thoroughbred race horse reflects traits which were passed down from his or her parents. Such influences can take the form of exceptional speed, the ability to run well on the turf, the ability to gain ground, or "off" track ability. Knowing the top "slop sires" can be beneficial to anyone's handicapping. **The demand for adjustment which accompanies wetter footing will affect any horse's performance.**

Example I

Sovereign Dancer, the sire of 1990 Eclipse Award winner Itsallgreektome, was known for his "off" track ability. Last fall, Itsallgreektome was sent off at odds of 37-1 in the Breeders' Cup Mile at Belmont Park on Saturday, October 27, 1990. The turf came up "good" and Itsallgreektome finished second by a neck to favored Royal Academy.

Example II

Ten Out of Ten's sire is Darby Creek Road. When making her first career start in Philadelphia Park's Race-3 on December 21, 1990, this filly did not have the most impressive workouts, but she did have impressive "slop sire" breeding. The Philadelphia crowd sent her off at 5-1. She led from the start, drawing off in the stretch to win by 5½ lengths in a clock stopping 1:11 flat.

Example III

Music in Time is sired by Stop the Music (with Graustark on the dam's side), another leading "off" track horse. This colt's third career start (Aqueduct's Race-4 on January 10, 1991) was against maiden $45,000 claimers. Music In Time finished seventh and showed little in his first two starts (also at Aqueduct). However, this time the colt stepped on a muddy track, took the lead at the half and drew off through the stretch to win by eight lengths under jockey Mike Smith, paying $11.80. In his victory, Music in Time came home in 1:45³/₅. In his previous start on a "fast" track he ran a 1:50³/₅—literally five seconds slower than his victory on an "off" track.

GREAT "SLOP SIRES"

Ack Ack	Al Near	Alleged
Alydar	Baederwood	Believe It
Big Spruce	Buckaroo	Buckfinder
Chief's Crown	Christopher R.	Cojak
Conquistador Cielo	Connorant	County Pine
Cox's Ridge	Crafty Prospector	Cure the Blues
Damascus	Danzig	Darby Creek Road
Deputy Minister	Dr. Blum	Flying Paster
Hagley	Halo	His Majesty
In Reality	Key to the Mint	Mr. Leader
Mr. Prospector	Naskra	Norcliffe
Northern Baby	Pleasant Colony	Private Account
Raja Baba	Relaunch	Rolicking
Sauce Boat	Secretariat	Smarten
Sovereign Dancer	Stalwart	State Dinner
Stop the Music	Valid Appeal	Vice Regent

Conclusion

The accompanying list presents some of the generally accepted great "off" track horses. Hence, give extra consideration to any entrants that reflect these sires in their pedigrees. Importantly, when handicapping "slop races," only be concerned with races run over the current track of interest. Combining known "slop sire" information with track bias can be a powerful handicapping tool.

Player-Network Arbitraging

In this age of simulcasting, getting the best payout can involve using a handicapping tool that lay outside the limits of past-performance lines, jockey-trainer standings, and similar statistics.

Many times particular races, like the Triple Crown, will be simulcast to numerous tracks which are each conducting their own independent betting pool. As such, handicappers who used to go to the same track as a group are now splitting up to find the best payout. Among horseplayers, the process of searching for the best possible payoff offered on a particular item (horse or multiple of horses) among a network of independent markets (pari-mutuals pools) is referred to as arbitraging.

Joe Mercurio, one of the best sports arbitragers in Las Vegas, has now "raided" the East Coast and turned his interests toward horses.

"There is a lot of money to be made, you just have to know where to bet it," Mercurio explains. "Also, it is unlike arbitraging in Las Vegas, with all you can lose in the vigorish."

"In horse racing, arbitraging is a little more risky, but why not take advantage of getting the best price you can? In the beginning of the week, I find out all the races that are being simulcast and I send one guy to each track. Do not get me wrong, you still have to pick the winner."

"Arbitraging has paid off. I bet almost everyday, and with the Aqueduct simulcasting, I have made out very well. On many occasions, I've made back-to-back hits on the same day."

"The most recent occurred on January 11, 1992, with the Appleton Handicap at Gulfstream and the Affectionately Handicap at Aqueduct. I had posted guys at Philadelphia, Aqueduct, Gulfstream, and, myself, at Garden State.

"In the Affectionately at Aqueduct, Get Lucky was a stand-out and the eventual winner. He won, paying $4.80 at Aqueduct, $4.20 at Philadelphia and $5.20 at Garden State. I had placed my wager at Aqueduct which proved not to be the highest payout, but if I would have placed my bet at Garden State it would have deflated the pool. Sixty cents might not seem like a lot of money but when you bet $2,000 to win $600.00, it is."

"In the Appleton, I liked a longshot named Royal Ninja. My guy in Florida reported 11-1 with three minutes to post and 9-1 at Philadelphia. With 12-1 odds at Garden State, I decided to place my wager there. Royal Ninja won, paying $26.80. Also, the exacta at Philadelphia paid $181.40 and if you were wagering at Garden State you would have collected $224.00. I will not deny that it's a lot of work, but why be robbed?"

This form of arbitraging is not necessarily limited to the handicapper who wagers a couple of thousand per play. For example, on Sunday, December 29, 1991, Aqueduct Ticonderoga Handicap was also simulcasted to Philadelphia Park. Cullinan Diamond won the race and paid $23.60 to win, trackside. Meanwhile, at Philadelphia Park that same horse paid $41.00. A $17.40 difference per $2 wagered is a spread that no player can afford to ignore. Furthermore, the ex-acta paid over $80 more at Philadelphia Park ($307.80, compared with Aqueduct's $221.60).

Also, two weeks later (Sunday, January 12) Aqueduct's Montauk Stakes yielded a $58.80 exacta trackside, compared with an inflated $111.60 at the Philadelphia Park simulcast outlet. For a $2 bettor, $53 extra dollars might account for a day's winnings.

Of course, not everyone can send people to different tracks to find out the best possible payout. But any time a group of gambling buddies can spread out and cooperate, they could all benefit from this form of arbitraging.

You can also do some of this by yourself. Use common sense. If the horse you like in a big race is from New York, go to a track in New Jersey rather than, say, Belmont. If you like a horse that is shipping from the midwest for a simulcast race, pick a smaller track where your horse may not be as well known.

The difference in mutual pay-off could be well worth the trouble.

Time Analysis

CHAPTER 4

Time Analysis is a procedure you can use to break down a horse's speed performance, thereby finding the horse with the most "raw speed." Time Analysis works in every class from claiming to stakes competition, such as the Belmont Stakes.

Executive Bid is a five-year-old gelding that we'll use to show how to perform Time Analysis.

Executive Bid — **B. g. 5, by Explosive Bid—Mary Mikeljohn, by Mike John G**
$22,500 **Br.—Sarkisian Norman (Fla)**
wn.—Mizrahi Ralph — **Tr.—Bottazzi Patrick L (85 8 15 13 .09)** — **114**

Lifetime						
53 11 9 7	**1992**	13	2	3	1	$34,285
$142,130	**1991**	18	5	4	3	$65,230
	Turf	2	0	0	0	$115
	Wet	8	0	1	1	$5,895

Jly92- 4Mth	fst	6f	:21^{2}	:45	1:11^{1}	3↑Clm 22000	**75**	8	2	5^{6}	$5^{4\frac{1}{2}}$	$5^{2\frac{3}{4}}$	$4^{3\frac{1}{2}}$	Vega A	L 116	9.30	81-14	SocblyJohnny116^{nk}RcngSplndr119$^{3\frac{1}{4}}$Alswy114	Late gain	9
Jly92- 6Mth	fst	6f	:21^{2}	:44^{4}	1:11^{1}	3↑Clm 25000	**77**	5	2	2^{2}	$3^{2\frac{1}{2}}$	1^{hd}	$3^{1\frac{3}{4}}$	Collazo L	L 116	3.50	83-17	RinbowQurtz116^{1}ClnndBold116$^{\frac{3}{4}}$ExcutvBd116	Tired late	8
Jun92- 7Mth	my	6f	:21^{2}	:44^{2}	1:10^{4}	3↑Clm 30000	**82**	4	3	4^{4}	$4^{2\frac{1}{2}}$	$4^{1\frac{1}{2}}$	$6^{3\frac{1}{4}}$	Collazo L	L 112	7.20	84-17	BrveAdventur116^{nk}DddyRx116$^{1\frac{1}{2}}$BigJwl119	In tight late	8
Jun92- 9Mth	fst	6f	:21^{4}	:44^{2}	1:08^{4}	3↑Alw 26000	**65**	4	7	7^{12}	$8^{9\frac{3}{4}}$	8^{12}	$7^{15\frac{1}{2}}$	Collazo L	L 115	49.80	81-13	Dyswhts115^{hd}TddyDrn122$^{7\frac{3}{4}}$NrthrnNTrmp115	Jostled st	8
May92- 3Mth	sly	6f	:21^{4}	:44^{2}	1:09^{2}	3↑Clm 32000	**86**	3	2	$1^{\frac{1}{2}}$	$1^{\frac{1}{2}}$	$2^{1\frac{1}{2}}$	2^{5}	Bravo J	L 116	*1.60	89-14	CrftyAlfl111^{5}ExctvBd116$^{3\frac{1}{2}}$SocblyJohnny114	No match	6
Mar92- 1Aqu	fst	6f	:21^{4}	:45	1:10^{3}	Clm 45000	**76**	2	1	$2^{\frac{1}{2}}$	$1^{\frac{1}{2}}$	3^{nk}	4^{6}	Bravo J	113	4.10	82-19	TopThRcord117$^{1\frac{3}{4}}$ScrtAlrt113^{3}PtncfJv117	Dueled, tired	6
Mar92- 5GS	fst	5½f	:22^{3}	:46^{4}	1:05^{3}	3↑Alw 15000	**71**	1	2	1^{hd}	$2^{\frac{1}{2}}$	$3^{3\frac{1}{2}}$	$4^{6\frac{1}{4}}$	Pennisi F A	L 117	5.00	78-26	Jesuit117^{nk}SamsTank119$^{4\frac{1}{4}}$NausetFlsh117	Used in pace	6
Mar92- 5Aqu	gd	6f	⊡:23^{1}	:46^{3}	1:11^{2}	Clm 35000	**95**	5	1	1^{1}	1^{2}	$1^{1\frac{1}{2}}$	$1^{\frac{1}{2}}$	Bravo J	113	5.10	86-16	ExecutiveBid113$^{\frac{1}{2}}$Talc'sBid113^{6}GallantHitter112	Driving	6
Feb92- 2Aqu	fst	6f	⊡:22^{4}	:46^{1}	1:10^{2}	Clm 45000	**73**	4	1	$2^{\frac{1}{2}}$	$2^{\frac{1}{2}}$	$5^{7\frac{3}{4}}$	$6^{15\frac{3}{4}}$	Bravo J	113	9.40	75-18	Rppl113$^{10\frac{1}{2}}$TrnChrmng113^{no}ChnPlsr117	Frcd pace, tired	7
Feb92- 9GS	my	6f	:22^{1}	:45^{2}	1:11^{3}	Alw 15000	**84**	5	1	1^{1}	$1^{1\frac{1}{2}}$	2^{hd}	4^{2}	Collazo L	L 119	5.80	82-28	Michel'sRep115^{1}Jesuit122^{nk}Miner'sDrem115	Weakened	6

ATEST WORKOUTS **May 26 Mth 4f fst :48^{3} B**

Courtesy of Daily Racing Form ©

Executive Bid's last start was the worst of his last three. The fractions of the race were 21$^{2}/_{5}$, 45 flat, and 1.11$^{1}/_{5}$. We adjust the race's fraction to find Executive Bid's actual times by adding $1/5$ of a second for each length he was off the leader. By doing this we get Executive Bid's actual racing time.

The first quarter in this particular race was run in $21^2/5$. To adjust this time we have to look at how many lengths Executive Bid was behind, which was six. Six lengths add up to one second and one-fifth. When added to the actual time, this raises the time from $21^2/5$ to Executive Bid's actual time of $22^3/5$. At the half, the actual time was 45 seconds flat, but when one full second is added, because he was behind four and one-half lengths (when we have a $1/2$ of length we round up to a full length), Executive Bid actually ran a :46 flat to the half-mile pole.

Handicappers must know the condition of the surrounding tracks to have success with Time Analysis. Understanding which tracks are faster and which are slower is required. In the New York/New Jersey area it is pertinent to know that Rockingham Park and Garden State are very deep and Monmouth Park and Philadelphia Park are lighting fast. How does this effect Time Analysis?

In figuring Time Analysis, the handicapper will have to set his own Speed Bias per track for the tracks in his surrounding area.

Suppose the track you are handicapping is Monmouth. Here are your adjustments:

Philadelphia Park—Even
Garden State— – 2 seconds
Rockingham— – $2^2/5$ seconds
Belmont— – $3/5$ of a second

These figures will vary on "off" tracks and the handicapper will have to use his own judgment. Remember: **Never fault a horse that has slow or medium fractions on a deep track.** These fractions will improve once a particular horse is placed on a faster surface. A good rule of thumb is to check the workouts to see how the particular horse has performed on this new surface.

On June 2, 1992, the fourth race featured nine fillies and mares going six furlongs on a muddy track. Claiming horses are erratic, but most will run approximately the same time every race when adjusted. This race was for claiming $5,000 horses. It will show how effective Time Analysis really is.

4 6 FURLONGS MONMOUTH PARK (START / FINISH)

6 FURLONGS. **(1.08) CLAIMING. Purse $5,500. Fillies and mares, 3-year-olds and upward. Weight, 3-year-olds, 115 lbs. Older, 122 lbs. Non-winners of two races since April 28 allowed 3 lbs. A race, 6 lbs. Claiming price $5,000. (Races where entered for $4,000 or less not considered.)**

Coupled—Top Tomato and Play It Hard.
LASIX—Go Lassie Go, Shayla's Prospect, Novel Wish, Freezing Run, Minnesota's Way, Top Tomato, Push Broom, Play It Hard, Well Assembled, Running Deal, Flying Pegemina.

Go Lassie Go

Dk. b. or br. f. 4, by Prince Valid—By the Stream, by New Prospect
$5,000 **Br.—Cohn Seymour (Md)**
Tr.—Serey Juan (—)
116
Own.—Ritter D & R

Lifetime	1992 7 1 0 3	$5,010
37 4 8 7	1991 22 3 7 4	$19,724
$26,704	Wet 4 0 2 1	$2,610

30Apr92- 7GS	fst	6f	$:22^2$	$:46^2$	$1:13^3$	3↑ⒻClm 8000	38	1	6	1^1	2^{hd}	4^3	$7^{4¾}$	Pennisi F A	Lb	117	2.50	69-23	SmplGldn117½SmldrngEmbrs117nkLnBld119	Weakened	10
10Apr92- 6GS	fst	6f	:23	$:46^4$	$1:13^2$	3↑ⒻClm c-6250	64	7	2	2^1	$3^{3½}$	3^2	3^2	Frates D	Lb	119	*2.50	73-23	KrtLdy117hdSilverholme1172GoLssieGo119	No late rally	7

10Apr92-Claimed from Schuster Fritz, Anthony Priscilla Trainer

26Mar92- 3GS	sly	6f	$:22^4$	$:47^2$	$1:14^1$	3↑ⒻClm 6250	46	4	2	5^3	$4^{3½}$	$2^{4½}$	3^4	Frates D	Lb	119	6.90	67-28	SyJoJo117½MyAnglJillin1153½GoLssGo119	No final rally	6
15Mar92- 6GS	fst	6f	$:22^3$	$:46^4$	1:14	ⒻClm 6000	59	7	5	4^2	1^1	$1^{3½}$	$1^{1½}$	Frates D	Lb	115	9.60	72-28	GoLssieGo1151½LepinLuren115¾IsleofBechs115	Driving	7
5Mar92- 7GS	fst	6f	$:22^3$	$:46^4$	$1:13^2$	ⒻClm 7000	52	8	3	3^{nk}	$2^{1½}$	2^5	7^{10}	Grabowski J A	Lb	116	16.80	65-25	LongClover1175LivingBold1154Voodoo'sSister117	Tired	11
16Feb92- 3GS	my	6f	$:22^2$	:47	1:15	ⒻClm 7000	55	3	4	$2^{2½}$	3^2	$3^{½}$	$4^{¾}$	Grabowski J A	Lb	115	9.90	66-28	MorningStrshin113hdLpnLurn119nkYvnn117	Outfinished	6
31Jan92- 4GS	fst	6f	$:22^1$	$:46^3$	$1:13^2$	ⒻClm 6250	53	4	6	$3^{2½}$	$3^{3½}$	2^5	$3^{6½}$	Grabowski J A	Lb	117	5.10	68-26	SyJoJo1175¼MorningStrshn1171¼GoLssGo117	Even trip	8
29Nov91- 2Med	fst	6f	$:22^1$	$:45^3$	1:12	ⒻClm 7500	46	9	5	$7^{5¼}$	$7^{5¾}$	$5^{5½}$	$5^{6¼}$	Vasquez M M	Lb	115	3.50	76-16	Nanlinli1152¾ Say Jo Jo1152½ Tenacious Fran115	Wide	9
19Nov91- 3Med	fst	6f	$:22^4$	$:46^2$	$1:11^4$	ⒻClm 7500	61	4	3	$2^{½}$	2^{hd}	$2^{1½}$	$2^{1½}$	Vasquez M M	Lb	118	*1.20	81-13	FieryDebutnte1141½GoLssiGo1184½Shopkpr115	2nd best	6
30Oct91- 2Med	fst	6f	$:22^4$	$:46^3$	$1:12^2$	ⒻClm 7500	59	3	8	$3^{1½}$	$3^{1½}$	3^1	$1^{1¼}$	Vasquez M M	Lb	115	8.10	80-17	GoLssieGo1151¼FiryDbutnt1091IrishLimrick115	Driving	6

Shayla's Prospect

Dk. b. or br. f. 4, by Tank's Prospect—Honey I'm Home, by Gaelic Dancer
$5,000 **Br.—Eaton Farms Inc & Red Bull Stable (Ky)**
Tr.—Crupi James J (2 1 0 0 .50)
111^5
Own.—Martucci William C

Lifetime	1992 1 0 0 0	
26 4 4 2	1991 14 2 3 1	$11,475
$28,290	Turf 1 0 0 0	

8Jan92- 7GS	fst	6f	$:22^4$	$:46^4$	$1:13^3$	ⒻClm 4000	39	1	4	6^7	$6^{4¾}$	$6^{6½}$	6^8	Marquez C HJr	Lb	119	3.80	66-22	ChrcnsTr1173QnlSdKc1172¼WnstsWhs112	Wide, outrun	8
27Dec91- 6GS	fst	$1\frac{1}{16}$	:47	$1:12^1$	$1:46^4$	3↑ⒻClm 6250	3	3	3	3^8	7^{17}	7^{28}	$6^{42¼}$	Ferrer J C	Lb	114	2.80	33-23	MorningJo1157Cstoutthedvil117¾GlowingWild110	Tired	7
5Dec91- 4Med	fst	1	$:11^3$		$1:38^1$	ⒻClm 5000	57	5	4	$1^{1½}$	$1^{2½}$	$1^{2½}$	1^3	Ferrer J C	Lb	114	2.70	88-11	Shyl'sProspct1143Wouldn'tYo1161½BlCnopy118	Driving	9
27Nov91- 4Med	fst	6f	$:22^4$	$:45^4$	$1:11^4$	ⒻClm 5000	56	6	2	$5^{3½}$	2^2	2^1	$2^{¾}$	Marquez C HJr	Lb	115	2.40	82-13	FrnnBrtchs118¾Shl'sPrspct1154OhMPrttPnn115	Gamely	8
19Nov91- 2Med	fst	6f	$:22^4$	$:46^3$	$1:12^2$	ⒻClm 5000	51	2	2	$5^{2½}$	$6^{4½}$	$3^{6½}$	$2^{2¼}$	Marquez C HJr	Lb	115	3.90	78-13	FrnnBrtchs1152¼Shl'sPrspct1151½LDst110	Gained place	9
22Oct91- 4Med	fst	6f	$:22^2$	$:45^3$	$1:11^3$	ⒻClm 5000	51	6	12	9^8	$5^{3½}$	$6^{4¾}$	$4^{6¼}$	Marquez C HJr	Lb	115	3.10	78-15	FryDbtnt1101SyJoJo1154BrfootAv115	Some gain, wide	12
18Oct91-11Med	fst	6f	:22	$:45^3$	$1:12^1$	ⒻClm 5000	53	3	8	$9^{6¼}$	$9^{8¾}$	$5^{4½}$	$2^{1¼}$	Marquez C HJr	Lb	115	8.60	80-17	KneLw1101¼Shyl'sProspect1152CntrlCsting115	Checked	11
7Oct91- 4Med	fst	6f	$:22^2$	$:46^2$	$1:12^2$	ⒻClm 5000	48	4	6	$7^{8½}$	$7^{5¼}$	7^7	$5^{4½}$	Marquez C HJr	Lb	115	3.60	75-13	Dark Mariha115no Sharp Sam1151¾ Kane Law110	Wide	8
27Sep91- 4Med	fst	6f	:22	$:45^3$	$1:10^2$	ⒻClm 7500	47	6	3	$7^{9½}$	$7^{5¼}$	$5^{6½}$	$5^{10½}$	BrocklbnkGV5	Lb	113	3.50	79-09	Chircvn'sTrx1155KnLw1081¾SlwMystqu112	Lacked rally	9
7Sep91-10Med	fst	6f	$:22^2$	$:45^3$	$1:11^4$	ⒻClm 7500	56	8	2	$8^{7½}$	5^6	$4^{2¼}$	1^1	BrocklbnkGV5	Lb	110	13.80	83-12	Shayla'sProspect1101SharpSm1151½LdyBliss111	Driving	9

LATEST WORKOUTS May 30 Mth 3f fst :36 B — May 25 Mth 6f fst 1:18 Bg — May 19 Mth 5f fst 1:02 Bg

Novel Wish

Ch. m. 6, by Text—Wish, by Wise Exchange
$5,000 **Br.—Weinsier Randolph (Ky)**
Tr.—Dollinger Susan M (—)
116
Own.—Dollinger Susan M

Lifetime	1992 6 1 1 1	$4,959
39 7 4 3	1991 14 4 1 0	$13,315
$29,892	Turf 3 0 0 0	
	Wet 6 4 1 0	$13,930

3May92- 1GS	fst	170	$:48^4$	1:16	$1:47^4$	3↑ⒻClm 5000	39	1	1	1^1	1^1	4^1	5^6	Grabowski J A	Lb	119	*1.20	57-31	LdyLIIB.1171½GlwngWld117hdPrdprmsdldy117	Gave way	7
30Mar92- 6Pha	fst	$1\frac{1}{16}$	$:47^1$	$1:12^3$	$1:47^4$	ⒻClm 6000	45	1	4	4^7	4^7	$5^{7½}$	$4^{5½}$	Capanas S	Lb	114	6.20	64-20	HghSprtd119nkMornngJ1124½MdtwnMldy115	No threat	8
19Mar92- 7GS	sly	$1\frac{1}{16}$	$:48^3$	1:14	$1:48^3$	3↑ⒻClm 5000	73	1	2	$2^{½}$	$2^{3½}$	$2^{1½}$	1^1	Capanas S	Lb	117	2.30	71-33	NovelWish1171BeachBallerina1121½Wachoot119	Driving	7
14Feb92- 2Pha	fst	$1\frac{1}{16}$	:49	$1:14^3$	$1:49^3$	ⒻClm 5000	66	2	3	2^2	2^3	$2^{2½}$	2no	Capanas S	Lb	116	8.00	61-42	Jnnfr'sCstody116noNvlWsh1165HtMAgn116	Just missed	8
3Feb92- 3Pha	fst	170	$:47^3$	$1:14^3$	$1:47^2$	ⒻClm 5000	57	8	3	$3^{2½}$	2^{hd}	2^2	$3^{1½}$	Capanas S	Lb	116	38.80	57-29	FastTrt119nkOnNturl1161½NovelWish116	Wide good try	8
3Jan92- 4Pha	fst	170	:48	$1:13^4$	$1:45^1$	ⒻClm 5000	23	9	4	$6^{5¾}$	10^{16}	11^{26}	$11^{25½}$	Capanas S	Lb	116	40.80	44-32	GrandTle116nkSvgeRebel1162¼ShmpooKtie108	Stopped	11
20Dec91- 2Pha	fst	170	$:47^4$	$1:13^4$	$1:45^1$	3↑ⒻClm 5000	16	4	5	$6^{6¼}$	10^{11}	10^{20}	$10^{22¾}$	Capanas S	Lb	116	11.10	47-23	Vllrco1161½MdivlDm1197½GloriousPrsnt116	Tired badly	10
11Nov91- 1Pha	sly	$1\frac{1}{16}$	$:47^4$	$1:12^3$	1:47	3↑ⒻClm 4000	68	5	4	$1^{1½}$	1^6	1^5	$1^{5½}$	Capanas S	Lb	119	4.90	74-22	NovlWish1195½InDwn'sLight1121¾AnniSpruc116	Driving	7
23Oct91- 2Pha	fst	$1\frac{1}{16}$	:47	$1:12^2$	$1:45^2$	3↑ⒻClm 5000	54	8	3	3^4	$4^{3½}$	6^{10}	$6^{9¾}$	Lloyd J S	Lb	116	44.50	72-18	On a Natural1164½AnnieSpruce116nkWolfLuck119	Tired	8
8Sep91- 4Pha	fst	170	:47	$1:13^4$	$1:44^3$	3↑ⒻClm 5000	27	6	6	7^{12}	$8^{4¾}$	7^{15}	$7^{22¼}$	Lloyd J S	Lb	116	7.10	51-24	IceCubes1195½AnnieSpruce1163OnaNaturl116	No threat	9

LATEST WORKOUTS Apr 29 GS 4f fst $:51^2$ B — Apr 11 GS 3f fst $:37^3$ B

Freezing Run

Ch. m. 7, by It's Freezing—Rollicking Runner, by Rollicking
$5,000 **Br.—Payson Virginia Kraft (NJ)**
Tr.—Spina Chuck (—)
116
Own.—Spina Chuck

Lifetime	1992 3 0 0 0	$240
61 10 8 9	1991 21 4 2 4	$17,733
$80,009	Turf 2 0 0 0	$322
	Wet 5 1 1 0	$5,680

2Feb92- 4GS	fst	5½f	:23	$:40^3$	1.08	ⒻClm 4000	32	7	4	1^{hd}	3^1	$5^{3½}$	$7^{9½}$	Gomez I	L	117	8.20	62-29	RacyPrincess1174¾SheIsGlint117nkJpr122	Used in pace	10
16Jan92-10GS	fst	6f	$:22^2$	:47	$1:13^3$	ⒻClm 4000	40	9	2	1^1	$1^{½}$	2^{hd}	$5^{5¼}$	Gomez I	L	119	5.80	69-23	LovbleLiz1171½[D]SheIsGlint117nkSilverOrGold117	Faded	10
7Jan92-10GS	fst	6f	$:22^3$	:47	$1:14^1$	ⒻClm 4000	40	6	5	2^{hd}	2^1	3^5	5^5	Gomez I	L	119	3.30	66-29	JossSprm117¾LovblLz1192NxtKndofmrcl114	Weakened	10
7Dec91-10Med	fst	6f	$:22^3$	$:46^2$	1:12	3↑ⒻⓈClm 5000	40	11	1	$1^{½}$	2^{hd}	3^6	$7^{11½}$	Gomez I	L	116	31.10	70-18	Kpn'Thoughts1162¾PushBroom1192GurdHous114	Faded	12
21Nov91- 4Med	gd	6f	:22	:46	$1:11^2$	3↑ⒻⓈClm 5000	40	4	3	$2^{2½}$	3^{nk}	$4^{4½}$	5^{15}	Gomez I	L	116	4.50	70-23	FrstFlghtOt1146½Fthrsn'Fn1164Wnstn'sWhms116	Tired	9
11Nov91- 2Med	sly	6f	$:22^2$	$:46^3$	$1:12^3$	3↑ⒻⓈClm 5000	53	7	1	2^{hd}	$1^{2½}$	$1^{½}$	2^5	Gomez I	L	116	4.00	74-20	GurdHous1145FrzngRun1164¾Lvnhrslv'116	Second best	8
20Oct91- 2Med	fst	6f	$:22^1$	$:46^1$	$1:11^3$	3↑ⒻⓈClm 5000	55	3	2	$2^{½}$	2^{hd}	2^{hd}	$3^{5¾}$	Gomez I	L	116	5.00	78-17	GurdHouse1113StgMothr1192¾FrzingRun116	Weakened	9
8Oct91- 9Pha	fst	5½f	$:22^1$	$:46^4$	1:07	3↑ⒻClm 4000	49	5	5	$5^{1¼}$	$5^{3¼}$	$4^{2½}$	$3^{2¼}$	Gomez I	L	116	16.80	77-22	Yvnne116nkPrivilegedClss1162FrezingRun116	No threat	9

8Oct91-Awarded second purse money
21Sep91-11Del fst 5½f :22 :46³ 1:05³ 3↑ⒻClm 4000 33 7 4 3½ 44 78 811½ Gomez I L 115 3.70 75-17 B.F.Egypt116²MyMomLnor110ⁿᵒLdydJur119 Thru early 9
13Sep91- 1Med fst 6f :22² :45² 1:11¹ 3↑ⒻⓈClm 5000 52 2 5 11½ 1hd 21½ 33¾ Olea R E⁵ L 111 4.60 82-14 SwnnisFinl1102½It'sLlyTm1161½FrzngRun111 Weakened 9
LATEST WORKOUTS May 19 Mth 5f fst 1:03⁴ B Apr 25 GS 3f fst :36 B Apr 18 GS 3f fst :37⁴ B

Minnesota's Way Dk. b. or br. f. 4, by Real Way—Minnesota Muriel, by Minnesota Mac
$5,000 Br.—Appleton Arthur I (Fla)
Own.—Blue Devil Stable Tr.—Reid Mark J (4 0 1 3 .00) 116
Lifetime 33 7 5 7 $42,360 | 1992 4 2 0 1 $5,480 | 1991 23 5 3 3 $31,435 | Wet 5 2 2 0 $11,325
21May92- 1GS fst 6f :22⁴ :46⁴ 1:12⁴ 3↑ⒻClm 4000 52 2 4 11 1hd 12 11½ King E L Jr Lb 119 6.30 78-21 Minnesota'sWy1191½Lis'sIslnd1171½Deceived117 Driving 7
7May92- 5GS fst 6f :23 :47³ 1:14 3↑ⒻClm 4000 50 3 6 31½ 1hd 1hd 1hd Lopez C E Jr⁵ Lb 112 *1.40 72-27 Mnnsot'sWy112ʰᵈGllRvrGl117ⁿᵏLs'sIslnd117 Long drive 8
11Apr92- 2GS fst 5½f :23¹ :47⁴ 1:07³ 3↑ⒻClm 4000 49 1 3 43 43½ 42½ 31 Lovato F Jr L 117 *1.50 73-25 Japar117½EndoftheNinth117½Minnesot'sWy117 Fin well 9
2Apr92- 7GS fst 6f :23 :47² 1:14⁴ ⒻClm 4000 48 3 3 2hd 1hd 1hd 41¾ Castillo F⁵ L 112 *1.70 66-28 CookieMker117ⁿᵏBengliBby117½MostImprovd117 Faded 9
29Nov91- 4Med fst 1¹⁄₁₆ :46³ 1:11⁴ 1:46¹ 3↑ⒻClm 5000 42 12 7 711 812 1012 1016½ Brockelbank G V L 116 27.10 60-20 SmrtySmrty1154½MornngJ115ⁿᵏCsttthdvl117 No factor 12
19Nov91- 3Med fst 6f :22⁴ :46² 1:11⁴ ⒻClm 7500 34 6 2 68 67 69½ 612½ Kamada E J L 115 4.80 70-13 FieryDebutnte1141½GoLssieGo1184½Shopkpr115 Outrun 6
22Oct91- 6Med fst 6f :22³ :46 1:11⁴ ⒻClm 10000 51 3 7 86½ 86½ 67½ 55½ Yang C C L 115 8.80 77-15 PrclnGddss115½IrshLmrc1111½Intnththts115 No factor 10
8Oct91- 4Med fst 6f :22² :46² 1:12² ⒻClm c-7500 54 5 9 62½ 63 54½ 43¾ Gryder A T L 115 3.70 76-19 PorclnGoddss115¾GLssG115ⁿᵏIrshLmrck115 No late bid 11
3Oct91- 3Med fst 6f :22³ :45⁴ 1:11² ⒻClm 14000 51 4 2 33 43 45 65¾ Gryder A T L 112 6.90 79-13 Brd'sTrbt1122¾Bno'sJodyTw1142AfrcnDsy115 No factor 6
11Sep91- 7Med fst 6f :22³ :46¹ 1:12¹ ⒻClm 16000 55 6 9 96 75 73½ 75¾ Bravo J L 115 4.70 75-17 Southbound1152Brd'sTrbut113ⁿᵏQukrLdy108 No str bid 11
LATEST WORKOUTS May 4 GS 3f fst :36² B

Top Tomato Dk. b. or br. m. 5, by Vittorioso—Lil Banner, by Minnesota Mac
$5,000 Br.—Shannon P Jr (NJ)
Own.—Shannon Peter H Jr Tr.—Forbes John H (3 0 0 1 .00) 111⁵
Lifetime 33 8 7 2 $69,632 | 1991 15 5 4 2 $33,952 | 1990 10 2 3 0 $29,080 | Wet 4 2 0 0 $25,200
6Dec91- 7Med fst 6f :22² :46 1:11² 3↑ⒻClm 10500 61 5 2 47 46 33½ 31½ Marquez C H Jr L 112⁴ *2.30 83-12 LvngBld1161½Mrs.Mny116ⁿᵏDHSmmrStrm116 Mild rally 9
6Dec91-Dead heat
18Nov91- 6Med fst 6f :22¹ :45¹ 1:10⁴ 3↑ⒻⓈClm 10500 67 6 2 38½ 27 25½ 24¾ Marquez C H Jr L 112 2.90 83-14 FlwlssMlody1164¾TopTmt1122LvOldDd111 Second best 6
17Oct91- 5Med sly 6f :22⁴ :46² 1:12 3↑ⒻⓈAlw 20000 67 3 1 2½ 2hd 1hd 1nk Marquez C H Jr L 116 5.10 82-12 TopTomato116ⁿᵏSisterRock1131RuleBreker113 Driving 6
7Oct91- 7Med fst 6f :22⁴ :45⁴ 1:11 3↑ⒻⓈAlw 20000 51 8 1 41½ 63½ 88 811½ Marquez C H Jr L 116 4.10 75-13 QckToBlm1134½BrghtstMomnt1131½SstrRck115 Outrun 8
22Sep91- 2Mth fst 6f :21⁴ :45² 1:11³ 3↑ⒻⓈClm 6250 65 3 4 55½ 43 2½ 12¾ Marquez C H Jr L 116 3.60 83-14 TopTomto1162¾RedyToBeGrt1163½JrsyFrsh116 Handily 7
13Sep91-10Med fst 6f :21⁴ :44⁴ 1:11 3↑ⒻⓈClm 5000 63 1 7 69 68½ 54 1½ Marquez C H Jr L 116 5.50 87-14 TopTomto116½CslssChttr119ⁿᵏDuplktProdst116 Driving 9
11Aug91-10Mth fst 1¹⁄₁₆ :46³ 1:12² 1:46⁴ 3↑ⒻClm 5000 58 6 2 35 33 34 47½ Marquez C H Jr L 115 8.50 67-20 Jimenette1171½ Trickle Up117⁶ Golden Dove115 Tired 10
19Jly91- 2Mth fst 1¹⁄₁₆ :47³ 1:12¹ 1:46² 3↑ⒻClm 5000 52 6 7 55¾ 35 27 29 Marquez C H Jr L 117 *1.50e 68-19 Jimenette115⁹ TopTomato117¹GuardHouse115 2nd best 9
10Jly91- 2Mth fst 170 :46³ 1:12 1:43¹ 3↑ⒻClm 5000 40 6 5 413 210 210 221 Marquez C H Jr L 117 *2.20 59-27 TrickleUp115²¹TopTomto1171½GoldenDove115 2nd best 8
28Jun91- 4Mth fst 1 :47³ 1:13² 1:40¹ 3↑ⒻClm 5000 62 4 3 32 2hd 1½ 11 Marquez C H Jr L 115 3.50 68-27 Top Tomato115¹ Trickle Up115⁷ BitsyWhite115 Driving 10
LATEST WORKOUTS May 27 Mth 4f fst :49² B May 21 Mth 5f fst 1:03¹ B May 16 Mth 4f gd :53⁴ B May 9 GS 4f my :53¹ B

Atlas Axis Ch. f. 4, by Lobsang-IR—Lady Ashmore, by Ashmore
$5,000 Br.—Dubel James W (NJ)
Own.—Dubel & Grimm Tr.—Grimm Wayne (—) 116
Lifetime 11 1 0 0 $11,520 | 1992 1 0 0 0 | 1991 10 1 0 0 $11,520 | Turf 3 1 0 0 $9,900
18Apr92- 7GS fst 6f :22⁴ :46² 1:13¹ 3↑ⒻⓈClm 7500 15 5 5 43 615 718 720½ Chavis S T 117 33.40 55-24 ClymoreGl11010½SisterGorg1173DvidsRoylty122 Outrun 9
9Oct91- 3Med fst 170 :46⁴ 1:12² 1:44 ⒻClm 5000 35 2 3 35 59 511 516½ MacMillan J R 114 14.80 62-24 TequilMoon114ⁿᵏBlueCnopy1148½IttyBittySlw114 Tired 7
30Sep91- 5Med fst 1¹⁄₁₆ :47¹ 1:13¹ 1:47 ⒻClm 12500 41 4 6 75¾ 82½ 67 513¾ Ferrer J C 114 24.30 59-27 SttchndSw1162ProdsPnch1145¾TonyLny114 Wide, tired 9
22Sep91- 8Del fm 1¹⁄₁₆ Ⓣ:48² 1:13⁴ 1:46⁴ 3↑ⒻAlw 8000 49 7 5 5⁵ 97½1015 716 Cabrera S b 116 17.90 60-17 Grassy Lane1101½ Gracies Riddle1101½Collatia116 Tired 12
27Aug91- 8Mth fm 1¹⁄₁₆ Ⓣ:47⁴ 1:12 1:43³ + 3↑ⒻAlw 18000 64 6 1 1hd 73¾ 613 615 MacMillan JR⁵ b 108 25.90 68-18 WhmsclMlody1163¾SpctrPhot-Ir112ʰᵈMt.Mrn109 Tired 8
16Aug91- 6Mth gd *1¹⁄₁₆ Ⓣ:48⁴ 1:13² 1:46² + 3↑ⒻMd Sp Wt 79 1 1 1½ 1½ 11 1nk MacMillan JR⁵ b 110 28.40 82-16 Atlas Axis110ⁿᵏKristening1153½TrioPrincess115 Driving 8
10Aug91- 4Mth gd 6f :22² :46⁴ 1:12³ 3↑ⓈMd Sp Wt 39 6 6 96¾1010½ 96 811 MacMillan JR⁵ b 107 60.20 67-18 HelloDere1173¾Robert'sFire117½QueensJstr117 Outrun 10
28Jly91- 7Mth fst 6f :22² :45⁴ 1:11⁴ 3↑ⓈMd Sp Wt 39 3 8 88½ 99½ 99½ 69½ Ferrer J C b 112 40.00 73-10 SonofPrincss1163½CrimsonCry1112Robrt'sFr116 Outrun 9
14Jly91-11Mth gd 6f :21⁴ :45² 1:11⁴ 3↑ⒻⓈMd Sp Wt 37 7 9 911 911 810 812 Edwards J W 116 23.60 70-08 OnryCstl1161½Flowrfrlxndr1168½GldnLf116 Lacked rally 11
4Jly91-11Mth fst 6f :22¹ :46² 1:12 3↑ⒻⓈMd Sp Wt 38 10 2 107 89½ 611 412½ Edwards J W 116 33.90 69-15 Luciente1167¾Srcende1162Flowerforlxndr116 Wide turn 12
LATEST WORKOUTS May 27 Mth 4f fst :53 B Apr 15 GS 4f fst :51 B

Push Broom B. m. 5, by To America—Sweep Me Away, by Barbizon
$5,000 Br.—Hemlock Cottage Inc (NJ)
Own.—Maple Crest Farm Tr.—Dowd John F (1 0 0 1 .00) 116
Lifetime 33 8 6 1 $47,790 | 1992 10 3 2 0 $12,776 | 1991 15 3 3 1 $16,778 | Wet 2 0 0 0 $486
8May92-10GS sly 6f :22 :45³ 1:11² 3↑ⒻⓈClm 5000 43 2 5 32 42 43½ 55 Sousonis S Lb 122 4.40 80-11 DundrumBy119½LuckyLpco1172¾Gs'Nghtmr119 No rally 6
25Apr92- 7GS fst 6f :23³ :47⁴ 1:14¹ 3↑ⒻⓈClm 6500 19 5 7 41½ 48 613 616½ Sousonis S Lb 113 3.90 54-27 ShrpSm1133½NrlySpnt1171CookiMkr114 Fractious gate 8
18Apr92- 3GS fst 6f :23¹ :46³ 1:13² 3↑ⒻⓈClm 5000 69 6 3 11 14 15 1½ Sousonis S Lb 119 3.60 75-23 PushBroom119½JustWink1192Kpn'Thoughts114 Driving 6
27Mar92- 4GS my 6f :22⁴ :46⁴ 1:13³ 3↑ⒻⓈClm 5000 47 3 4 13½ 1hd 22 42¾ Sousonis S Lb 122 2.60 71-26 JustAired1142¾JustWink119ⁿᵒBlueMistrss119 Gave way 8
15Mar92- 7GS fst 5½f :23 :47⁴ 1:08 3↑ⒻⓈClm 5000 58 1 5 3½ 11 13 1½ Sousonis S Lb 119 4.30 72-28 PushBroom119½LuckyLipco117½Nicol'sGold119 Driving 7
6Mar92- 2GS fst 6f :22³ :47 1:14¹ ⒻClm 4000 59 1 5 21½ 21½ 21½ 22¾ Sousonis S Lb 119 3.30 68-31 Maris'sNight1142¾PushBroom1191½Winellie117 2nd best 7
20Feb92- 6GS gd 6f :22¹ :46 1:13¹ ⒻⓈClm 6500 44 2 4 23½ 36 59 510¾ Sousonis S Lb 113 6.60 65-28 Kepin'Thoughts113¾DupliktiProdst1142KrtLdy117 Tired 6
9Feb92- 4GS fst 6f :22² :46³ 1:14² ⒻClm 9000 38 5 3 22½ 33½ 35½ 59¾ Sousonis S Lb 113 4.60 60-27 Fethersn'Fun1193¾DupliktiProdst1102JustAird113 Tired 8
28Jan92- 9GS fst 6f :22² :46² 1:12¹ ⒻⓈClm 5000 65 2 5 32 31 12½ 14 Sousonis S Lb 119 *1.60 81-19 PushBroom1194LuckyLipco1172WishMRoss114 Driving 8
9Jan92- 2GS gd 6f :22² :46¹ 1:12⁴ ⒻⓈClm 5000 64 8 5 3½ 2hd 11 2hd Sousonis S Lb 119 *2.20 78-25 Kpn'Thoghts122ʰᵈPshBrom1194SwnnsFnl117 Not quite 8

Play It Hard B. m. 9, by Advocator—Play Bold, by Master Bold
$5,000 Br.—Wimborne Farm Inc (Ky)
Own.—Shannon Peter H Jr Tr.—Forbes John H (3 0 0 1 .00) 111⁵
Lifetime 89 16 18 9 $127,937 | 1991 14 2 3 2 $14,562 | 1990 17 2 5 3 $25,026 | Turf 50 8 12 6 $82,363 | Wet 8 0 2 1 $4,979

7Dec91- 2Med	fst	170	:462	1:12	1:443	3↑ⒻClm 5000	53	2	4	59	816	511	56	Marquez C HJr	Lb	119	*.60	69-18	MorningJo1163¼Cstoutthedevil1191¼JustJzzy116	No rally	11	
21Nov91- 2Med	gd	170	:473	1:133	1:443	3↑ⒻClm 5000	67	3	3	33½	1½	14	17½	Marquez C HJr	Lb	115	2.00	75-25	PlayItHard1157½Cojak'sTurn115¾BnditProof115	Driving	9	
28Oct91- 6Med	gd	1 1/16	Ⓣ:473	1:12	1:433	3↑ⒻAlw 8000s	69	4	1	2½	74½	77½	77½	Marquez C HJr	Lb	115	2.90	71-18	DrmingJni115nkMissBrownEys110½MissMstlto117	Tired	8	
15Oct91- 1Med	sly	170	:474	1:124	1:443	3↑ⒻAlw 5000s	64	3	2	21½	22	22½	22½	Marquez C HJr	Lb	115	1.70	72-27	Shecnmove1132½PlyItHrd1154¾HoldMForvr115	2nd best	7	
15Oct91-Originally scheudled on turf																						
28Sep91- 2Med	gd	1 1/16	Ⓣ:473	1:131	1:462	3↑ⒻAlw 8000s	72	1	4	65½	44½	64¾	64¾	Marquez C HJr	Lb	117	4.60	60-29	MystcLr110¾Wnstn'sWhms1151MssMcCnn109	Bid, tired	12	
12Sep91- 7Med	fm	1 1/16	Ⓣ:462	1:11	1:43	3↑ⒻAlw 5000s	72	9	8	914	99	69	46½	Marquez C HJr	Lb	117	4.30	75-12	PrncssFddld1153¼MAndMPrd110noSrtSrt115	Mild rally	10	
27Aug91- 1Mth	fm	1	Ⓣ:47	1:124	1:391	3↑ⒻAlw 5000s	74	2	5	68½	51¼	22	1hd	Marquez C HJr	Lb	115	*1.50	77-18	PlyItHrd115hdMystcLr110¾BlwBy115	Fanned wide,drvg	8	
10Aug91- 6Atl	fm	*1⅛	Ⓣ:482	1:134	1:543	3↑ⒻClm 10000	72	5	8	65½	52¼	42	32¼	Marquez C HJr	Lb	115	*2.10	88-07	LdyB.Good1061¾PetitFlurist113½PlyItHrd115	Mild rally	10	
20Jly91- 2Mth	fm	1	Ⓣ:46	1:103	1:352	3↑ⒻClm 20000	70	10	8	812	85½	78	510¾	Krone J A	Lb	111	10.30	85-11	WhmsclMld1155MOthrHn1152B.J.Brnnr115	Lacked rally	11	
3Jly91- 5Mth	fm	1 1/16	Ⓣ:481	1:121	1:434 +	3↑ⒻAlw 5000s	86	8	6	86¼	64¼	41½	23	Marquez C HJr	Lb	115	7.80	79-18	SmartySmrty1193PlyItHrd1152½Didejol111	Second best	8	

LATEST WORKOUTS May 29 Mth 4f fst :53 B May 25 Mth 4f fst :54 B May 19 Mth 6f fst 1:20 B May 14 Mth 5f fst 1:062 B

Well Assembled

B. f. 4, by General Assembly—Weeping Willow, by Naskra
$5,000 Br.—Firestone Mr-Mrs B R (Ky)
Own.—Cort & Trak Stable
Tr.—Thompson J Willard (2 0 0 0 .00)
116

Lifetime								
18 2 4 3	1992	3	0	0	1	$965
$23,557	1991	15	2	4	2	$22,592
	Turf	2	0	1	0	$4,572
	Wet	2	0	1	1	$1,970

1Feb92- 2GS	fst	1 1/16	:501	1:16	1:493	ⒻClm 7500	61	1	1	2hd	34½	47½	55¾	Landicini C Jr	Lb	115	2.50	60-34	Castoutthedevil1142¾Fnnie'sThunder1171Persi113	Tired	8
23Jan92- 5GS	sly	170	:474	1:134	1:461	ⒻClm 10000	55	4	2	2½	21½	24½	36½	Jocson G J	Lb	117	10.60	64-32	ShsSTgh1176½OpsShsLc117nkWllAssmbld117	Weakened	6
11Jan92-10GS	fst	6f	:22	:452	1:13	ⒻClm 9000	18	2	9	915	920	923	819¼	Diaz L F	Lb	113	49.80	58-27	Lucky Linda117¾ Shabarra1191 LuckyAtLast113	Outrun	9
1Dec91- 2Med	gd	1	:48	1:13	1:392	ⒻClm 10000	42	6	3	53	69	612	612¾	Edwards J W	Lb	116	8.60	69-19	StrSpngl1142½GnrlWhsh1161¾PrncssCndy114	No factor	7
20Nov91- 2Med	fst	1	:47	1:122	1:392	ⒻClm 10000	51	7	4	511	59	411	411¼	Santagata N	Lb	114	3.60	71-19	GnrlWhoosh1097Nnlinli1143¾Ginny'sSlwpy116	No factor	8
12Nov91- 5Med	fst	170	:481	1:13	1:433	ⒻClm 10500	55	6	3	21½	23½	26	27½	Gryder A T	Lb	112	5.50	72-30	SrtogAprl1107½WllAssmbld1122PrncssCndy114	2nd best	6
23Oct91- 5Med	fst	1 1/16	:47	1:122	1:451	ⒻClm 12500	54	6	5	52	42½	46½	48½	Gryder A T	L	114	2.90	72-20	CremetheCat1163MiniVan1145PebblePower114	No rally	7
12Oct91- 3Med	fst	170	:464	1:121	1:432	ⒻClm 16000	48	3	6	76	74¾	77¾	710	Gryder A T	L	116	7.30	71-12	DtblMss114¾SmoldrngEmbrs1143½SlvrOrGld114	Outrun	8
21Sep91- 3Med	fst	170	:462	1:114	1:414	ⒻClm 15000	70	5	5	46½	31½	32½	32½	Gryder A T	L	114	*1.90	86-14	SrtAprl114¾SldrnEbrs1141¾WllAssbld114	Lacked fin bid	8
8Sep91- 3Mth	fst	1 1/16	:47	1:121	1:461	ⒻClm 12500	62	2	4	43½	32	2½	1½	Gryder A T	L	116	*2.20	78-28	WllAssmbld116½SmldrnEmbrs1116¼WhtTrph114	Driving	7

LATEST WORKOUTS May 26 Mth 5f fst 1:033 B May 20 Mth 5f fst 1:022 B ●May 14 Mth 4f fst :474 H May 2 GS 3f fst :363 B

Running Deal

B. m. 8, by Be a Rullah—Big Scare, by Break Up the Game
$5,000 Br.—Murphy J P (Fla)
Own.—Red Check One
Tr.—Tammaro John J III (2 0 0 0 .00)
116

Lifetime						
48 8 8 7	1992	6	1	1	1	$4,006
$104,386	1991	4	0	1	1	$2,665
	Turf	1	0	0	0	
	Wet	6	0	0	2	$5,176

8May92- 3GS	sly	6f	:234	:473	1:132	3↑ⒻClm 4000	36	1	4	45	34½	33	31½	Black A S	L	119	2.10	73-11	Chrcvn'sTrx117½NntmMstrss1171RnnngDl119	Even trip	6
24Apr92- 2GS	fst	6f	:224	:471	1:44	3↑ⒻClm 4000	51	6	4	31	2½	2½	1nk	Black A S	L	117	4.50	72-24	RunningDel117nkAprilKizzi1175¼FinlFlsh117	Long drive	8
3Apr92- 3Pim	fst	6f	:233	:472	1:124	ⒻClm 5000	46	6	2	75¾	67½	68	58½	Johnston M T	L	114	13.80	72-16	April Diva1124½ Alcoolu114no Chilly Luv'in122	No thrat	11
30Jan92- 5Lrl	fst	6½f	:24	:48	1:191	ⒻClm 5000	48	9	2	42	53½	56½	97½	Sarvis D A	L	114	8.40	73-21	Mideast119noHstyleRegin1194NtiveMicki109	Weakened	13
19Jan92- 3Lrl	fst	6f	:23	:47	1:132	ⒻClm 5000	52	5	4	54	56	33½	22¼	Sarvis D A	L	114	3.60	72-19	Rj'sDrlin1142¼RunningDel114½Mt.AiryDynsty114	Rallied	10
5Jan92-10Lrl	fst	7f	:233	:471	1:252	ⒻClm 7500	33	3	1	2½	2hd	78½	720	Sarvis D A	Lb	113	4.60	60-20	P. P. Dancer1193½ Rosalta114nk Contarina114	Faltered	7
30Nov91- 2Med	fst	6f	:221	:463	1:123	3↑ⒻClm 5000	62	6	1	26	2hd	2hd	2½	Sarvis D A	Lb	116	*2.30	78-19	SilverDesigner119½RunningDeal116¾LdyRick116	Gamely	10
26Jly91- 2Mth	fst	6f	:213	:45	1:112	3↑ⒻClm 10000	65	7	2	55¾	54¾	31½	32¾	Sarvis D A	L	116	11.60	81-12	Fragua1122¾LoppieLove116noRunningDel116	Hung late	8
12Jly91- 4Mth	fst	6f	:22	:452	1:114	3↑ⒻClm c-8000	63	1	6	22½	22	22½	54¾	Edwards J W	L	116	5.80	77-17	Loppie Love1151 Real Windy1122¾ Bold Erica116	Tired	10
25Jun91- 5Mth	fst	6f	:214	:45	1:111	3↑ⒻClm 7000	62	7	1	22½	22½	22	44½	Edwards J W	L	115	16.10	80-15	LoppieLove1121¾CeslssChttr1162¾BtOnDuchss116	Tired	7

LATEST WORKOUTS May 29 Mth 3f fst :363 B

Flying Pegemina

B. m. 5, by Paavo—Get Off My Case, by Upper Case
$5,000 Br.—Heard Frank (Fla)
Own.—J A V Stables Inc
Tr.—Serpe Philip M (—)
116

Lifetime						
35 5 10 4	1992	10	1	3	1	$9,330
$93,905	1991	4	0	1	0	$4,960
	Turf	5	0	1	1	$6,485
	Wet	3	1	0	0	$9,608

6May92- 3Crc	fst	7f	:233	:474	1:28	ⒻClm 7500	44	5	3	74¼	87½	68	610½	Ferrer J C	L	112	*.50	69-13	Frgu112hdBrookegrovmrilyn1064½OnMorPss106	10-wide	8
22Apr92- 4Crc	fst	7f	:222	:461	1:253	ⒻClm 7500	73	1	7	52	22½	1hd	2¾	Ferrer J C	L	112	2.70	91-08	TpTester112¾FlyingPegmin1123Sjoni112	Best of others	8
8Apr92- 1Crc	fst	6f	:221	:462	1:124	ⒻClm 8500	66	8	3	54	31	21½	21½	Ferrer J C	L	116	4.30	86-10	SilntKnight1161½FlyingPgmin116½MriDncr116	Willingly	11
22Mar92- 2Crc	fst	6f	:221	:46	1:13	ⒻClm 10000	61	9	5	74	75	46½	34½	Ferrer J C	L	116	3.80	— —	Most Kas114hd Silent Knight1124½ FlyingPegemina116		11
22Mar92-5 wide str, lugged in inside 3/16																					
4Mar92- 4GP	fst	7f	:23	:461	1:251	ⒻClm 7500	65	1	6	31	1½	1½	2½	Ferrer J C	L	112	*2.50	79-14	FlyingCuti113½FlyingPgmin112hdHowGrt108	Cldn't last	11
17Feb92- 4GP	fst	7f	:223	:451	1:242	ⒻClm 11000	55	7	4	3nk	41½	710	89¾	Fires E	L	116	*3.30	74-12	NiceIsle1161TpTstr1161TwicAMorning116	Led, faltered	11
8Feb92- 6GP	fst	1 1/16	:462	1:12	1:462	ⒻClm 20000	50	2	1	1½	2hd	55	815¾	Lee M A	L	116	7.30	64-22	For Nando111nk Askrawhy1132 Tea Rosy116	Gave way	10
31Jan92- 4GP	fst	6f	:224	:464	1:122	ⒻClm 25000	69	3	5	51¼	52¼	43½	53½	Fires E	L	120	7.00	77-21	D.Lady116½MasterPrint117½SunnyTune120	Lost ground	11
15Jan92- 4GP	fst	1 1/16	:474	1:132	1:462	ⒻClm 35000	58	9	4	35	31½	46	914	Guerra W A		112	23.30	66-24	OrientlGme1122IronndSilvr1164½Codydonit116	Faltered	9
3Jan92- 8Hia	gd	7f	:232	:463	1:252	ⒻClm 20000	75	9	7	85¼	75¾	2½	11½	Guerra W A		117	5.90	76-26	FlyingPgmin1171½DlicousSurprs113nkTpTstr113	Driving	12

Courtesy of Daily Racing Form ©

Go Lassie Go is a Maryland bred that has been racing on the New Jersey circuit for the past year. The time of Go Lassie Go's last five races have been 1:14⅗, 1:13⅘, 1:15, 1:14, and 1:14⅖. The 1:14 flat was on March 15, 1992. Since that victory she has been claimed and finished seventh in her last race. The best time Go Lassie Go can do is 1:13⅘ and 1:14 flat as a winning time.

Shayla's Prospect, a four-year-old by Tank's Prospect, is making her first start of the year besides a sixth place finish on January 8. She has been working well for her debut and could be tough if ready. Her consistent performance throughout last year makes her a main contender here. She would be a standout if she had a race under her belt.

Novel Wish is not a good horse. The problem with Novel Wish is she loves a deep track. She needs track variants that average around twenty to thirty. Garden State is a perfect example. Because of the deep surface here Novel Wish has better footing plus slow fractions. Here she can compete, but the best she can do is about 1:14 and change.

Freezing Run is a tired old horse who will on occasion come up with a big race, but she doesn't offer much here.

Minnesota's Way is a four-year-old filly that woke up with the addition of blinkers in her last two starts. Minnesota's Way is a proven $4,000 claimer and is stepping up to claiming $5,000 competition. Her last race time of 1:12^{4}/$_{5}$ makes her a horse to contend with, but her fraction split makes her the horse to beat. No one in this contest can beat 22^{4}/$_{5}$, 46^{4}/$_{5}$, and 1:12^{4}/$_{5}$. She has shown improvement in every one of her starts this year.

Atlas Axis is a winner of one in eleven outings and is steadily declining with every start.

Push Broom is a consistent $5,000 claimer that has compiled three wins this year. Her winning times of 1:13^{2}/$_{5}$, 1:08 at five furlongs, and 1:12^{1}/$_{5}$ put her in a perfect position to be right there with these horses. The only problem with her is that in this contest there is too much speed inside of her. If you look at her past performances she has to be on the lead or very close to have a chance. The speed inside of her will hinder her chances drastically.

Play It Hard, a winner of sixteen, is dropping back to the sprints once again. She has the times but like Push Broom will have a tough time getting to the front. Most horses who are dropping back in distance will tend to try to steal this on the front end.

Well Assembled is nothing but a cheap claimer that will come up with a big race once in a while. With her times lately, she should be watching everyone from the back of the pack.

Minnesota's Way outhustled Shayla's Prospect in the last few strides to get up and win. It was Shayla's Prospect's first start of the

FOURTH RACE

Monmouth

JUNE 2, 1992

6 FURLONGS. (1.08) CLAIMING. Purse $5,500. Fillies and mares, 3-year-olds and upward. Weight, 3-year-olds, 115 lbs. Older, 122 lbs. Non-winners of two races since April 28 allowed 3 lbs. A race, 6 lbs. Claiming price $5,000. (Races where entered for $4,000 or less not considered.)

Value of race $5,500; value to winner $3,300; second $1,045; third $605; fourth $275; balance of starters $55 each. Mutuel pool $57,606. Exacta Pool $61,753 Trifecta Pool $90,562

Last Raced	Horse	M/Eqt.A.Wt	PP	St	¼	½	Str	Fin	Jockey	Cl'g Pr	Odds $1
21May92 1GS1	Minnesota's Way	Lb 4 116	5	7	4hd	22	11	1½	King E L Jr	5000	3.00
8Jan92 7GS6	Shayla's Prospect	Lb 4 111	2	6	56	4½	22	25½	Homistr RB Jr5	5000	6.80
2Feb92 4GS7	Freezing Run	Lb 7 116	4	4	1hd	1hd	32	3nk	Gomez I	5000	24.10
3May92 1GS5	Novel Wish	Lb 6 116	3	9	71½	61	61½	41½	Colton R E	5000	4.80
1Feb92 2GS5	Well Assembled	Lb 4 116	9	1	6hd	72	71½	5no	Gryder A T	5000	7.40
8May92 10GS5	Push Broom	Lb 5 116	7	3	3½	53	5hd	6nk	Sousonis S	5000	9.50
7Dec91 2Med5	Play It Hard	Lb 9 111	8	2	9	83½	87	71¾	Frost G C5	5000	20.50
30Apr92 7GS7	Go Lassie Go	Lb 4 116	1	8	21½	31	4½	87	Vega A	5000	1.80
18Apr92 7GS7	Atlas Axis	4 116	6	5	8½	9	9	9	Lovato F Jr	5000	73.40

OFF AT 2:23 Start good Won driving Time, :214, :453, :583, 1:121 Track muddy.

$2 Mutuel Prices:	5-MINNEOSTA'S WAY	8.00	3.60	3.40
	2-SHAYLA'S PROSPECT		5.80	5.00
	4-FREEZING RUN			11.80

$2 EXACTA 5-2 PAID $60.60 $2 TRIFECTA 5-2-4 PAID $738.20

Dk. b. or br. f, by Real Way—Minnesota Muriel, by Minnesota Mac. Trainer Reid Mark J. Bred by Appleton Arthur I (Fla).

MINNEOSTA'S WAY advanced on the turn, drew clear then held off SHAYLA'S PROSPECT. The latter eased outside top one in midstretch and finished well. FREEZING RUN posted early fractions, raced removed from the rail and tired in the drive. NOVEL WISH offered a mild bid. WELL ASSEMBLED lacked a rally. PUSH BROOM had little left entering the lane. GO LASSIE GO advanced along inside soon after start to challenge for the lead, saved ground and gave way in upper stretch. SHAYLA'S PROSPECT and PLAY IT HARD wore mud calks.

Owners— 1, Blue Devil Stable; 2, Martucci William C; 3, Spina Chuck; 4, Dollinger Susan M; 5, Cort & Trak Stable; 6, Maple Crest Farm; 7, Shannon Peter H Jr; 8, Ritter D & F; 9, Dubel & Grimm.

Trainers— 1, Reid Mark J; 2, Crupi James J; 3, Spina Chuck; 4, Dollinger Susan M; 5, Thompson J Willard; 6, Dowd John F; 7, Forbes John H; 8, Serey Juan; 9, Grimm William.

Scratched—Top Tomato (6Dec91 7Med3); Running Deal (8May92 3GS3); Flying Pegemina (6May92 3Crc6).

Courtesy of Daily Racing Form ©

year and she will improve off of that effort. Freezing Run, the pacesetter, tired to third. The favorite "Go Lassie Go" could not keep up with the early fractions and tired to eighth. For Minnesota's Way it was her third victory in a row, once again improving on her time. The final time was 1:12¹/₅.

Handicap races can be very difficult because there is usually a mix of improving horses and horses that are on the decline. That's exactly what the feature event at Belmont offered.

Lost Mountain was a declining Kentucky Derby and Belmont Stakes contender and Isn't That Special and Fighting Fantasy were on the rise. In this example, Time Analysis will show the better bet, and though many may say that Lost Mountain has a lot more class than the rest of the field, that would be true only if this race was run last year. Lost Mountain is now a different horse, as he displayed in his last start. He did finish third, beaten by six and a quarter lengths, but he also only beat one horse.

---

8 — START — 1 1/16 MILES — BELMONT PARK — FINISH

1 1/16 MILES. **(1.402) HANDICAP. Purse $47,000. 3-year-olds and upward. Weights Monday, July 6. Declarations by 10:00 A.M., Wednesday, July 8. Closed Monday, July 6 with 7 nominations.**

Whiz Along

DAVIS R G (147 17 19 9 .12)
Own.—Andy-Mart Stable

Dk. b. or br. h. 7, by Cormorant—Answer Back, by Northern Answer
Br.—Kinderhill Farm (NY)
Tr.—Figueroa Carlos R Jr (12 2 4 0 .17)

113

Lifetime						
65 9 9 10	1991	15	1	3	1	$191,106
$539,897	1990	18	2	2	4	$143,432
	Turf	3	0	0	0	$810
	Wet	7	2	1	1	$92,604

9Sep91- 3Bel fst 7f	:23	:452	1:224	3↑Clm c-70000	71	5	3	32	79	98½	913¼	Smith M E		117	3.30	77-15	SctlshMnk108nkDrmmndLn1134KngfWll113	Brief speed	10
19Aug91- 8Sar sly 1⅛	:463	1:112	1:502	3↑Ⓡ Upset	93	2	1	1½	1hd	32	37¾	Krone J A		115	4.40	77-24	Midas1154¼FrewellWve1223½WhizAlong115	Speed, tired	6
20Jly91-11Rkmfst 1⅛	:471	1:113	1:492	3↑New Eng Clsc	95	2	2	27	24½	34½	411¼	Marquez C H Jr	LB	115	25.60	102-04	Mrqutry1213Fstin-Ar1245SilvrSurvivor121	Bid, bore out	5
13Jly91- 9Det fst 1⅛	:474	1:12	1:494	Mich Mile H	106	7	2	32	21	21½	22½	Marquez C H Jr	L	110	52.40	92-16	BlckTAffr-Ir1222½WhzAlong1102SlMtt113	Game second	11
13Jly91-Grade II																			
6Jly91-10FL fst 6f	:214	:444	1:102	3↑Bud Brd Cup	98	5	4	78¼	76¼	55½	54	Marquez C H Jr		113	24.50	90-19	ClvrTrvor1131½BrvlyBold113¾MrcdsWn113	Lacked rally	7
10Jun91- 8Bel fm 1 1/16 Ⓣ	:462	1:094	1:402	3↑Handicap	51	4	2	32	87¼	816	826½	Krone J A		112	22.70	67-12	HghlndPnny113½SftngGold114½ScottthGrt111	Gave way	8
17May91- 8Bel fst 1	:464	1:11	1:361	3↑Handicap	88	1	2	2½	42½	47	49¾	Krone J A		113	10.90	79-14	FrewellWve114noSoundofCnnons1164¾Rhythm122	Tired	5
27Apr91- 7Spt sly 1⅛	:471	1:122	1:502	N Jky Clb H	99	8	2	21	2½	1hd	21¼	Marquez C H Jr	L	110	13.10	93-06	Alljb1161¼WhzAlong110¾SondofCnnns115	Game second	8
27Apr91-Grade III																			
17Apr91- 8Aqu gd 1⅛	:471	1:114	1:512	3↑Alw 47000	95	4	4	416	413	25	21¼	Vasquez M O5		114	3.40	78-21	ApplCrrnt1241¼WhAln1147AdncnEnsn119	Finished well	4
16Mar91- 8Aqu fst 1⅛	:463	1:104	1:471	3↑Grey Lag H	86	2	1	1½	31	58	513	Velazquez J R		111	35.10	87-21	Apple Current1121¼BolshoiBoy1132KillerDiller115	Tired	7
16Mar91-Grade III																			

LATEST WORKOUTS ●Jun 25 Aqu Ⓣ 4f sf :493 H (d) ●Jun 18 Aqu Ⓣ 5f fm 1:013 H (d) ●Jun 8 Aqu 5f fst 1:01 B May 28 Aqu 5f fst 1:031 B

Isn't That Special

VELAZQUEZ J R (179 12 25 25 .07)
Own.—C'est Tout Stable

Gr. g. 6, by Private Account—Lucy Belle, by Raise a Native
Br.—Raphaelson Robert B (Ky)
Tr.—Daggett Michael H (31 2 2 8 .06)

115

Lifetime						
33 9 5 4	1992	6	2	2	0	$48,068
$191,986	1991	10	1	2	1	$51,160
	Turf	2	0	0	0	$540
	Wet	5	2	1	1	$35,496

6Jun92- 2Bel my 1 1/16	:451	1:092	1:413	3↑Affirmed	96	6	2	33	32½	53½	25	Velazquez J R		115	9.90	89-08	MchllCnPss1195Isn'tThtSpcl115hdFrllWv115	Held place	8
22May92- 5Bel fst 7f	:232	:462	1:213	Clm 70000	102	4	2	1½	1½	1hd	1nk	Velazquez J R		113	7.60	96-11	Isn'tThtSpecil113nkRelMinx1132FrostyWish117	Driving	7
30Apr92- 6Aqu fst 1	:454	1:094	1:344	Clm 47500	96	5	2	1½	1hd	1hd	2nk	Velazquez J R		115	12.40	88-25	PcktStrkr117nkIsn'tThtSpcl1156DrssdShppr113	Gamely	7
13Apr92- 8Aqu gd 1	:462	1:101	1:343	3↑Alw 47000	63	7	3	63	62½	610	617½	Velazquez J R		117	9.90	71-18	KidRussell1121VouchforMe1171½RedRitul117	Four wide	7
26Mar92- 5Aqu fst 1	:461	1:102	1:361	Clm 47500	95	1	1	1½	1½	11	1no	Velazquez J R		115	11.90	81-21	Isn'tThtSpcl115noPcktStrkr113½AnMntMn117	Drftd drv	6
14Mar92- 7Aqu fst 7f	:221	:45	1:232	Clm 70000	77	1	10	1014	1020	1011	814¼	Velazquez J R		113	20.90	74-23	HrrVnKnnchn115½TrndBl1135¾ArgylLk117	Broke slowly	10
9Sep91- 3Bel fst 7f	:23	:452	1:224	3↑Clm 75000	52	8	4	86¼	912	1013	1022¼	Migliore R		117	6.00	68-15	ScottshMonk108nkDrmmondLn1134KngfWll113	Outrun	10
19Aug91- 8Sar sly 1⅛	:463	1:112	1:502	3↑Ⓡ Upset	56	4	5	59	69¼	68½	630¾	Santos J A		115	2.90	54-24	Midas1154¼ Farewell Wave1223½ Whiz Along115	Outrun	6
12Aug91- 7Sar fst 7f	:222	:443	1:212	3↑Alw 41000	89	2	7	711	713	68	47¼	Santos J A		115	4.10	91-09	Crckedbell1221½ForRlly119nkSntorToB119	Belated rally	7
28Jly91- 5Sar fst 1⅛	:482	1:121	1:492	3↑Handicap	100	1	1	1½	1½	1hd	2¾	Migliore R		111	9.80	89-08	I'mSkyHgh119¾Isn'tThtSpcl111hdChllngMDt113	Gamely	7

LATEST WORKOUTS Jun 27 Bel 4f fst :491 B Jun 19 Bel 4f fst :49 B May 30 Bel tr.t 3f fst :361 H May 19 Bel tr.t 4f fst :494 B

Lost Mountain

PERRET C (80 19 10 16 .24)
Own.—Loblolly Stable

B. c. 4, by Cox's Ridge—Space Angel, by To the Quick
Br.—Loblolly Stable & Hochner A Jr (Ky)
Tr.—Bohannan Thomas (19 2 2 4 .11)

122

Lifetime						
19 4 2 4	1992	1	0	0	1	$4,920
$843,236	1991	12	3	2	1	$699,380
	Wet	4	0	0	3	$20,456

24Jun92- 8Bel my 6½f	:222	:45	1:15	3↑Handicap	91	3	3	44½	41¾	32½	36¼	Perret C	b	121	3.70	92-09	Crckdbll118nkTkMOt1226LstMntn121	Broke awkwardly	4
22Sep91-10LaD fst 1¼	:462	1:36	2:004	Super Derby	96	6	5	417	66½	59	512½	Perret C	b	126	10.20	93-02	Free Spirit'sJoy1262½Olympio1261Zeeruler126	Bid, tired	7
22Sep91-Grade I																			
2Sep91- 8Bel fst 1	:451	1:092	1:34	Jerome H	99	8	8	83¾	71¾	52¼	47	Perret C	b	121	3.30	93-12	Scan1174ExcellentTipper1131½KingMutesa113	6-wide,tn	8
2Sep91-Grade I																			
17Aug91- 8Sar fst 1¼	:472	1:36	2:011	Travers	98	6	5	513	53½	55½	57¼	Perret C	b	126	6.30	91-06	CorporteRport126nkHnsl1262½FlySoFr126	Flattened out	6
17Aug91-Grade I																			
27Jly91-10Mth gd 1⅛	:46	1:101	1:48	Haskell H	107	5	5	57	43½	21½	1hd	Perret C	b	118	5.80	98-15	LostMountin118hdCorporteReport12013Hnsl126	Driving	5
27Jly91-Grade I																			
7Jly91- 8Bel fst 1⅛	:454	1:10	1:491	Dwyer	102	4	7	56¼	52½	2hd	11	Perret C	b	123	8.60	83-17	LostMontn1231SmoothPrfrmnc1142½FlySFr126	Driving	7
7Jly91-Grade II																			
8Jun91- 8Bel fst 1½	:463	2:02	2:28	Belmont	84	4	8	911	812	715	722	Perret C	b	126	19.10	68-08	Hansel126hdStrikeTheGold1263ManeMinister126	Outrun	11
8Jun91-Grade I																			
26May91- 8Bel fst 1⅛	:461	1:102	1:492	Peter Pan	104	6	6	65	52½	31	1hd	Perret C	b	114	1.80	82-31	Lost Mountain114hd Man Alright1141½ Scan126	Driving	6
26May91-Grade II																			
4May91- 8CD fst 1¼	:462	1:372	2:03	Ky Derby	89	9	11	76½	94¾	108¼	1211¼	McCauley W H	Bb	126	72.60	84-04	Strike the Gold1261¾ Best Pal1261¾ Mane Minister126		16

4May91-Grade I; Forced into rail on far turn

20Apr91- 8Aqu fst 1⅛ :463 1:104 1:482 Wood Mem 104 7 6 56½ 41¾ 21½ 23 McCauley W H b 126 40.90 91-23 ChillRod1263LostMountn1266HppyJzzBnd126 Sharp try 10

20Apr91-Grade I

LATEST WORKOUTS Jly 7 Bel 6f fst 1:133 B ●Jun 20 Bel tr.t 5f my 1:014 B Jun 9 Bel 5f fst 1:014 B Jun 3 Bel 4f fst :483 H

Farewell Wave

Ch. g. 6, by Topsider—Farewell Letter, by Arts and Letters

BAILEY J D (190 37 38 20 .19)

Own.—Rokeby Stables

Br.—Mellon Paul (Va)

Tr.—Miller Mack (40 10 11 8 .25)

116

Lifetime 36 10 9 5 $360,623

1992	2	1	0	1	$31,128
1991	10	4	1	0	$131,752
Turf	4	0	0	1	$10,551
Wet	6	2	2	1	$58,312

6Jun92- 2Bel my 1 1/16 :451 1:092 1:413 3↑Affirmed 96 5 8 86¾ 63½ 63¾ 35 Bailey J D b 115 *1.50 89-08 MchllCnPss1195Isn'tThtSpcl115hdFrllWv115 Wide trip 8

6May92- 7Bel fst 7f :232 :461 1:22 3↑Alw 41000 96 5 1 42 31 2½ 1hd Bailey J D b 117 3.40 94-09 FrewellWv117hdShiningBid119nkFirstndOnly122 Driving 5

2Nov91- 8Aqu fst 1⅛ :472 1:111 1:481 3↑Stuyv'snt H 94 1 9 96 85¾ 55½ 48½ Samyn J L b 111 3.40e 86-15 Mntb-Ar1105½MntnLr112hdTmlyWrnng114 Broke slowly 9

2Nov91-Grade III

26Oct91- 8Aqu fst 1 :444 1:083 1:333 3↑N Y R A Mle 98 13 13 135¾124¾149½146½ Samyn J L b 111 92.90 87-08 Rubiano116hd Sultry Song1111 Diablo112 Outrun, wide 15

26Oct91-Grade I

2Oct91- 8Bel fst 1 :472 1:11 1:352 3↑Handicap 87 5 5 53½ 52¼ 55½ 59 Bailey J D b 120 2.30 84-07 Rubino121noCrckdbll1185ShotsArRingng108 Speed,tired 5

2Sep91- 1Bel fst 1 1/16 :464 1:103 1:413 3↑Handicap 108 3 5 53¼ 2hd 11 12½ Smith M E b 119 2.60 94-12 Farewell Wave1192½ Zee Best118hd Slavic117 Driving 5

19Aug91- 8Sar sly 1⅛ :463 1:112 1:502 3↑ⓇUpset 99 5 4 45 33½ 2½ 24¼ Smith M E b 122 *1.70e 81-24 Mids1154¼FrewellWv1223½WhizAlong115 Saved ground 6

28Jly91- 5Sar fst 1⅛ :482 1:121 1:492 3↑Handicap 89 2 3 52 64 74¼ 77½ Bailey J D b 117 *.90 82-08 ImSHgh119¾IsntThtSpcl111hdChllngMDt113 Done early 7

6Jly91- 3Bel gd 1 1/16 :46 1:101 1:413 3↑Handicap 98 4 4 41½ 2hd 11½ 16 Bailey J D b 116 *.70 94-05 Farewell Wave1166Slavic11816Congeleur113 Ridden out 4

10Jun91- 8Bel fm 1 1/16 Ⓣ:462 1:094 1:402 3↑Handicap 91 2 4 42 42½ 43 54 Bailey J D b 115 7.00 90-12 HghlndPnn113½SftnGld114½ScttthGrt111 Saved ground 8

LATEST WORKOUTS Jly 6 Bel tr.t 6f my 1:164 B (d) Jun 27 Bel 4f fst :484 B Jun 13 Bel 4f fst :483 B May 31 Bel 6f fst 1:131 H

Polonium

Dk. b. or br. g. 3(Mar), by Summing—Polo, by Forli

KRONE J A (280 55 48 33 .20)

Own.—Leveen Lenard

Br.—Guest Raymond R (Ky)

Tr.—Margotta Anthony Jr (11 1 1 1 .09)

109

Lifetime 9 2 4 0 $39,910

1992	7	1	4	0	$30,910
1991	2	1	0	0	$9,000
Turf	1	0	0	0	
Wet	2	0	2	0	$11,020

21May92- 4Bel fst 7f :222 :453 1:223 Clm 70000 89 2 6 33½ 31½ 22½ 22¾ Bailey J D 113 2.10 88-16 Permit1132¾ Polonium1132½ RomanChorus113 2nd best 7

6May92- 6Bel fm 1¼ Ⓣ:491 1:373 2:021 3↑Alw 31000 71 8 4 43 52½ 86 89½ Bailey J D 110 *3.20 70-17 ProSrv119nkMuchoPrcos119nkExplosvRl119 Tired at fin 8

17Apr92- 6Aqu sly 1 :46 1:103 1:352 3↑Alw 31000 90 6 4 42½ 1½ 11 2nk Samyn J L 110 *1.00 85-18 Best Offer119nk Polonium1104½ Glance Of Gold119 6

17Apr92-Wide, drifted out, lost whip 1/16 pole; Originally scheduled on turf

17Mar92- 7Crc fst 170 :471 1:124 1:441 3↑Alw 19600 72 4 3 45½ 68 610 614¾ Vasquez J 114 *2.10 — — Bts'nBc1172BddngPrd1133MnchnNsh113 Bmp wide str. 6

21Feb92- 8GP sly 1⅛ :483 1:133 1:521 Alw 21000 78 5 3 32½ 2hd 2hd 25 Vasquez J 114 1.30 71-23 DshForDotty1175Polnm1149Frtn'sGn115 Led, no match 6

21Feb92-Originally Scheduled on Turf

30Jan92- 9GP fst 1 1/16 :463 1:111 1:441 Alw 19000 79 3 3 34½ 33½ 25 26½ Vasquez J 115 2.40 84-16 Goldwater1206½ Polonium1151 Randy115 Best of rest 5

15Jan92- 6GP fst 7f :223 :461 1:26 Alw 17000 74 5 9 64¾ 21½ 2½ 1no Vasquez J 114 7.00 76-21 Polonm114noProprBondr112noContryDrv114 Up at wire 11

20Oct91- 3Bel fst 1 :47 1:122 1:381 Md 50000 74 3 2 32 1hd 17 110½ Lidberg D W 118 *1.80 79-21 Polonium11810½Cheese1184½Grrettson109 Kept to drive 8

16Aug91- 6Sar fst 7f :221 :451 1:234 Md Sp Wt 36 2 10 95¾108¼1011 918¾ Smith M E 118 40.90 67-11 Pine Bluff1181½HarrytheHat1182Noactor118 Brk slowly 10

LATEST WORKOUTS Jly 3 Bel 5f fst :59 H Jun 27 Bel 7f fst 1:30 B Jun 18 Bel 6f fst 1:183 B May 19 Bel 3f fst :37 B

Fighting Fantasy

Ch. h. 5, by Fighting Fit—Ice Fantasy, by It's Freezing

ANTLEY C W (243 41 24 35 .17)

Own.—Cottrell Ray H Sr

Br.—Lamonica Bettie T & J A (Ky)

Tr.—McPeek Kenneth G (—)

114

Lifetime 37 8 9 7 $339,035

1992	9	3	3	1	$77,083
1991	6	0	1	4	$28,744
Turf	1	0	0	0	
Wet	8	3	0	1	$125,306

24Jun92- 8CD fst 1 1/16 :472 1:114 1:441 3↑Alw 39500 96 2 1 12 13 12½ 1½ Miller D A Jr B 115 11.60 93-18 FghtngFnts115½FlngCntnntl1154BgCrg117 Steady drive 7

14Jun92- 6CD fst 1 :453 1:103 1:364 3↑Alw 38100 67 2 3 2hd 2hd 54¾ 712½ Stacy A T B 122 4.60 80-15 Arbc115nkBtEmTogthr1122CoolCorbtt110 Bid gave way 7

29May92- 8CD sly 1 1/16 :49 1:141 1:462 3↑Alw 39450 92 1 1 1½ 11½ 12 12 Miller D A Jr B 115 6.10 82-27 FghtngFnts1152SpcdCff1191OnthEdg117 Driving, clear 6

19May92- 6CD fst 6f :213 :452 1:103 3↑Alw 31290 83 5 5 62¼ 62¼ 41½ 32½ Hernandez R B 115 8.40 90-12 Arbc1152½NITyrnt115hdFghtngFnts115 Lean in bumped 8

9May92- 4RD gd 5½f :223 :462 1:052 3↑Alw 6000 85 1 3 33 22½ 13 13 Mella S A B 115 *.30 94-11 FightingFntsy1153Tigr'sFnst1144½GnrlBrntt120 Handily 8

2May92- 7CD fst 7f :224 :452 1:221 C Downs H 91 8 1 1½ 1½ 62¼ 86 Smith M E B 112 9.70 93-02 PlsntTp120noTkMOt1202CntrllRod113 Wde trip fltered 9

2May92-Grade III

23Apr92- 7Kee fst 7f :224 :453 1:22 Alw 30000 106 3 1 11½ 11½ 1hd 2nk Arguello F A Jr Bb 112 6.00 99-09 Tlmrkt118nkFghtngFnts1121Dscvr115 Bumped gametry 5

3Apr92- 7Kee fst 6½f :222 :45 1:17 Alw 28800 94 2 3 1½ 1hd 21 2¾ Stacy A T B 112 3.60 91-15 SnnyGG112¾FghtngFntsy1122½FrndlLvr114 Dueled alter 8

21Mar92- 8OP fst 6f :214 :451 1:10 Alw 33000 91 4 2 2hd 1½ 21½ 23½ Stacy A T b 115 5.00 85-16 Dvlyn1153½FightingFntsy115½Albrt'sFirst115 Held place 7

16Jun91- 8CD fst 6½f :222 :452 1:172 3↑Alw 34360 89 3 4 3nk 1hd 1½ 34½ McDowell M LB 118 5.30 88-14 CntrllRod1183LVoygur1181½FightingFntsy118 Game try 8

Isn't That Special is a six-year-old gelding that is still going strong, judging from his last race. In the Affirmed Stakes, Isn't That Special's fractions were 45⁴⁄₅, 1:09⁴⁄₅, and 1:42³⁄₅. With a little slower pace, as in his second to last race in claiming $70,000, he will have enough left to stick around at the end. His speed will dominate this race if no one challenges him.

Lost Mountain is a colt that should be called "Mr. Hardluck." The end of 1991 took its toll on Lost Mountain. Though he stretches out to a distance here that is more suitable to him, even on his best performance his speed figures could not keep up with Isn't That Special. He is also taking on older horses again.

Farewell Wave's speed figures are as close as they come to Isn't That Special. These two geldings were a neck apart in their last race. He may be the most competition to Isn't That Special. Like Lost Mountain, Farewell Wave is making only his third start of the year and his workouts are not as impressive as those he was running on June 6, 1992.

Polonium has put up some decent speed figures in the past, but he is in over his head today.

Although Fighting Fantasy finished only six lengths behind Pleasant Tap in the Churchill Downs Handicap, he does not look like he has what it takes here.

Fighting Fantasy led most of the way and relinquished the lead at the three quarter pole to Isn't That Special. Farewell Wave and Polonium trailed most of the way trading fourth and fifth with each other. Lost Mountain started making his run about the same time as Isn't That Special. Isn't That Special took over the lead from Fighting Fantasy and drew off to a two length advantage. Lost Mountain made his run throughout the stretch and had plenty of time at the end to catch Isn't That Special but just ran out of gas. At 3-5, Lost Mountain performed like a horse that was bet on past form and realistically is on the decline.

EIGHTH RACE
Belmont
JULY 10, 1992

1 $\frac{1}{16}$ MILES. (1.40²) HANDICAP. Purse $47,000. 3-year-olds and upward. Weights Monday, July 6. Declarations by 10:00 A.M., Wednesday, July 8. Closed Monday, July 6 with 7 nominations.

Value of race $47,000; value to winner $28,200; second $10,340; third $5,640; fourth $2,820. Mutuel pool $142,413, Minus show pool $1,334.97. Exacta Pool $270,031

Last Raced	Horse	M/Eqt.A.Wt	PP St	¼	½	¾	Str	Fin	Jockey	Odds $1
6Jun92 2Bel2	Isn't That Special	6 115	1 2	2¹	2¹½	2¹	1hd	1½	Velazquez J R	6.10
24Jun92 8Bel3	Lost Mountain	b 4 122	2 3	3hd	3½	3³	3⁵	2½	Perret C	.60
24Jun92 8CD1	Fighting Fantasy	5 114	5 1	1¹	1½	1hd	2hd	3⁶½	Antley C W	5.50
6Jun92 2Bel3	Farewell Wave	b 6 116	3 4	4hd	4hd	5	5	4nk	Bailey J D	3.30
21May92 4Bel2	Polonium	3 109	4 5	5	5	4¹	4hd	5	Samyn J L	13.90

OFF AT 4:28 Start good, Won driving. Time, :23², :46³, 1:10², 1:35³, 1:42² Track fast.

$2 Mutuel Prices:

1-(B)-ISN'T THAT SPECIAL	....	14.20	3.00	2.10
2-(C)-LOST MOUNTAIN	....		2.20	2.10
5-(F)-FIGHTING FANTASY	....			2.10

$2 EXACTA 2-3 PAID $36.80

Gr. g, by Private Account—Lucy Belle, by Raise a Native. Trainer Daggett Michael H. Bred by Raphaelson Robert B (Ky).

ISN'T THAT SPECIAL saved ground moved up to challenge leaving the backstretch and held on gamely in the drive to prove best. LOST MOUNTAIN moved up to loom menacingly behind the dueling leaders on the turn, had aim while outside through the stretch and gained the place with a determined late bid. FIGHTING FANTASY set the early pace and held on well to deep stretch, then weakened slightly. FAREWELL WAVE was always outrun. POLONIUM was always outrun.

Owners— 1, C'est Tout Stable; 2, Loblolly Stable; 3, Cottrell Ray H Sr; 4, Rokeby Stables; 5, Leveen Lenard.

Trainers— 1, Daggett Michael H; 2, Bohannan Thomas; 3, McPeek Kenneth G; 4, Miller Mack; 5, Margotta Anthony Jr.

Scratched—Whiz Along (9Sep91 3Bel9).

Courtesy of Daily Racing Form ©

In big races, such as the 1992 Belmont Stakes, huge fields are common. These races usually attract many horses that do not belong, and this race was no different. Look at Al Sabin, Jacksonport, Crisofori, Agincourt, Robert's Hero, and Montreal Marty. Some of these horses would qualify for Time Analysis under different circumstances but they did not achieve their times in the class of horses they will be racing against in the Belmont Stakes.

8

Belmont *Stakes*
1-1/2 Miles

1 1/2 MILES. (2.24) 124th Running THE BELMONT STAKES (Grade I). Purse $500,000 added. 3-year-olds. Scale Weight. $5,000 to pass the entry box; $5,000 to start with $500,000 added. At any time prior to Closing. Thursday, June 4, 1992, horses may be nominated to The Belmont Stakes upon payment of a supplementary fee of $50,000 to The New York Racing Association Inc. The added money and all fees to be divided 60% to the winner, 22% to second, 12% to third and 6% to fourth. Colts and Geldings, 126 lbs.; Fillies, 121 lbs. Starters to be named at the closing time of entries. The Belmont field will be limited to sixteen (16) starters. In the event that more than 16 entries pass through the entry box at the closing, the starters will be determined at the closing with 50% of the field (8 starters) given preference by accumulating the highest earnings in Graded Stakes (lifetime), including all money paid for performances in such Graded Stakes. The next five (5) starters (approximate 30%) will be determined by accumulating the highest earnings (lifetime) in all races except restricted races (i.e., any stake containing eligibility conditions other than sex and age). The remaining 3 starters (approximate 20%) shall be determined by accumulating the highest earnings (lifetime) in all races. Should this preference produce any ties the additional starter(s) shall be determined by lot. If the rules described result in the exclusion of any horse, the $5,000 entry fee will be refunded to the owner of said horse. The winning owner will be presented with the August Belmont Memorial Cup, to be retained for one year, as well as a trophy for permanent possession and trophies will be presented to the winning trainer and jockey. Nominations to each of all of the Triple Crown races, The Kentucky Derby, The Preakness and The Belmont (the "Races") may be made only by payment of a single subscription fee to Triple Crown Productions, Inc., as agent for Churchill Downs Incorporated, The Maryland Jockey Club and the New York Racing Association Inc. (the "Associations"). The subscription fee for 389 nominations received by January 18, 1992, is $600 and for 18 nominations received by April 1, 1992, is $4,500. (These fees are to be apportioned equally among the three Associations to be part of the total purse for each of the three races.) After April 1, at any prior time to Closing for the Kentucky Derby, additional nominations to all three races will be accepted and the nominee

will be eligible for the Chrysler Triple Crown Challenge bonus, upon payment of a supplementary fee of $150,000 to Churchill Downs Incorporated. Following the running of The Kentucky Derby, but an any time prior to Closing for the Preakness Stakes, horses may be nominated to the remaining Races but will not be eligible for the Chrysler Triple Crown Challenge bonus, upon payment of a supplementary fee of $100,000 to The Maryland Jockey Club of Baltimore City, Inc. At any time prior to the Closing for the Belmont Stakes, horses may be nominated to The Belmont Stakes upon payment of a supplementary fee of $50,000 to the New York Racing Association Inc. All supplemental fees will be included in the purse distribution of the respective Races for which paid. Horses nominated by payment of supplementary fee ("supplemental nominees") will not be allowed to enter any Race in which the maximum number of starters has otherwise been reached prior to the time of Closing. If the number of supplemental nominees exceed the number of available starting positions at Closing, the conditions of each respective Race shall be applied to determine which supplemental nominees wil be allowed to start in such Race. All nominees will be allowed to start in such Race. All nominees, supplemental or otherwise, will be requested to pay entry and starting fees for the Race or Races to which they have been nominated. Triple Crown Productions, Inc. is guaranteeing total earnings of $5,000,000 to the owner of any horse which wins all of the 1992 Kentucky Derby, Preakness and Belmont Stakes races (the "Races") and is offering a $1,000,000 bonus to the owner of a horse with the best, most consistent finishes in the Races. The "Triple Crown Challenge" monies will be paid to the owner of a horse which meets these criteria: 1. Finishes in all three Triple Crown Races as listed above; 2. Earns points by finishing first, second, third or fourth in at least one of the Triple Crown Races; and 3. Earns the highest number of points over the course of the three Races. Points are assigned for each race: Win—10, Place—5, Show—3, Fourth—1. In the event of a tie, the $1 million bonus will be distributed equally among the top point-getters. In the event of a dead-heat, equal pionts will be awarded in full. For example, 10 points for each horse in a dead-heat to win. Triple Crown Productions Inc. will pay to the owner of a horse winning all of the Races that amount necessary to bring total earnings for the Triple Crown winner to $5,000,000. The total will include the winner's purse distributed by each racing association. The total include the winner's purse distributed by each racing association; and the $1 million point bonus described above; and a further bonus guaranteed by Triple Crown Productions to reach the $5 million total. Triple Crown Productions will present the Triple Crown Trophy to the owner of a horse that sweeps the Kentucky Derby, Preakness Stakes and Belmont Stakes. Closed with 1 Supplemental Nominee: MY MEMORIES—GB.

Coupled—Agincourt and Robert's Hero.

A.P. Indy

Dk. b. or br. rig. 3(Mar), by Seattle Slew—Weekend Surprise, by Secretariat
Br.—Farish W S & Kilroy W S (Ky)
Tr.—Drysdale Neil (1 1 0 0 1.00)
DELAHOUSSAYE E (6 1 2 0 .17)
Own.—Tsurumaki Tomonori
126
Lifetime 7 6 0 0 $828,935 | 1992 3 3 0 0 $471,680 | 1991 4 3 0 0 $357,255 | Wet 1 1 0 0 $13,750

24May92- 8Bel fst 1⅛ :453 1:10 1:472 Peter Pan 108 6 5 53½ 1½ 12½ 15½ Delahoussaye E 126 *.50 92-08 A.P.Indy1205½ColonyLight1144¾BrklyFitz114 Ridden out 7
24May92-Grade II
4Apr92- 5SA fst 1⅛ :461 1:102 1:491 S A Derby 95 3 4 42½ 43 31 11¾ Delahoussaye E B 122 *.90 84-11 A.P.Indy1221¾Bertrando122nkCsulLies122 Wide, driving 7
4Apr92-Grade I
29Feb92- 8SA fst 1 :46 1:10 1:352 San Rafael 100 5 3 31½ 2½ 22½ 1¾ Delahoussaye E B 121 *.50 90-12 A.P.Indy121¾Treekster1169PrinceWild118 Determinedly 6
29Feb92-Grade II
22Dec91- 5Hol fst 1 1/16 :464 1:11 1:424 Hol Fut 96 11 9 95¾ 63¼ 1hd 1nk Delahoussaye E B 121 3.20 87-17 A. P. Indy121nk Dance Floor1215½ Casual Lies121 14
22Dec91-Grade I; Wide trip, ridden out
4Dec91- 8BM fst 1 :464 1:112 1:362 Alw 21000 82 1 1 1hd 1hd 11 13 Delahoussaye E B 117 *.20 88-19 A.P.Indy1173KlooknBoy1173½FbulousPol117 Ridden out 8
27Oct91- 6SA sl 6½f :214 :453 1:181 Md Sp Wt 88 4 8 87¼ 63½ 31½ 14 Delahoussaye E B 117 *1.30 79-24 A. P. Indy1174 Dr Pain1173½ Hickman Creek117 9
27Oct91-Lacked room 1/4, swung out, handily
24Aug91- 4Dmr fst 6f :221 :451 1:101 Md Sp Wt 71 2 5 54½ 46½ 47 45½ Delahoussaye E B 117 *2.30 82-11 ShrpBndt1172½Annsl1172¾RchrdOfEnld117 Gaining late 7

LATEST WORKOUTS ●Jun 2 Aqu 6f gd 1:173 B May 19 Bel 6f fst 1:133 B ●Apr 27 CD 6f fst 1:15 B ●Apr 22 CD 7f fst 1:30 B

Casual Lies

B. c. 3(May), by Lear Fan—Morna, by Blakeney
Br.—Meadowhill (Ky)
Tr.—Riley Shelley L (—)
STEVENS G L (—)
Own.—Riley Shelley L
126
Lifetime 11 5 1 3 $665,108 | 1992 5 2 1 2 $514,480 | 1991 6 3 0 1 $150,628 | Turf 1 0 0 0 $8,438

16May92-10Pim gd 1 3/16 :461 1:104 1:553 Preakness 101 8 5 78 65½ 43 32¼ Stevens G L L 126 5.60 82-18 PineBluff126¾Alydeed1261½CasualLies126 Angled in str. 14
16May92-Grade I
2May92- 8CD fst 1¼ :464 1:363 2:03 Ky Derby 106 4 3 64½ 21½ 1hd 21 Stevens G L LB 126 29.90 94-06 LilE.Tee1261CsulLies1263¼DnceFloor126 Brushd ltly str 18
2May92-Grade I
4Apr92- 5SA fst 1⅛ :461 1:102 1:491 S A Derby 92 2 3 32½ 31½ 2½ 32 Patterson A LB 122 9.50 82-11 A.P.Indy1221¾Bertrando122nkCasulLies122 Steadied 3/4 7
4Apr92-Grade I
7Mar92- 8GG fst 1 1/16 :453 1:094 1:421 Sausalito 93 2 3 41 2hd 11½ 12 Patterson A LB 122 *.70 86-13 CsulLies1222WstrnMn1193FifthBusinss115 Rallied wide 6
25Jan92- 7BM fst 1 1/16 :452 1:101 1:42 El Cam Dby 90 6 4 41½ 31 1½ 1½ Patterson A LB 117 5.10 89-15 CasualLies117½SehwkGold1151SilverRy122 Rallied wide 11
25Jan92-Grade III
22Dec91- 5Hol fst 1 1/16 :464 1:11 1:424 Hol Fut 86 5 2 21 31½ 43½ 35¾ Patterson A LB 121 52.10 81-17 A.P.Indy121nkDanceFloor1215½CsulLies121 Kept to task 14
22Dec91-Grade I
1Dec91- 6Hol fm 1 Ⓣ:461 1:10 1:342 Hst The Flg 85 3 4 45¼ 43¾ 35½ 45¾ Patterson A LB 121 13.90 87-07 CntstdBd1141¾TrblntKrs1144Snrnprs114 4-wide stretch 9
1Dec91-Grade III; Run in divisions
12Oct91- 8BM fst 1 :462 1:104 1:354 Foster City 81 3 2 21½ 2½ 2hd 1hd Patterson A LB 115 8.60 91-11 CasualLies115hdMterilEyes1152½BigPl115 Bumped start 7
18Sep91- 6BM fst 6f :223 :461 1:12 Alw 20000 63 4 6 52¼ 42 1½ 11½ Patterson A LB 117 9.60 76-24 CasualLies1171½BigPl1171NtiveExpress117 Rallied wide 6
15Aug91-11Bmf fst 6f :221 :45 1:10 Mdpeninsula 58 7 7 73 64¼ 56 58½ Rollins C J LB 116 5.40 81-14 NrthrnTrct1166TrsrExprss1161CnstdrL121 Brushed 3/16 7
23Jly91- 9SR fst 5½f :231 :47 1:053 Md Sp Wt 51 5 4 54 56 21½ 12 Rollins C J B 118 7.20 86-13 CslLs1182NrthrnTrct1181RmrkblWll118 Erratic stretch 10

LATEST WORKOUTS Jun 3 Bel 3f fst :36 B May 10 CD 5f fst 1:07 B ●Apr 28 CD 5f fst 1:00 H Apr 19 CD 7f fst 1:31 H

Pine Bluff

B. c. 3(May), by Danzig—Rowdy Angel, by Halo
Br.—Loblolly Stable (Ky)
Tr.—Bohannan Thomas (4 0 0 0 .00)
MCCARRON C J (6 2 0 1 .33)
Own.—Loblolly Stable
126
Lifetime 12 6 1 2 $1,164,108 | 1992 5 3 1 0 $879,120 | 1991 7 3 0 2 $284,988

16May92-10Pim gd 1 3/16 :461 1:104 1:553 Preakness 104 4 8 67½ 53½ 32½ 1¾ McCarron C J 126 *3.50 84-18 PineBluff126¾Alydeed1261½CsulLis126 Brushed str, drv 14
16May92-Grade I
2May92- 8CD fst 1¼ :464 1:363 2:03 Ky Derby 96 12 4 32 43½ 53¼ 57¼ Perret C B 126 10.50 88-06 LilE.Te1261CsulLis1263¼DncFloor126 Lckd lte response 18
2May92-Grade I
18Apr92- 9OP fst 1⅛ :473 1:113 1:492 Ark Derby 106 2 3 31 31½ 1hd 1nk Bailey J D 122 *.80 89-19 Pine Bluff122nk Lil E. Tee1227 Desert Force122 6
18Apr92-Grade II; Steadied 1st turn, taken back 1/2 and out, driving
28Mar92- 9OP fst 1 1/16 :461 1:10 1:424 Rebel 105 7 2 1hd 1hd 11 12½ Bailey J D 122 *.30 87-19 PineBluff1222½DsrtForc1173½LooksLikMony113 Driving 7
28Mar92-Grade III
7Mar92-10OP fst 1 :463 1:11 1:363 Southwest 105 3 3 3½ 2hd 21½ 22½ Perret C 122 *1.00 91-17 Big Sur1192½ PineBluff122hdLilE.Tee115 Bid, weakened 6
7Dec91- 8Aqu fst 1 1/16 ⊡:471 1:12 1:46 Nashua 98 6 3 21 21 1½ 12½ Perret C 124 *1.10 78-26 PineBluff1242½Spekerphone1142BestDcortd114 Driving 11
7Dec91-Grade III
16Nov91- 8Aqu fst 1⅛ :472 1:121 1:504 Remsen 93 1 2 21½ 2½ 12 14¾ Perret C 113 5.20 82-23 Pine Bluff1134¾ Offbeat1131¼ Cheap Shades122 Driving 8
16Nov91-Grade II
2Nov91- 6CD fst 1 1/16 :463 1:12 1:443 Br Cp Juv 78 3 7 33 44 612 713½ Perret C B 122 27.50 78-09 Arazi1225Bertrndo1223½SnppyLnding122 Tight 1st turn 14
2Nov91-Grade I
12Oct91- 8Bel fst 1 :45 1:102 1:363 Champagne 74 4 7 73¼ 32 57¾ 311 Perret C 122 9.10 76-16 TrtWtch1227½SnppyLndng1223½PnBlff122 Bobbled brk 15
12Oct91-Grade I
15Sep91- 8Bel fst 7f :214 :44 1:234 Futurity 78 1 7 76¾ 54 31 31 Perret C 122 5.40 84-13 Agincourt1221 Tri toWatch122noPineBluff122 Bid, hung 7
15Sep91-Grade I
16Aug91- 6Sar fst 7f :221 :451 1:234 Md Sp Wt 76 5 8 42½ 42½ 2½ 11½ Perret C 118 3.00 86-11 Pine Bluff1181½ Harry theHat1182Noactor118 Wide drv 10
13Jun91- 4Bel fst 5f :212 :44 :561 Md Sp Wt 66 7 8 54 54 45½ 510¾ Smith M E 118 4.30 96-05 Lure1185 In a Walk1182¾ Money Run118 Brk slowly 8

LATEST WORKOUTS Jun 2 Bel 4f sly :502 B ●May 27 Bel 6f fst 1:10 H May 12 Bel 4f fst :463 B Apr 28 CD 4f fst :472 H

Al Sabin

Ch. c. 3(Mar), by Alydar—Sabin, by Lyphard
Br.—Kennelot Stables Ltd (Ky)
Tr.—Lukas D Wayne (39 3 6 3 .08)
PINCAY L JR (—)
Own.—de Kwiatkowski Henryk
126
Lifetime 14 3 2 1 $132,477 | 1992 7 2 1 1 $99,580 | 1991 7 1 1 0 $32,897 | Turf 2 0 1 0 $6,600

2May92- 8CD fst 1¼ :464 1:363 2:03 Ky Derby 95 1 6 53½ 78¾ 75¼ 68 Nakatani C S B 126 33.30e 87-06 Lil E. Tee1261 Casual Lies1263¼ Dance Floor126 18
2May92-Grade I; Came out in stretch, tired
18Apr92- 6Aqu gd 1⅛ :471 1:11 1:491 Cahill Road 99 3 4 54 34 22 1nk Desormeaux K J 117 2.90 90-10 Al Sabin117nk Justfortherecord1174¾JayGee117 Driving 8
4Apr92- 8Aqu fst 1 :434 1:081 1:353 Gotham 83 3 6 53½ 64 77½ 79¼ Santos J A 118 6.50 75-21 [DH]Lur1144¼[DH]DvlHsD1144¼BstDcortd114 Saved ground 8
4Apr92-Grade II
15Mar92- 8SA fst 1 1/16 :454 1:101 1:423 San Felipe 78 3 4 45 44 56½ 511 Stevens G L B 116 10.40 79-13 Bertrando122¾ Arp1161¾ Hickman Creek116 No mishap 6
15Mar92-Grade II

19Feb92- 8SA fst 1⅛ :461 1:102 1:491 ®Bradbury 94 7 3 31½ 2½ 11 2hd Stevens G L B 117 *1.70 84–18 NaturlNine115hdAlSbin1172½ChinOfLife115 Sharp effort 8
29Jan92- 8SA fst 1 1/16 :462 1:113 1:441 ®S Catalina 86 9 9 96½ 74½ 33½ 33½ Stevens G L B 117 *1.60 78–20 VyngVctor1153TurbulntKrs114½AlSbn117 Flattened out 11
11Jan92- 7SA fst 1 1/16 :46 1:103 1:432 Alw 35000 90 6 4 45½ 32 31½ 1½ Stevens G L B 115 2.80 86–17 Al Sabin115½ TurbulentKris1182¼VyingVictor115 Got up 7
1Dec91- 4Hol fm 1 Ⓣ:46 1:101 1:35 Hst The Flg 73 2 6 64 73¾ 64½ 62¾ Smith M E B 114 *1.70 87–07 SilverRy1141¼Thinkrnot115hdAfricnColony117 Wide trip 9
1Dec91-Grade III; Run in divisions
15Nov91- 8Hol fm 1 Ⓣ:47 1:11 1:36 Alw 33000 80 1 7 611 510 44 2nk Stevens G L B 119 *2.80 85–17 Bossanova111nk Al Sabin119½ Thinkernot119 Rallied 10
20Oct91- 8Kee fst 1 1/16 :474 1:12 1:441 Brds Fut 81 6 5 53¾ 44½ 47½ 411 Pedroza M A LB 121 18.10 72–23 DnceFloor1213StrRecruit1217CounttheTim121 No rally 7
20Oct91-Grade II
28Sep91- 9TP fst 1 1/16 :471 1:113 1:453 Alysheba 65 1 3 32 45 711 717 Desormeaux KJ Bb 120 4.50 66–21 StrRcrut1202PckUpthPhon1205Bttnbrg120 Svd ground 9
28Sep91-Grade III
8Sep91- 8AP fst 7f :221 :451 1:243 Arch Ward 62 10 1 42½ 54 43 54¼ Velasquez J 116 *1.90 76–16 GCnHDnc1171FrightTrnr1161½Dnc'nJk116 4 wide evenly 11
16Aug91- 3Sar gd 7f :222 :454 1:241 Md Sp Wt 72 4 4 11 11 12½ 12 Antley C W 118 6.00 84–11 Al Sabin1182 Winver Ridge118nkSplinterRed118 Driving 10
4Jly91- 4Bel fst 5½f :222 :453 1:052 Md Sp Wt 53 7 4 31½ 31 43 85¾ Stevens G L 118 4.10 86–11 SeattleShuffle1181¼ShyawyFox118¾MoneyRun118 Tired 9
LATEST WORKOUTS Jun 3 Bel 4f fst :48 B May 27 Bel 7f fst 1:261 H May 20 Bel 5f fst 1:033 B Apr 28 CD 5f fst 1:013 B

Jacksonport

Dk. b. or br. c. 3(Mar), by Vigors—On the Brink, by Cox's Ridge
Br.—Loblolly Stable (Ky)
Tr.—Garren Murray M (21 1 0 2 .05)
CRUGUET J (62 10 8 5 .16)
Own.—Garren Murray M
126

Lifetime						
16 3 1 4	1992	13	2	1	3	$74,213
$84,593	1991	3	1	0	1	$10,380
	Turf	3	0	0	0	
	Wet	1	0	0	1	$1,680

23May92- 4Bel fm 1⅜ T:484 1:364 2:131 3↑Alw 31000 80 4 4 31½ 21 32½ 64¼ Cruguet J b 110 18.00 81–07 GryGumbo115nkExplosivRul119¾CptivTun121 Bid, tired 9
6May92- 6Bel fm 1¼ T:491 1:373 2:021 3↑Alw 31000 73 6 7 76 63 64½ 77¼ Madrid A Jr b 110 6.50 72–17 ProSrv119nkMuchoPrcious119nkExplosivRul119 Outrun 8
27Apr92- 6Aqu yl 1⅛ Ⓣ:493 1:151 1:54 3↑Alw 31000 — 5 5 64 62½ — — Madrid A Jr b 110 7.90 — — Cantinero119½ King's Gent119hd Rainlough119 8
27Apr92-Clipped heels, stumbled 1/4 pole, lost rider
18Apr92- 8Aqu gd 1⅛ :47 1:11 1:491 Wood Mem 81 9 11 127¼ 129 1010 911 Velasquez J b 126 95.60 79–10 DvlHsD1261WstbyWst1262Rokby-GB126 Checked, wide 12
18Apr92-Grade I
6Apr92- 7Aqu fst 7f :233 :464 1:234 3↑Alw 28000 80 6 3 62¼ 63¼ 44½ 47½ Madrid A Jr b 110 4.30e 78–21 AftrThBp1143¾HntngHorn1193AlwysAshly119 No threat 8
28Mar92- 8GS gd 1 :481 1:132 1:39 Cherry Hill 77 3 5 42½ 53 67½ 612 Santagata N b 117 6.00 74–19 PieinYourEye115noSurlySix1151¾DixiBrss117 No factor 7
28Mar92-Grade III
13Mar92- 8Aqu fst 1⅛ :463 1:114 1:512 Gate Dancer 90 6 6 69½ 43½ 34 35¼ Antley C W b 117 4.20e 74–32 ThndrRmbl1195StpOtFront117nkJcksnprt117 Bid, wknd 8
29Feb92- 7Aqu fst 1 1/16 ⊡:473 1:132 1:471 Flag Raiser 96 6 8 78½ 33 33½ 1nk Antley C W b 115 4.60 72–36 Jcksonport115nkStpOutFront1171¾NinsWild119 Driving 9
15Feb92- 8Aqu fst 1 1/16 ⊡:481 1:13 1:441 Whirlaway 80 6 10 106¼ 41½ 47½ 411¼ Antley C W b 117 7.60e 76–26 DrUnrht1195½TnsNmbr1173½ThndrRbl126 Tk up st, wide 10
7Feb92- 6Aqu fst 170 ⊡:474 1:14 1:444 Alw 29000 85 2 3 31 12 11 2no Madrid A Jr b 117 *1.40 81–29 RomnChorus117noJcksonport1174½GongAwy117 Gamely 6
27Jan92- 7Aqu fst 1 1/16 ⊡:474 1:123 1:454 Alw 29000 81 7 3 33 2½ 31½ 35 Madrid A Jr b 117 2.30 74–27 HghTr1173¾SothrnRomnc1171¼Jcksonprt117 Weakened 7
16Jan92- 7Aqu fst 170 ⊡:47 1:133 1:451 Alw 29000 76 2 1 12 11 2hd 31¼ Madrid A Jr b 117 3.30 78–27 Tnk'sNmbr119¾Sonfmswk117½Jcksnprt117 Chckd, wknd 8
9Jan92- 1Aqu fst 1 1/16 ⊡:482 1:131 1:463 Clm c-35000 87 4 1 12 13½ 16 110½ Antley C W b 119 *2.10 75–26 Jcksonport11910½GttSccss117nkDHRmnChrs117 Driving 7
15Dec91- 3Aqu fst 170 ⊡:49 1:143 1:451 Md 35000 73 8 2 1hd 1hd 18 16½ Antley C W b 118 *1.00 79–12 Jacksonport1186½NkeTheSnke1112NobleKsi114 Driving 8
22Nov91- 4Aqu sly 7f :222 :454 1:234 Md 45000 64 9 6 74 55½ 33 38¼ Antley C W b 118 2.50 75–21 PyfrPly1186¾LrdWllstn1141¼Jcksnprt118 Bid, weakened 10
14Nov91- 4Aqu fst 1 :473 1:13 1:381 Md 50000 49 2 10 118¼ 73¼ 52¾ 44½ Antley C W 118 14.20 66–12 DovrCost114nkJss'sd'Accrd1142½ArTrty114 Rallied wide 11
LATEST WORKOUTS Jun 1 Bel 5f sly 1:024 B May 18 Bel tr.t 4f fst :47 H ●Apr 13 Bel tr.t 5f gd :592 H

Cristofori

Dk. b. or br. c. 3(May), by Fappiano—Somfas, by What a Pleasure
Br.—Groves Carolyn T (Ky)
Tr.—Fabre Andre (—)
CAUTHEN S (—)
Own.—Sheikh Mohammed
126

Lifetime						
7 2 1 0	1992	2	0	0	0	$5,446
$58,766	1991	5	2	1	0	$53,320
	Turf	7	2	1	0	$58,766

10May92♦5Longchamp(Fra) gd*1½ 2:371 Ⓣ Prix Hocquart(Gr2) 42¾ Jarnet T 128 *.70e — — AduARo1281½ Glnvll128nk PrncPolno128 Led to midstr 6
26Apr92♦4Longchamp(Fra) gd*1 3/16 2:143 Ⓣ Pirx Greffulhe(Gr2) 53½ Cauthen S 128 *1.00 — — AppleTr1282 BrkBrd128hd SilvrKit128 Prom, led, wknd 7
13Oct91♦3Longchamp(Fra) yl*1⅛ 1:552 Ⓣ Prix de Conde(Gr3) 11½ Cauthen S 121 3.40 — — Cristofori1211½ ShrpCounsl1181¼ BrkBrd121 Prom,drvg 6
15Sep91♦1Longchamp(Fra) gd*1 1:384 Ⓣ Prix la Rochette(Gr3) 42½ Jarnet T 123 2.90e — — [illegible]
19Aug91♦4Deauville(Fra) gd*7f 1:274 Ⓣ PrixHaras de la Huderie 42¼ Cauthen S 123 6.50 — — Code Breaker123hd SliverKite1281½ Amizour123 Evenly 5
27Jly91♦2Evry(Fra) gd*7f 1:271 Ⓣ Prix d'Arbonne 2¾ Jarnet T 128 *1.50 — — Guislaine 128¾ Cristofori 1281½ Alzarina 126 Fin. well 10
8Jly91♦1Compiegne(Fra) gd*7f 1:252 Ⓣ Prix Henri Foy(Mdn) 13 Jarnet T 123 *1.70 — — *Cristofori 1233 Innergy 1231 Mon Domino 123* *Easily* 11

Agincourt

B. c. 3(Apr), by Capote—Conquistador Blue, by Conquistador Cielo
Br.—Heins & McGee Mmes (Ky)
Tr.—Zito Nicholas P (9 2 1 0 .22)
MADRID A JR (72 6 11 7 .08)
Own.—Perez Robert
126

Lifetime						
9 3 0 1	1992	4	1	0	1	$33,505
$141,045	1991	5	2	0	0	$107,540
	Wet	1	0	0	1	$13,705

16May92-10Pim gd 1 3/16 :461 1:104 1:553 Preakness 80 1 9 1113 1110 713 715¼ Madrid A Jr 126 70.10 69–18 PineBluff126¾Alydeed1261½CasulLies126 Bore out, rank 14
16May92-Grade I
21Apr92- 8Kee my 1 1/16 :471 1:122 1:44 Lexington 93 5 1 21 31 32½ 34¼ Chavez J F B 115 6.10 82–16 MyLckRnsNorth115nkLr1184Agncort115 Bore out, rank 5
21Apr92-Grade II
6Apr92- 8Aqu fst 1 :471 1:113 1:373 3↑Alw 33000 95 2 2 1½ 1hd 13 12½ Chavez J F 110 1.90 74–35 Agncourt1102½PnsonFrd1211¼DrssdShppr119 Mild drive 5
21Mar92- 8Aqu gd 7f :22 :443 1:213 Bay Shore 76 10 1 42 43 611 813 Chavez J F 119 8.10 84–11 ThreePeat1143¼Goldwater117noBestDecorated114 Tired 10
21Mar92-Grade II
2Nov91- 6CD fst 1 1/16 :463 1:12 1:443 Br Cp Juv 83 2 2 21½ 32 49 510¼ Chavez J F LB 122 62.30 82–09 Arazi1225 Bertrando1223½ SnappyLanding122 Gave way 14
2Nov91-Grade I
12Oct91- 8Bel fst 1 :45 1:102 1:363 Champagne 10 5 3 95¼ 1210 1428 1445¼ Chavez J F 122 11.20e 42–16 TrtoWtch1227½SnppyLndng1223½PnBlff122 Brief speed 15
12Oct91-Grade I
15Sep91- 8Bel fst 7f :214 :44 1:234 Futurity 80 2 2 23 22 1hd 11 Chavez J F 122 19.90 85–13 Agincourt1221 Tri to Watch122no Pine Bluff122 Driving 7
15Sep91-Grade I
12Aug91- 3Sar fst 6f :222 :454 1:11 Md Sp Wt 76 7 1 1hd 11½ 11 15 Chavez J F 118 8.30 89–09 Agincourt1185 Appointee118nk Hoover Dam118 Driving 11
25Jly91- 5Sar fst 5f :214 :451 :581 Md Sp Wt 33 8 8 54 55 79½ 517 Black C A 118 3.30 76–06 ProspctorJ1187CortngPlsr1183¾IslndProspct118 Faded 8
LATEST WORKOUTS Jun 3 Bel 4f fst :483 B May 29 Bel 5f fst 1:001 B May 23 Bel 6f fst 1:024 B May 13 Pim 4f fst :472 H

Robert's Hero — Dk. b. or br. c. 3(Mar), by King of the North—Robert's Heroine, by Slewpy
CHAVEZ J F (96 13 14 8 .14) — Br.—Perez Robert (NY)
Own.—Perez Robert — Tr.—Callejas Alfredo (8 0 3 1 .00) — 126
Lifetime 7 1 2 1 $31,720 | 1992 5 1 1 1 $26,000 | 1991 2 M 1 0 $5,720 | Turf 2 0 1 1 $9,860

27May92- 7Bel fm 1 1/16 [T]:473 1:114 1:424 3↑[S]Alw 29000 82 5 4 21 2½ 21½ 2½ Chavez J F 110 3.70 83-16 MkBrk109½Robrt'sHr1102½PlckWthLck119 Good effort 9
6May92- 9Bel fm 1¼ [T]:472 1:362 2:02 3↑[S]Alw 29000 77 4 1 11 2hd 3nk 36¼ Chavez J F 110 14.40 74-17 Pchnto119¾Ptrt'sThndr1155½Rbrt'sHr110 Bid, weakened 12
28Mar92- 8TP fst 1 1/16 :473 1:131 1:47 Rushaway 52 8 4 31 42½ 921 822¾ Chavez J F B 110 54.20 49-28 Dignits110nkTnSns1143½RturnVoyg110 Bumped soundly 9
24Feb92- 6Aqu fst 1 1/16 [•]:483 1:143 1:472 [S]Alw 29000 51 4 2 31 34½ 412 421 Madrid A Jr 117 2.90 50-26 Amberjack1199 Need's Fixin1179 O Matty117 Tired 5
29Jan92- 9Aqu fst 6f [•]:233 :48 1:144 [S]Md Sp Wt 53 1 5 1½ 1½ 12 1½ Madrid A Jr 122 *.80 69-24 Robert'sHero122½NicShot1223½KhrtoumKid122 Driving 8
22Dec91- 8Aqu fst 1 1/16 [•]:472 1:124 1:473 [S]B Bongard 44 4 1 11 55 915 919½ Madrid A Jr 113 3.80e 50-32 PhntomFinn1222JyG119nkQunofTriumph116 Used early 11
16Dec91- 9Aqu fst 1 1/16 [•]:491 1:151 1:491 [S]Md Sp Wt 71 3 3 2hd 1hd 2hd 2hd Chavez J F 118 7.80 62-31 LoclProblem118hdRobrt'sHro118nkLivrStnd118 Gamely 11
LATEST WORKOUTS Jun 3 Bel 5f fst 1:022 B — May 25 Bel 3f fst :371 Bg — May 20 Bel 4f fst :491 B — Apr 27 Bel tr.t 4f fst :491 B

My Memoirs–GB — B. c. 3(Apr), by Don't Forget Me—Julip, by Track Spare
BAILEY J D (85 16 19 9 .19) — Br.—Hinley Mrs J J & Smart Mrs S (GB)
Own.—Team Valor — Tr.—Hannon Richard M (—) — 126
Lifetime 8 3 1 1 $61,658 | 1992 3 1 0 1 $46,330 | 1991 5 2 1 0 $15,328 | Turf 8 3 1 1 $46,330

7May92♦2Chester(Eng) gd*1¼ 2:091 (T) Dee Stakes(L) 1no Reid J 128 10.00 — — My Memoirs 128no Profusion 1241½ Torrey Canyon128 7
7May92-Led 3 fur, dropped back to last, up final strides
11Apr92♦3Thirsk(Eng) gd 1 1:391 (T) TetleyBitterClassicTrial 47½ McGlone A 128 7.00 — — Jeune 123hd Zaahi 1235 Big Blue 118 With pace 6f 6
21Mar92♦3Doncaster(Eng) gd 1 1:43 (T) DoncasterMileStks(L) 31½ McGlone A 112 7.80 — — Daros 112hd Tanfith 1291½ MyMemoirs112 Bid, blocked 8
20ct91♦5Newmarket(Eng) gd 7f 1:241 (T) TattersalTiffnyHiflyrStk 148½ Reid J 126 25.00 — — YoungSnor126hd DrDvious126nk AlnsrAlwshk126 Led 4f 30
29Aug91♦5Lingfield(Eng) gd 7f 1:224 (T) RedlandPlasterboardStk 2hd Perham R5 128 5.00 — — Alhijz130hd MyMmoirs128½ Alflor123 Set pace, headed 11
1Aug91♦1Goodwood(Eng) gd 7f 1:283 (T) LansonChampagneVintgeS(G3 67¾ Eddery P 123 7.50 — — DrDvous1261½ MdofGold1232 GovrnorsImp123 Prom 5f 7
13Jly91♦2York(Eng) gd*7f 1:264 (T) FriargateGraduationStk 1½ Raymont S 126 4.50 — — MyMmoirs126½ Alhijz1281½ JwllryQurtr126 Led thruout 5
29Jun91♦1Chepstow(Wales) gd*6f 1:14 (T) EBF WoodpeckerStks(Mdn) 11 McGlone A 126 5.50 — — MyMemoirs1261 Cochabmb1212 Dj126 With pace, drvg 16

Montreal Marty — Ch. c. 3(May), by Mt Livermore—Reason to Act, by Bold Reason
SANTOS J A (101 10 10 19 .10) — Br.—Goichman Lawrence (NY)
Own.—Vendome Stable — Tr.—Schulhofer Flint S (26 3 5 4 .12) — 126
Lifetime 10 3 5 0 $224,273 | 1992 3 1 2 0 $100,690 | 1991 7 2 3 0 $123,583 | Turf 1 1 0 0 $56,340 | Wet 1 1 0 0 $74,400

17May92- 8Bel my 1 :453 1:10 1:352 [S]Mike Lee H 92 3 4 42 32 2½ 12¼ Krone J A 118 *1.60 93-23 MontrelMrty1182¼Detox1132¾RoylCormornt112 Driving 12
24Apr92- 8Aqu fst 1 :453 1:092 1:36 3↑Alw 31000 92 6 4 41½ 32 2½ 2nk Santos J A 113 1.70 82-29 CrrptCncl110nkMntrlMrt1133½HntnHrn119 Rallied wide 7
5Apr92- 8Aqu fst 7f :232 :472 1:261 [S]D Clinton H 84 5 3 53½ 32 2½ 2½ Krone J A 118 2.10 73-25 BllOfRghts113½MntrlMrty1181½PghkpsGyps112 Gamely 8
16Nov91- 8Aqu fst 1⅛ :472 1:121 1:504 Remsen 72 8 7 64½ 54½ 65½ 713¼ Santos J A 119 6.10 69-23 Pine Bluff1134¾ Offbeat1131¼ Cheap Shades122 4-wide 8
16Nov91-Grade II
4Nov91- 8Aqu fm 1 (T):462 1:122 1:373 [S]DmonRnyon 78 5 6 67½ 3½ 13 1no Krone J A 117 3.30 88-11 MontrealMrty117noBudgetCrisis1171¾JyGee122 Driving 11
23Oct91- 8Aqu fst 7f :214 :44 1:223 Cowdin 83 8 3 77½ 66½ 35 26½ Krone J A 122 13.30 82-13 SaltLake1226½MontrelMrty122nkOffbet122 Up for place 9
23Oct91-Grade II
7Oct91- 4Bel fst 6½f :23 :47 1:18 [S]Md Sp Wt 80 8 4 2½ 1hd 11½ 1¾ Krone J A 118 *.40 87-11 MontrelMrty118¾HirHouse1181LivrStnd118 Ridden out 11
5Sep91- 8Bel fst 6f :222 :451 1:094 [S]Empire 76 9 5 63¼ 31 21 23¼ Krone J A 115 *1.00 88-13 TVHrtThrb1173¼MntrlMrt1152WthIt115 Lugged in-ralld 10
22Aug91- 6Sar gd 6f :222 :453 1:11 [S]Md Sp Wt 78 9 2 31 2hd 12½ 17½ Krone J A 118 *.90[D] 89-11 [D]Montreal Marty1187½ With It118nk Just Show Up118 10
22Aug91-Disqualified and placed fourth; Lugged in stretch, greenly
11Aug91- 3Sar fst 6f :22 :453 1:113 [S]Md Sp Wt 67 10 1 31 31 1hd 2½ Krone J A 118 2.40 85-09 PoughkeepsieGypsy118½MontrlMrty118¾JyG118 Gamely 11
LATEST WORKOUTS Jun 4 Bel 4f fst :473 B — May 30 Bel 5f fst :594 Hg — May 25 Bel 4f fst :474 B — May 13 Bel 4f fst :462 H

Colony Light — Dk. b. or br. c. 3(Mar), by Pleasant Colony—Great Light, by Rube the Great
KRONE J A (129 24 29 14 .19) — Br.—Lone Star Breeding Associates (Ky)
Own.—Peace John H — Tr.—Arnold George R II (12 3 2 2 .25) — 126
Lifetime 7 1 2 1 $75,566 | 1992 5 1 2 1 $74,006 | 1991 2 M 0 0 $1,560

24May92- 8Bel fst 1⅛ :453 1:10 1:472 Peter Pan 99 2 7 76 31½ 22½ 25½ Krone J A 114 14.80 86-08 A.P.Indy1205½ColonyLight1144¾BerklyFitz114 Wide trip 7
24May92-Grade II
11Apr92- 9Kee fst 1⅛ :471 1:112 1:49 Blue Grass 76 10 4 63¾ 74¾ 911 1016¾ Krone J A B 121 4.70 73-10 PistolsndRoss121nkContDiSvoy1212½EcstticRd121 Tired 11
11Apr92-Grade II
21Mar92-10FG fst 1 1/16 :472 1:12 1:432 La Derby 95 8 3 48 33½ 11 11¼ Krone J A 112 7.30[D] 97-05 [D]ClnLht1121¼LIThSd1171HllPss117 Lug-in,impede foe 9
21Mar92-Grade III; Disqualified and placed third
3Mar92- 9GP fst 1⅛ :483 1:13 1:503 Alw 20000 89 2 5 53½ 65 53½ 23½ Krone J A 112 2.60 80-15 JstLPrfct1173½ClnLht1121½ChlThrt113 Crred out 4 wide 6
1Feb92- 2GP fst 7f :23 :463 1:244 Md Sp Wt 83 7 8 85¼ 64¾ 21½ 1nk Krone J A 120 7.70 82-15 ColonyLight120nkPrivtTrsurr1208½Wstrng120 Wide turn 12
29Sep91- 4Bel fst 1 :463 1:113 1:364 Md Sp Wt 64 12 12 1210 84½ 38½ 412 Smith M E 118 39.80 74-18 Onlooker11810HrrytheHt1181DesrtProspctor118 5-wide 14
16Sep91- 4Bel fst 7f :23 :463 1:234 Md Sp Wt 54 7 6 2½ 5¾ 77½ 510 Smith M E 118 3.80 75-15 SnppyLndng118½FrzngFun1183½DsrtProspctor118 Tired 7
LATEST WORKOUTS Jun 1 Bel 6f sly 1:16 B — May 18 Bel 6f fst 1:11 H — May 12 Bel 6f fst 1:15 B — Apr 27 CD 5f fst 1:022 B

Casual Lies made a good account of himself in the first two legs of the Triple Crown. In both races, the Kentucky bred came up a little short in the stretch, tiring slightly. Casual Lies cannot cut the pace setting the fractions, or he will tire. He must come off the pace hoping to run down the early pacesetters as he has done in the past. Against the class of horses in the Kentucky Derby and Preakness he tried these tactics and still came up short.

Pine Bluff, winner of the Preakness Stakes, is in a prime spot if he goes the 1½ miles in the Belmont. The Rebel Stakes and the Preakness were two different types of races for Pine Bluff, even though he was successful in both. In the Rebel Stakes, he showed high speed on the front end. The problem, though, was at a mile and a sixteenth. The Preakness had a different twist for Pine Bluff. He rallied from behind to chase down Alydeed. In the mile-and-a-half Belmont Stakes the best chance Pine Bluff is going to have is to go out and set very slow fractions and hope to have enough in the tank at the end. Pine Bluff will have to be in front by setting fractions such as 47²/₅, 1:12, 1:37³/₅ to have any chance. If the fractions are that slow Pine Bluff will have to fight off more than just A.P. Indy and Casual Lies.

A.P. Indy is one of the lightly raced colts in the race. He has an injury to blame for his absence in the first two legs of the Triple Crown. A.P. Indy's Time Analysis is superior to any horse in the Belmont Stakes. In the San Rafael Stakes at Santa Anita, A.P. Indy set adjusted speed fractions of 46¹/₅, 1:10¹/₅, and 1:35²/₅. These fractions are unmatchable by any contender. Many people thought that the only reason A.P. Indy could run tremendous fractions was because the tracks on the West Coast were lightning fast. When A.P. Indy came to the East Coast, his "acid test" came in the Peter Pan Stakes at Belmont. This was A.P. Indy's first race since his injury on the day of the Kentucky Derby. In this race, A.P. Indy took over at the half and pulled away leaving the rest stunned. He set super fractions on his way to victory. In the Belmont Stakes, A.P. Indy can dictate the race any way he likes. His speed could take it all the way on the front end or he could pick up the pieces coming from behind.

The only reason Colony Light is even considered is because of his efforts in the Peter Pan Stakes. If he could improve off of that performance he may have enough to be in the gimmicks.

My Memoirs is an England bred colt that made our contender list only because of a few races in Europe. **Horses that come from foreign countries are usually at a disadvantage because they don't run on dirt.** Time Analysis must be used to examine most foreign horse performances. The conditions of foreign tracks vary tremendously. You have to adjust final times only. Comparing these times to other races that have occurred that day is the best way to get a read on these foreigners. The Belmont Stakes' track conditions (good) will help My Memoirs. Also, the addition of jockey Jerry Bailey will not hurt. His last race makes him good enough for the gimmicks. My Memoirs led, then came back to win that race. Two horses that My Memoirs beat in the Dee Stakes came back to win. Each won in $100,000 purse stakes races.

EIGHTH RACE

Belmont

JUNE 6, 1992

1 ½ MILES. (2.24) 124th Running THE BELMONT STAKES (Grade I). Purse $500,000 added. 3–year–olds. Scale Weight. $5,000 to pass the entry box; $5,000 to start with $500,000 added. At any time prior to Closing, Thursday, June 4, 1992, horses may be nominated to The Belmont Stakes upon payment of a supplementary fee of $50,000 to The New York Racing Association Inc. The added money and all fees to be divided 60% to the winner, 22% to second, 12% to third and 6% to fourth. Colts and Geldings, 126 lbs.; Fillies, 121 lbs. Starters to be named at the closing time of entries. The Belmont field will be limited to sixteen (16) starters. In the event that more than 16 entries pass through the entry box at the closing, the starters will be determined at the closing with 50% of the field (8 starters) given preference by accumulating the highest earnings in Graded Stakes (lifetime), including all money paid for performances in such Graded Stakes. The next five (5) starters (approximate 30%) will be determined by accumulating the highest earnings (lifetime) in all races except restricted races (i.e., any stake containing eligibility conditions other than sex and age). The remaining 3 starters (approximate 20%) shall be determined by accumulating the highest earnings (lifetime) in all races. Should this preference produce any ties the additional starter(s) shall be determined by lot. If the rules described result in the exclusion of any horse, the $5,000 entry fee will be refunded to the owner of said horse. The winning owner will be presented with the August Belmont Memorial Cup, to be retained for one year, as well as a trophy for permanent possession and trophies will be presented to the winning trainer and jockey. Nominations to each and all of the Triple Crown races, The Kentucky Derby, The Preakness and The Belmont (the "Races") may be made only by payment of a single subscription fee to Triple Crown Productions, Inc., as agent for Churchill Downs Incorporated, The Maryland Jockey Club and the New York Racing Association Inc. (the "Associations"). The subscription fee for 389 nominations received by January 18, 1992, is $600 and for 18 nominations received by April 1, 1992, is $4,500. (These fees are to be apportioned equally among the three Associations to be part of the total purse for each of the three races.) After April 1, at any time prior to Closing for the Kentucky Derby, additional nominations to all three races will be accepted and the nominee will be eligible for the Chrysler Triple Crown Challenge bonus, upon payment of a supplementary fee of $150,000 to Churchill Downs Incorporated. Following the running of The Kentucky Derby, but at any time prior to Closing for the Preakness Stakes, horses may be nominated to the remaining Races but will not be eligible for the Chrysler Triple Crown Challenge bonus, upon payment of a supplementary fee of $100,000 to The Maryland Jockey Club of Baltimore City, Inc. At any time prior to the Closing for the Belmont Stakes, horses may be nominated to The Belmont Stakes upon payment of a supplementary fee of $50,000 to the New York Racing Association Inc. All supplemental fees will be included in the purse distribution of the respective Races for which paid. Horses nominated by payment of supplementary fee ("supplemental nominees") will not be allowed to enter any Race in which the maximum number of starters has otherwise been reached prior to the time of Closing. If the number of supplemental nominees exceed the number of available starting positions at Closing, the conditions of each respective Race shall be applied to determine which supplemental nominees will be allowed to start in such Race. All nominees, supplemental or otherwise, will be requested to pay entry and starting fees for the Race or Races to which they have been nominated. Triple Crown Productions, Inc. is guaranteeing total earnings of $5,000,000 to the owner of any horse which wins all of the 1992 Kentucky Derby, Preakness Stakes and Belmont Stakes races (the "Races") and is offering a $1,000,000 bonus to the owner of a horse with the best, most consistent finishes in the Races. The "Triple Crown Challenge" monies will be paid to the owner of a horse which meets these criteria: 1. Finishes in all three Triple Crown Races as listed above; 2. Earns points by finishing first, second, third or fourth in at least one of the Triple Crown Races; and 3. Earns the highest number of points over the course of the three Races. Points are assigned for each race: Win–10, Place–5, Show–3, Fourth–1. In the event of a tie, the $1 million bonus will be distributed equally among the top point–getters. In the event of a dead–heat, equal points will be awarded in full. For example, 10 points for each horse in a dead–heat to win. Triple Crown Productions Inc. will pay to the owner of a horse winning all of the Races that amount necessary to bring total earnings for the Triple Crown winner to $5,000,000. The total will include the winner's purse distributed by each racing association; the $1 million point bonus described above; and a further bonus guaranteed by Triple Crown Productions to reach the $5 million total. Triple Crown Productions will present the Triple Crown Trophy to the owner of a horse that sweeps the Kentucky Derby, Preakness Stakes and Belmont Stakes. Closed with 1 Supplemental Nominee: My Memoirs–GB.

Value of race $1,764,800; value to winner $458,880; second $168,256; third $1,091,776; fourth $45,888. Mutuel pool $2,570,867. Exacta Pool $1,879,213 Triple Pool $1,905,000

Last Raced	Horse	M/Eqt.A.Wt	PP	$\frac{1}{4}$	$\frac{1}{2}$	1	$1\frac{1}{4}$	Str	Fin	Jockey	Odds $1
24May92 8Bel^1	A.P. Indy	3 126	1	2^1	4^4	$4^{1\frac{1}{2}}$	$3^{2\frac{1}{2}}$	$2^{1\frac{1}{2}}$	$1^{\frac{3}{4}}$	Delahoussaye E	1.10
7May92 2Eng^1	(S)My Memoirs-GB	3 126	9	$5^{1\frac{1}{2}}$	$5^{\frac{1}{2}}$	$6^{\frac{1}{2}}$	4^2	3^6	2^{nk}	Bailey J D	18.00
16May92 10Pim^1	Pine Bluff	3 126	3	4^1	$3^{\frac{1}{2}}$	3^1	$1^{\frac{1}{2}}$	$1^{\frac{1}{2}}$	$3^{13\frac{1}{2}}$	McCarron C J	3.80
10May92 5Fra^4	Cristofori	b 3 126	6	$8^{\frac{1}{2}}$	6^{hd}	5^{hd}	$6^{1\frac{1}{2}}$	5^4	$4^{1\frac{3}{4}}$	Cauthen S	7.50
16May92 10Pim^3	Casual Lies	3 126	2	$1^{\frac{1}{2}}$	$2^{1\frac{1}{2}}$	1^{hd}	2^{hd}	4^2	5^4	Stevens G L	4.60
24May92 8Bel^2	Colony Light	3 126	11	$9^{1\frac{1}{2}}$	$9^{1\frac{1}{2}}$	7^1	$7^{1\frac{1}{2}}$	6^2	$6^{6\frac{1}{2}}$	Krone J A	20.70
16May92 10Pim^7	Agincourt	3 126	7	$3^{\frac{1}{2}}$	1^{hd}	$2^{1\frac{1}{2}}$	5^1	7^2	7^3	Madrid A Jr	a-24.30
17May92 8Bel^1	Montreal Marty	3 126	10	7^{hd}	$8^{\frac{1}{2}}$	8^4	8^8	8^{16}	8^{23}	Santos J A	24.20
27May92 7Bel^2	Robert's Hero	3 126	8	11	11	11	11	11	$9^{\frac{1}{2}}$	Chavez J F	a-24.30
2May92 8CD^6	Al Sabin	3 126	4	$6^{\frac{1}{2}}$	7^1	$9^{1\frac{1}{2}}$	$9^{\frac{1}{2}}$	$10^{2\frac{1}{2}}$	10	Pincay L Jr	21.90
23May92 4Bel^6	Jacksonport	b 3 126	5	10^1	10^2	10^6	10^6	$9^{\frac{1}{2}}$	—	Cruguet J	44.40

Jacksonport, Eased.
a–Coupled: Agincourt and Robert's Hero.
(S) Supplementary nomination.
OFF AT 5:31 Start good. Won driving. Time, :23^1, :47 , 1:11^4, 1:36^1, 2:01^1, 2:26 , Track good.

$2 Mutuel Prices:

2-(B)–A.P. INDY	4.20	3.80	3.00
8-(H)–MY MEMOIRS-GB		11.60	6.60
4-(D)–PINE BLUFF			4.20

$2 EXACTA 2-8 PAID $73.20 $2 TRIPLE 2-8-4 PAID $240.00

Dk. b. or br. rig, (Mar), by Seattle Slew—Weekend Surprise, by Secretariat. Trainer Drysdale Neil. Bred by Farish W S & Kilroy W S (Ky).

A.P. INDY, away alertly from the inside, raced forwardly while saving ground until near the backstretch, came out after being eased back off the leaders before going six furlongs, made a run four wide approaching the stretch, caught PINE BLUFF inside the final furlong and proved best under strong handling. MY MEMOIRS-GB, well placed along the inside on the first turn, was allowed to drop back nearing the backstretch, made a run while racing well out in the track nearing the stretch and finished strongly. PINE BLUFF away in good order, followed the leaders while in hand for a mile, rallied to reach the front from between horses approaching the stretch and held on well in a long drive. CRISTOFORI, off slowly, was steadied along the inside around the first turn, moved within easy striking distance at the far turn, came out nearing the stretch but lacked a further response. CASUAL LIES showed good early foot, alternated for the lead while racing slightly out from the rail held on well to the stretch and gave way. COLONY LIGHT, wide throughout moved up nearing the end of the backstretch but had nothing left. AGINCOURT raced outside CASUAL LIES while vying for the lead for more than a mile and tired badly. MONTREAL MARTY had no apparent excuse. ROBERT'S HERO steadied in tight quarters following the start, was never close. AL SABIN, finished early, was not perservered with late. JACK-SONPORT, never close was eased after entering the stretch. AGINCOURT wore mud caulks.

Owners— 1, Tsurumaki Tomonori; 2, Team Valor; 3, Loblolly Stable; 4, Sheikh Mohammed; 5, Riley Shelley L; 6, Peace John H; 7, Perez Robert; 8, Vendome Stable; 9, Perez Robert; 10, de Kwiatkowski Henryk; 11, Garren Murray M.

Trainers— 1, Drysdale Neil; 2, Hannon Richard M; 3, Bohannan Thomas; 4, Fabre Andre; 5, Riley Shelley L; 6, Arnold George R II; 7, Zito Nicholas P; 8, Schulhofer Flint S; 9, Callejas Alfredo; 10, Lukas D Wayne; 11, Garren Murray M.

Pine Bluff, Agincourt, and Casual Lies set the early fractions. These fractions were slow but, as they hit the top of the stretch, Agincourt and Casual Lies were tiring and A.P. Indy was hitting his best stride. My Memoirs dueled with Pine Bluff down the stretch competing for second while A.P. Indy drew off in a hand ride. The early fractions were slow enough for all to compete, but as the race wore down to the end no one could keep up with A.P. Indy.

Breaking down the fractions of every horse will show you the obvious play based on speed through Time Analysis. At times there will be two or three horses with the same Time Analysis. When this occurs we must revert back to other factors such as workouts, trainers + jockey combos, or just staying off that particular race. If Minnesota's Way and Go Lassie Go were both even with Time Analysis and all other factors were even, Minnesota's Way would have been a better bet based on odds. **Time Analysis will produce longshots, so do not be intimidated by odds. NEVER let the board influence your selection.**

Handicapping the Maidens

CHAPTER 5 This chapter on workouts and maidens may be the most important chapter in this book. This area of handicapping is my specialty. Many times I have been called the best Maiden Handicapper on the East Coast, and maybe in the United States. In this chapter I will cover twelve different angles in betting maiden races. I'll also try to show you how to fit workouts into your handicapping.

12 Keys to Handicapping the Maidens

1—Looking Up Workouts

This is the most important angle in handicapping maiden races. If you learn anything from this book, I want you to learn to look up workouts and learn how to use the "Latest Workouts" page. Once you learn the benefits from the "Latest Workouts" page you will be able to use it for all types of races.

2—Dissecting Breeding

Knowing which horses are currently producing is essential. Just because certain sires were good runners does not mean the foals are doing well.

3—Workouts From Other Tracks
It is a challenge to find workouts that are performed at a different track and are not provided in the Daily Racing Form. These workouts might not be published because the current days had to go to print. Always look at the next day's Daily Racing Form for additional workouts. This point will be made clear in an upcoming example.

4—Class Edge Over Field
Certain maidens will have an edge based on all-around class. Great workouts, excellent breeding, and master handlers constitute all-around class.

5—Watching The Board
This is one of the more obvious techniques used by most handicappers in maiden races. First time starters money often finds "hot horses."

6—Layoffs
Layoffs with maidens are usually because of injuries. These injuries to two-year-olds are often minor. You should learn how to use this angle to your advantage by either throwing these horses out or by betting them.

7—Consistency Of Workouts
Many times horses will have workouts spaced more than seven days apart. This usually means an injury is involved. These horses should be watched closely.

8—Two-To-Three-Start Theory
The two-to-three-start theory is very simple. **If a maiden has not won after his second start he is not playable.** The only way we could possibly play a horse on his third start is if the particular horse had an excuse in one of those first two starts. Obviously, if a maiden race is compiled of horses that have all made more than three starts, this theory cannot be used. This theory is essential in maiden special weights races, where false favorites can occur.

9—Bouncing Back

A maiden loses to a horse that goes on to win again versus better. The loser in that race could be "live." I'll show you how to find such horses.

10—Knowing Trainers, Owners, And Jockeys

Be aware! Every handicapper should know which trainer uses certain jockeys on a regular basis. If there is a maiden with great workouts and his trainer is not using his regular jockey, be careful.

11—Maiden Claiming Races

Watch out for maidens that have impressive workouts and are in a claiming race. If these horses were that good they would not be running for a tag.

12—Maidens Who Do Not Win, But Are Still Bet Down

Certain maidens will always come close to winning but never win. They will continue to be bet down. I will show you how to eliminate these non-contenders and take advantage of throwing out the favorite.

Let's get going with some actual race examples!

On July 1, 1992, Monmouth Park offered a six furlong maiden claiming $25,000 event. As our handicapping began, we first eliminated All Desire because he had more than three starts. He does not figure into our handicapping because of the two-to-three-start theory. These horses usually draw sucker money and are not playable anyway. These horses can only be used if they have an excuse, as in the case of North Dakota. B.B. Wild has had two starts, but both of these starts came in 1990, so he is considered as a first-time starter.

---

1   **6 FURLONGS.** (1.08) MAIDEN CLAIMING. Purse $9,000. 3-year-olds and upward. Weight, 3-year-olds, 116 lbs. Older, 122 lbs. Claiming price $25,000; for each $2,500 to $20,000 allowed, 2 lbs.

LASIX—Prospect Singer, North Dakota, All Desire.

Mr. J. J. Jr.   Dk. b. or br. c. 3(Mar), by Kona Tenor—Misguided, by Clue Chips

$25,000 Br.—Ernie St. John, Jesse Cooper & Bud (Fla)

Own.—Turvan Stable   Tr.—Fisher John L (3 0 0 0 .00)   **116**

	Lifetime	1992	1 M	0	0	$155
	1 0 0 0	1991	0 M	0	0	
	$155					

23Jun92- 7Mth fst 6f :22 :453 1:113 3↑Md Sp Wt 45 5 10 89¾ 88½ 811 710½ Picon J 115 79.10 72-16 Heff110½ All Desire122¾CumberlandBlues115 In tight st 10
LATEST WORKOUTS Jun 15 Mth 7f fst 1:33 B Jun 9 Mth 5f fst 1:023 B Jun 4 Mth 5f fst 1:051 B

B.B. Wild B. c. 4, by Wild Again—Beer and Bananas, by Nostrum
$25,000 Br.—Kustee Mr-Mrs & Reynolds Mr-Mrs (Ky)
Own.—Buntain Derek H L Tr.—Meyer Jerome C (—) 1175
Lifetime 2 0 1 1 $5,440 1990 2 M 1 1 $5,440 1989 0 M 0 0

5Jun90- 2Pim fst 5f :223 :462 :592 Md Sp Wt 49 7 6 46 34 34 32¾ Luzzi M J 120 *1.30 88-14 Ducere1151¾ Haymaker1201 B.B. Wild120 Wide 8
25May90- 1Pim fst 5f :224 :471 :594 Md Sp Wt 42 3 6 45 43 21 23 Luzzi M J 120 9.10 86-15 Secret Notion1203B.B.Wild1201CrazyCanuck120 Rallied 8
LATEST WORKOUTS ●Jun 19 Aqu 3f fst :362 H

Cipi Ch. c. 3(May), by Mulberry—You Won't Be Sorry, by Hold Your Peace
$20,000 Br.—Maraspin L (NJ)
Own.—BottazzoPatrickL-MizrhiRlphM Tr.—Bottazzi Patrick L (50 6 10 7 .12) 112
Lifetime 0 0 0 0 1991 0 M 0 0
LATEST WORKOUTS Jun 26 Mth 3f fst :372 Bg Jun 23 Mth 4f fst :491 B Jun 16 Mth 5f fst 1:05 B Jun 10 Mth 4f fst :512 Bg

Changeisgood B. c. 3(Apr), by Henrywuzwrong—Hurri Queenie, by Hurricane Ed
$20,000 Br.—Sharon Hild (Ark)
Own.—Hild Sharon Tr.—Hild Glenn L (9 2 0 0 .22) 1075
Lifetime 1 0 1 0 $4,000 1992 1 M 1 0 $4,000 1991 0 M 0 0

26Mar92- 10P fst 6f :214 :451 1:111 Ⓢ Md Sp Wt 62 11 5 21½ 21 22½ 27 Lovelace A K 120 8.80 76-21 MissonComplt1207Chngsgood1207LttlBoldBlu120 Tired 12
LATEST WORKOUTS Jun 22 Mth 4f fst :494 B Jun 16 Mth 4f fst :482 H Jun 11 Mth 3f fst :363 B

Prospect Singer B. c. 3(Mar), by North Prospect—Morena, by Highbinder
$25,000 Br.—Rahesa Farm Inc (Mn)
Own.—Rahesa Farm Tr.—Romero Jorge E (28 5 3 4 .18) 116
Lifetime 1 0 0 0 $90 1992 1 M 0 0 $90 1991 0 M 0 0
12Jun92- 10Mth fst 6f :213 :451 1:114 3↑Md 22500 39 7 6 32½ 31 85½ 812¼ Romero J A 113 18.40 70-15 ChoicPrz1094¾NorthDkot122½RockyMrcno115 Gave way 11
LATEST WORKOUTS Jun 20 Mth 4f my :51 B Jun 9 Mth 3f fst :362 B May 30 Mth 3f fst :371 Bg May 23 Mth 3f fst :364 B

North Dakota B. c. 4, by Cox's Ridge—Desert Chill, by Damascus
$25,000 Br.—Ryehill Farm (Md)
Own.—OverbrookFarm-SugarMpleFrm Tr.—Lukas D Wayne (16 1 4 1 .06) 122
Lifetime 2 0 1 0 $1,710 1992 2 M 1 0 $1,710 1990 0 M 0 0
12Jun92- 10Mth fst 6f :213 :451 1:114 3↑Md 25000 58 8 10 42¾ 41¼ 3nk 24¾ Bravo J L 122 *2.00 77-15 ChoicPriz1094¾NorthDkot122½RockyMrcno115 Good try 11
9Apr92- 5OP fst 6f :211 :451 1:112 3↑Md Sp Wt 49 4 8 76¾ 78¼ 912 913¼ Guillory D L 120 *2.20 69-20 Wht'sthPnch1144PlcKt1202OldTmStn120 Clipped heels 12
LATEST WORKOUTS Jun 26 Mth 4f fst :493 B Jun 7 Mth 4f fst :48 B May 25 Mth 5f fst 1:032 B May 19 Mth 5f fst 1:012 B

All Desire B. c. 4, by Au Point—Am Desireable, by Red Monk
$20,000 Br.—Pemstein Rachel & Troncone (Ky)
Own.—Troncone Richard J Tr.—Forbes John H (56 6 4 11 .11) 118
Lifetime 8 0 2 2 $15,200 1992 5 M 2 0 $12,000 1991 3 M 0 2 $3,200 Turf 1 0 0 0 $1,560 Wet 2 0 1 0 $6,720
23Jun92- 7Mth fst 6f :22 :453 1:113 3↑Md Sp Wt 70 6 3 55¾ 43 22½ 2½ Krone J A Lb 122 3.10 82-16 Heff110½AllDesire122¾CumberlndBlues115 Drfd out late 10
14Jun92- 1Mth fst 6f :22 :443 1:102 3↑Md Sp Wt 72 3 6 42 43½ 43 42½ Bravo J L 122 3.50 86-11 DnNZc1152½PecRoyl115nkTwntyTwoNGon115 Mild gain 8
25May92- 6Bel fm 1 Ⓣ :45 1:09 1:344 3↑Md Sp Wt 65 5 3 33 35 46½ 48¼ McMahon H I7 117 10.70 80-14 ThQun'sPrinc115¾CollnsCrt1155RtBuck115 Lacked rally 12
10May92- 7Bel sly 6f :221 :453 1:103 3↑Md Sp Wt 70 7 3 32½ 31½ 22½ 44¼ Krone J A 124 3.10 83-12 StrtFght1083¼Wdmn'sDn1151CrrdIntrst115 Lacked rally 8
17Apr92- 4Aqu sly 6f :222 :46 1:104 3↑Md Sp Wt 63 1 4 1½ 1hd 2½ 22½ Smith M E 124 4.30 84-13 Renimte1192½AllDesir1243RunwyStorm115 Second best 5
2Jly91- 6Mth fst 6f :221 :46 1:114 3↑Md Sp Wt 69 6 3 53 51¼ 2hd 32 Marquez C H Jr 116 7.30 80-19 SmokeyO.116noImpropriety1162AllDesir116 Blocked 1/4 7
15Feb91- 9Aqu fst 6f ⊡:224 :472 1:14 Md 35000 60 11 7 105½ 42¾ 43½ 3¾ Krone J A 122 13.40 72-20 LikeItorLeveIt122½YukonMn118nkAllDesir122 Five wide 12
8Feb91- 2Aqu fst 6f ⊡:224 :471 1:112 Md 35000 42 4 9 99¼ 65½ 512 513¼ Krone J A 122 8.80 73-13 CoolBu1229½FlinRight1182CommndNorth118 Four wide 10
LATEST WORKOUTS Jun 9 Mth 5f fst 1:02 B May 21 Bel 5f fst 1:02 B May 7 Bel tr.t 4f fst :514 B

Namascus Ch. g. 3(Apr), by Naskra—Syrian Circle, by Damascus
$25,000 Br.—Hurstland Farm (Ky)
Own.—Candy Stables Tr.—Perkins Ben W Jr (24 5 5 5 .21) 116
Lifetime 0 0 0 0 1992 0 M 0 0 1991 0 M 0 0
LATEST WORKOUTS Jun 23 Mth 3f fst :362 Bg Jun 13 Mth 5f fst 1:024 Bg Jun 8 Mth 5f fst 1:023 B Jun 3 Mth 5f fst 1:021 B

Courtesy of Daily Racing Form ©

Mr. J. J. Jr., showed nothing in his first start and was not expected to by his final odds in that race of 79-1. His workouts going into that race were not good and he has not worked since then.

B.B. Wild is a four-year-old colt that has not raced since 1990. He has had a lot of money invested in him during that period. Obviously, he was injured in his last race and is now ready to make his third start. Is he ready? His races in 1990 show his ability to run well. If he could run as well as he did in those efforts he should be right in the hunt. To evaluate the condition of B.B. Wild we have to look at his most current workouts. He has only one at Aqueduct on June 19, three furlongs in a swift 36³/5 handily. When we look up his workout on the "Latest Workouts" sheet we find that he has received a "Black Type Comment" from the Daily Racing Form's Clockers. B.B. Wild (3f) "is razor sharp." This comment tells us that he is conditioned, in form, and ready to go.

Cipi is a three-year-old colt that has slow and inconsistent workouts. He does not look to be too much of a threat here. Also, the fact that Luis Collazo has the mount secures our gauge on this colt. Pat Bottazzi never uses this jockey and usually uses a top-rated jockey when he knows he has a decent animal.

Changeisgood is another shipper, like B.B. Wild, who has a good performance in his only start. But there are a few drawbacks to this colt, although he is going to draw money because of his second place finish. First, the colt who beat Changeisgood is now racing in claiming $5,000 races in Arkansas. Second, his finishing time of 1:12⁴/5 will not get it done today. Third, his workouts are consistent but not impressive. An in-the-money finish would not be surprising. He is a good bet in the gimmicks.

Prospect Singer tired in his only start this year and has come back with a slow workout in preparation for his second start. He will not be a factor.

North Dakota is a four-year-old that ran a good second in the second start of his career in 1:12⁴/5. He has a top-notch trainer and jockey and has been well-backed by the public. He has very good breeding and would be a major threat for B.B. Wild if his latest workout on June 26 was not so slow. Also, he must improve on his past time of 1:12⁴/5.

All Desire could not be selected for top spot because of his number of starts. He would be a good play in the gimmicks.

Namascus has very good breeding and good workouts, but if he is so good, why is he in a claiming race? If Ben Perkins thought anything of this animal he would be in a Maiden Special Weight contest.

Changeisgood set the pace but could not hold off the late stretch running B.B. Wild. B.B. Wild settled into fifth gear in front of 6-5 favorite All Desire and outkicked the favorite to the wire. Namascus, who went off at odds of 7-2, drew all the sucker money. It is a well known fact at Monmouth Park that Ben Perkins is very good with maidens and he was using his top jockey, Rick Wilson. Yet, as I mentioned above, if this maiden was any good he would be in a Maiden Special Weight event.

FIRST RACE 6 FURLONGS. (1.08) MAIDEN CLAIMING. Purse $9,000. 3–year–olds and upward.
Monmouth
Weight, 3–year–olds, 116 lbs. Older, 122 lbs. Claiming price $25,000; for each $2,500 to $20,000 allowed, 2 lbs. (25TH DAY. WEATHER CLOUDY. TEMPERATURE 84 DEGREES).

JULY 1, 1992

Value of race $9,000; value to winner $5,400; second $1,800; third $990; fourth $450; balance of starters $90 each. Mutuel pool $36,775. Exacta Pool $54,768

Last Raced	Horse	M/Eqt.A.Wt	PP St	¼	½	Str	Fin	Jockey	Cl'g Pr	Odds $1
5Jun90 2Pim3	B.B. Wild	b 4 122	2 8	51½	5½	4½	1½	MrquezCHJrt	25000	8.00
26Mar92 10P2	Changeisgood	3 107	4 4	1hd	1hd	1½	2no	Ybarra R E5	20000	6.70
23Jun92 7Mth2	All Desire	Lb 4 118	7 2	61½	66	3hd	31	Gryder A T	20000	1.20
12Jun92 10Mth8	Prospect Singer	L 3 116	5 3	2hd	2½	2hd	42½	Romero J A	25000	19.50
23Jun92 7Mth7	Mr. J. J. Jr.	3 116	1 6	31	3hd	54½	510½	Picon J	25000	16.30
	Namascus	b 3 116	8 1	76	78	79	67	Wilson R	25000	3.80
12Jun92 10Mth2	North Dakota	L 4 122	6 5	4hd	4hd	64	77½	Bravo J	25000	4.60
	Cipi	3 112	3 7	8	8	8	8	Collazo L	20000	26.10

OFF AT 1:06 Start good, Won driving. Time, :221, :451, :581, 1:12 Track fast.

Official Program Numbers

$2 Mutuel Prices:

2–B.B. WILD	18.00	8.40	4.20
4–CHANGEISGOOD		7.40	3.40
7–ALL DESIRE			2.60

$2 EXACTA 2–4 PAID $115.40

B. c, by Wild Again—Beer and Bananas, by Nostrum. Trainer Meyer Jerome C. Bred by Kustee Mr–Mrs & Reynolds Mr–Mrs (Ky).

B.B. WILD steadied off heels nearing the turn, moved between foes in upper stretch, bumped with PROSPECT SINGER then finished gamely to prevail. CHANGEISGOOD held a narrow edge into the lane while between foes and held on gamely. ALL DESIRE, six wide into the stretch, loomed boldly a furlong out then hung in the closing stages. PROSPECT SINGER pressed the pace into the lane, was bumped in midstretch and tired late. MR. J. J. JR. saved ground and tired in the drive. NAMASCUS lacked a response. NORTH DAKOTA advanced outside nearing the quarter pole, and gave way in upper stretch and was not urged late.

Owners— 1, Buntain Derek H L; 2, Hild Sharon; 3, Troncone Richard J; 4, Rahesa Farm; 5, Turvan Stable; 6, Candy Stables; 7, Overbrook Farm-Sugar Maple Farm; 8, Bottazzo Patrick L-Mizrahi Ralph M.

Trainers— 1, Meyer Jerome C; 2, Hild Glenn L; 3, Forbes John H; 4, Romero Jorge E; 5, Fisher John L; 6, Perkins Ben W Jr; 7, Lukas D Wayne; 8, Bottazzi Patrick L.

† Apprentice allowance waived: B.B. Wild 5 pounds.

Courtesy of Daily Racing Form ©

The tenth race at Monmouth Park featured eleven maidens, nine of which were first time starters, going five furlongs. The conditions were two-year-olds, Maiden Special Weight with a purse of $15,500.

Smart money knows! This is especially true with first time starters. In most maiden races, the favorite will be a horse with many starts under his belt that seems to always come close. When first time starters are bet down heavily it's usually due to one of two reasons. First, a horse has a lot of obvious talent through his workouts. Second, a horse has been tipped around the track. It might not show much, but smart money knows about this maiden. Great Navigator was at odds of 8-1 in the program. When betting opened on the 10th race this two-year-old opened at 3-2. Great Navigator had consistent workouts, with the last two being better that the first, but the word was obviously out about this son of Gulch.

5 FURLONGS. (.56¹) MAIDEN SPECIAL WEIGHT. Purse $15,500. 2–year–olds, weights, 118 lbs.

Coupled—Wasiota and Gerson.

Thriller Chiller
B. c. 2(Apr), by Copelan—Elegant Exit, by Bailjumper
Br.—Allor Fred Michael (Ky)
Tr.—Velez Roberto (1 0 0 1 .00)
Lifetime 0 0 0 0 — 1992 0 M 0 0 — **118**
Own.—Canonie Anthony C
LATEST WORKOUTS Jun 26 Mth 4f fst :48⁴ B — Jun 19 Mth 5f fst 1:02 B — Jun 11 Mth 5f fst 1:03 B — Jun 4 Mth 4f fst :49 B

Russian Freedom
B. g. 2(Mar), by Sir Jinsky—Russian Night, by Czar Alexander
Br.—Bailey Richard E (Ky)
Tr.—Huston Sharon T (4 0 0 1 .00)
Lifetime 0 0 0 0 — 1992 0 M 0 0 — **113⁵**
Own.—Bailey Patricia K
LATEST WORKOUTS Jun 22 Mth 4f fst :50 B — May 26 Mth 5f fst 1:02⁴ Bg — May 19 Mth 4f fst :49¹ B — May 13 Mth 4f fst :49 B

What's It's Face
B. c. 2(Mar), by Lucky North—More Hilarious, by Fast Hilarious
Br.—John Franks (Fla)
Tr.—Vincitore Michael J (12 0 2 2 .00)
Lifetime 0 0 0 0 — 1992 0 M 0 0 — **118**
Own.—Mele Louie
LATEST WORKOUTS Jun 26 Mth 4f fst :50 B — Jun 19 Mth 3f fst :35 H — Jun 13 Mth 5f fst 1:02⁴ B — Jun 7 Mth 4f fst :48³ H

Strand of Blue
Gr. c. 2(Mar), by Blue Ensign—Strand of Gems, by Accipiter
Br.—Francis W. Lucas (Fla)
Tr.—Perkins Ben W Jr (24 5 5 5 .21)
Lifetime 0 0 0 0 — 1992 0 M - 0 0 — **118**
Own.—Char–Mari Stable
LATEST WORKOUTS ●Jun 27 Mth 4f fst :47¹ Hg — Jun 22 Mth 4f fst :50 B — Jun 17 Mth 4f fst :48⁴ B — Jun 2 Mth 3f my :36¹ Bg

Great Navigator
B. c. 2(Mar), by Gulch—Nonoalca, by Nonoalco
Br.—Foxfield (Ky)
Tr.—Mazza John F (26 3 2 4 .12)
Lifetime 0 0 0 0 — 1992 0 M 0 0 — **118**
Own.—Roron Stables
LATEST WORKOUTS Jun 27 Mth 5f fst 1:00² H — Jun 21 Mth 5f fst 1:00² Hg — Jun 16 Mth 4f fst :49 Bg — Jun 10 Mth 4f fst :48³ H

Ultimate Luck
B. c. 2(Mar), by Lucky North—Steel Penny Black, by Cutlass
Br.—John Franks (Fla)
Tr.—Serpe Philip M (27 6 5 5 .22)
Lifetime 0 0 0 0 — 1992 0 M 0 0 — **118**
Own.—Vermeire Albert
LATEST WORKOUTS ●Jun 24 Mth 4f fst :48 H — Jun 13 Mth 4f fst :48¹ Bg — ●Jun 7 Mth 3f fst :34³ H — May 13 Mth 5f fst 1:03⁴ B

Northern Witness
Dk. b. or br. g. 2(Feb), by Ankara—Silent Times, by Silent Screen
Br.—Starsfell Farms Inc (Fla)
Tr.—Thrasher Clint D (10 2 1 0 .20)
Lifetime 0 0 0 0 — 1992 0 M 0 0 — **118**
Own.—Asper Grant Stable
LATEST WORKOUTS Jun 23 Mth 4f fst :52 B — Jun 10 Mth 4f fst :48⁴ H

Rajab's Promise
Ch. c. 2(Apr), by Rajab—Gettin' There, by Promised Land
Br.—Howell Bill & Sandra (Fla)
Tr.—Dowd John F (13 1 3 3 .08)
Lifetime 1 0 0 0 $50 — 1992 1 M 0 0 — **118**
Own.—Hemlock Cottage
Entered 30Jun92- 4 M I H
19Jun92- 5Atl fst 4½f :23 :47 :53³ Md 20000 7 4 2 42 58½ 811½ Sousonis S 118 1.50 82-17 Picalow118⁵¼NativeTongue118¹WrighttKnight118 Tired 8
LATEST WORKOUTS Jun 17 Mth 3f fst :37 Bg — ●May 18 GS 3f fst :37 B — May 11 GS 3f gd :39⁴ B

Wasiota
B. c. 2(Mar), by Tyrant—Connemara Miss, by L'Enjoleur
Br.—Eugene Goss (Ky)
Tr.—Griffitt D Hal (2 0 1 1 .00)
Lifetime 0 0 0 0 — 1992 0 M 0 0 — **118**
Own.—Goss Eugene
LATEST WORKOUTS Jun 23 Mth 5f fst 1:01 H — Jun 16 Mth 4f fst :48 Hg — Jun 10 Mth 3f fst :35³ Hg — Jun 5 Mth 3f fst :35⁴ B

Gerson
B. c. 2(Mar), by Play On—White Hot, by Whitesburg
Br.—William G. Munn (Pa)
Tr.—Griffitt D Hal (2 0 1 1 .00)
Lifetime 0 0 0 0 — 1992 0 M 0 0 — **118**
Own.—Munn William G

LATEST WORKOUTS   Jun 10 Mth   3f fst :36   B   ● Jun 5 Mth   3f fst :35¹ H

No Stalling

               B. c. 2(Mar), by Groovy—Reason to Please, by Boldnesian

Own.—Krakower Lawrence J

               Br.—Loradale & Racing Investment Corp. (Ky)

               Tr.—Taylor Ronald J (9 1 1 1 .11)   **118**

Lifetime   1992   1   M   0   1 $1,485
   1   0   0   1
    $1,485

22Jun92- 4Pha fst 5f   :22³   :47¹ 1:00²   Md Sp Wt   42   6   2   2½   2½   2nd 3¹   Gryder A T   118   *1.30   79–21 UlyssesKnight118¼Arrolink118¼NoStlling118   Weakened 8

LATEST WORKOUTS   ● Jun 14 Mth   4f fst :48   Hg   Jun 10 Mth   5f fst 1:01⁴ Hg   Jun 5 Mth   4f fst :48³ Hg

Carnival Knight

               Dk. b. or br. c. 2(Apr), by Carnivalay—Codette, by Codex

Own.—Armbrister Carl D

               Br.—Ivy Dell Stud (Pa)

               Tr.—Armbrister Carl D (—)   **118**

Lifetime   1992   0   M   0   0
   0   0   0   0

LATEST WORKOUTS   Jun 27 Atl   3f fst :35³ H   ● Jun 19 Atl   5f fst 1:01   Hg   Jun 13 Atl   5f fst 1:01³ Bg   Jun 9 Atl   4f fst :50³ B

10

MAIDEN
PURSE $15,500

START↓
5 Furlongs
↑FINISH

FOR MAIDEN TWO-YEAR-OLDS. Weight: 118 lbs.

↓ **MAKE SELECTION BY PROGRAM NUMBER**

PP	OWNER / TRAINER		HORSE	WT	JOCKEY	MORNING LINE
PP-9	EUGENE GOSS	D. H. GRIFFITT				8
	Blue, White "MP", Blue Cap				HEBERTO	
	1 **WASIOTA**			118	CASTILLO, JR.	
	B. c.'90, Tyrant-Connemara Miss, by L' Enjoleur					
PP-10	WILLIAM G. MUNN	D. H. GRIFFITT				8
	Blue, Yellow Sash, Blue Chevrons on Yellow Sleeves, Blue Cap				HEBERTO	
	1A **GERSON**			118	CASTILLO, JR.	
	Dk.b/br. c.'90, Play On-White Hot, by Whitesburg					
PP-1	ANTHONY C. CANONIE	R. VELEZ				10
	Hot Pink, Pink "TC" on White Ball, Pink Chevrons on White Sleeves, Pink Cap				C. H.	
	2 **THRILLER CHILLER**			118	MARQUEZ, JR.	
	B. c.'90, Copelan-Elegant Exit, by Bailjumper					
PP-2	PATRICIA K. BAILEY	SHARON T. HUSTON				12
	Yellow, Purple Braces, Purple Emblem In Shield, Purple Bars on Sleeves, Yellow Cap				ROSEMARY	
	3 **RUSSIAN FREEDOM**			*113	HOMEISTER	
	B. g.'90, Sir Jinsky-Russian Night, by Czar Alexander					
PP-3	LOUIS MELE	M. VINCITORE				12
	Purple, Gold "D", Purple and Gold Cap				FRANK	
	4 **WHAT'S IT'S FACE**			118	LOVATO, JR.	
	B. c.'90, Lucky North-More Hilarious, by Fast Hilarious					
PP-4	CHAR-MARI STABLE	B. W. PERKINS, JR.				9/2
	Light Blue, Dark Blue "CM" and Braces, Light Blue and Dark Blue Halved Sleeves, Blue Cap				RICK	
	5 **STRAND OF BLUE**			118	WILSON	
	Gr. c.'90, Blue Ensign-Strand Of Gems, by Accipiter					
PP-5	RORON STABLES	J. F. MAZZA				8
	Blue, Blue "R" on Pink Block, Pink Sleeves, Pink Cap				AARON T.	
	6 **GREAT NAVIGATOR**			118	GRYDER	
	B. c.'90, Gulch-Nonoalca, by Nonoalco					
PP-6	ALBERT VERMEIRE	P. M. SERPE				6
	Red, Blue Star, Blue Chevrons on Sleeves, Red Cap				JOSE C.	
	7 **ULTIMATE LUCK**			118	FERRER	
	B. c.'90, Lucky North-Steel Penny Black, by Cutlass					

PP-7	ASPERGRANT STABLE	C. D. THRASHER	12
	Red, White "A", White Chevrons on Sleeves, Red Cap		ROBERT
8	**NORTHERN WITNESS**	118	MCKNIGHT
	Dk.b/br. g.'90, Ankara-Silent Times, by Silent Screen		
PP-8	HEMLOCK COTTAGE	J. F. DOWD	20
	Black, Yellow Diamonds, Red Bars on Sleeves, Black Cap		STEVE
9	**RAJAB'S PROMISE**	118	SOUSONIS
	Ch. c.'90, Rajab-Gettin' There, by Promised Land		
PP-11	LAWRENCE J. KRAKOWER	R. J. TAYLOR	5/2
	Black, Turquoise Dots, Turquoise Sleeves, Black Cap		JUAN
10	**NO STALLING**	118	PICON
	B. c.'90, Groovy-Reason To Please, by Boldnesian		
PP-12	CARL D. ARMBRISTER	OWNER	10
	White, Black Spades, Black Spades on Sleeves, White Cap		EMILIO
11	**CARNIVAL KNIGHT**	118	RODRIGUEZ
	Dk.b/br. c.'90, Carnivalay-Codette, by Codex		

* 5 Lbs. Apprentice Allowance
1 - 1A - Eugene Goss - William G. Munn - entry
Equipment Change: (BLINKERS ON) NO STALLING

PROBABLE FAVORITES 10 - 5 - 7

The morning line favorite was No Stalling. This Kentucky bred made his first start at Philadelphia Park. Aaron Gryder was aboard the colt in this start. He cut slow fractions and still tired. Aaron Gryder got off of No Stalling and switched to Great Navigator.

Northern Witness and Strand of Blue were second and third choices. They both had decent workouts and breeding and deserved to be used in the gimmicks.

Great Navigator took the lead at the half and drew off to an eight length victory in 57³/₅ paying $5.80.

TENTH RACE 5 FURLONGS. (.56¹) MAIDEN SPECIAL WEIGHT. Purse $15,500. 2-year-olds,

Monmouth weights, 118 lbs.

JULY 1, 1992
Value of race $15,500; value to winner $9,300; second $2,945; third $1,550; fourth $620; balance of starters $155 each.
Mutuel pool $73,065. Exacta Pool $65,590 Trifecta Pool $92,258

Last Raced	Horse	M/Eqt.A.Wt	PP St	⅟₁₆	¾	Str	Fin	Jockey	Odds $1
	Great Navigator	2 118	5 1	12½	13	16½	1⁸	Gryder A T	1.90
	Strand of Blue	2 118	4 7	31	3½	32½	2²	Wilson R	3.50
	Northern Witness	2 118	7 2	5²	52½	4¹	31½	McKnight R E	2.40
	Wasiota	2 118	9 4	6½	6½	5ʰᵈ	41½	Castillo H Jr	47.30
22Jun92 ⁴Pha³	No Stalling	b 2 118	10 3	2²	2²	2ʰᵈ	5½	Picon J	10.60
	What's It's Face	2 118	3 9	7²	72½	7²	6ⁿᵏ	Lovato F Jr	16.10
	Thriller Chiller	b 2 118	1 11	94½	8⁵	8⁸	72½	Marquez C H Jr	13.40
	Ultimate Luck	2 118	6 6	4½	42½	6²	89½	Ferrer J C	13.10
	Russian Freedom	2 113	2 10	10¹	10²	9½	9²	Homeister R BJr⁵	61.00
	Carnival Knight	b 2 118	11 8	8¹	9¹	10³	10²	Rodriguez E	39.30
19Jun92 ⁵Atl⁸	Rajab's Promise	2 118	8 5	11	11	11	11	Sousonis S	105.60

OFF AT 5:12 Start good, Won easily Time, :22 , :45² , :57³ Track fast.

$2 Mutuel Prices:

6—GREAT NAVIGATOR	———————	5.80	4.40	3.40
5—STRAND OF BLUE	———————		4.60	3.20
8—NORTHERN WITNESS	———————			3.80

$2 EXACTA 6–5 PAID $23.20 $2 TRIFECTA 6–5–8 PAID $119.00

B. c, (Mar), by Gulch—Nonoalca, by Nonoalco. Trainer Mazza John F. Bred by Foxfield (Ky).

GREAT NAVIGATOR quickly drew clear, was rated on the lead to the lane then gradually widened while well within himself. STRAND OF BLUE, outside into the lane, earned the place. NORTHERN WITNESS, well out in the strip into the stretch, offered a belated gain. WASIOTA was gaining some ground at the end. NO STALLING chased the winner into the lane and tired in the drive. WHAT'S IT'S FACE saved ground on the turn and lacked a bid. THRILLER CHILLER lacked the needed rally. ULTIMATE LUCK, bothered some at the start, saved ground on the turn and tired. RAJAB'S PROMISE broke through the gate and unseated the rider then was no threat.

Owners— 1, Roron Stables; 2, Char-Mari Stable; 3, Asper Grant Stable; 4, Goss Eugene; 5, Krakower Lawrence J; 6, Mele Louie; 7, Canonie Anthony C; 8, Vermeire Albert; 9, Bailey Patricia K; 10, Armbrister Carl D; 11, Hemlock Cottage.

Trainers— 1, Mazza John F; 2, Perkins Ben W Jr; 3, Thrasher Clint D; 4, Griffitt D H; 5, Taylor Ronald J; 6, Vincitore Michael J; 7, Velez Roberto; 8, Serpe Philip M; 9, Huston Sharon T; 10, Armbrister Carl D; 11, Dowd John F.

Scratched—Gerson.

Courtesy of Daily Racing Form ©

Don't be scared of odds! If a long shot on the morning line is bet down in the first couple of minutes, do not be turned off if his odds go up. More than likely this early money is money from the connections tied to the animal.

In the following example, the emphasis is placed on checking for Black Type comments on the "Latest Workout" sheet.

This Maiden Special Weight contest was at five furlongs with seven going on a rain soaked surface at Monmouth Park. When we are blessed with an "off" track, we must check every horse's bloodlines to ensure that he will like an imperfect surface.

3

5 FURLONGS. (.56¹) MAIDEN SPECIAL WEIGHT. Purse $15,500. 2–year–olds. Weight 118 lbs.

Proofs Echo

Ch. c. 2(Apr), by Proof—Sweet Echo, by Stiff Sentence

Br.—Ljoka Daniel J (NJ)

Own.—Outlaw Biker Stable

Tr.—Serey Juan (2 0 1 0 .00)   **118**

LATEST WORKOUTS   Jun 2 Mth 3f my :36 B   May 26 Mth 4f fst :52 B   May 19 GS 4f fst :50 Bg

Lifetime   1992   0 M   0   0

0 0 0 0

Ragucci Clan

B. c. 2(Mar), by Slew O Gold—River Sue, by Riverman

Br.—Elmendorf Farm Inc (Ky)

Own.—Martucci William C

Tr.—Crupi James J (7 1 1 2 .14)   **1135**

LATEST WORKOUTS   May 30 Mth 5f fst 1:02² B   May 23 Mth 4f fst :48⁴ Bg

Lifetime   1992   0 M   0   0

0 0 0 0

Storm Tower

B. c. 2(Mar), by Irish Tower—Storm Doll, by Storm Bird

Lifetime   1992   0 M   0   0

0 0 0 0

```
                              Br.—Parrish Hill Farm (Ky)
Own.—Char-Mari Stable         Tr.—Perkins Ben W Jr (8 2 2 2 .25)          118
LATEST WORKOUTS    Jun 2 Mth  3f my  :36¹ Bg
```

Nickieman

```
                              Ch. g. 2(Jan), by Shananie—Carolyn's Charm, by Inverness Drive    Lifetime    1992  1 M  0  0
                              Br.—Campbell Gilbert G                                            1 0 0 0
Own.—Campbell Gilbert G       Tr.—Allard Edward T (2 0 2 0 .00)                      118
16May92-10Suf fst  5f  :22³   :46³  :59³   Paul Revere  —0 8 10 55½ 6¹¹ 6¹⁴ 723¾ Vargas J L    b 114  7.90  76–16 DncsWthFr116½ErthsF114¾DAccrdrss119  Hesitated brk 10
LATEST WORKOUTS    May 27 Suf  4f fst :51² Hg        May 13 Suf  3f fst :37  Hg     May 11 Suf  4f fst :49³ Hg      ●Apr 27 Suf  3f my  :36¹ H
```

Papaskids

```
                              B. c. 2(Apr), by Silver Supreme—Re Re's Gala, by Gala Harry       Lifetime    1992  0 M  0  0
                              Br.—Steve Atkins (NJ)                                             0 0 0 0
Own.—Atkins Steven            Tr.—Jolin Louis F (2 0 1 0 .00)                        118
LATEST WORKOUTS    May 22 GS  4f fst :50² Bg         May 16 GS  4f my :50² Bg        May 12 GS  4f fst :51² B
```

Chief John

```
                              Ch. g. 2(Jan), by To America—Dancing Frog, by Sibelius II         Lifetime    1992  0 M  0  0
                              Br.—Dollinger Susan & Dowd Virginia M (NJ)                        0 0 0 0
Own.—Maple Crest Farm         Tr.—Dowd John F (0 0 0 0 .00)                          118
LATEST WORKOUTS    May 30 Mth  4f fst :49¹ B         May 23 Mth  5f fst 1:02³ B      May 17 GS  4f my :48  Hg       May 10 GS  4f sly :49¹ Bg
```

Armagh County

```
                              Dk. b. or br. g. 2(Mar), by Distinctive Pro—Black Bess, by Riverman   Lifetime  1992  0 M  0  0
                              Br.—Lusararian Inc (Fla)                                          0 0 0 0
Own.—Equity Horse Farm        Tr.—Thrasher Clint D (1 0 0 0 .00)                     118
LATEST WORKOUTS    May 26 Mth  3f fst :37  Bg        ●May 20 Mth  3f fst :35  H
```

Eagles Crest

```
                              B. c. 2(May), by El Raggaas—Fille Ruse, by Lonny's Secret          Lifetime    1992  0 M  0  0
                              Br.—Russo Carmine V (NY)                                          0 0 0 0
Own.—Russo Carmine V          Tr.—Hammond Wilbur C (2 0 1 0 .00)                     113⁵
LATEST WORKOUTS    May 26 Mth  3f fst :39¹ Bg        May 22 Mth  3f fst :37⁴ Bg
```

Saber Three

```
                              Ch. c. 2(May), by Blade—Marlodge, by Tentam                        Lifetime    1992  0 M  0  0
                              Br.—Classic Lines Partnership (Fla)                                0 0 0 0
Own.—Fowler Anderson          Tr.—Raines Virgil W (6 0 1 1 .00)                      118
LATEST WORKOUTS    Jun 2 Mth  3f my :38  B          May 28 Mth  3f fst :37³ Bg       May 19 Mth  4f fst :51³ B      May 13 Mth  3f fst :39¹ B
```

Courtesy of Daily Racing Form ©

Papaskins and Eagles Crest are not playable because of slow workouts and low caliber breeding.

Proofs Echo had two awful workouts on May 19 and 26 but did turn in a nice effort on June 2. This workout was at three furlongs on a muddy track in 36 (breezing). Her breeding hints that she would not like a sloppy track, so she should not be considered.

Ragucci Clan and Chief John both show impressive workouts on the Monmouth Park surface. Both sires also like an "off" track.

Storm Tower teaches a lesson. To the average handicapper it would appear that this two-year-old colt has only one workout. If we looked at the "Latest Workout" sheet in the Racing Form as well as to-day's entries, we find additional workouts for Storm Tower at Bowie race course.

BOWIE – Track Fast

Three Furlongs		Four Furlongs— :46³		Prince Ivy :48³ H		Wild Zone 1:02 H	
AssertiveCounsl	:36⁴ H	Kelly's Class	:47² H	Five Furlongs— :58		Six Furlongs—1:08	
Busy Woman	:38 B	Luramore	:48 H	Crowned 1:00² H		Hooliganisim 1:14³ H	
Silver Tango	:35³ B	Mardeka	:50² B	Semi Explodent 1:01 H		StrlightSurprise 1:15³ H	

SILVER TANGO (3f) is at her best. **KELLY'S CLASS (4f)** was razor sharp. **CROWNED (5f)** appears to be peaking for a top effort. Additional Workout: 5/15 STORM TOWER (3f) fst 36.3hg 5/21 STORM TOWER (4f) fst 49bg 5/28 STORM TOWER (4f) fst 48.3h

Courtesy of Daily Racing Form ©

Storm Tower has workouts on this track because trainer Ben Perkins has a track in Maryland. Sorry, this you just have to know!

THIRD RACE

Monmouth

JUNE 5, 1992

5 FURLONGS. (.56¹) MAIDEN SPECIAL WEIGHT. Purse $15,500. 2-year-olds. Weight, 118 lbs.

Value of race $15,500; value to winner $9,300; second $3,100; third $1,860; fourth $775; balance of starters $155 each. Mutuel pool $45,117. Exacta Pool $66,292 Trifecta Pool $47,419

Last Raced	Horse	M/Eqt.A.Wt	PP	St	¼	¾	Str	Fin	Jockey	Odds $1
	Storm Tower	2 118	3	1	11½	12	13½	17	Wilson R	.50
	Ragucci Clan	2 113	2	7	42½	2ʰᵈ	25	216	Homeister R BJr⁵	5.20
	Chief John	2 118	6	5	5½	54½	41	32	Sousonis S	5.50
16May92¹⁰Suf⁷	Nickieman	b 2 118	4	3	23	35½	34	41½	Rivera L Jr	7.50
	Eagles Crest	2 113	7	4	7	6ʰᵈ	61½	57½	Lopez C E Jr⁵	42.20
	Papaskids	b 2 118	5	2	61	7	7	6ⁿᵏ	Collazo L	37.70
	Proofs Echo	2 118	1	6	3½	41½	52	7	Grabowski J A	9.30

OFF AT 1:58 Start good, Won easily. Time, :22³, :45⁴, :57⁴ Track sloppy.

$2 Mutuel Prices:

3-STORM TOWER	3.00	2.60	2.10
2-RAGUCCI CLAN		3.40	2.40
6-CHIEF JOHN			2.80

$2 EXACTA 3-2 PAID $10.00 $2 TRIFECTA 3-2-6 PAID $18.80

B. c, (Mar), by Irish Tower—Storm Doll, by Storm Bird. Trainer Perkins Ben W Jr. Bred by Parrish Hill Farm (Ky).

STORM TOWER, broke alertly and showed the way to the lane while removed from the rail, responded when asked turning for home and drew off while not being asked through the late stages. RAGUCCI CLAN, slow to find his best stride, advanced rounding the turn and was clearly best. CHIEF JOHN stayed outside and lacked a solid bid. NICKIEMAN, a bit slow to load, broke well and prompted the early issue then tired through the lane. EAGLES CREST, a bit slow to load, was outrun. PAPASKIDS showed little. PROOFS ECHO had little left turning for home. SABER THREE UNSEATED THE RIDER WHILE WARMING UP, RAN OFF AND WAS SCRATCHED WITH REGULAR EXACTA AND TRIFECTA WAGERS BEING ORDERED REFUNDED. HIS PICK THREE SELECTIONS WERE SWITCHED TO THE FAVORITE STORM TOWER. PROOFS ECHO WORE MUD CALKS.

Owners— 1, Char-Mari Stable; 2, Martucci William C; 3, Maple Crest Farm; 4, Campbell Gilbert G; 5, Russo Carmine V; 6, Atkins Steven; 7, Outlaw Biker Stable.

Trainers— 1, Perkins Ben W Jr; 2, Crupi James J; 3, Dowd John F; 4, Allard Edward T; 5, Hammond Wilbur J; 6, Jolin Louis F; 7, Serey Juan.

Scratched—Armagh County; Saber Three.

Courtesy of Daily Racing Form ©

Looking for extra workouts can prove profitable, as it did with Storm Tower. He only brought a win mutual of $3.00 but when we play the exacta with the only other two horses with "off" track breeding we turn a 2-5 shot into a $10.00 exacta or $18.80 trifecta. Two of the main reasons Storm Tower was such a big favorite were his following with Ben Perkins as trainer and his three furlong workout on an "off" track. When handicapping future maiden races with this angle you will often come away with higher payouts.

Great breeding and very good workouts can be deadly for other competitors and profitable for the handicapper who uses the "Latest Workout" sheet. The seventh race offered a Maiden Special Weight contest at five-and-a-half furlongs. This race featured a horse that we looked at previously in this chapter, Strand of Blue.

5 ½ FURLONGS. (1.02⁴) MAIDEN SPECIAL WEIGHT. Purse $15,500. 2-year-olds.
Weight: 118 lbs.

Coupled—Shu Fellow and Super Nip.
LASIX—Inagroove.

Inagroove
Ch. c. 2(May), by Groovy—Rose Of Darby, by Roberto
Br.—Prestonwood Farm (Ky)
Own.—Spina Nicholas   Tr.—Spina Chuck (12 0 1 2 .00)   **118**
Lifetime 1992 0 M 0 0
0 0 0 0
LATEST WORKOUTS   Jly 19 Mth   6f fst 1:14² Bg   Jly 15 Mth   5f fst 1:01³ Hg

Wading Castelli
B. c. 2(Apr), by Leo Castelli—Wading Power, by Balance of Power
Br.—Edwards Robert L (NJ)
Own.—Castelli Stables   Tr.—Anderson William D (31 3 5 1 .10)   **118**
Lifetime 1992 0 M 0 0
0 0 0 0
LATEST WORKOUTS   ●Jly 15 Mth   3f fst :35   H   Jly 10 Mth   5f fst 1:02² Bg   Jly 1 Mth   5f fst 1:03   B   Jun 30 Mth   5f fst 1:06   B

Stately Fighter
Dk. b. or br. c. 2(Apr), by Fit To Fight—Statuesque, by Gay Mecene
Br.—Wakefield Farm (Ky)
Own.—Polin Mrs Charlotte C   Tr.—Forbes John H (101 15 6 18 .15)   **118**
Lifetime 1992 0 M 0 0
0 0 0 0
LATEST WORKOUTS   Jun 29 Mth   4f fst :51   B

Armagh County
Dk. b. or br. g. 2(Mar), by Distinctive Pro—Black Bess, by Riverman
Br.—Lusararian Inc (Fla)
Own.—Equity Horse Farm   Tr.—Thrasher Clint D (18 2 3 1 .11)   **118**
Lifetime 1992 0 M 0 0
0 0 0 0
LATEST WORKOUTS   Jly 17 Mth   4f fst :48³ Bg   Jly 10 Mth   5f fst 1:01¹ H   Jly 2 Mth   4f fst :49   B   Jun 16 Mth   3f fst :36³ B

Strand of Blue
Gr. c. 2(Mar), by Blue Ensign—Strand of Gems, by Accipiter
Br.—Francis W. Lucas (Fla)
Own.—Char-Mari Stable   Tr.—Perkins Ben W Jr (34 6 8 7 .18)   **118**
Lifetime 1992 1 M 1 0 $2,945
1 0 1 0
$2,945
1Jly92-10Mth fst 5f   :22   :45² :57³   Md Sp Wt   70 4 7 34½ 35   Wilson R   118   3.50   85-17 GrtNgtr118⁸StrndfBl118¾NrthrnWtnss118   Earned place 11
LATEST WORKOUTS   Jly 21 Mth   4f fst :50   B   Jly 14 Mth   4f fst :50⁴ B   ●Jun 27 Mth   4f fst :47¹ Hg   Jun 22 Mth   4f fst :50   B

Shu Fellow
B. c. 2(Feb), by Saratoga Six—Video Babe, by T V Commercial
Br.—Red Bull Stable Inc & Eaton Farms (Ky)
Own.—Due Process Stables   Tr.—Nobles Reynaldo H (24 2 4 4 .08)   **118**
Lifetime 1992 0 M 0 0
0 0 0 0
LATEST WORKOUTS   Jly 15 Mth   4f fst :49   Bg   Jly 8 Mth   4f fst :49   Bg   Jly 3 Mth   5f fst 1:02¹ Bg   Jun 28 Mth   4f fst :48³ Bg

Carnival Knight
Dk. b. or br. c. 2(Apr), by Carnivalay—Codette, by Codex
Br.—Ivy Dell Stud (Pa)
Own.—Armbrister Carl D   Tr.—Armbrister Carl D (1 0 0 0 .00)   **118**
Lifetime 1992 2 M 1 0 $1,485
2 0 1 0
$1,485
10Jly92- 1Atl fst 5½f   :22³   :47³ 1:07¹   Md Sp Wt   30 1 4 2² 3¹ 1½ 2¾ Rodriguez E   b 118   19.50   80-14 KickthTr118¾CrnvlKnght118¾¾QuckScootr118   Bid tired 10
1Jly92-10Mth fst 5f   :22   :45² :57³   Md Sp Wt   12 11 8 8¹¹ 9¹⁹10²³10²⁶¼ Rodriguez E   b 118   39.30   66-17 GrtNvgtor118⁸StrndofBlu118¾NorthrnWtnss118   Outrun 11
LATEST WORKOUTS   ●Jly 21 Atl   3f fst :35² H   Jun 27 Atl   3f fst :35³ H   ●Jun 19 Atl   5f fst 1:01   Hg   Jun 13 Atl   5f fst 1:01³ By

Carnival Knight could be played because of the two-to-three start theory.

Wading Castelli, Stately Fighter, Strike Commander, Major Manila, and Super Nip all have awful workouts and no breeding. They are not playable for those reasons. Strand of Blue would be the top choice because of a decent performance against Great Navigator, but he has had two horrible workouts since that race and should be used only in the gimmicks. Tricky Catman also has one start but he faced weaker competition in Atlantic City and should not be effective here.

This left two major competitors: Armagh County and Inagroove. Armagh County had decent workouts but was a little inconsistent from June 16 to July 2. Consider his breeding, however, and he is better than anything else in this race and should be used under Inagroove in the gimmicks. Inagroove has very good breeding, a top jockey and two very good workouts. He was the better of the two on July 10 at six furlongs in 1:14⁴/₅ breezing. Some of these horses could not run six furlongs in 1:14. Inagroove is working out in this time. Also, when horses work out at greater distances than they are running, fitness is not a problem.

MONMOUTH PARK – Track Fast

Three Furlongs		Four Furlongs		Five Furlongs— :56¹		Six Furlongs—1:08	
		VimndVigorous	:36² B	Quick Flick	:49² B	Maston	1:01³ H
Alaskan Frost	:40 B	**Four Furlongs**		S. I. Ritz	:50 Bg	Musical Lights	1:02³ Bg
Calling for Rain	:36² B	Arlene'sVlentine	:52 B	Seaside Appeal	:48 H	Party Secret's	1:04 B
Crimson Cry	:35 B	Back Nine	:50 Bg	Sofgne	:51 B	PrestigiousDncr	1:04 B
DecidedPlesure	:38 B	Chill Factor	:49 B	Sunflower Field	:52 B	**Princess I. R. A.**	1:00² Hg
Entrotski	:36³ Bg	Coastal Caress	:49 B	Tommy Halo	:50 Bg	Serefe	1:04² B
Fishy Business	:36⁴ B	Deador's Pine	:48² H	**Five Furlongs— :56¹**			
Git Western	:38¹ B	Eager Salute	:49 B	Andover Square	1:07 B	**Six Furlongs—1:08**	
Last Capade	:38 B	Gallant Amber	:48¹ Hg	Angel Us	1:03 B	**Fatal Beauty**	1:13² H
Lockenbridge	:36² B	Grand Betty	:49³ B	Caroselambra	1:07 B	In the Groove	1:14² Hg
One Reality	:39 B	Onery Julie	:49 B	ChristmsVirgini	1:02⁴ B	Into the Woods	1:18 B
So Long Waj	:37² B	**Out for Gold**	:47² H	Denison	1:02 Bg	Iron n' Silk	1:15 Bg
Takeanip	:36² H	Patty L.	:48 H	Kay Oh Kat	1:02⁴ B	Jav'sGoldenGirl	1:16 Bg
TsunamiSpngler	:35² Hg	PeppermintLne	:50 B	Lively Oak	1:02¹ H	Steven Frost	1:15 Bg

PATTY L. (4F) appears sharp. PRINCESS I.R.A. (5F) went well with blinkers. IN THE GROOVE (6F) continues to train well.

Courtesy of Daily Racing Form ©

When we look up this workout on July 19 we see that Inagroove has been given a Black Type comment: "Inagroove continues to train well." This comment tells us that Inagroove is fit and ready to dominate this field.

SEVENTH RACE Monmouth — 5 ½ FURLONGS. (1.02^{4}) MAIDEN SPECIAL WEIGHT. Purse $15,500. 2-year-olds. Weight: 118 lbs.

JULY 24, 1992

Value of race $15,500; value to winner $9,300; second $2,945; third $1,705; fourth $620; balance of starters $155 each. Mutuel pool $78,688. Exacta Pool $85,266 Trifecta Pool $97,746

Last Raced	Horse	M/Eqt.	A.	Wt	PP	St	¼	⅜	Str	Fin	Jockey	Odds $1
	Inagroove	Lb	2	118	1	8	3^{2}	3^{3}	$2\frac{1}{2}$	$1\frac{3}{4}$	Marquez C H Jr	7.80
	Armagh County		2	118	4	4	1^{hd}	$1\frac{1}{2}$	$1\frac{1}{2}$	$2^{1\frac{1}{2}}$	Vega A	2.20
1Jly92^{10}Mth^{2}	Strand of Blue		2	118	5	7	$4^{1\frac{1}{2}}$	4^{5}	3^{hd}	$3^{1\frac{3}{4}}$	Wilson R	1.80
	Major Manila	Lb	2	118	9	1	8^{2}	$7\frac{1}{2}$	$5\frac{1}{2}$	4^{nk}	Purdom M D	22.10
28Jun92 ^{1}Atl^{2}	Tricky Catman		2	118	8	2	2^{2}	2^{2}	$4^{5\frac{1}{2}}$	$5\frac{3}{4}$	Gryder A T	7.40
	Super Nip		2	118	10	5	6^{3}	$6\frac{1}{2}$	6^{1}	$6^{2\frac{1}{4}}$	Santagata N	6.20
10Jly92 ^{1}Atl^{2}	Carnival Knight	b	2	118	6	3	$5\frac{1}{2}$	5^{2}	7^{3}	7^{2}	McCormick M L	43.60
	Wading Castelli		2	118	2	9	$9\frac{1}{2}$	10	8^{2}	$8^{2\frac{1}{2}}$	Romero J A	12.20
	Stately Fighter		2	118	3	10	10	9^{hd}	9^{hd}	$9^{3\frac{1}{2}}$	Lidberg D W	35.50
	Strike Commander	b	2	118	7	6	$7\frac{1}{2}$	8^{3}	10	10	Picon J	67.50

OFF AT 3:51 Start good, Won driving. Time, :22^{1}, :46^{1}, 1:06^{1} Track fast.

$2 Mutuel Prices:			
1-INAGROOVE	17.60	8.60	4.40
4-ARMAGH COUNTY		4.00	3.20
5-STRAND OF BLUE			2.80

$2 EXACTA 1-4 PAID $73.40 $2 TRIFECTA 1-4-5 PAID $273.00

Ch. c, (May), by Groovy—Rose Of Darby, by Roberto. Trainer Spina Chuck. Bred by Prestonwood Farm (Ky).

INAGROOVE, angled out nearing the turn, advanced into the lane and challenged in upper stretch, came over approaching the sixteenth pole then bested ARMAGH COUNTY. The latter held a narrow edge into the lane while removed from the rail and gave way grudgingly. STRAND OF BLUE advanced along the rail through upper stretch and tired late. MAJOR MANILA offered a late gain from the outside. TRICKY CATMAN showed the early way, raced outside of ARMAGH COUNTY into the lane, steadied nearing the sixteenth pole and tired. SUPER NIP lacked the needed rally. WADING CASTELLI was outrun. STATELY FIGHTER failed to menace.

Owners— 1, Spina Nicholas; 2, Equity Horse Farm; 3, Char-Mari Stable; 4, Marla Farm; 5, Canonie Tony Jr; 6, Due Process Stables; 7, Armbrister Carl D; 8, Castelli Stables; 9, Polin Mrs Charlotte C; 10, Carabelli Robert.

Trainers— 1, Spina Chuck; 2, Thrasher Clint D; 3, Perkins Ben W Jr; 4, Crupi James J; 5, Velez Roberto; 6, Nobles Reynaldo H; 7, Armbrister Carl D; 8, Anderson William D; 9, Forbes John H; 10, Tronco William L.

Scratched—Shu Fellow.

Inagroove shook loose of Armagh County in the deep stretch to win. Inagroove returned $17.60 to win and keyed a $273 trifecta with our horses for the gimmicks. **The workout sheet is the most important page in the Daily Racing Form.** I can not emphasize this enough. This sheet proves it worth time and time again.

On June 18, 1992, Belmont Park featured a Maiden Special Weight at five furlongs. This race had eight two-year colts, seven of which were first time starters. This is an example of good all-around breeding: horses that have a class level over the entire field.

4 START **5 FURLONGS** BELMONT PARK FINISH

5 FURLONGS. (.56¹) MAIDEN SPECIAL WEIGHT. Purse $24,000. 2-year-olds. Weight, 118 lbs.

Circle Trick
B. c. 2(Apr), by Clever Trick—Indian Circle, by Troon Road
Br.—Farish William S III (Ky)
Tr.—Kimmel John C (16 2 1 3 .13)
MIGLIORE R (114 16 17 10 .14)
Own.—Ellenburg Kenneth
118
Lifetime 0 0 0 0   1992 0 M. 0 0
LATEST WORKOUTS   Jun 11 Bel 5f fst 1:00² Hg   Jun 4 Bel 4f fst :49² Hg   May 30 Bel 4f fst :51 B   May 24 Bel 4f fst :49 H

Meadow Roue
Ch. c. 2(Feb), by Meadowlake—Boldancia, by Iron Warrior
Br.—Wright Del & Joan (Fla)
Tr.—O'Connell Richard (20 4 2 1 .20)
SANTOS J A (148 17 11 26 .11)
Own.—Dor-Sea Stable
118
Lifetime 0 0 0 0   1992 0 M 0 0
LATEST WORKOUTS   Jun 15 Bel 5f fst :59 H   Jun 9 Bel 4f fst :49 B   Jun 4 Bel 4f fst :47 Hg   May 28 Bel 3f fst :36 Hg

England Expects
B. c. 2(Mar), by Topsider—Victoria Cross, by Spectacular Bid
Br.—Paul Mellon (Va)
Tr.—Miller Mack (26 5 10 4 .19)
BAILEY J D (129 21 29 12 .16)
Own.—Rokeby Stable
118
Lifetime 0 0 0 0   1992 0 M 0 0
LATEST WORKOUTS   Jun 15 Bel 3f fst :35⁴ Bg   ●Jun 10 Bel 4f fst :46 H   Jun 4 Bel 3f fst :36 Hg   May 29 Bel 5f fst 1:01 B

Living Vicariously
Dk. b. or br. c. 2(Apr), by Time for a Change—Extravagant Woman, by Alydar
Br.—Ogden Mills Phipps (Ky)
Tr.—McGaughey Claude III (17 2 2 5 .12)
ANTLEY C W (160 29 11 23 .18)
Own.—Phipps O M
118
Lifetime 0 0 0 0   1992 0 M 0 0
LATEST WORKOUTS   Jun 11 Bel 5f fst 1:01³ Hg   Jun 4 Bel 4f fst :50 Bg   May 29 Bel 4f fst :48¹ B   May 23 Bel 3f fst :36 B

Bet Hudson
B. c. 2(Apr), by Bet Big—My Reigndance, by Sovereign Dancer
Br.—Petelain Stable (Fla)
Tr.—Shapoff Stanley R (28 2 4 7 .07)
PEZUA J M (124 8 14 21 .06)
Own.—Cohen Robert B
118
Lifetime 0 0 0 0   1992 1 M 0 0 $1,440
LATEST WORKOUTS   Jun 14 Bel tr.t 4f fst :49¹ B   Jun 10 Bel 4f fst :48³ Hg   Jun 5 Bel tr.t 4f fst :48³ H   May 28 Bel 3f fst :37³ Bg

D'Orazio
Ch. c. 2(May), by Gulch—Whidah, by Codex
Br.—Brant Peter M & Evans Edward P (Ky)
Tr.—Jolley Leroy (17 1 5 1 .06)
CRUGUET J (86 12 10 9 .14)
Own.—Brant Peter M
118
Lifetime 1 0 0 0   1992 1 M 0 0 $1,440
7Jun92- 5Bel gd 5½f   :22   :45 1:04²   Md Sp Wt   50 1 5 5⁵ 6⁵¼ 4⁷ 4⁸   Day P   118 *.60 85–14 PcBby118⁴BgWhsk118²¾InsrdWnnr118   Stead'd greenly 8
LATEST WORKOUTS   Jun 15 Bel 4f fst :48¹ B   Jun 4 Bel 3f fst :34⁴ H   May 28 Bel 5f fst 1:00 H   May 20 Bel 4f fst :49² Hg

Exceeded
Ro. c. 2(Jan), by Affirmed—Lovingness, by Spectacular Bid
Br.—Harbor View Farm (Ky)
Tr.—Kelly Patrick J (33 7 0 2 .21)
MAPLE E (98 14 14 14 .14)
Own.—Live Oak Plantation
118
Lifetime 0 0 0 0   1992 0 M 0 0
LATEST WORKOUTS   Jun 12 Bel 4f fst :49¹ B   Jun 8 Bel 3f fst :37² Bg   May 22 Bel 4f fst :49 B   May 18 Bel tr.t 4f fst :50² B

Satellite Signal
B. c. 2(Feb), by Valid Appeal—La Feria, by Elocutionist
Br.—Mangurian Harry T Jr (Fla)
Tr.—Hough Stanley M (20 4 2 7 .20)
DAVIS R G (54 10 5 1 .19)
Own.—Triumviri Stable
118
Lifetime 0 0 0 0   1992 0 M 0 0
LATEST WORKOUTS   Jun 15 Bel 4f fst :48¹ H   Jun 10 Bel 4f fst :48 H

Also Eligible (Not in Post Position Order):

Ocean Wave
Ro. c. 2(Apr), by Tsunami Slew—Bid Me Adieu, by Spectacular Bid
Br.—Whelan David J & Elizabeth P (Ky)
Tr.—Terrill William V (27 5 5 3 .19)
CARR D (115 18 16 11 .16)
Own.—Royal Lines Stable
118
Lifetime 0 0 0 0   1992 0 M 0 0
LATEST WORKOUTS   Jun 15 Bel 3f fst :36¹ H   Jun 4 Bel 4f fst :49³ Hg   May 27 Bel 5f fst 1:01¹ Hg   May 21 Bel 4f fst :48² Hg

Jak Ten Straight
B. c. 2(Mar), by Smarten—Skyjak, by Cojak
Br.—Albert H. Cohen, Randy L. Cohen & R (Md)
Tr.—Dutrow Richard E (29 2 5 4 .07)
KRONE J A (194 38 36 21 .20)
Own.—Hickory Plains Farm
118
Lifetime 0 0 0 0   1992 0 M 0 0
LATEST WORKOUTS   Jun 5 Aqu 5f fst 1:02³ B   May 30 Aqu 5f fst 1:03⁴ B   May 23 Aqu 4f fst :51 Bg

Classic Jet

CHAVEZ J F (135 20 17 14 .15)
Own.—Hooper Fred W

B. c. 2(Feb), by Tri Jet—School Princess, by Crozier
Br.—Hooper F W (Fla)
Tr.—Domino Carl J (14 4 1 4 .29)

Lifetime	1992	2	M	0	2	$5,760
	2	0	0	2		
118	$5,760					

15May92- 4Bel fst 5f :22 :46 :59^2 Md Sp Wt 54 2 1 1$\frac{1}{2}$ 1hd 2hd 3^1 Velazquez J R 118 *1.40 83-11 BbsCrrnt118^{1}WthtDsst118^{no}ClsscJt118 Bumped stretch 6

6May92- 4Bel fst 5f :22^2 :45^4 :58^1 Md Sp Wt 62 2 2 1$\frac{1}{2}$ 1$\frac{1}{2}$ 2hd 3$^4\frac{1}{2}$ Smith M E 118 4.90 86-09 DieLughing118^{nk}MmorblDt118^{4}ClssicJt118 Speed, tired 6

LATEST WORKOUTS · Jun 13 Bel 5f fst 1:02 H   May 26 Bel 5f fst 1:03^4 B   May 2 Bel 4f fst :49^2 Hg   Apr 27 Bel 4f fst :51^1 B

Courtesy of Daily Racing Form ©

Circle Trick, Bet Hudson, Exceeded, Satellite Signal, and Jak Ten Straight were all first time starters with average to below average workouts and breeding. This left three contenders: Living Vicariously, D'Orazio, and England Expects.

Living Vicariously made our contender list solely because of his trainer, Claude McGaughey. He is known for working his horses slow and for that reason Living Vicariously can be used in the gimmicks.

D'Orazio is a son of Gulch trained by Leroy Jolley. This colt went off at 3-5 in his first start and finished a disappointing fourth, beaten by eighth lengths in 1:06 for five-and-a-half furlongs. His adjusted speed fractions of 23, 46, and 1:06 are very slow. Unless he can dramatically improve, he will not have any effect on the outcome of this contest.

England Expects is by Topsider and Victoria Cross, who was sired by Spectacular Bid. England Expects has top breeding and one of the most potent trainer-owner-breeder combinations. As we analyze each individual workout, one stands out from the rest. On June 10 at Belmont Park, England Expects worked out in 46 seconds flat handily. When we look up this workout on the "Latest Workout" sheet, England Expects received a Black type comment: "England Expects delivered in fine style."

Wednesday, June 10, 1992
BELMONT PARK – Track Fast

Three Furlongs						
Annies Money	:39 Bg	Barron Mohawk	:48^2 H	Mistee Vee	:49^4 B	DancingDevlette 1:00^1 H
Apprentice	:38^3 B	Bet Hudson	:48^3 Hg	Mr. Sledge	:48^3 Hg	Dark Palette	1:00^1 H
Baatish	:38 B	BlondeOnBlond	:49^2 B	Mr. T. V.	:50 B	Easy Peices	1:01^2 H
Buffalino	:39 B	Candy Diver	:49^2 B	MyFriendBernie	:54 B	Flying Colonel	1:03^4 Bg
Carsey's Pal	:37^3 B	Cearas Dancer	:51^3 B	My Girl Rodes	:51^3 B	ForeverFighting 1:01^1 H
		CrtinConvictons	:52 B	My Necessity	:49 B	Grenade	1:03^4 Bg

Charleston	:38⁴ B	ChampgneCkes	:49 B	NewYorkAppeal	:47¹ H	High Talent	1:02 Hg
Cross of Honor	:37² B	Close Play	:49³ B	No Holme Keys	:48 H	Inner Truth	1:01 H
EnderingDancer	:36⁴ H	Country Lassie	:50 B	Option Contract	:50² B	Joe Hardwick	1:02⁴ Hg
Engraving	:38¹ B	Crystal Gazing	:50¹ B	Paper Hat	:47 H	Lady Sage	1:00³ H
Flashy Deb	:39 Bg	Dance Colony	:49⁴ B	Peeler Bend	:51³ B	Lord Wollaston	1:02² H
I of the Vortex	:34⁴ H	Dancing Hunter	:48¹ H	Port O Silver	:48⁴ Hg	Lugh	1:01⁴ H
I'm Majestic	:36³ H	Darien Deacon	:49³ B	PrancingBllerin	:49³ B	Majestys Time	1:00⁴ H
Johnny Glory	:37³ B	DecoratedQueen	:49 Hg	QueensOvrSvns	:50 Bg	Masterclass	1:01³ H
Julie Apple	:36⁴ H	**England Expects**	:46 H	RmmbrMidnight	:51² Bg	Michael Chris	1:03 H
Magic Mount	:38⁴ B	Environment	:48³ H	Rollicking Edge	:50³ Bg	Napale	1:00⁴ H
Mr. BoomBoom	:36 H	Free At Last	:49¹ B	Rose Colony	:48³ H	O'Star	1:00³ H
New Deal	:36 B	Freezing Fun	:48¹ H	Satellite Signal	:48 H	Old Ulm	1:02 H
One Bid Only	:37² B	Gin Joint	:49 B	Scout Setter	:52 B	Pension Fraud	1:02¹ B
Personal Bid	:39 Bg	Gulpha Gorge	:51³ B	Shared Interest	:48³ B	Perhaps Grass	1:02² B
Rain Alert	:38³ B	Hidden Desire	:48³ Hg	Slew O Tunes	:48⁴ B	Rebecca Lauren	1:02² B
Rowing	:37 B	Holiday Ake	:49 B	Sound Prospect	:50 Bg	**Ryan'sGroomsmn**	:58³ B
Salt Shaker	:34³ H	HollywoodSmile	:49² B	Sunshine Magic	:50 B	Saucey Latin	1:00³ H
Social Delima	:37 B	Home Base	:48⁴ H	Tri to Trade	:50¹ B	Skinny Dipper	1:01³ H
States Rights	:36³ H	It's S. S. Maria	:49⁴ B	TrumpetTongud	:48² B	Southern Slew	1:00¹ H
Steady On	:37 B	Java Drems	:48² B	Virginia Rapids	:48² H	SpectacularTide	1:02³ B
Thrill Courier	:34⁴ H	Key Contender	:48 H	Whisper Hello	:49 B	Technoflash	1:04 B
Toe Loop	:38¹ B	Lady Wollaston	:50 Bg	Win the Pace	:50 B	Walk the Walk	1:01⁴ Hg
Valuable Lady	:37³ B	Lhasa	:47³ H	Wonder Wave	:51² Bg	Weather Gage	1:02 H
Four Furlongs		Loam	:50 Bg	Wonderbuck	:48³ H	Wild Assets	1:01¹ H
A PrivateMatter	:49⁴ B	Majesty's Man	:48⁴ B	Zimmerman	:51³ B		
Aimaam	:48² H	MajorMcCallum	:47² H	**Five Furlongs— :56¹**		**Six Furlongs—1:07⁴**	
AllMyPrincesses	:49² B	McPine	:49² Hg	Ada Cort	1:03 B		
Alpha Rascal	:47² H	Mick	:48² B	**Bless Our Home**	:58³ H	Exotic Slew	1:14⁴ H
Axe Creek	:48¹ H	Mile High Glory	:48¹ H	Bonky	1:01¹ H	**Slamya**	1:13³ H

SALT SHAKER (3F) was put on his toes. ENGLAND EXPECTS (4F) delivered in fine style. MASTERCLASS (5F) was in hand throughout – M. Smith aboard. RYANS GROOMSMAN (5F) remains sharp. SOUTHERN SLEW (5F) is doing well. SLAMYA (6F) had early speed – Rojas up.

Courtesy of Daily Racing Form ©

England Expects has the breeding, the right handlers, and has the Black Type comment in a race where there is not much competition. This is the icing on the cake. England Expects worked out in the same time that D'Orazio ran his half in his first start.

FOURTH RACE 5 FURLONGS. (.56¹) MAIDEN SPECIAL WEIGHT. Purse $24,000. 2-year-olds. Weight, 118 lbs.

Belmont
JUNE 18, 1992

Value of race $24,000; value to winner $14,400; second $5,280; third $2,880; fourth $1,440. Mutuel pool $152,382. Quinella Pool $94,242 Exacta Pool $335,585

Last Raced	Horse	M/Eqt.A.Wt	PP St	⅛	¾	Str	Fin	Jockey	Odds $1
	England Expects	2 118	2 2	11½	11½	13	13½	Bailey J D	1.00
	Living Vicariously	2 118	3 5	5hd	4½	2hd	21½	Antley C W	8.40
	Satellite Signal	b 2 118	7 7	31	3½	41½	3no	Davis R G	6.80
7Jun92 5Bel⁴	D'Orazio	2 118	5 4	21	2hd	3½	42	Cruguet J	2.00
	Exceeded	2 118	6 6	64	52½	5½	5no	Maple E	18.00
	Bet Hudson	2 118	4 3	7½	62	66	615½	Pezua J M	49.30
	Jak Ten Straight	2 118	8 8	8	8	7⁴	7	Krone J A	24.50
	Circle Trick	2 118	1 1	4hd	71	8	—	Migliore R	27.30

Circle Trick, Eased.

OFF AT 2:31 Start good, Won handily. Time, :22², :46, :58² Track fast.

$2 Mutuel Prices:

2–(C)–ENGLAND EXPECTS	4.00	2.80	2.80
3–(D)–LIVING VICARIOUSLY		5.20	4.20
7–(H)–SATELLITE SIGNAL			3.80

$2 QUINELLA 2–3 PAID $19.40 $2 EXACTA 2–3 PAID $22.20

B. g, (Mar), by Topsider—Victoria Cross, by Spectacular Bid. Trainer Miller Mack. Bred by Paul Mellon (Va).

ENGLAND EXPECTS, outsprinted rivals for the early advantage widened his margin in upper stretch then was never threatened while drawing off in hand. LIVING VICARIOUSLY settled in good position while slightly off the rail to the turn then finished willingly to best the others. SATELLITE SIGNAL stalked the pace while three wide into upper stretch and lacked a strong closing response. D'ORAZIO forced the pace outside the winner for a half and weakened. EXCEEDED was never a serious threat. BET HUDSON was never a factor while racing wide. JAK TEN STRAIGHT never reached contention. CIRCLE TRICK was taken in hand after showing brief early speed and was eased in the stretch.

Owners— 1, Rokeby Stable; 2, Phipps O M; 3, Triumviri Stable; 4, Brant Peter M; 5, Live Oak Plantation; 6, Cohen Robert B; 7, Hickory Plains Farm; 8, Ellenburg Kenneth.

Trainers— 1, Miller Mack; 2, McGaughey Claude III; 3, Hough Stanley M; 4, Jolley Leroy; 5, Kelly Patrick J; 6, Shapoff Stanley R; 7, Dutrow Richard E; 8, Kimmel John C.

Scratched— Meadow Roue; Ocean Wave; Classic Jet (15May92 4Bel3).

Courtesy of Daily Racing Form ©

As expected, England Expects dominated, going wire to wire in a swift 58²/₅. D'Orazio could not keep up when England Expects went slow to the half, and there was no way D'Orazio could make a stretch run when England Expects came home quickly, running the last quarter in 12²/₅. Living Vicariously hung in there and battled to get up for second.

Since Living Vicariously ran so good against a monster, England Expects, we can use the bounce back theory on Living Vicariously. Living Vicariously's next start did not come until September 17, 1992. In addition to the good performance against England Expects, Living Vicariously worked five furlongs from the gate on September 9 in 59²/₅ handily.

Wednesday, September 9, 1992
BELMONT PARK – Track Fast

Three Furlongs							
Ashley Spumoni	:39⁴ B	Anybody'sGuess	:50 Bg	Olympic Ridge	:51 B	BasinStreetEast	1:03² Hg
Asking Park	:38² Bg	Apprentico	:50 Bg	One Great Lady	:49³ B	Bright Penny	1:00 H
Bermuda Gal	:37² D	Atarsara	:48³ Hg	Opinionator	:47 H	Chief Honcho	1:02 B
Bland	:38² B	Datcat	:47¹ H	Priceless One	.51 Bg	Dance Floor	1:00⁷ H
Colonial Affair	:37² Hg	Bless Our Home	:48¹ B	Private Pennant	:50² B	Diggin In	1:00 H
Cool Flower	:37² Hg	Burn Fair	:47¹ H	ProspectiveWif	:50¹ Bg	Dr. Alfoos	1:01⁴ B
Danger Lurks	:38⁴ B	Celeste Cielo	:46¹ H	ProspctorsPick	:48 Hg	Dr. Hemlock	1:02⁴ B
Dixie Reef	:35 Hg	Curvy Cat	:50³ Bg	Quiet Crusader	:49³ Bg	Eli's Bruno	1:01² B
For My Jet	:37² B	Decanter	:51⁴ Bg	Royal Lap	:49⁴ B	Jicarella	1:01⁴ Hg
Frau Bucharest	:38² B	Decision Maker	:48 B	Russian Bride	:47⁴ H	Kissin Kris	1:01¹ H
Gold Cortez	:37⁴ B	Dreminthedywy	:49 B	Sacque	:49¹ B	Lite Light	1:01² B
I'mSoAgreeable	:36¹ B	Elytis	:48 H	Safrinella	:49⁴ B	LivingVicariously	:59² Hg
		Expensiveness	:49⁴ B	Salt Lake	:49¹ B	Lugh	1:02 B

Indian Ace	$:36^{1}$ Hg	Graysportcoat	$:48^{1}$ H	Scam	$:48^{1}$ Hg	Mein Liebschen	1:03 Bg
It's A BoyScout	$:37^{4}$ B	Heavy Treasure	$:50^{2}$ B	Senor Rex	$:48^{3}$ Hg	Memory Green	$1:01^{1}$ H
Java Spice	$:38^{4}$ Bg	I'm ASportsFan	$:49^{3}$ Bg	Sibling Sword	$:47^{4}$ H	MissedtheStorm	$1:01^{4}$ B
Key tothePeace	$:38^{4}$ Bg	Landslide Lynn	$:49^{3}$ Bg	SpanishPssport	$:49^{3}$ Bg	Multimara	1:02 B
Marbella	$:36^{2}$ H	LnngrdSymphny	$:48^{3}$ B	Staple Queen	:50 B	My Vote	$1:02^{2}$ H
MissImportance	$:36^{4}$ B	Loatsa Talc	$:49^{2}$ Hg	Stop the Rain	$:47^{4}$ Hg	Pencil	$1:01^{4}$ H
Noble Sheba	$:36^{2}$ Hg	Lojakono	$:49^{4}$ Bg	Suite Tasso	$:47^{4}$ H	RomanticDinner	1:05 B
Pedicure	$:38^{2}$ B	Lucky Port	$:51^{2}$ B	Teeshuck	$:50^{3}$ Bg	Sea Carman	$1:02^{3}$ Hg
Personalized	$:36^{1}$ Bg	Maggie Day	$:50^{3}$ Bg	Thakib	$:49^{2}$ B	Sharia	$1:02^{3}$ B
Premier Flag	$:37^{1}$ B	Magic Tower	:49 B	Thunderbolted	:51 B	Somthngscndlos	1:00 H
Sakura Fabuki	$:36^{1}$ Hg	**Major McCallum**	**$:46^{1}$ H**	Timely Accord	$:49^{1}$ Hg	Starry Prophecy	$1:02^{3}$ Hg
Seul Ring	:38 B	Meadow Victory	:48 Hg	Top the Record	$:47^{4}$ H	Trimious	1:05 Bg
Tight Fit	$:38^{2}$ B	Miss Balete	:49 Hg	Tough Heart	$:49^{3}$ B	**Six Furlongs—$1:07^{4}$**	
TrumpetTongud	$:36^{1}$ B	Movietone	$:49^{3}$ Bg	Track Favorite	$:49^{3}$ Bg	**Dazzling Dixie**	**$1:12^{4}$ H**
Venturist	$:35^{2}$ H	Mt. Shannon	$:48^{3}$ Hg	Tribulation	$:48^{2}$ Hg	Marquis de Soie	1:17 B
World Flag	$:36^{2}$ H	My Girl Delana	$:48^{4}$ B	Upstate Flyer	$:48^{2}$ Hg	Our Tomboy	$1:13^{2}$ H
Four Furlongs		Naulakha	$:52^{2}$ B	Wise Skipper	$:51^{2}$ B	Palace Piper	1:17 B
Acero	$:47^{4}$ H	New Deal	$:50^{1}$ B	**Five Furlongs— $:56^{1}$**		Stolen Zeal	$1:13^{2}$ H
Alwasmi's Tony	$:50^{3}$ B	O My Darling	:48 H	Aimaam	$1:02^{2}$ B		

EXPENSIVENESS (4f) was in hand Baily up. CELESTE CIELO (4f) woke up. OPINIONATOR (4f) is doing well. LITE LIGHT (5f) looked good physically. CHIEF HONCHO (5f) had an easy trial. LIVING VICARIOUSLY (5f) broke running. DAZZLING DIXIE (6f) is in form. OUR TOMBOY (6f) had McCauley in the irons. Additional Workouts: 9/7 track fast: FLY SO FREE (3f) :33.4bg RINKA DAS (3f) :34.2bg.

Courtesy of Daily Racing Form ©

Living Vicariously — **Dk. b. or br. c. 2(Apr), by Time for a Change—Extravagant Woman, by Alydar** — Lifetime 1 0 1 0 $5,280 — 1992 1 M 1 0 $5,28

MCCAULEY W H (43 13 5 3 .30) — **Br.—Ogden Mills Phipps (Ky)**

Own.—Phipps O M — **Tr.—McGaughey Claude III (12 6 1 3 .50)** — **118**

18Jun92- 4Bel fst 5f $:22^{2}$:46 $:58^{2}$ Md Sp Wt **60** 3 5 $5^{3\frac{1}{2}}$ 4^{2} 2^{3} $2^{3\frac{1}{2}}$ Antley C W 118 8.40 85-13 EnglndEpcts$118^{3\frac{1}{2}}$LvngVcrsl$118^{1\frac{1}{4}}$StlltSgnl118 2nd best

LATEST WORKOUTS ●**Sep 9 Bel 5f fst $:59^{2}$ Hg** **Sep 3 Bel 4f gd $:48^{4}$ B** **Aug 30 Sar tr.t 4f fst $:49^{3}$ B** **Aug 27 Sar tr.t 3f fst $:37^{3}$ B**

Courtesy of Daily Racing Form ©

Apparently Living Vicariously was hurt after his first start. It's obvious that whatever was bothering him then has been cleared up.

FIFTH RACE **6 FURLONGS. (1.07^{4}) MAIDEN SPECIAL WEIGHT. Purse $24,000. 2–year–olds. Weight 118 lb.**

Belmont

SEPTEMBER 17, 1992

Value of race $24,000; value to winner $14,400; second $5,280; third $2,880; fourth $1,440. Mutuel pool $217,776. Exacta Pool $416,008

Last Raced	Horse	M/Eqt.A.Wt	PP	St	¼	½	Str	Fin	Jockey	Odds $1
18Jun92 ^{4}Bel^{2}	Living Vicariously	2 118	12	4	3^{hd}	2^{hd}	2^{2}	$1^{\frac{3}{4}}$	McCauley W H	2.30
	Man's Hero	2 118	5	1	$1^{\frac{1}{2}}$	$1^{\frac{1}{2}}$	$1^{1\frac{1}{2}}$	2no	Velazquez J R	5.40
	Digging In	2 118	14	13	$7^{1\frac{1}{2}}$	$3^{1\frac{1}{2}}$	$3^{2\frac{1}{2}}$	$3^{6\frac{3}{4}}$	Smith M E	15.90
6Sep92 ^{9}Bel^{2}	Seattle Ore	2 118	8	6	$4^{1\frac{1}{2}}$	4^{hd}	4^{3}	4^{4}	Davis R G	1.70
	Press On Jesse	2 118	3	5	12^{3}	$11^{1\frac{1}{2}}$	6^{hd}	$5^{1\frac{3}{4}}$	Bailey J D	11.30
	Mastership	2 118	4	11	$11^{\frac{1}{2}}$	$8^{\frac{1}{2}}$	5^{2}	$6^{2\frac{1}{2}}$	Perret C	24.40
	Showpower	b 2 118	9	7	6^{1}	$7^{1\frac{1}{2}}$	7^{1}	$7^{2\frac{3}{4}}$	Gryder A T	27.90
	Khaleefa	2 118	6	9	5^{hd}	6^{hd}	8^{1}	8^{nk}	Romero R P	53.80
	Twilight Looming	2 118	13	14	$9^{\frac{1}{2}}$	$10^{1\frac{1}{2}}$	10^{3}	9^{3}	Solis A	42.40
16Aug92 ^{4}Sar^{3}	Spartan Leader	2 118	7	10	$10^{2\frac{1}{2}}$	12^{1}	$12^{\frac{1}{2}}$	10^{hd}	Maple E	15.00
5Aug92 ^{7}Mth^{8}	Rideofyourlife	2 118	2	3	8^{1}	9^{1}	9^{hd}	11^{nk}	King E L Jr	112.60
29Aug92 ^{9}Sar^{8}	Silent Passage	2 118	1	8	13^{1}	$13^{\frac{1}{2}}$	13^{1}	$12^{\frac{3}{4}}$	Madrid A Jr	150.50
26Aug92 ^{4}Sar^{3}	Te Caliente	2 118	11	2	$2^{1\frac{1}{2}}$	$5^{\frac{1}{2}}$	11^{1}	$13^{1\frac{3}{4}}$	Carr D	22.90
7Jun92 ^{5}Bel^{6}	John's Storm	2 118	10	12	14	14	14	14	Santagata N	57.80

OFF AT 3:04 Start good, Won driving. Time, $:22^{3}$, $:46^{1}$, $:58^{1}$, 1:11 Track fast.

$2 Mutuel Prices:

12—(L)—LIVING VICARIOUSLY	6.60	3.80	3.20
5—(E)—MAN'S HERO		6.40	6.80
14—(N)—DIGGING IN			9.20

$2 EXACTA 12-5 PAID $59.00

Dk. b. or br. c, (Apr), by Time for a Change—Extravagant Woman, by Alydar. Trainer McGaughey Claude III. Bred by Ogden Mills Phipps (Ky).

LIVING VICARIOUSLY, stalked the pace from outside into upper stretch then wore down MAN'S HERO under brisk urging. MAN'S HERO set the pace under pressure into deep stretch but couldn't hold the winner safe. DIGGING IN, far back early after breaking slowly, made a run four wide to threaten on the turn then finished willingly to gain a share. SEATTLE ORE raced in close contention along the inside into upper stretch and lacked a strong closing response. PRESS ON JESSE, outrun for a half, failed to threaten while improving his position through the lane. MASTERSHIP was never a serious threat. SHOWPOWER raced four wide to the turn then lacked a strong closing response. KHALEEFA steadied between horses in the early stages, raced within striking distance to the turn then tired. TWILIGHT LOOMING never reached contention after breaking slowly. SPARTAN LEADER saved ground to no avail. RIDEOFYOURLIFE saved ground to no avail. SILENT PASSAGE was outrun as was JOHN'S STORM. TE CALIENTE was used up forcing the early pace.

Owners— 1, Phipps O M; 2, Dileo Philip; 3, Christiana Stable; 4, Centennial Farms; 5, Cohen Bertram I; 6, Nydrie Stud; 7, Masterson Robert E; 8, Hassan Shoni B; 9, Moyglare Stud; 10, Reineman Russell L; 11, Talarico Jacqueline; 12, Singer Joseph B; 13, Marquard William A; 14, Murrell John R.

Trainers— 1, McGaughey Claude III; 2, Hertler John O; 3, Badgett William Jr; 4, Schulhofer Flint S; 5, O'Connell Richard; 6, Mott William I; 7, Goldberg Alan E; 8, Carroll Del W II; 9, Lukas D Wayne; 10, Gleaves Philip A; 11, Stoklosa Richard; 12, Daggett Michael H; 13, Tammaro John J; 14, Dutrow Richard E.

Scratched—All Private (12Aug92 4Sar9); Iron Gavel.

Using the bounce back theory can be very profitable and could give the handicapper that needed advantage. By the time that Living Vicariously made his second start, England Expects already had over $75,000 in earnings and was headed towards the Breeder's Cup. This shows that Living Vicariously has enough class to keep with a future superstar. When we see a maiden who has a lot of class and wins in a very good time, learning and remembering who lost to him can be profitable in the future.

The bounce back theory may be even more evident in the case of Roxaneda.

Many times a maiden will run second, come back to run again, and be bet very heavily. Is this horse worth a bet? The best way to judge is by watching the winner of that race and see how that horse performs against stiffer competition. Roxaneka is a perfect example of this.

5

START
6 FURLONGS
MONMOUTH PARK
FINISH

6 FURLONGS. **(1.08) MAIDEN SPECIAL WEIGHT. Purse $15,500. Fillies and mares, weights, 3-year-olds, 116 lbs. Older, 122 lbs.**

LASIX—A Nip Holme-Ir.

Georgia Anna — B. f. 3(Apr), by Stutz Blackhawk—Exclusive Needle, by Needles — Lifetime 1 0 0 0 $155 — 1992 1 M 0 0 $155 — 1991 0 M 0 0

Br.—Leanheart Steven (Fla)

Own.—Gross & Leanheart — Tr.—Gross George F (25 2 1 4 .08) — **116** — Wet 1 0 0 0 $155

20Jun92- 5Mth my 6f :221 :45 1:103 3+Ⓕ Md Sp Wt 51 8 3 66 65¼ 59½ 59½ King E L Jr 115 22.50 78-13 LadySage1151¾Roxaneka115noPastaEFgioli115 No rally 8

LATEST WORKOUTS Jun 16 Mth 4f fst :502 B — Jun 5 Mth 5f fst 1:05 B

Roxaneka — Dk. b. or br. f. 3(Apr), by Cox's Ridge—Aneka, by Believe It — Lifetime 1 0 1 0 $3,100 — 1992 1 M 1 0 $3,100 — 1991 0 M 0 0

Br.—Jayeff B Stables (Ky)

Own.—Mottola Gary — Tr.—Cash Russell J (10 2 2 0 .20) — **116** — Wet 1 0 1 0 $3,100

20Jun92- 5Mth my 6f :221 :45 1:103 3+Ⓕ Md Sp Wt 71 3 6 76½ 53¾ 44½ 21¾ Gryder A T 115 5.20 86-13 LadySge1151¾Roxnek115noPstEFgioli115 Frcd wide 1/4 8

LATEST WORKOUTS Jun 27 Mth 3f fst :36 B — Jun 14 Mth 5f fst 1:021 B — Jun 7 Mth 3f fst :35 H — May 25 Mth 5f fst 1:024 Bg

Baby North — Ch. f. 3(Mar), by Northern Baby—Rose Above, by Hagley — Lifetime 2 0 0 0 $775 — 1992 2 M 0 0 $775 — 1991 0 M 0 0

Br.—Hi-Rock Stable (Va)

Own.—Evans Edward P — Tr.—Lukas D Wayne (16 1 4 1 .06) — **116** — Wet 1 0 0 0 $775

20Jun92- 5Mth my 6f :221 :45 1:103 3+Ⓕ Md Sp Wt 71 2 8 2½ 1hd 2½ 41¾ Lovato F Jr 115 7.70 86-13 LadySage1151¾Roxaneka115noPastEFgioli115 Tired late 8

30May92- 3Bel fst 6f :222 :454 1:113 3+Ⓕ Md Sp Wt 41 1 7 47 55 57 512½ Antley C W 115 11.90 69-12 Brvly1241MySstrJlt1152½Slpththnmy115 Brk slw, drftd 7

LATEST WORKOUTS Jun 11 Bel 5f fst 1:011 H — May 24 Bel 3f fst :37 Bg — May 20 Bel 4f fst :491 Hg — May 12 Bel 5f fst 1:011 B

A Nip Holme-Ir — Ch. f. 3(Apr), by Fools Holme—Blink, by Dike — Lifetime 5 0 1 0 $2,970 — 1992 3 M 1 0 $2,970 — 1991 2 M 0 0 — Turf 2 0 0 0

Br.—Carroll Ivor (Ire)

Own.—Rowe Virginia — Tr.—Gaffney Ronald (—) — **116**

10May92- 2Crc fst 1 :49 1:144 1:431 3+Ⓕ Md Sp Wt 53 7 6 610 69 67½ 46 Lester R N b 113 *2.40 — — SpptDD1081½I'mStT1133Sl'sPlmGld114 Late rally, 7-wd 7

25Apr92- 3Crc fst 7f :221 :452 1:273 3+Ⓕ Md Sp Wt 57 2 6 76 79½ 54 4¾ Fires E b 114 5.70 81-10 Zubdubdoo113¾MssVIllong105hdBrdlShow113 Late rally 10

2Apr92- 4Crc fst 6f :224 :464 1:134 Ⓕ Md 30000 55 1 7 33 44 25 21½ Cruguet J b 116 13.00 81-07 DDsPrncss1161½ANpHl-Ir1163½PhscsPc116 Good effort 10

21Jun91♦3Dundalk(Ire) gd*1 1:363 Ⓣ Omeath Clm Race (Mdn) 821½ O'Donohoe D J 109 *2.75 — — Sarstro1166 DoubleLetter1048 Greter109 Reins slipped 9

21Jun91-Raced for a claiming price of $14,865

15Jun91♦1Naas(Ire) gd 6f 1:12 Ⓣ Monread Auction Race 1110¾ O'Donohoe D J 106 6.00 — — SuiteApplus1034 MgicGlow1152½ Shindw105 No threat 19

LATEST WORKOUTS Jun 26 Mth 4f fst :53 B — Jun 17 Mth 4f fst :49 B — Jun 10 Mth 3f fst :364 B

Moodtomove — B. f. 4, by Ruthie's Native—Dewanocatch, by Dewan — Lifetime 1 0 1 0 $3,100 — 1992 1 M 1 0 $3,100 — 1991 0 M 0 0

Br.—Tinsle Sonia C (Ky)

Own.—Gorman Allen — Tr.—Serpe Philip M (27 6 5 5 .22) — **122**

Entered 30Jun92- 6 MTH

30May92- 1Mth fst 6f :214 :452 1:113 3+Ⓕ Md Sp Wt 59 2 7 31 31½ 23 23½ Ferrer J C 122 7.90 79-12 ShpOtFrst1143½Moodtomv1222½FshnDsgnr114 2nd best 9

LATEST WORKOUTS Jun 13 Mth 3f fst :37 B — ●May 25 Mth 5f fst 1:012 Hg — May 19 Mth 5f fst 1:024 B — May 13 Mth 5f fst 1:03 B

Fine China Gal — Ch. f. 3(Mar), by Sauce Boat—Katherine's Gal, by State Dinner — Lifetime 0 0 0 0 — 1992 0 M 0 0 — 1991 0 M 0 0

Br.—Sims Robert C (Ky)

Own.—Mims Ted J — Tr.—Mims Ted J (6 1 1 0 .17) — **116**

Entered 30Jun92- 1 MTH

LATEST WORKOUTS Jun 25 Mth 4f fst :504 B — Jun 16 Mth 5f fst 1:022 Bg — Jun 10 Mth 4f fst :51 B — Jun 4 Mth 5f fst 1:06 B

Banner Dancer — B. f. 3(Mar), by Danzig—Nalees Flying Flag, by Hoist The Flag — Lifetime 1 0 0 0 — 1991 1 M 0 0

Br.—Humphrey G Watts Jr (Ky)

Own.—Humphrey G Watts Jr — Tr.—Pierce Joseph H Jr (23 1 4 5 .04) — **116**

15Aug91- 4Sar fst 6f :221 :453 1:112 Ⓕ Md Sp Wt 38 2 8 52 51¾ 64½ 610¼ Smith M E 117 *1.00 77-10 Flattery1173¾ Artful Tri1172I'mProud117 Saved ground 8

LATEST WORKOUTS Jun 10 Mth 4f fst :493 B

John's Angel — B. f. 3(Mar), by Skip Trial—Native Angel, by Exclusive Native — Lifetime 0 0 0 0 — 1991 0 M 0 0

Br.—Appleton Arthur I (Fla)

Own.—Appleton Arthur I — Tr.—Jennings Lawrence Jr (22 5 2 2 .23) — **116**

LATEST WORKOUTS Jun 29 Mth 3f fst :35 H — Jun 23 Mth 5f fst 1:012 H — Jun 16 Mth 5f fst 1:034 B — Jun 9 Mth 5f fst 1:02 B

Tassotasse — Ch. f. 3(Apr), by Tasso—Demitasse, by Young Emperor — Lifetime 1 0 0 0 — 1992 1 M 0 0 — 1991 0 M 0 0 — Turf 1 0 0 0

Br.—Robins Gerald (Ky)

Own.—Robins Gerald — Tr.—Drysdale Neil (—) — **116**

13Jun92- 5Bel fm 1 Ⓣ:464 1:111 1:354 3+Ⓕ Md Sp Wt 38 8 10 96½ 107¼ 917 820½ Bailey J D 114 2.50 63-13 Insurprise1142½Kte'sPride114¾Herto'Mine114 No factor 12

13Jun92-Placed seventh through disqualification

LATEST WORKOUTS Jun 22 Bel 3f fst :374 B — Jun 11 Bel 3f fst :382 B — May 19 Bel tr.t 7f fst 1:273 B

In her first start Roxaneka was runner-up to Lady Sage. After her victory Lady Sage went to Belmont and was victorious in an Allowance $27,000 event on June 27, 1992. Roxaneka was reentered on July 1, 1992 and placed in an easy field. After seeing Lady Sage win back at Belmont, there is a good chance that Roxaneka will be able to handle this field today. On July 1 she had eight rivals.

A Nip Holme, a three-year-old filly, could not be used because of the two-to-three-start rule.

Georgia Anna was eight lengths behind Lady Sage in her first start and will have to improve tremendously: doubtful bet.

Baby North had an excuse in her first start and ran very well in her second, but she did not work out since her last race and could be a little stale.

Mood To Move is a four-year-old who cannot produce the times to keep up with these.

Fine China Gal's workouts are not competitive.

Banner Dancer is coming off an eleven month layoff and the lone workout is not impressive.

Tassotasse is a filly that did not want anything to do with the turf. We will let this one beat us. Unplayable.

This left one other horse besides Roxaneka: John's Angel. John's Angel has good breeding and a solid owner-trainer combination. His workouts are decent but he did not receive any Black Type comments on the workout sheet, so the edge must be given to Roxaneka.

| **FIFTH RACE** | | **6 FURLONGS. (1.08) MAIDEN SPECIAL WEIGHT. Purse $15,500. Fillies and mares, weights, 3-year-olds, 116 lbs. Older, 122 lbs.** | | | | | | | | | |

Monmouth
JULY 1, 1992

Value of race $15,500; value to winner $9,300; second $2,945; third $1,705; fourth $775; balance of starters $155 each.
Mutuel pool $67,912. Exacta Pool $77,941 Trifecta Pool $76,390

Last Raced	Horse	M/Eqt.A.Wt	PP St	¼	½	Str	Fin	Jockey	Odds $1
20Jun92 5Mth2	Roxaneka	3 116	2 6	4²	56½	2hd	1½	Gryder A T	*1.80
	John's Angel	3 116	8 1	5⁵	3 1½	12	2⁶	Bravo J	1.80
15Aug91 4Sar6	Banner Dancer	3 116	7 4	3hd	1hd	3½	32½	Wilson R	8.90
20Jun92 5Mth5	Georgia Anna	3 116	1 7	6²	6².	5²	41½	King E L Jr	33.70
20Jun92 5Mth4	Baby North	3 116	3 5	1½	2½	45	51½	Lovato F Jr	6.10
10May92 2Crc4	A Nip Holme-Ir	Lb 3 116	4 9	7½	7½	71½	62½	Romero J A	16.40
	Fine China Gal	b 3 116	6 8	81½	8½	8hd	7½	McKnight R E	59.60
13Jun92 5Bel7	Tassotasse	3 116	9 2	9	9	9	81½	Lidberg D W	25.60
30May92 1Mth2	Moodtomove	4 122	5 3	2½	4hd	6hd	9	Ferrer J C	7.70

*—Actual Betting Favorite.

OFF AT 2:54 Start good, Won driving. Time, :21³, :45³, :58², 1:11² Track fast.

$2 Mutuel Prices:

2-ROXANEKA	5.60	3.20	2.40
8-JOHN'S ANGEL		3.20	2.80
7-BANNER DANCER			4.00

$2 EXACTA 2-8 PAID $19.80 $2 TRIFECTA 2-8-7 PAID $111.60

Dk. b. or br. f, (Apr), by Cox's Ridge—Aneka, by Believe It. Trainer Cash Russell J. Bred by Jayeff B Stables (Ky).
ROXANEKA, behind rivals on the turn, moved out for room at the top of the lane and finished steadily while edging JOHN'S ANGEL. The latter advanced outside nearing the stretch, drew well clear a furlong out then continued on gamely while unable to contain the top one. BANNER DANCER moved to the lead nearing the five-sixteenths pole and tired in the drive. GEORGIA ANNA offered a belated gain. BABY NORTH vied for the lead to the drive and gradually tired through the final eighth. FINE CHINA GAL was jostled between rivals at the start. MOODTOMOVE prompted the early issue between foes, dropped back nearing the quarter pole and faded through the lane.
Owners— 1, Mottola Gary; 2, Appleton Arthur I; 3, Humphrey G Watts Jr; 4, Gross & Leanheart; 5, Evans Edward P; 6, Graf Paul; 7, Mims Ted J; 8, Robins Gerald; 9, Gorman Allen.
Trainers— 1, Cash Russell J; 2, Jennings Lawrence Jr; 3, Pierce Joseph H Jr; 4, Gross George F; 5, Lukas D Wayne; 6, Gaffney Ronald; 7, Mims Ted J; 8, Drysdale Neil; 9, Serpe Philip M.

Courtesy of Daily Racing Form ©

Roxaneka prevailed, winning by a half of a length as the co-favorite at 8-5. John's Angel's inexperience showed as she tired and lugged out in the final sixteenth. The bounce back angle worked again with John's Angel as she came back to win in her next start.

Maiden races are shied away from by many handicappers. If these twelve rules are followed, especially #1, as a handicapper you will have greater success in the future. **Look up workouts and pay special attention to maidens that receive Black Type mention.**

Inside Stuff on Trainers and Jockeys

CHAPTER 6 The more you know about the trainers and owners from the track you are handicapping the better off you'll be. In this chapter I have done most of the homework for you. These trainers and jockeys might not be from the particular track you are handicapping but don't worry, you can still use this information. All trainer and jockey statistics can be recalled from The Jockey Club Information Systems in Kentucky.

The first of ten trainers and jockeys that we will analyze is Gary Jones. Jones currently trains on the California circuit. He had 329 starts in 1992 with 71 winners. He is most profitable in allowance and claiming races. He has a plus $35.00 in allowance and plus $26.00 in claiming races. This means if you bet $2.00 on every horse Gary Jones entered in an allowance race you would be ahead $35.00. One third (34%) of his winners came from horses that have won in allowance races. This is a very profitable betting percentage. Also, on the turf, Jones shows a profit. In graded stakes races, he has placed his horses well: 54% finished in the money. His weakness: "off" tracks. He has only won on "off" tracks 11% of the time. With first-time starters, he has only a 22% winning percentage. With maiden horses starting more than once this percentage again drops to 11.

JONES, GARY – TRAINER SUMMARY FOR SPECIFIC YEAR FOR ALL TRACKS IN
NORTH AMERICA

IN NORTH AMERICA FOR ALL TRACKS:

	1976–1992
STARTERS	1,133
WINNERS	562 (49%)
PLACERS	662 (58%)
STARTS	6,740
WINS	1,223 (18%)
PLACES	1,744 (25%)

1992 IN NORTH AMERICA

	STARTS	1ST	(%)	2ND	(%)	3RD	(%)	UNPL%	EARNINGS	ROWB
TOTALS	329	71	(22)	50	(15)	45	(14)	(49)	$4,720,519	–$57
AVERAGE FOR ALL TRAINERS			(9)		(9)		(10)	(72)		–$18
COLTS	169	38	(22)	27	(16)	23	(14)	(48)	$3,070,025	–$23
FILLIES	160	33	(21)	23	(14)	22	(14)	(51)	$1,650,494	–$34
GRADED BLACKTYPE	43	14	(33)	5	(12)	4	(9)	(46)	$2,911,950	+ $0
ALL BLACKTYPE	70	18	(26)	8	(11)	9	(13)	(50)	$3,268,994	–$17
ALLOWANCE	88	24	(27)	14	(16)	18	(20)	(37)	$782,675	+ $35
CLAIMING	74	14	(19)	16	(22)	11	(15)	(44)	$369,775	+ $26
MAIDEN	97	15	(15)	12	(12)	7	(7)	(66)	$299,075	–$102
DIRT	209	41	(20)	33	(16)	24	(11)	(53)	$2,749,494	–$87
FAST TRACK	171	37	(22)	28	(16)	15	(9)	(53)	$2,590,844	–$33
OFF TRACK	38	4	(11)	5	(13)	9	(24)	(52)	$158,650	–$54
TURF	120	30	(25)	17	(14)	21	(18)	(43)	$1,971,025	+ $30
FIRM TURF	114	29	(25)	16	(14)	21	(18)	(43)	$1,890,350	+ $34
OFF TURF	6	1	(17)	1	(17)	0	(0)	(66)	$80,675	–$4
MILE OR MORE	171	37	(22)	28	(16)	28	(16)	(46)	$3,704,375	+ $7
< 1 MILE	158	34	(22)	22	(14)	17	(11)	(53)	$1,016,144	–$63
FAVORITES	86	36	(42)	10	(12)	12	(14)	(32)	$2,763,125	–$1
ODDS < 5 TO 1	105	24	(23)	21	(20)	19	(18)	(39)	$1,343,850	–$6
ODDS 5 TO 1– 10 TO 1	81	9	(11)	15	(19)	8	(10)	(60)	$413,144	–$12
ODDS > 10 TO 1	57	2	(4)	4	(7)	6	(11)	(78)	$200,400	–$38
FIRST TIME STARTERS	37	8	(22)	4	(11)	4	(11)	(56)	$177,000	–$12
RACES WITH APPRENTICES	2	0	(0)	1	(50)	0	(0)	(50)	$6,800	–$4

Ronald McAnally trains horses across America but, like Gary Jones has his tack on the California circuit. McAnally has a solid 57% in the money with first time starters. His lowest ratios come in claiming races where he has his smallest win percentage and highest unplacement. Also, in graded Black Type races McAnally has a tremendous winning percentage of 24. Otherwise McAnally is a relatively even trainer and does not stand out in any category. This shows the consistency in his training. Though his horses are not a good bet every time out in any separate category, he has his best showing in graded stakes races.

MCANALLY, RONALD – TRAINER SUMMARY FOR SPECIFIC YEAR FOR ALL TRACKS
IN NORTH AMERICA

IN NORTH AMERICA FOR ALL TRACKS:

	1976–1992
STARTERS	1,016
WINNERS	544 (53%)
PLACERS	662 (65%)
STARTS	8,222
WINS	1,242 (15%)
PLACES	2,107 (25%)

1992 IN NORTH AMERICA

	STARTS	1ST	(%)	2ND	(%)	3RD	(%)	UNPL%	EARNINGS	ROWB
TOTALS	613	103	(17)	108	(18)	78	(13)	(52)	$8,041,663	–$326
AVERAGE FOR ALL TRAINERS			(9)		(9)		(10)	(72)		–$18
COLTS	317	50	(16)	53	(17)	41	(13)	(54)	$3,947,508	–$185
FILLIES	296	53	(18)	55	(19)	37	(13)	(50)	$4,094,155	–$142
GRADED BLACKTYPE	102	24	(24)	18	(18)	8	(8)	(50)	$5,337,165	–$21
ALL BLACKTYPE	170	30	(18)	28	(16)	21	(12)	(54)	$5,929,943	–$111
ALLOWANCE	193	29	(15)	44	(23)	25	(13)	(49)	$1,219,355	–$134
CLAIMING	73	9	(12)	11	(15)	12	(16)	(57)	$239,777	–$67
MAIDEN	177	35	(20	25	(14)	20	(11)	(55)	$652,588	–$13
DIRT	418	73	(17)	68	(16)	50	(12)	(55)	$5,607,413	–$219
FAST TRACK	353	60	(17)	61	(17)	44	(12)	(54)	$4,975,843	–$180
OFF TRACK	65	13	(20)	7	(11)	6	(9)	(60)	$631,570	–$39
TURF	195	30	(15)	40	(21)	28	(14)	(50)	$2,434,250	–$109
FIRM TURF	190	30	(16)	37	(19)	28	(15)	(50)	$2,393,650	–$99
OFF TURF	5	0	(0)	3	(60)	0	(0)	(40)	$40,600	–$10

1992 IN NORTH AMERICA (continued)

	STARTS	1ST	(%)	2ND	(%)	3RD	(%)	UNPL%	EARNINGS	ROWB
MILE OR MORE	362	72	(20)	70	(19)	46	(13)	(48)	$7,066,639	−$115
< 1 MILE	251	31	(12)	38	(15)	32	(13)	(60)	$975,024	−$211
FAVORITES	119	39	(33)	29	(24)	14	(12)	(31)	$2,824,049	−$54
ODDS < 5 TO 1	196	47	(24)	43	(22)	23	(12)	(42)	$3,793,068	−$12
ODDS 5 TO 1–										
10 TO 1	134	11	(8)	20	(15)	21	(16)	(61)	$597,662	−$106
ODDS > 10 TO 1	164	6	(4)	16	(10)	20	(12)	(74)	$826,884	−$156
FIRST TIME										
STARTERS	52	9	(17)	9	(17)	12	(23)	(43)	$288,700	+$0
RACES WITH										
APPRENTICES	5	0	(0)	1	(20)	1	(20)	(60)	$8,200	−$10

Courtesy of The Jockey Club Information Systems ©

Mario Beneito is not as well known as most trainers in this chapter but he had more victories than D.W. Lukas in 1992. Beneito has his tack at a less competitive track: Penn National. He excels in maiden and claiming races where he runs 91% of his starts. In the maiden area, Beneito is much better when his horses already have one start under their belts. His maiden horses win 23% of their races but only 13% the first time out. Beneito is also much better on the dirt. His horses run 24% on dirt compared to 13% on the turf. In Black Type races, Beneito has won only 6%.

BENEITO, MARIO – TRAINER SUMMARY FOR SPECIFIC YEAR FOR ALL TRACKS IN
NORTH AMERICA

IN NORTH AMERICA FOR ALL TRACKS:

	1976–1992
STARTERS	1,221
WINNERS	733 (60%)
PLACERS	837 (68%)
STARTS	11,285
WINS	2,035 (18%)
PLACES	3,203 (28%)

1992 IN NORTH AMERICA

	STARTS	1ST	(%)	2ND	(%)	3RD	(%)	UNPL%	EARNINGS	ROWB
TOTALS	1,029	239	(23)	177	(17)	156	(15)	(45)	$1,055,518	−$442
AVERAGE FOR ALL TRAINERS			(9)		(9)		(10)	(72)		−$18

1992 IN NORTH AMERICA (continued)

	STARTS	1ST	(%)	2ND	(%)	3RD	(%)	UNPL%	EARNINGS	ROWB
COLTS	599	141	(24)	98	(16)	88	(15)	(45)	$690,247	−$290
FILLIES	430	98	(23)	79	(18)	68	(16)	(43)	$365,271	−$153
GRADED BLACKTYPE	1	0	(0)	0	(0)	0	(0)	(100)	$4,641	−$2
ALL BLACKTYPE	17	1	(6)	4	(24)	1	(6)	(64)	$64,849	−$29
ALLOWANCE	78	15	(19)	14	(18)	15	(19)	(44)	$150,854	−$47
CLAIMING	842	204	(24)	150	(18)	129	(15)	(43)	$770,948	−$382
MAIDEN	92	19	(21)	9	(10)	11	(12)	(57)	$68,867	+$14
DIRT	983	233	(24)	172	(17)	150	(15)	(44)	$1,011,301	−$412
FAST TRACK	739	172	(23)	133	(18)	119	(16)	(43)	$776,737	−$320
OFF TRACK	244	61	(25)	39	(16)	31	(13)	(46)	$234,564	−$92
TURF	46	6	(13)	5	(11)	6	(13)	(63)	$44,217	−$32
FIRM TURF	31	3	(10)	4	(13)	4	(13)	(64)	$23,219	−$43
OFF TURF	15	3	(20)	1	(7)	2	(13)	(60)	$20,998	+$11
MILE OR MORE	372	83	(22)	61	(16)	61	(16)	(46)	$358,251	−$188
< 1 MILE	657	156	(24)	116	(18)	95	(14)	(44)	$697,267	−$256
FAVORITES	426	152	(35)	84	(20)	67	(16)	(29)	$534,795	−$144
ODDS < 5 TO 1	310	68	(22)	57	(18)	56	(18)	(42)	$364,429	−$75
ODDS 5 TO 1– 10 TO 1	180	16	(9)	29	(16)	24	(13)	(62)	$108,161	−$130
ODDS > 10 TO 1	110	3	(3)	7	(6)	9	(8)	(83)	$48,133	−$95
FIRST TIME STARTERS	15	2	(13)	2	(13)	1	(7)	(67)	$10,087	−$12
RACES WITH APPRENTICES	48	7	(15)	3	(6)	9	(19)	(60)	$21,779	−$5

Courtesy of The Jockey Club Information Systems ©

Perhaps the best known trainer in the thoroughbred industry is D.W. Lukas. **Lukas' reputation has carried him through the last couple of years, but he has slipped a little and does not have the best horses anymore.** This knowledge will create underlays and help you decide to throw these horses out. In 1992, D.W. Lukas won 12% of the time in graded Black Type races. This figure is his lowest in eight years. Over the last seven years Lukas' horses hit the board 50% of the time. In 1992 that figure dropped to 40%. His earnings tell the story on how good his horses really are. Lukas has averaged $15,085,295 in earnings over the last seven seasons. In 1992 he recorded about $9,500,000—$5.5 million under his average. He still is tough in graded Black Type races but in 1992, for the first time in Lukas' training career, his biggest winning percentage was in claiming races.

LUKAS, D. WAYNE – TRAINER SUMMARY FOR SPECIFIC YEAR FOR ALL TRACKS IN NORTH AMERICA

IN NORTH AMERICA FOR ALL TRACKS:

	1977–1992
STARTERS	1,691
WINNERS	1,019 (60%)
PLACERS	1,183 (69%)
STARTS	15,106
WINS	2,753 (18%)
PLACES	4,244 (28%)

1985 IN NORTH AMERICA

	STARTS	1ST	(%)	2ND	(%)	3RD	(%)	UNPL%	EARNINGS	ROWB
TOTALS	1,140	218	(19)	183	(16)	135	(12)	(53)	$11,155,188	–$309
AVERAGE FOR ALL TRAINERS			(8)		(9)		(9)	(74)		–$22
COLTS	553	117	(21)	81	(15)	63	(11)	(53)	$5,058,631	+$29
FILLIES	587	101	(17)	102	(17)	72	(12)	(54)	$6,096,557	–$338
GRADED BLACKTYPE	144	38	(26)	20	(14)	18	(13)	(47)	$6,799,415	+$3
ALL BLACKTYPE	410	89	(22)	77	(19)	54	(13)	(46)	$9,178,351	–$209
ALLOWANCE	294	54	(18)	36	(12)	34	(12)	(58)	$908,495	–$41
CLAIMING	136	25	(18)	18	(13)	12	(9)	(60)	$328,538	+$30
MAIDEN	300	50	(17)	52	(17)	35	(12)	(54)	$739,804	–$91
DIRT	1013	207	(20)	172	(17)	123	(12)	(51)	$10,786,488	–$175
FAST TRACK	906	189	(21)	154	(17)	103	(11)	(51)	$9,616,581	–$154
OFF TRACK	107	18	(17)	18	(17)	20	(19)	(47)	$1,169,907	–$21
TURF	127	11	(9)	11	(9)	12	(9)	(73)	$368,700	–$133
FIRM TURF	105	9	(9)	9	(9)	8	(8)	(74)	$323,840	–$113
OFF TURF	22	2	(9)	2	(9)	4	(18)	(64)	$44,860	–$20
MILE OR MORE	457	82	(18)	61	(13)	63	(14)	(55)	$6,586,602	–$274
< 1 MILE	683	136	(20)	122	(18)	72	(11)	(51)	$4,568,586	–$35
FAVORITES	291	115	(40)	61	(21)	33	(11)	(28)	$5,996,436	–$101
ODDS < 5 TO 1	306	62	(20)	71	(23)	42	(14)	(43)	$3,278,390	–$96
ODDS 5 TO 1– 10 TO 1	240	26	(11)	32	(13)	34	(14)	(62)	$1,068,605	–$59
ODDS > 10 TO 1	303	15	(5)	19	(6)	26	(9)	(80)	$811,757	–$54
FIRST TIME STARTERS	89	10	(11)	13	(15)	9	(10)	(64)	$175,840	–$45
RACES WITH APPRENTICES	18	2	(11)	0	(0)	1	(6)	(83)	$28,875	+$24

LUKAS, D WAYNE – TRAINER SUMMARY FOR SPECIFIC YEAR FOR ALL TRACKS IN
NORTH AMERICA

IN NORTH AMERICA FOR ALL TRACKS:

	1977–1992
STARTERS	1,691
WINNERS	1,019 (60%)
PLACERS	1,183 (69%)
STARTS	15,106
WINS	2,753 (18%)
PLACES	4,244 (28%)

1986 IN NORTH AMERICA

	STARTS	1ST	(%)	2ND	(%)	3RD	(%)	UNPL%	EARNINGS	ROWB
TOTALS	1,509	259	(17)	230	(15)	210	(14)	(54)	$12,344,520	−$876
AVERAGE FOR ALL TRAINERS			(8)		(9)		(9)	(74)		−$23
COLTS	694	120	(17)	108	(16)	91	(13)	(54)	$5,100,933	+$303
FILLIES	815	139	(17)	122	(15)	119	(15)	(53)	$7,243,587	−$575
GRADED BLACKTYPF	179	36	(20)	35	(20)	29	(16)	(44)	$7,433,197	-$137
ALL BLACKTYPE	355	62	(17)	64	(18)	57	(16)	(49)	$9,043,885	−$298
ALLOWANCE	496	80	(16)	58	(12)	83	(17)	(55)	$1,723,700	−$321
CLAIMING	164	31	(19)	26	(16)	14	(9)	(56)	$443,532	+$9
MAIDEN	494	86	(17)	82	(17)	56	(11)	(55)	$1,133,403	−$268
DIRT	1363	248	(18)	222	(16)	189	(14)	(52)	$11,989,550	−$740
FAST TRACK	1100	202	(18)	173	(16)	158	(14)	(52)	$9,960,821	−$587
OFF TRACK	263	46	(17)	49	(19)	31	(12)	(52)	$2,028,729	−$153
TURF	146	11	(8)	8	(5)	21	(14)	(73)	$354,970	−$138
FIRM TURF	124	7	(6)	7	(6)	19	(15)	(73)	$287,480	−$174
OFF TURF	22	4	(18)	1	(5)	2	(9)	(68)	$67,490	+$36
MILE OR MORE	637	109	(17)	94	(15)	86	(14)	(54)	$8,317,876	−$385
< 1 MILE	872	150	(17)	136	(16)	124	(14)	(53)	$4,026,644	−$492
FAVORITES	388	129	(33)	82	(21)	55	(14)	(32)	$5,922,956	−$222
ODDS < 5 TO 1	466	86	(18)	82	(18)	72	(15)	(49)	$3,912,579	−$217
ODDS 5 TO 1– 10 TO 1	317	32	(10)	39	(12)	52	(16)	(62)	$1,474,466	−$121
ODDS > 10 TO 1	338	12	(4)	27	(8)	31	(9)	(79)	$1,034,519	−$318
FIRST TIME STARTERS	113	11	(10)	13	(12)	8	(7)	(71)	$161,261	−$130
RACES WITH APPRENTICES	77	11	(14)	8	(10)	8	(10)	(66)	$171,418	−$40

LUKAS, D WAYNE – TRAINER SUMMARY FOR SPECIFIC YEAR FOR ALL TRACKS IN
    NORTH AMERICA

IN NORTH AMERICA FOR ALL TRACKS:

	1977–1992
STARTERS	1,691
WINNERS	1,019 (60%)
PLACERS	1,183 (69%)
STARTS	15,106
WINS	2,753 (18%)
PLACES	4,244 (28%)

1987 IN NORTH AMERICA

	STARTS	1ST	(%)	2ND	(%)	3RD	(%)	UNPL%	EARNINGS	ROWB
TOTALS	1,735	343	(20)	296	(17)	238	(14)	(49)	$17,502,110	–$633
AVERAGE FOR ALL TRAINERS			(8)		(9)		(9)	(74)		–$22
COLTS	860	154	(18)	140	(16)	117	(14)	(52)	$8,037,115	–$301
FILLIES	875	189	(22)	156	(18)	121	(14)	(46)	$9,464,995	–$336
GRADED BLACKTYPE	272	53	(19)	46	(17)	30	(11)	(53)	$9,841,974	–$145
ALL BLACKTYPE	474	92	(19)	84	(18)	64	(14)	(49)	$12,598,843	–$265
ALLOWANCE	597	126	(21)	103	(17)	83	(14)	(48)	$3,019,958	–$276
CLAIMING	161	31	(19)	21	(13)	19	(12)	(56)	$417,200	+$88
MAIDEN	503	94	(19)	88	(17)	72	(14)	(50)	$1,466,109	–$187
DIRT	1600	331	(21)	279	(17)	227	(14)	(48)	$17,081,044	–$482
FAST TRACK	1308	276	(21)	225	(17)	189	(14)	(48)	$14,893,346	–$267
OFF TRACK	292	55	(19)	54	(18)	38	(13)	(50)	$2,187,698	–$215
TURF	135	12	(9)	17	(13)	11	(8)	(70)	$421,066	–$152
FIRM TURF	106	10	(9)	13	(12)	8	(8)	(71)	$334,228	–$109
OFF TURF	29	2	(7)	4	(14)	3	(10)	(69)	$86,838	–$43
MILE OR MORE	837	164	(20)	153	(18)	106	(13)	(49)	$11,737,306	–$409
< 1 MILE	898	179	(20)	143	(16)	132	(15)	(49)	$5,764,804	–$225
FAVORITES	484	164	(34)	93	(19)	66	(14)	(33)	$7,429,123	–$265
ODDS < 5 TO 1	530	124	(23)	113	(21)	72	(14)	(42)	$6,354,072	–$56
ODDS 5 TO 1– 10 TO 1	385	41	(11)	59	(15)	61	(16)	(58)	$2,541,958	–$124
ODDS > 10 TO 1	336	14	(4)	31	(9)	39	(12)	(75)	$1,176,957	–$189
FIRST TIME STARTERS	125	20	(16)	17	(14)	9	(7)	(63)	$319,480	+$0
RACES WITH APPRENTICES	44	5	(11)	9	(20)	7	(16)	(53)	$70,455	–$21

LUKAS, D WAYNE – TRAINER SUMMARY FOR SPECIFIC YEAR FOR ALL TRACKS IN
NORTH AMERICA

IN NORTH AMERICA FOR ALL TRACKS:

	1977–1992
STARTERS	1,691
WINNERS	1,019 (60%)
PLACERS	1,183 (69%)
STARTS	15,106
WINS	2,753 (18%)
PLACES	4,244 (28%)

1988 IN NORTH AMERICA

	STARTS	1ST	(%)	2ND	(%)	3RD	(%)	UNPL%	EARNINGS	ROWB
TOTALS	1,500	318	(21)	238	(16)	193	(13)	(50)	$17,852,600	–$366
AVERAGE FOR ALL TRAINERS			(8)		(8)		(9)	(75)		–$21
COLTS	782	162	(21)	126	(16)	118	(15)	(48)	$9,605,891	–$178
FILLIES	718	156	(22)	112	(16)	75	(10)	(52)	$8,246,709	–$189
GRADED BLACKTYPE	241	43	(18)	39	(16)	37	(15)	(51)	$9,994,302	–$138
ALL BLACKTYPE	423	82	(19)	64	(15)	68	(16)	(50)	$12,672,022	–$102
ALLOWANCE	496	113	(23)	79	(16)	64	(13)	(48)	$3,022,117	–$155
CLAIMING	172	29	(17)	42	(24)	17	(10)	(49)	$628,680	–$108
MAIDEN	409	94	(23)	53	(13)	44	(11)	(53)	$1,529,781	–$1
DIRT	1348	297	(22)	213	(16)	174	(13)	(49)	$16,368,948	–$240
FAST TRACK	1131	246	(22)	175	(15)	150	(13)	(50)	$12,516,773	–$209
OFF TRACK	217	51	(24)	38	(18)	24	(11)	(47)	$3,852,175	–$31
TURF	152	21	(14)	25	(16)	19	(13)	(57)	$1,483,652	–$128
FIRM TURF	133	18	(14)	23	(17)	18	(14)	(55)	$1,072,714	–$110
OFF TURF	19	3	(16)	2	(11)	1	(5)	(68)	$410,938	–$18
MILE OR MORE	759	147	(19)	118	(16)	97	(13)	(52)	$12,048,494	–$255
< 1 MILE	741	171	(23)	120	(16)	96	(13)	(48)	$5,804,106	–$112
FAVORITES	484	170	(35)	91	(19)	58	(12)	(34)	$8,025,632	–$252
ODDS < 5 TO 1	498	100	(20)	88	(18)	84	(17)	(45)	$5,738,096	–$208
ODDS 5 TO 1– 10 TO 1	307	34	(11)	38	(12)	41	(13)	(64)	$3,095,017	–$48
ODDS > 10 TO 1	211	14	(7)	21	(10)	10	(5)	(78)	$993,855	+$139
FIRST TIME STARTERS	119	26	(22)	15	(13)	7	(6)	(59)	$451,964	+$34
RACES WITH APPRENTICES	6	0	(0)	0	(0)	1	(17)	(83)	$5,625	–$12

LUKAS, D WAYNE – TRAINER SUMMARY FOR SPECIFIC YEAR FOR ALL TRACKS IN NORTH AMERICA

IN NORTH AMERICA FOR ALL TRACKS:

	1977–1992
STARTERS	1,691
WINNERS	1,019 (60%)
PLACERS	1,183 (69%)
STARTS	15,106
WINS	2,753 (18%)
PLACES	4,244 (28%)

1989 IN NORTH AMERICA

	STARTS	1ST	(%)	2ND	(%)	3RD	(%)	UNPL%	EARNINGS	ROWB
TOTALS	1,398	305	(22)	231	(17)	162	(12)	(49)	$16,103,998	–$612
AVERAGE FOR ALL TRAINERS			(8)		(9)		(9)	(74)		–$19
COLTS	630	134	(21)	110	(17)	64	(10)	(52)	$8,447,043	–$380
FILLIES	768	171	(22)	121	(16)	98	(13)	(49)	$7,656,955	–$232
GRADED BLACKTYPE	238	50	(21)	34	(14)	23	(10)	(55)	$8,997,930	–$161
ALL BLACKTYPE	393	89	(23)	62	(16)	39	(10)	(51)	$11,403,739	–$242
ALLOWANCE	501	108	(22)	88	(18)	67	(13)	(47)	$2,832,323	–$198
CLAIMING	101	22	(22)	11	(11)	16	(16)	(51)	$406,040	–$40
MAIDEN	403	86	(21)	70	(17)	40	(10)	(52)	$1,461,896	–$129
DIRT	1159	266	(23)	198	(17)	135	(12)	(48)	$13,164,497	–$439
FAST TRACK	990	225	(23)	168	(17)	112	(11)	(49)	$11,593,312	–$387
OFF TRACK	169	41	(24)	30	(18)	23	(14)	(44)	$1,571,185	–$52
TURF	239	39	(16)	33	(14)	27	(11)	(59)	$2,939,501	–$167
FIRM TURF	192	28	(15)	26	(14)	24	(13)	(58)	$1,895,598	–$194
OFF TURF	47	11	(23)	7	(15)	3	(6)	(56)	$1,043,903	+$27
MILE OR MORE	710	131	(18)	120	(17)	88	(12)	(53)	$10,882,645	–$457
< 1 MILE	688	174	(25)	111	(16)	74	(11)	(48)	$5,221,353	–$154
FAVORITES	450	174	(39)	83	(18)	49	(11)	(32)	$7,843,894	–$173
ODDS < 5 TO 1	453	92	(20)	96	(21)	68	(15)	(44)	$5,273,839	–$184
ODDS 5 TO 1– 10 TO 1	279	31	(11)	38	(14)	29	(10)	(65)	$1,995,497	–$76
ODDS > 10 TO 1	216	8	(4)	14	(6)	16	(7)	(83)	$990,768	–$178
FIRST TIME STARTERS	220	38	(17)	27	(12)	18	(8)	(63)	$994,077	–$163
RACES WITH APPRENTICES	20	3	(15)	3	(15)	1	(5)	(65)	$68,333	–$22

LUKAS, D WAYNE – TRAINER SUMMARY FOR SPECIFIC YEAR FOR ALL TRACKS IN
    NORTH AMERICA
IN NORTH AMERICA FOR ALL TRACKS:

	1977–1992
STARTERS	1,691
WINNERS	1,019 (60%)
PLACERS	1,183 (69%)
STARTS	15,106
WINS	2,753 (18%)
PLACES	4,244 (28%)

1990 IN NORTH AMERICA

	STARTS	1ST	(%)	2ND	(%)	3RD	(%)	UNPL%	EARNINGS	ROWB
TOTALS	1,449	272	(19)	224	(15)	170	(12)	(54)	$14,696,426	–$509
AVERAGE FOR ALL TRAINERS			(9)		(9)		(9)	(73)		–$19
COLTS	754	158	(21)	97	(13)	81	(11)	(55)	$9,278,070	+$18
FILLIES	695	114	(16)	127	(18)	89	(13)	(53)	$5,418,356	-$526
GRADED BLACKTYPE	243	42	(17)	31	(13)	33	(14)	(56)	$8,175,911	–$73
ALL BLACKTYPE	412	70	(17)	51	(12)	55	(13)	(58)	$9,857,718	–$97
ALLOWANCE	501	111	(22)	97	(19)	59	(12)	(47)	$3,018,671	–$238
CLAIMING	117	19	(16)	18	(15)	16	(14)	(55)	$358,632	–$37
MAIDEN	419	72	(17)	58	(14)	40	(10)	(59)	$1,461,405	–$133
DIRT	1225	246	(20)	191	(16)	146	(12)	(52)	$12,674,900	–$320
FAST TRACK	985	191	(19)	148	(15)	120	(12)	(54)	$10,138,611	–$220
OFF TRACK	240	55	(23)	43	(18)	26	(11)	(48)	$2,536,289	–$100
TURF	224	26	(12)	33	(15)	24	(11)	(62)	$2,021,526	–$190
FIRM TURF	187	21	(11)	28	(15)	18	(10)	(64)	$1,430,612	–$162
OFF TURF	37	5	(14)	5	(14)	6	(16)	(56)	$590,914	–$28
MILE OR MORE	745	139	(19)	102	(14)	95	(13)	(54)	$10,417,369	–$320
< 1 MILE	704	133	(19)	122	(17)	75	(11)	(53)	$4,279,057	–$188
FAVORITES	389	137	(35)	80	(21)	41	(11)	(33)	$4,850,282	–$180
ODDS < 5 TO 1	483	88	(18)	87	(18)	73	(15)	(49)	$5,573,212	–$262
ODDS 5 TO 1– 10 TO 1	330	36	(11)	39	(12)	39	(12)	(65)	$3,440,903	–$81
ODDS > 10 TO 1	247	11	(4)	18	(7)	17	(7)	(82)	$832,029	+$14
FIRST TIME STARTERS	136	14	(10)	11	(8)	17	(13)	(69)	$337,468	-$189
RACES WITH APPRENTICES	14	1	(7)	1	(7)	2	(14)	(72)	$37,365	–$12

LUKAS, D WAYNE – TRAINER SUMMARY FOR SPECIFIC YEAR FOR ALL TRACKS IN NORTH AMERICA

IN NORTH AMERICA FOR ALL TRACKS:

	1977–1992
STARTERS	1,691
WINNERS	1,019 (60%)
PLACERS	1,183 (69%)
STARTS	15,106
WINS	2,753 (18%)
PLACES	4,244 (28%)

1991 IN NORTH AMERICA

	STARTS	1ST	(%)	2ND	(%)	3RD	(%)	UNPL%	EARNINGS	ROWB
TOTALS	1,497	289	(19)	250	(17)	189	(13)	(51)	$15,942,223	–$676
AVERAGE FOR ALL TRAINERS			(8)		(9)		(9)	(74)		–$20
COLTS	781	169	(22)	125	(16)	91	(12)	(50)	$11,343,819	–$96
FILLIES	716	120	(17)	125	(17)	98	(14)	(52)	$4,598,404	–$584
GRADED BLACKTYPE	227	36	(16)	33	(15)	24	(11)	(58)	$8,910,826	–$158
ALL BLACKTYPE	371	56	(15)	60	(16)	44	(12)	(57)	$10,809,349	–$289
ALLOWANCE	518	115	(22)	93	(18)	75	(14)	(46)	$2,972,638	–$154
CLAIMING	137	29	(21)	18	(13)	18	(13)	(53)	$462,679	–$24
MAIDEN	471	89	(19)	79	(17)	52	(11)	(53)	$1,697,557	–$211
DIRT	1316	266	(20)	233	(18)	172	(13)	(49)	$14,713,203	–$599
FAST TRACK	1102	223	(20)	189	(17)	140	(13)	(50)	$12,918,779	–$468
OFF TRACK	214	43	(20)	44	(21)	32	(15)	(44)	$1,794,424	–$131
TURF	181	23	(13)	17	(9)	17	(9)	(69)	$1,229,020	–$80
FIRM TURF	161	20	(12)	15	(9)	15	(9)	(70)	$1,054,277	–$65
OFF TURF	20	3	(15)	2	(10)	2	(10)	(65)	$174,743	–$15
MILE OR MORE	722	145	(20)	115	(16)	80	(11)	(53)	$11,683,464	–$347
< 1 MILE	775	144	(19)	135	(17)	109	(14)	(50)	$4,258,759	–$330
FAVORITES	386	139	(36)	90	(23)	49	(13)	(28)	$5,205,857	–$158
ODDS < 5 TO 1	498	107	(21)	87	(17)	70	(14)	(48)	$4,999,722	–$146
ODDS 5 TO 1– 10 TO 1	333	33	(10)	48	(14)	42	(13)	(63)	$3,854,817	–$142
ODDS > 10 TO 1	280	10	(4)	25	(9)	28	(10)	(77)	$1,881,827	–$234
FIRST TIME STARTERS	123	20	(16)	14	(11)	13	(11)	(62)	$377,144	-$48
RACES WITH APPRENTICES	14	1	(7)	1	(7)	2	(14)	(72)	$37,365	–$12

LUKAS, D WAYNE – TRAINER SUMMARY FOR SPECIFIC YEAR FOR ALL TRACKS IN
NORTH AMERICA

IN NORTH AMERICA FOR ALL TRACKS:

	1977–1992
STARTERS	1,691
WINNERS	1,019 (60%)
PLACERS	1,183 (69%)
STARTS	15,101
WINS	2,753 (18%)
PLACES	4,244 (28%)

1992 IN NORTH AMERICA

	STARTS	1ST	(%)	2ND	(%)	3RD	(%)	UNPL%	EARNINGS	ROWB
TOTALS	1,278	215	(17)	166	(13)	156	(12)	(58)	$9,502,232	–$429
AVERAGE FOR ALL TRAINERS			(9)		(9)		(10)	(72)		–$18
COLTS	712	124	(17)	90	(13)	92	(13)	(57)	$6,713,431	–$223
FILLIES	566	91	(16)	76	(13)	64	(11)	(60)	$2,788,801	-$207
GRADED BLACKTYPE	170	21	(12)	15	(9)	18	(11)	(68)	$4,283,864	–$124
ALL BLACKTYPE	285	45	(16)	28	(10)	32	(11)	(63)	$5,616,965	–$97
ALLOWANCE	487	84	(17)	72	(15)	62	(13)	(55)	$2,376,495	–$185
CLAIMING	144	27	(19)	22	(15)	15	(10)	(56)	$467,854	–$64
MAIDEN	362	59	(16)	44	(12)	47	(13)	(59)	$1,040,918	–$84
DIRT	1106	185	(17)	147	(13)	150	(14)	(56)	$8,248,075	–$484
FAST TRACK	905	151	(17)	122	(13)	122	(13)	(57)	$7,108,935	–$358
OFF TRACK	201	34	(17)	25	(12)	28	(14)	(57)	$1,139,140	–$126
TURF	172	30	(17)	19	(11)	6	(3)	(69)	$1,254,157	+$53
FIRM TURF	146	27	(18)	17	(12)	5	(3)	(67)	$1,087,564	+$66
OFF TURF	26	3	(12)	2	(8)	1	(4)	(76)	$166,593	–$13
MILE OR MORE	638	112	(18)	87	(14)	64	(10)	(58)	$6,540,054	–$176
< 1 MILE	640	103	(16)	79	(12)	92	(14)	(58)	$2,962,178	–$255
FAVORITES	282	83	(29)	47	(17)	37	(13)	(41)	$3,600,950	–$192
ODDS < 5 TO 1	361	74	(20)	64	(18)	51	(14)	(48)	$2,908,316	–$74
ODDS 5 TO 1–10 TO 1	358	46	(13)	35	(10)	43	(12)	(65)	$1,903,594	+$1
ODDS > 10 TO 1	277	12	(4)	20	(7)	25	(9)	(80)	$1,089,372	–$165
FIRST TIME STARTERS	102	11	(11)	8	(8)	12	(12)	(69)	$214,743	–$79
RACES WITH APPRENTICES	11	1	(9)	0	(0)	0	(0)	(91)	$6,940	–$12

Ben Perkins Jr. is well known on the East Coast and has his tack in the state of Maryland. Despite having a good year in 1992, Ben Perkins is lacking in a few areas. In graded Black Type races, he is 0 for 13, but in non-graded events he has done very well, boasting a 24% winning percentage. It is obvious that Perkins is better on dirt than turf. This is evident with his in-the-money percentages: 56% compared to 33% on turf. Perkins has performed tremendously well with favorites, winning 42% and with first time starters 26%. Perkins is not a good bet is when he is longer than 10-1: only 17% in the money. When he uses an apprentice, he wins 14% and is in the money with 28%.

PERKINS, BEN W. JR. – TRAINER SUMMARY FOR SPECIFIC YEAR FOR ALL TRACKS IN NORTH AMERICA

IN NORTH AMERICA FOR ALL TRACKS:

	1982–1992
STARTERS	244
WINNERS	161 (65%)
PLACERS	178 (72%)
STARTS	1,690
WINS	381 (22%)
PLACES	496 (29%)

1992 IN NORTH AMERICA

	STARTS	1ST	(%)	2ND	(%)	3RD	(%)	UNPL%	EARNINGS	ROWB
TOTALS	407	102	(25)	70	(17)	51	(13)	(45)	$1,823,601	–$65
AVERAGE FOR ALL TRAINERS			(9)		(9)		(9)	(73)		–$18
COLTS	207	56	(27)	35	(17)	21	(10)	(46)	$1,062,094	–$34
FILLIES	200	46	(23)	35	(18)	30	(15)	(44)	$761,507	–$31
GRADED BLACKTYPE	13	0	(0)	2	(15)	1	(8)	(77)	$100,883	–$26
ALL BLACKTYPE	55	10	(18)	8	(15)	6	(11)	(56)	$621,311	–$34
ALLOWANCE	148	40	(27)	27	(18)	21	(14)	(41)	$677,255	+$3
CLAIMING	70	16	(23)	15	(21)	8	(11)	(45)	$165,958	–$16
MAIDEN	134	36	(27)	20	(15)	16	(12)	(46)	$359,077	–$18
DIRT	373	95	(25)	67	(18)	50	(13)	(44)	$1,722,339	–$52
FAST TRACK	303	79	(26)	58	(19)	37	(12)	(43)	$1,384,776	+$1
OFF TRACK	70	16	(23)	9	(13)	13	(19)	(45)	$337,563	–$53
TURF	34	7	(21)	3	(9)	1	(3)	(67)	$101,262	–$14

1992 IN NORTH AMERICA (continued)

	STARTS	1ST	(%)	2ND	(%)	3RD	(%)	UNPL%	EARNINGS	ROWB
FIRM TURF	32	7	(22)	3	(9)	1	(3)	(66)	$101,107	−$10
OFF TURF	2	0	(0)	0	(0)	0	(0)	(100)	$155	−$4
MILE OR MORE	123	27	(22)	20	(16)	10	(8)	(54)	$605,801	−$34
< 1 MILE	284	75	(26)	50	(18)	41	(14)	(42)	$1,217,800	−$33
FAVORITES	143	62	(43)	29	(20)	22	(15)	(22)	$900,262	+ $6
ODDS < 5 TO 1	144	26	(18)	29	(20)	18	(13)	(49)	$567,987	−$65
ODDS 5 TO 1–										
10 TO 1	74	12	(16)	10	(14)	7	(9)	(61)	$254,574	+ $40
ODDS > 10 TO 1	46	2	(4)	2	(4)	4	(9)	(83)	$100,778	−$46
FIRST TIME										
STARTERS	46	11	(24)	10	(22)	2	(4)	(50)	$141,495	−$19
RACES WITH										
APPRENTICES	14	2	(14)	2	(14)	0	(0)	(72)	$23,691	−$12

Mack Miller is one of the most respected trainers on the New York Circuit. His consistency was outstanding in 1992, placing 60% of what he sent out. Mack Miller's strongest showing comes in allowance company. Here he has 70% in the money and a 31% winning percentage. On an "off" track, Miller has visited the winners circle 9 out of 24 times (38%). He is much more consistent in races over a mile than he is in sprints. When Miller is the favorite he has finished in the money in 82% of his starts. Miller does not do very well in all Black Type races: 5 for 45 in 1992. In races where his horses are more than 5-1 he is 2 for 40. Miller is 0 for 13 when he uses an apprentice.

MILLER, MACK – TRAINER SUMMARY FOR SPECIFIC YEAR FOR ALL TRACKS IN
NORTH AMERICA

IN NORTH AMERICA FOR ALL TRACKS:

	1976–1992
STARTERS	248
WINNERS	163 (65%)
PLACERS	194 (78%)
STARTS	2,444
WINS	516 (21%)
PLACES	787 (32%)

1992 IN NORTH AMERICA

	STARTS	1ST	(%)	2ND	(%)	3RD	(%)	UNPL%	EARNINGS	ROWB
TOTALS	146	33	(23)	34	(23)	21	(14)	(40)	$1,396,929	−$86
AVERAGE FOR ALL TRAINERS			(9)		(9)		(9)	(73)		−$18
COLTS	75	17	(23)	19	(25)	11	(15)	(37)	$913,035	−$53
FILLIES	71	16	(23)	15	(21)	10	(14)	(42)	$483,894	−$33
GRADED BLACKTYPE	21	2	(10)	3	)(14)	2	(10)	(66)	$529,799	−$16
ALL BLACKTYPE	24	3	(13)	3	(13)	3	(13)	(61)	$572,069	−$14
ALLOWANCE	61	19	(31)	16	(26)	8	(13)	(30)	$544,780	−$2
CLAIMING	5	2	(40)	1	(20)	0	(0)	(40)	$23,000	+$0
MAIDEN	56	9	(16)	14	(25)	10	(18)	(41)	$257,080	−$70
DIRT	86	16	(19)	15	(17)	14	(16)	(48)	$841,686	−$77
FAST TRACK	62	7	(11)	12	(19)	11	(18)	(52)	$352,206	−$83
OFF TRACK	24	9	(38)	3	(13)	3	(13)	(36)	$489,480	+$6
TURF	60	17	(28)	19	(32)	7	(12)	(28)	$555,243	−$9
FIRM TURF	38	12	(32)	10	(26)	7	(18)	(24)	$337,899	+$8
OFF TURF	22	5	(23)	9	(41)	0	(0)	(36)	$217,344	−$17
MILE OR MORE	91	26	(29)	26	(29)	10	(11)	(31)	$1,121,409	−$16
< 1 MILE	55	7	(13)	8	(15)	11	(20)	(52)	$275,520	−$70
FAVORITES	62	23	(37)	18	(29)	10	(16)	(18)	$659,008	−$30
ODDS < 5 TO 1	44	8	(18)	11	(25)	6	(14)	(43)	$315,153	−$32
ODDS 5 TO 1– 10 TO 1	20	1	(5)	3	(15)	2	(10)	(70)	$365,188	−$20
ODDS > 10 TO 1	20	1	(5)	2	(10)	3	(15)	(70)	$57,580	−$4
FIRST TIME STARTERS	11	2	(18)	1	(9)	1	(9)	(64)	$46,800	−$15
RACES WITH APPRENTICES	13	0	(0)	3	(23)	2	(15)	(62)	$25,800	−$26

Courtesy of The Jockey Club Information Systems ©

One trainer who may have an upper hand on Mack Miller in placing horses is Noel Hickey, currently training on the Illinois circuit. Hickey placed 61% in 1992. **Hickey is the only trainer covered in this chapter that has a plus figure in overall total starts.** His record shows his two successful areas are allowance and maiden races. In allowance company Hickey is winning one-third of the time and winning 32% in maiden races. In allowance company Hickey's horses have finished in the money 72%. On a fast track, Hickey produces winners at a rate of 34% and only 17% on an off surface. Hickey's weaknesses lay in graded blacktype, claiming, sprints, and horses that are over 10-1.

HICKEY, P NOEL – TRAINER SUMMARY FOR SPECIFIC YEAR FOR ALL TRACKS IN
   NORTH AMERICA

IN NORTH AMERICA FOR ALL TRACKS:

	1976–1992
STARTERS	358
WINNERS	199 (55%)
PLACERS	221 (61%)
STARTS	3,076
WINS	512 (16%)
PLACES	787 (25%)

1992 IN NORTH AMERICA

	STARTS	1ST	(%)	2ND	(%)	3RD	(%)	UNPL%	EARNINGS	ROWB
TOTALS	287	79	(28)	54	(19)	41	(14)	(39)	$1,984,148	+$4
AVERAGE FOR ALL TRAINERS			(9)		(9)		(9)	(73)		–$18
COLTS	193	52	(27)	33	(17)	29	(15)	(41)	$1,367,996	+$19
FILLIES	94	27	(29)	21	(22)	12	(13)	(36)	$616,152	–$14
GRADED BLACKTYPE	19	3	(16)	1	(5)	2	(11)	(68)	$305,185	–$1
ALL BLACKTYPE	53	9	(17)	14	(26)	5	(9)	(48)	$892,269	–$39
ALLOWANCE	99	32	(32)	18	(18)	19	(19)	(31)	$604,356	+$10
CLAIMING	75	19	(25)	16	(21)	10	(13)	(41)	$246,567	+$26
MAIDEN	60	19	(32)	6	(10)	7	(12)	(46)	$240,956	+$7
DIRT	138	38	(28)	26	(19)	21	(15)	(38)	$797,057	-$24
FAST TRACK	90	30	(33)	14	(16)	12	(13)	(38)	$519,995	+$27
OFF TRACK	48	8	(17)	12	(25)	9	(19)	(39)	$277,062	–$51
TURF	149	41	(28)	28	(19)	20	(13)	(40)	$1,187,091	+$28
FIRM TURF	113	32	(28)	24	(21)	15	(13)	(38)	$983,920	+$46
OFF TURF	36	9	(25)	4	(11)	5	(14)	(50)	$203,171	–$18
MILE OR MORE	221	62	(28)	39	(18)	38	(17)	(37)	$1,638,642	+$17
< 1 MILE	66	17	(26)	15	(23)	3	(5)	(46)	$345,506	–$14
FAVORITES	132	52	(39)	26	(20)	16	(12)	(29)	$1,097,972	–$18
ODDS < 5 TO 1	80	15	(19)	18	(23)	18	(23)	(35)	$499,517	–$20
ODDS 5 TO 1– 10 TO 1	56	11	(20)	10	(18)	3	(5)	(57)	$301,852	+$50
ODDS > 10 TO 1	19	1	(5)	0	(0)	4	(21)	(74)	$84,807	–$8
FIRST TIME STARTERS	28	8	(29)	2	(7)	2	(7)	(57)	$108,375	+$3
RACES WITH APPRENTICES	40	10	(25)	7	(18)	7	(18)	(39)	$130,895	+$8

Courtesy of The Jockey Club Information Systems ©

Though Noel Hickey has his tack on the Chicago circuit, some of his best performances and best bets for handicappers come when Noel ships to other tracks. When this occurs his unknown ability on these tracks opens the doors for a very profitable meet as happened at the 1992 Gulfstream Park meet. He is a major force on the turf. Hickey started 18 horses at Gulfstream with six wins, six seconds, and three thirds. That is an 83% in the money ratio. Also, Hickey had a total return on winning bets of $54.00. Considering the success that Hickey had, a trip back to Gulfstream Park in 1993 and succeeding years is very likely and potentially profitable.

Just like the trainers, certain jockeys perform better in different classes and under certain circumstances. Know when to bet and when to throw them out.

Julie Krone is the best female jockey and one of the best jockeys overall. Julie has some obvious areas where she is to be bet and be thrown out. A whopping 72% of Julie's winners come in allowance and claiming company. She has an overall 49% in-the-money ratio and 73% with favorites. On the turf course, Julie has a plus $14.00 in all types of races. In maiden races, Julie is at her worst, only bringing 40% in the money and a winning percentage of 13. With colts, Julie has brought home 21% compared to 17% with fillies: a minus $34.00 for colts compared to minus $188.00 with fillies. Even though Julie does not have a plus figure with colts she still does considerably better with colts than fillies. **Julie is the only jockey that we are reviewing that has a plus figure when the odds on her horse are over 10-1. That shows she always tries no matter what the odds.**

KRONE, J.A. – JOCKEY SUMMARY FOR SPECIFIC YEAR FOR ALL TRACKS IN
      NORTH AMERICA

IN NORTH AMERICA FOR ALL TRACKS:

		1981–1992
MOUNTS		14,922
WINS		2,547 (17%)
PLACES		4,357 (29%)

1992 IN NORTH AMERICA

	STARTS	1ST	(%)	2ND	(%)	3RD	(%)	UNPL%	EARNINGS	ROWB
TOTALS	1,438	278	(19)	242	(17)	188	(13)	(51)	$9,178,848	–$222
AVERAGE FOR ALL JOCKEYS			(7)		(8)		(9)	(76)		–$96

1992 IN NORTH AMERICA (continued)

	STARTS	1ST	(%)	2ND	(%)	3RD	(%)	UNPL%	EARNINGS	ROWB
COLTS	783	167	(21)	127	(16)	98	(13)	(50)	$5,578,405	−$34
FILLIES	655	111	(17)	115	(18)	90	(14)	(51)	$3,600,443	−$188
GRADED BLACKTYPE	113	19	(17)	15	(13)	18	(16)	(54)	$2,971,206	−$26
ALL BLACKTYPE	198	33	(17)	35	(18)	31	(16)	(49)	$4,027,804	+$38
ALLOWANCE	491	117	(24)	84	(17)	64	(13)	(46)	$2,844,248	+$49
CLAIMING	402	82	(20)	65	(16)	43	(11)	(53)	$1,311,779	−$67
MAIDEN	347	46	(13)	58	(17)	50	(14)	(56)	$995,017	−$244
DIRT	1025	194	(19)	174	(17)	139	(14)	(50)	$6,379,442	−$237
FAST TRACK	800	150	(19)	135	(17)	112	(14)	(50)	$5,024,003	−$150
OFF TRACK	225	44	(20)	39	(17)	(27)	(12)	(51)	$1,355,439	−$87
TURF	413	84	(20)	68	(16)	49	(12)	(52)	$2,799,406	+$14
FIRM TURF	313	67	(21)	53	(17)	36	(12)	(50)	$2,076,261	+$31
OFF TURF	100	17	(17)	15	(15)	13	(13)	(55)	$723,145	−$17
MILE OR MORE	787	166	(21)	125	(16)	104	(13)	(50)	$5,871,901	−$88
< 1 MILE	651	112	(17)	117	(18)	84	(13)	(52)	$3,306,947	−$136
FAVORITES	323	127	(39)	67	(21)	42	(13)	(27)	$3,317,190	−$62
ODDS < 5 TO 1	457	97	(21)	92	(20)	65	(14)	(45)	$3,065,475	−$85
ODDS 5 TO 1– 10 TO 1	373	39	(10)	53	(14)	53	(14)	(62)	$1,582,060	−$102
ODDS > 10 TO 1	285	15	(5)	30	(11)	28	(10)	(74)	$1,214,123	+$26
FIRST TIME STARTERS	98	16	(16)	16	(16)	8	(8)	(60)	$369,015	+$28
RACES AS AN APPRENTICE	0	0	(0)	0	(0)	0	(0)	(0)	$0	+$0

Courtesy of The Jockey Club Information Systems ©

Pat Day is known world-wide for his achievements. He rode more horses in 1992 than he had in the last five years. Only one class has a plus figure for Day. Day has won 27% of claiming races for a plus figure of $98.00. In all races, Pat has a tremendous 56% in the money ratio and a 24% winning percentage. On an "off" track, he isn't as effective, winning only 19% compared to 26% on a fast track.

DAY, P. – JOCKEY SUMMARY FOR SPECIFIC YEAR FOR ALL TRACKS IN NORTH AMERICA

IN NORTH AMERICA FOR ALL TRACKS:

	1976–1992
MOUNTS	23,525
WINS	5,284 (22%)
PLACES	7,306 (31%)

1992 IN NORTH AMERICA (continued)

	STARTS	1ST	(%)	2ND	(%)	3RD	(%)	UNPL%	EARNINGS	ROWB
TOTALS	1,208	291	(24)	228	(19)	160	(13)	(44)	$12,321,973	−$433
AVERAGE FOR ALL JOCKEYS			(7)		(8)		(9)	(76)		−$96
COLTS	665	159	(24)	124	(19)	77	(12)	(45)	$8,495,037	−$142
FILLIES	543	132	(24)	104	(19)	83	(15)	(42)	$3,826,936	−$292
GRADED BLACKTYPE	113	22	(19)	19	(17)	11	(10)	(54)	$6,720,429	−$53
ALL BLACKTYPE	194	39	(20)	37	(19)	20	(10)	(51)	$7,837,493	−$95
ALLOWANCE	410	100	(24)	82	(20)	55	(13)	(43)	$2,495,479	−$253
CLAIMING	343	94	(27)	59	(17)	38	(11)	(45)	$1,032,479	+$98
MAIDEN	261	58	(22)	50	(19)	47	(18)	(41)	$956,522	−$185
DIRT	1016	250	(25)	195	(19)	130	(13)	(43)	$8,591,789	−$302
FAST TRACK	794	207	(26)	149	(19)	97	(12)	(43)	$7,426,276	−$145
OFF TRACK	222	43	(19)	46	(21)	33	(15)	(45)	$1,165,513	−$157
TURF	192	41	(21)	33	(17)	30	(16)	(46)	$3,730,184	−$130
FIRM TURF	155	33	(21)	28	(18)	22	(14)	(47)	$3,059,760	−$105
OFF TURF	37	8	(22)	5	(14)	8	(22)	(42)	$670,424	−$25
MILE OR MORE	591	145	(25)	106	(18)	88	(15)	(42)	$9,190,904	−$204
< 1 MILE	617	146	(24)	122	(20)	72	(12)	(44)	$3,131,069	−$230
FAVORITES	571	186	(33)	128	(22)	65	(11)	(34)	$7,023,656	−$273
ODDS < 5 TO 1	376	81	(22)	60	(16)	58	(15)	(47)	$3,199,944	−$64
ODDS 5 TO 1− 10 TO 1	193	21	(11)	32	(17)	29	(15)	(57)	$859,326	−$75
ODDS > 10 TO 1	68	3	(4)	8	(12)	8	(12)	(72)	$1,239,047	−$21
FIRST TIME STARTERS	74	14	(19)	16	(22)	9	(12)	(47)	$265,675	−$51
RACES AS AN APPRENTICE	0	0	(0)	0	(0)	0	(0)	(0)	$0	+$0

Courtesy of The Jockey Club Information Systems ©

Kent Desormeaux left Maryland and made a big name for himself in California. Desormeaux took California by storm and became one of the leading jockeys in the country before being injured late in 1992. Desormeaux is the only jockey in the United States to have a plus figure ($29.00) in total mounts with as many as he has ridden, which means if you bet $20 on the horse he was riding every time he rode a horse you would be ahead $290.00 overall. This is a tremendous achievement. In big money races many jockeys do not have the success Desormeaux has. In graded stakes races, Kent has a 28% winning percentage. This is the best in any of the classes that he competes in. He also has a plus figure in graded stakes, Black Type stakes and allowance classes. The biggest plus comes in allowance company, where he is a plus $174.00. He is not a value bet in maiden races, but he is slightly better with first time starters. In distance races he is far superior to how he fares in sprints, with a plus $249.00 compared to a minus $219.00 in sprints.

Listed below are all the years that Desormeaux has been riding, from 1986–1992. If we go over and examine each year we can spot several patterns that can be inserted in our handicapping. In my opinion, 1993 is going to be a tremendous betting year for Kent Desormeaux's fans. As I explained above, Kent showed a plus $29.00 in total starts and was dominant in distance and turf races. When Desormeaux started in 1986 he was an apprentice on the Maryland circuit. It took him four years to dominate those tracks. He did not show a profit because he was overwhelmingly the best and was always the favorite. Now that Desormeaux has moved to the West Coast he has stiffer competition and is not always the favorite, as shown in his 1992 stats. In 1989, Desormeaux's peak year on the Maryland circuit, he rode 598 winners with a 26% winning percentage. When he produces that dominance, as he should in 1993, (his fourth year on the west coast) he will not be the favorite. Be ready to cash in. **Remember: the best time to bet Desormeaux is when he is in distance races or on the turf.** These two together are a powerful combination. Let's hope he gets well soon.

DESORMEAUX, K. J. – JOCKEY SUMMARY FOR SPECIFIC YEAR FOR ALL TRACKS IN NORTH AMERICA

IN NORTH AMERICA FOR ALL TRACKS:

	1986–1992
MOUNTS	11,339
WINS	2,370 (20%)
PLACES	3,352 (29%)

1986 IN NORTH AMERICA

	STARTS	1ST	(%)	2ND	(%)	3RD	(%)	UNPL%	EARNINGS	ROWB
TOTALS	525	55	(10)	56	(11)	80	(15)	(64)	$539,769	–$190
AVERAGE FOR ALL JOCKEYS			(7)		(8)		(9)	(76)		–$110

1986 IN NORTH AMERICA (continued)

	STARTS	1ST	(%)	2ND	(%)	3RD	(%)	UNPL%	EARNINGS	ROWB
COLTS	254	28	(11)	27	(11)	42	(17)	(61)	$302,823	−$78
FILLIES	271	27	(10)	29	(11)	38	(14)	(65)	$236,946	−$112
GRADED BLACKTYPE	0	0	(0)	0	(0)	0	(0)	(0)	$0	+$0
ALL BLACKTYPE	6	3	(50)	0	(0)	1	(17)	(33)	$108,713	+$27
ALLOWANCE	59	3	(5)	5	(8)	9	(15)	(72)	$60,130	−$61
CLAIMING	298	37	(12)	36	(12)	52	(17)	(59)	$281,704	−$60
MAIDEN	162	12	(7)	15	(9)	18	(11)	(73)	$89,222	−$94
DIRT	510	54	(11)	56	(11)	77	(15)	(63)	$531,209	−$206
FAST TRACK	357	43	(12)	40	(11)	56	(16)	(61)	$430,040	−$21
OFF TRACK	153	11	(7)	16	(10)	21	(14)	(69)	$101,169	−$185
TURF	15	1	(7)	0	(0)	3	(20)	(73)	$8,560	+$15
FIRM TURF	13	1	(8)	0	(0)	3	(23)	(69)	$8,560	+$19
OFF TURF	2	0	(0)	0	(0)	0	(0)	(100)	$0	−$4
MILE OR MORE	173	19	(11)	24	(14)	26	(15)	(60)	$250,926	−$119
< 1 MILE	352	36	(10)	32	(9)	54	(15)	(66)	$288,843	−$71
FAVORITES	56	14	(25)	14	(25)	12	(21)	(29)	$104,840	−$25
ODDS < 5 TO 1	76	18	(24)	10	(13)	13	(17)	(46)	$197,395	+$10
ODDS 5 TO 1– 10 TO 1	111	12	(11)	15	(14)	27	(24)	(51)	$117,678	−$29
ODDS > 10 TO 1	282	11	(4)	17	(6)	28	(10)	(80)	$119,856	−$144
FIRST TIME STARTERS	23	1	(4)	1	(4)	1	(4)	(88)	$10,410	−$14
RACES AS AN APPRENTICE	525	55	(10)	56	(11)	80	(15)	(64)	$539,769	−$190

DESORMEAUX, K. J. – JOCKEY SUMMARY FOR SPECIFIC YEAR FOR ALL TRACKS IN NORTH AMERICA

IN NORTH AMERICA FOR ALL TRACKS:

	1986–1992
MOUNTS	11,339
WINS	2,370 (20%)
PLACES	3,352 (29%)

1987 IN NORTH AMERICA

	STARTS	1ST	(%)	2ND	(%)	3RD	(%)	UNPL%	EARNINGS	ROWB
TOTALS	2,207	450	(20)	370	(17)	294	(13)	(50)	$5,122,633	−$309
AVERAGE FOR ALL JOCKEYS			(7)		(8)		(9)	(76)		−$113
COLTS	1225	233	(19)	215	(18)	170	(14)	(49)	$2,578,828	−$295
FILLIES	982	217	(22)	155	(16)	124	(13)	(49)	$2,543,805	−$13

1987 IN NORTH AMERICA (continued)

	STARTS	1ST	(%)	2ND	(%)	3RD	(%)	UNPL%	EARNINGS	ROWB
GRADED BLACKTYPE	20	3	(15)	1	(5)	3	(15)	(65)	$478,578	+$7
ALL BLACKTYPE	121	20	(17)	18	(15)	19	(16)	(52)	$1,310,498	+$17
ALLOWANCE	384	76	(20)	61	(16)	50	(13)	(51)	$1,089,006	−$94
CLAIMING	1121	230	(21)	195	(17)	154	(14)	(48)	$1,811,158	−$220
MAIDEN	581	124	(21)	96	(17)	71	(12)	(50)	$911,971	−$11
DIRT	2074	430	(21)	351	(17)	270	(13)	(49)	$4,529,050	−$304
FAST TRACK	1654	353	(21)	275	(17)	214	(13)	(49)	$3,598,101	−$91
OFF TRACK	420	77	(18)	76	(18)	56	(13)	(51)	$930,949	−$213
TURF	133	20	(15)	19	(14)	24	(18)	(53)	$593,583	−$6
FIRM TURF	124	19	(15)	18	(15)	22	(18)	(52)	$549,566	−$9
OFF TURF	9	1	(11)	1	(11)	2	(22)	(56)	$44,017	+$3
MILE OR MORE	883	175	(20)	165	(19)	104	(12)	(49)	$2,516,715	−$152
< 1 MILE	1324	275	(21)	205	(15)	190	(14)	(50)	$2,605,918	−$156
FAVORITES	649	217	(33)	131	(20)	93	(14)	(33)	$1,876,269	−$109
ODDS < 5 TO 1	742	147	(20)	141	(19)	113	(15)	(46)	$1,790,743	−$198
ODDS 5 TO 1– 10 TO 1	542	67	(12)	76	(14)	66	(12)	(62)	$891,483	−$63
ODDS > 10 TO 1	274	19	(7)	22	(8)	22	(8)	(77)	$564,138	+$62
FIRST TIME STARTERS	121	23	(19)	14	(12)	11	(9)	(60)	$171,150	+$29
RACES AS AN APPRENTICE	1429	295	(21)	233	(16)	190	(13)	(50)	$2,884,253	−$205

DESORMEAUX, K. J. – JOCKEY SUMMARY FOR SPECIFIC YEAR FOR ALL TRACKS IN NORTH AMERICA

IN NORTH AMERICA FOR ALL TRACKS:

	1986–1992
MOUNTS	11,339
WINS	2,370 (20%)
PLACES	3,352 (29%)

1988 IN NORTH AMERICA

	STARTS	1ST	(%)	2ND	(%)	3RD	(%)	UNPL%	EARNINGS	ROWB
TOTALS	1,897	474	(25)	295	(16)	276	(15)	(44)	$6,276,241	−$260
AVERAGE FOR ALL JOCKEYS			(7)		(8)		(8)	(77)		−$95
COLTS	1138	298	(26)	171	(15)	167	(15)	(44)	$3,720,286	$75
FILLIES	759	176	(23)	124	(16)	109	(14)	(47)	$2,555,955	−$184
GRADED BLACKTYPE	22	2	(9)	3	(14)	3	(14)	(63)	$377,396	−$21

1988 IN NORTH AMERICA (continued)

	STARTS	1ST	(%)	2ND	(%)	3RD	(%)	UNPL%	EARNINGS	ROWB
ALL BLACKTYPE	117	22	(19)	22	(19)	20	(17)	(45)	$1,653,837	–$79
ALLOWANCE	355	104	(29)	51	(14)	59	(17)	(40)	$1,645,954	–$15
CLAIMING	961	238	(25)	146	(15)	141	(15)	(45)	$2,060,876	–$102
MAIDEN	464	110	(24)	76	(16)	56	(12)	(48)	$915,574	–$64
DIRT	1786	451	(25)	278	(16)	263	(15)	(44)	$5,777,717	–$194
FAST TRACK	1558	393	(25)	235	(15)	228	(15)	(45)	$5,007,048	–$131
OFF TRACK	228	58	(25)	43	(19)	35	(15)	(41)	$770,669	–$63
TURF	111	23	(21)	17	(15)	13	(12)	(52)	$498,524	–$66
FIRM TURF	103	22	(21)	15	(15)	13	(13)	(51)	$467,954	–$57
OFF TURF	8	1	(13)	2	(25)	0	(0)	(62)	$30,570	–$9
MILE OR MORE	759	196	(26)	117	(15)	106	(14)	(45)	$3,112,157	–$129
< 1 MILE	1138	278	(24)	178	(16)	170	(15)	(45)	$3,164,084	–$131
FAVORITES	795	274	(34)	146	(18)	117	(15)	(33)	$3,180,228	–$215
ODDS < 5 TO 1	673	148	(22)	115	(17)	105	(16)	(45)	$2,155,113	–$71
ODDS 5 TO 1– 10 TO 1	343	43	(13)	27	(8)	44	(13)	(66)	$806,882	–$52
ODDS > 10 TO 1	86	9	(10)	7	(8)	10	(12)	(70)	$134,018	+$77
FIRST TIME STARTERS	95	12	(13)	14	(15)	9	(9)	(63)	$139,530	–$88
RACES AS AN APPRENTICE	0	0	(0)	0	(0)	0	(0)	(0)	$0	+$0

DESORMEAUX, K. J. – JOCKEY SUMMARY FOR SPECIFIC YEAR FOR ALL TRACKS
IN NORTH AMERICA

IN NORTH AMERICA FOR ALL TRACKS:

	1986–1992
MOUNTS	11,339
WINS	2,370 (20%)
PLACES	3,352 (29%)

1989 IN NORTH AMERICA

	STARTS	1ST	(%)	2ND	(%)	3RD	(%)	UNPL%	EARNINGS	ROWB
TOTALS	2,312	598	(26)	384	(17)	309	(13)	(44)	$9,107,563	–$287
AVERAGE FOR ALL JOCKEYS			(7)		(8)		(9)	(76)		–$92
COLTS	1367	361	(26)	238	(17)	177	(13)	(44)	$5,345,483	–$25
FILLIES	945	237	(25)	146	(15)	132	(14)	(46)	$3,762,080	–$263
GRADED BLACKTYPE	30	10	(33)	1	(3)	2	(7)	(57)	$1,086,142	+$30
ALL BLACKTYPE	135	36	(27)	17	(13)	18	(13)	(47)	$2,762,344	–$23
ALLOWANCE	517	129	(25)	99	(19)	75	(15)	(41)	$2,351,716	+$41
CLAIMING	1125	303	(27)	188	(17)	154	(14)	(42)	$2,789,898	–$192
MAIDEN	535	130	(24)	80	(15)	62	(12)	(49)	$1,203,605	–$113

1989 IN NORTH AMERICA (continued)

	STARTS	1ST	(%)	2ND	(%)	3RD	(%)	UNPL%	EARNINGS	ROWB
DIRT	2166	567	(26)	367	(17)	289	(13)	(44)	$7,847,243	−$491
FAST TRACK	1787	457	(26)	299	(17)	244	(14)	(43)	$6,501,820	−$432
OFF TRACK	379	110	(29)	68	(18)	45	(12)	(41)	$1,345,423	−$59
TURF	146	31	(21)	17	(12)	20	(14)	(53)	$1,260,320	+$204
FIRM TURF	112	22	(20)	14	(13)	16	(14)	(53)	$662,510	+$210
OFF TURF	34	9	(26)	3	(9)	4	(12)	(53)	$597,810	−$6
MILE OR MORE	864	244	(28)	149	(17)	118	(14)	(41)	$4,875,021	+$160
< 1 MILE	1448	354	(24)	235	(16)	191	(13)	(47)	$4,232,542	−$447
FAVORITES	1098	372	(34)	205	(19)	159	(14)	(33)	$4,779,772	−$374
ODDS < 5 TO 1	765	170	(22)	134	(18)	102	(13)	(47)	$2,804,017	−$94
ODDS 5 TO 1− 10 TO 1	348	51	(15)	38	(11)	39	(11)	(63)	$1,276,592	+$59
ODDS > 10 TO 1	101	5	(5)	7	(7)	9	(9)	(79)	$247,182	+$124
FIRST TIME STARTERS	193	51	(26)	24	(12)	23	(12)	(50)	$768,042	+$21
RACES AS AN APPRENTICE	0	0	(0)	0	(0)	0	(0)	(0)	$0	+$0

DESORMEAUX, K. J. − JOCKEY SUMMARY FOR SPECIFIC YEAR FOR ALL TRACKS IN NORTH AMERICA

IN NORTH AMERICA FOR ALL TRACKS:

	1986−1992
MOUNTS	11,339
WINS	2,370 (20%)
PLACES	3,352 (29%)

1990 IN NORTH AMERICA

	STARTS	1ST	(%)	2ND	(%)	3RD	(%)	UNPL%	EARNINGS	ROWB
TOTALS	1,435	220	(15)	221	(15)	182	(13)	(57)	$7,204,712	−$84
AVERAGE FOR ALL JOCKEYS			(8)		(8)		(9)	(75)		−$89
COLTS	841	128	(15)	128	(15)	110	(13)	(57)	$4,280,746	−$307
FILLIES	594	92	(15)	93	(16)	72	(12)	(57)	$2,923,966	+$224
GRADED BLACKTYPE	84	7	(8)	15	(18)	11	(13)	(61)	$1,732,465	−$70
ALL BLACKTYPE	163	16	(10)	27	(17)	23	(14)	(59)	$2,533,699	−$136
ALLOWANCE	300	60	(20)	53	(18)	41	(14)	(48)	$1,904,781	+$22
CLAIMING	577	90	(16)	88	(15)	73	(13)	(56)	$1,651,242	+$56
MAIDEN	395	54	(14)	53	(13)	45	(11)	(62)	$1,114,990	−$26
DIRT	1146	175	(15)	179	(16)	145	(13)	(56)	$4,435,820	−$80
FAST TRACK	1091	166	(15)	168	(15)	137	(13)	(57)	$4,190,145	−$74
OFF TRACK	55	9	(16)	11	(20)	8	(15)	(49)	$245,675	−$6

1990 IN NORTH AMERICA (continued)

	STARTS	1ST	(%)	2ND	(%)	3RD	(%)	UNPL%	EARNINGS	ROWB
TURF	289	45	(16)	42	(15)	37	(13)	(56)	$2,768,892	−$2
FIRM TURF	275	42	(15)	41	(15)	35	(13)	(57)	$2,565,447	+$0
OFF TURF	14	3	(21)	1	(7)	2	(14)	(58)	$203,445	−$2
MILE OR MORE	659	93	(14)	106	(16)	83	(13)	(57)	$4,388,974	−$182
< 1 MILE	776	127	(16)	115	(15)	99	(13)	(56)	$2,815,738	+$98
FAVORITES	236	73	(31)	51	(22)	38	(16)	(31)	$1,504,310	−$91
ODDS < 5 TO 1	361	81	(22)	71	(20)	58	(16)	(42)	$2,513,537	+$4
ODDS 5 TO 1– 10 TO 1	373	38	(10)	57	(15)	54	(14)	(61)	$1,671,620	−$169
ODDS > 10 TO 1	465	28	(6)	42	(9)	32	(7)	(78)	$1,515,245	+$171
FIRST TIME STARTERS	124	12	(10)	16	(13)	10	(8)	(69)	$453,552	−$105
RACES AS AN APPRENTICE	1	0	(0)	0	(0)	0	(0)	(100)	$0	−$2

DESORMEAUX, K. J. – JOCKEY SUMMARY FOR SPECIFIC YEAR FOR ALL TRACKS IN NORTH AMERICA

IN NORTH AMERICA FOR ALL TRACKS:

	1986–1992
MOUNTS	11,339
WINS	2,370 (20%)
PLACES	3,352 (29%)

1991 IN NORTH AMERICA

	STARTS	1ST	(%)	2ND	(%)	3RD	(%)	UNPL%	EARNINGS	ROWB
TOTALS	1,395	212	(15)	217	(16)	200	(14)	(55)	$7,552,712	−$490
AVERAGE FOR ALL JOCKEYS			(7)		(8)		(9)	(76)		−$97
COLTS	806	101	(13)	120	(15)	117	(15)	(57)	$4,102,071	−$562
FILLIES	589	111	(19)	97	(16)	83	(14)	(51)	$3,450,641	+$73
GRADED BLACKTYPE	62	8	(13)	10	(16)	6	(10)	(61)	$1,655,320	+$61
ALL BLACKTYPE	142	22	(15)	25	(18)	19	(13)	(54)	$2,909,510	+$29
ALLOWANCE	292	44	(15)	52	(18)	41	(14)	(53)	$1,679,512	−$98
CLAIMING	553	92	(17)	84	(15)	88	(16)	(52)	$1,812,843	−$161
MAIDEN	408	54	(13)	56	(14)	52	(13)	(60)	$1,150,847	−$261
DIRT	1127	176	(16)	173	(15)	162	(14)	(55)	$4,842,371	−$449
FAST TRACK	1014	163	(16)	147	(14)	143	(14)	(56)	$4,381,096	−$332
OFF TRACK	113	13	(12)	26	(23)	19	(17)	(48)	$461,275	−$117
TURF	268	36	(13)	44	(16)	38	(14)	(57)	$2,710,341	−$40
FIRM TURF	263	33	(13)	44	(17)	38	(14)	(56)	$2,588,016	−$90
OFF TURF	5	3	(60)	0	(0)	0	(0)	(40)	$122,325	+$50

1991 IN NORTH AMERICA (continued)

	STARTS	1ST	(%)	2ND	(%)	3RD	(%)	UNPL%	EARNINGS	ROWB
MILE OR MORE	584	76	(13)	106	(18)	90	(15)	(54)	$4,238,584	−$289
< 1 MILE	811	136	(17)	111	(14)	110	(14)	(55)	$3,314,128	−$200
FAVORITES	227	88	(39)	49	(22)	38	(17)	(22)	$2,379,480	+$24
ODDS < 5 TO 1	345	62	(18)	67	(19)	69	(20)	(43)	$1,869,492	−$146
ODDS 5 TO 1–										
10 TO 1	368	44	(12)	55	(15)	49	(13)	(60)	$1,899,543	−$48
ODDS > 10 TO 1	455	18	(4)	46	(10)	44	(10)	(76)	$1,404,197	−$320
FIRST TIME										
STARTERS	139	23	(17)	10	(7)	12	(9)	(67)	$564,940	−$23
RACES AS AN										
APPRENTICE	0	0	(0)	0	(0)	0	(0)	(0)	$0	+$0

DESORMEAUX, K. J. – JOCKEY SUMMARY FOR SPECIFIC YEAR FOR ALL TRACKS
IN NORTH AMERICA

IN NORTH AMERICA FOR ALL TRACKS:

	1986–1992
MOUNTS	11,327
WINS	2,367 (20%)
PLACES	3,348 (29%)

1992 IN NORTH AMERICA

	STARTS	1ST	(%)	2ND	(%)	3RD	(%)	UNPL%	EARNINGS	ROWB
TOTALS	1,556	358	(23)	258	(17)	206	(13)	(47)	$14,128,431	+$29
AVERAGE FOR ALL JOCKEYS			(7)		(8)		(9)	(76)		−$96
COLTS	892	211	(24)	142	(16)	124	(14)	(46)	$9,004,427	+$100
FILLIES	664	147	(22)	116	(17)	82	(12)	(49)	$5,124,004	−$70
GRADED										
BLACKTYPE	97	27	(28)	11	(11)	19	(20)	(41)	$5,834,230	+$17
ALL BLACKTYPE	185	46	(25)	26	(14)	28	(15)	(46)	$7,779,118	+$29
ALLOWANCE	325	77	(24)	63	(19)	38	(12)	(45)	$2,419,328	+$174
CLAIMING	605	148	(24)	102	(17)	78	(13)	(46)	$2,401,806	−$45
MAIDEN	441	87	(20)	67	(15)	62	(14)	(51)	$1,528,179	−$127
DIRT	1225	287	(23)	204	(17)	152	(12)	(48)	$9,764,031	−$73
FAST TRACK	1090	263	(24)	177	(16)	135	(12)	(48)	$8,751,850	−$44
OFF TRACK	135	24	(18)	27	(20)	17	(13)	(49)	$1,012,181	−$29
TURF	331	71	(21)	54	(16)	54	(16)	(47)	$4,364,400	+$103
FIRM TURF	327	71	(22)	53	(16)	52	(16)	(46)	$4,269,400	+$111
OFF TURF	4	0	(0)	1	(25)	2	(50)	(25)	$95,000	−$8
MILE OR MORE	647	160	(25)	101	(16)	93	(14)	(45)	$9,730,833	+$249
< 1 MILE	909	198	(22)	157	(17)	113	(12)	(49)	$4,397,598	−$219
FAVORITES	447	175	(39)	86	(19)	54	(12)	(30)	$6,064,983	−$52

1992 IN NORTH AMERICA (continued)

	STARTS	1ST (%)	2ND (%)	3RD (%)	UNPL%	EARNINGS	ROWB
ODDS < 5 TO 1	457	120 (26)	96 (21)	66 (14)	(39)	$4,476,184	+$106
ODDS 5 TO 1– 10 TO 1	394	49 (12)	55 (14)	57 (14)	(60)	$1,898,379	+$12
ODDS > 10 TO 1	258	14 (5)	21 (8)	29 (11)	(76)	$1,688,885	–$36
FIRST TIME STARTERS	155	27 (17)	18 (12)	18 (12)	(59)	$684,455	–$56
RACES AS AN APPRENTICE	0	0 (0)	0 (0)	0 (0)	(0)	$0	+$0

Courtesy of The Jockey Club Information Systems ©

Lafit Pincay Jr. is one the best jockeys of all time, though he is not kind to the gambler. Pincay does not show a plus figure anywhere except in graded and regular Black Type races. He has slipped a little over the years. **As the statistics below show, Pincay is not worth a bet.** The fact that most of his mounts are at 10-1 or higher tells the handicapper that the public is not betting him because he is not winning. In most of Pincay's categories he is out of the money over 60%. He is out of the money 83% with a horse more than 10-1, where most of his mounts are. Pincay still might ride very well in stakes races but that is the only spot where he is playable.

PINCAY, L. JR. – JOCKEY SUMMARY FOR SPECIFIC YEAR FOR ALL TRACKS IN NORTH AMERICA

IN NORTH AMERICA FOR ALL TRACKS:

	1976–1992
MOUNTS	23,752
WINS	4,774 (20%)
PLACES	7,133 (30%)

1992 IN NORTH AMERICA

	STARTS	1ST (%)	2ND (%)	3RD (%)	UNPL%	EARNINGS	ROWB
TOTALS	1,196	178 (15)	178 (15)	119 (10)	(60)	$6,717,373	–$465
AVERAGE FOR ALL JOCKEYS		(7)	(8)	(9)	(76)		–$96
COLTS	696	111 (16)	103 (15)	64 (9)	(60)	$4,376,968	–$274
FILLIES	500	67 (13)	75 (15)	55 (11)	(61)	$2,340,405	–$192
GRADED BLACKTYPE	76	15 (20)	7 (9)	8 (11)	(60)	$2,623,746	+$13
ALL BLACKTYPE	138	25 (18)	14 (10)	16 (12)	(60)	$3,195,846	+$65

1992 IN NORTH AMERICA (continued)

	STARTS	1ST	(%)	2ND	(%)	3RD	(%)	UNPL%	EARNINGS	ROWB
ALLOWANCE	235	34	(14)	36	(15)	26	(11)	(60)	$1,203,022	−$123
CLAIMING	467	71	(15)	71	(15)	46	(10)	(60)	$1,337,650	−$212
MAIDEN	356	48	(13)	57	(16)	31	(9)	(62)	$980,855	−$194
DIRT	951	146	(15)	151	(16)	94	(10)	(59)	$4,464,173	−$261
FAST TRACK	836	128	(15)	138	(17)	79	(9)	(59)	$4,037,599	−$204
OFF TRACK	115	18	(16)	13	(11)	15	(13)	(60)	$426,574	−$57
TURF	245	32	(13)	27	(11)	25	(10)	(66)	$2,253,200	−$204
FIRM TURF	237	30	(13)	26	(11)	25	(11)	(65)	$1,943,625	−$208
OFF TURF	8	2	(25)	1	(13)	0	(0)	(62)	$309,575	+$4
MILE OR MORE	516	80	(16)	76	(15)	57	(11)	(58)	$4,380,633	−$238
< 1 MILE	680	98	(14)	102	(15)	62	(9)	(62)	$2,336,740	−$226
FAVORITES	209	63	(30)	47	(22)	25	(12)	(36)	$2,264,347	−$115
ODDS < 5 TO 1	340	71	(21)	75	(22)	42	(12)	(45)	$2,470,250	−$52
ODDS 5 TO 1– 10 TO 1	276	31	(11)	32	(12)	26	(9)	(68)	$1,011,664	−$60
ODDS > 10 TO 1	371	13	(4)	24	(6)	26	(7)	(83)	$971,112	−$239
FIRST TIME STARTERS	107	9	(8)	8	(7)	8	(7)	(78)	$210,300	−$66
RACES AS AN APPRENTICE	0	0	(0)	0	(0)	0	(0)	(0)	$0	+$0

Courtesy of The Jockey Club Information Systems ©

Money Management

7

The vast majority of gamblers who wager on horse racing have no sense of money management. Money management is half the battle in any type of gambling. Many times handicappers will win six or seven out of a nine race card and have a losing day. To the novice this may seem impossible, but the serious horseplayer understands.

Win, Place, and Show betting used to be the most popular form of wagering in horseracing. Now, in our advanced age of exotic wagering, this has become a side bet. Some of the best handicappers do not play the basic Win, Place, and Show at all. They stick with the exotics.

Betting the exotics alone is not the smartest way of betting, however. A combination of the two will measureably increase your bankroll, if bet properly. The reason I recommend that the average horseplayer not just bet the exactas and trifectas is that many times the horseplayer will handicap a race and come up with two horses that he would like to bet in a particular race. For example, say one horse is 2-1 and the other 10-1. The handicapper bets an exacta box and a trifecta part-wheel with all, 2-1 with 10-1 with all and 10-1 with 2-1 with all. This means if the two selected horses run first and second it would not matter who ran third. The handicapper would hit the trifecta as well as the exacta. Great, right? Wrong! The horse that is 10-1 wins and the 2-1 runs out of the money and our handicapper lost all his bets even though he picked a $22.00 winner. This tragedy occurs everyday to horseplayers. Money management will correct these losses.

Our bankroll should be broken down and set before we start betting. If we decide to bet $100.00 a race that is fine, but we must always bet $100.00. No more and no less. I am not saying that you have to bet $100.00 per race. This is just a convenient example. You will have to adjust the amount to your bankroll. As I mentioned, you must bet the same amount per race, but not necessarily on every race. Bet the same amount on each race that you have handicapped where you have come up with a horse you think is worth betting. Discipline and money management must guide your handicapping. Most successful handicappers will go to the track and bet only two or three races out of nine. If you want to be successful, be selective. **Only bet horse that you feel confident with.** Discipline is not easy. Most horseplayers want to have action in every race. This leads to an unsuccessful day at the track.

In distributing his or her bankroll, each handicapper will have his or her own style. Here is mine. I bet 60% win, place, and show, 15% Exactas, 15% Trifectas, 10% Daily Double, and 5% Hunch Bets, Pick-3, or Pick-6. You will have to adjust for your type of wagering. Just remember, always have a balanced bankroll structure. The following is NOT a balanced structure.

0% Win, Place, Show, 40% Exactas, 40% Trifectas, 10% Daily Double, and 10% Pick-3. Nothing is wrong with this structure if you like losing. Occasionally you will win but the odds are against you. Remember, Exactas and Trifectas have the biggest take-out percentages by the state (more money is deducted by the track for its profit here than Win, Place, and Show betting). So, you are not getting the same payout as you would with the across-the-board wagering. **The handicapper that likes to bet Exactas and Trifectas is not betting wrong but he must proportion his betting to make it profitable.** By not proportioning our betting, the following could occur.

John Doe (our pretend handicapper) liked two horses in the fifth race at the Meadowlands on December 4th. These two horses were Doorbuster Special and Living Bold. John liked Doorbuster Special more, but he only bets Exactas and Trifectas, so he bet his usual $20 exacta box. They both came in, producing a $17.00 exacta payout and

$170.00 for a $20 exacta. The only problem with this is if John Doe was a Win, Place, and Show bettor and put that same $40 to win on Doorbuster Special, he would have received $176.00 for his bet and would not have to worry about who ran second.

5th—$6,000, 6f, 3 YO & up, Off—9:01. Claiming ($6,250-$6,000) F & M. Winner—b m 6 At The Threshold-Watanga Native by Our Native. Owner—Y Knot Sta. Trainer—J. Orseno.

PP Horse & Weight	St.	¼	½	Str.	Fin.	Eq.
6-Doorbuster Specll (117)	3	4:½	3:hd	4:7	1:nk	3.40
5-Living Bold (116)	1	2:2½	2:2½	1:½	2:2	1.00
4-Galleria (119)	6	5:hd	4:3	3:hd	3:3	2.90
2-Anlta Lass (114)	5	1:1	1:1	2:hd	4:7	10.00
3-J Cs Miss (113)	2	3:½	5:4½	5:2	5:4	7.60
1-Callfon (114)	4	6	6	6	6	33.10

Time: 22 4/5, :46 1/5, :59, 1:11 3/5.

7-Doorbuster Special (Marquez)	8.80	3.60	2.60
6-Living Bold (Santagata)		2.80	2.20
5-Galleria (King)			2.40

SCRATCHED: Yangs Last. **EXACTA (7-6) PAID $17.00**

There is another wagering technique that has been around for years and is gaining new-found popularity throughout tracks across the country: parlaying bets instead of using the Daily Double (DD). Parlaying can be performed in any race. It is not limited to selected races like the DD. Parlaying is simple. When you have a winner, take the winnings and bet it all on the next handicapped select row you like. This angle gives the bettor and edge over the DD in a few ways. First, as I mentioned, the DD limits the bettor to two particular races. Parlaying can be used on any races the handicapper likes. When you wager on the DD you are locked in to those two horses. If you parlay your bets after you win the first race, you have the option to change the horse you originally selected in the next betting race. Parlays frequently have larger payouts.

FIRST RACE
Phila Park
NOVEMBER 22, 1992

$1\frac{1}{16}$ MILES. (1.40^{4}) CLAIMING. Purse $5,500. Fillies and Mares, 3-year-olds and upward. Weights, 3-year-olds 118 lbs.; Older 122 lbs. Non-winners of two races at one mile or over since September 22 allowed 3 lbs. Such a race since then 6 lbs. Claiming Price $4,000. (101ST DAY WEATHER SHOWERY TEMPERATURE 60 DEGREES)

Value of race $5,500; value to winner $3,300; second $1,100; third $605; fourth $330; fifth $165. Mutuel pool $26,711. Exacta Pool $31,903 Trifecta Pool $15,574

Last Raced	Horse	M/Eqt.	A.Wt	PP	St	¼	½	¾	Str	Fin	Jockey	Cl'g Pr	Odds $1
8Nov92 ^{4}Pha^{2}	Needs No Reason	Lb	4 111	4	5	5^{hd}	$6^{2\frac{1}{2}}$	2^{hd}	$1^{1\frac{1}{2}}$	$1^{5\frac{1}{2}}$	Umana J L^{5}	4000	5.80
13Nov92 ^{6}Pha^{8}	I'ma Decided	Lb	4 113	3	4	$1^{1\frac{1}{2}}$	$1^{\frac{1}{2}}$	$1^{1\frac{1}{2}}$	$2^{2\frac{1}{2}}$	$2^{1\frac{1}{4}}$	Castaneda K	4000	11.20
8Nov92 ^{6}Pha^{2}	Roodle	Lb	4 111	6	2	$3^{1\frac{1}{2}}$	2^{2}	3^{hd}	3^{hd}	3^{nk}	Somsanith N^{3}	4000	7.00
8Nov92 ^{6}Pha^{6}	This Ones Easy	Lb	5 116	2	7	$6^{2\frac{1}{2}}$	5^{hd}	4^{3}	4^{3}	$4^{1\frac{1}{2}}$	Petersen J L	4000	11.50
8Nov92 ^{4}Pha^{5}	High Spirited	L	6 116	9	8	8^{7}	7^{1}	5^{1}	5^{2}	5^{7}	Lukas M	4000	1.70
8Nov92 ^{6}Pha^{7}	Wajadama	Lb	4 119	5	3	$2^{1\frac{1}{2}}$	$4^{1\frac{1}{2}}$	6^{5}	6^{8}	$6^{4\frac{1}{2}}$	Cruz C	4000	5.00
8Nov92 ^{6}Pha^{1}	Slady Janey	Lb	7 119	8	9	9	9	9	7^{2}	$7^{4\frac{1}{2}}$	Landicini C Jr	4000	5.00
16Nov92 ^{2}Pha^{1}	Kathleen's Follie	L	4 119	7	1	4^{2}	3^{hd}	7^{hd}	9	$8^{2\frac{1}{2}}$	Barbazon D S	4000	19.60
8Nov92 ^{4}Pha^{7}	Sultry Princess	Lb	4 116	1	6	7^{3}	8^{7}	8^{2}	8^{hd}	9	Bisono J†	4000	39.80

OFF AT 12:31 Start good Won driving Time, :23^{1}, :47^{4}, 1:14 , 1:42^{2}, 1:49^{4} Track muddy.

Official Program Numbers↘

$2 Mutuel Prices:			
4–NEEDS NO REASON	13.60	6.40	4.80
3–I'MA DECIDED		11.40	7.20
6–ROODLE			4.00

$2 EXACTA 4–3 PAID $189.60 $2 TRIFECTA 4–3–6 PAID $1,038.20

Dk. b. or br. f, by Royal Reasoning—Je Vous A'dore, by Mo Bay. Trainer Gruwell Bessie S. Bred by Pennfield Farms Inc (Pa).

NEEDS NO REASON saving ground throughout, rallied to take lead in early stretch and pulled clear. I'MA DECIDED set pace just off rail, opened clar lead on final turn but couldn't keep pace late. ROODLE was outside and just off pace, moved to inside near lane and gae way. THIS ONES EASY advanced racing well ut from rail and flattened out. HIGH SPIRITED was wide. WAJADAM tired.

Owners— 1, Foraker Diana; 2, Capelli & Carapella; 3, Fallon Martin L; 4, Murray Audrey R; 5, Bradan Stable; 6, Cap J & Sons Stable; 7, Baker Mrs Thomas W Jr; 8, Scorese Carmen; 9, Clifford Carol P & White Kevin.

Trainers— 1, Gruwell Bessie S; 2, Scanlan John F; 3, Fallon Martin L; 4, Sanders Harland; 5, Jenkins Suzanne H; 6, Solano Rafael; 7, Gilday James A; 8, Scorese Carmen; 9, Taylor Ronald E.

† **Apprentice allowance waived:** Sultry Princess 5 pounds. **Corrected weight:** I'ma Decided 113 pounds.

Needs No Reason was claimed by Emerald Isle Stable; trainer, McCarthy William E.

Scratched—Joli Princess (8Nov92 ^{4}Pha^{6}); Shuffling Sokey (15Nov92^{11}Pha^{7}).

SECOND RACE
Phila Park
NOVEMBER 22, 1992

7 FURLONGS. (1.21^{2}) CLAIMING. Purse $4,500. 3-year-olds and upward which have not won two races since May 22, 1992. Weights, 3-year-olds 119 lbs.; Older 122 lbs. Non-winners of two races since April 22 allowed 3 lbs. A race since then 6 lbs. Claiming Price $4,000.

Value of race $4,500; value to winner $2,700; second $900; third $495; fourth $270; fifth $135. Mutuel pool $36,288. Exacta Pool $47,002 Trifecta Pool $27,704

Last Raced	Horse	M/Eqt.	A.Wt	PP	St	¼	½	Str	Fin	Jockey	Cl'g Pr	Odds $1
11Nov92 ^{1}Pha^{1}	Medieval Prospect	Lb	4 114	12	7	5^{hd}	5^{2}	3^{2}	$1^{\frac{3}{4}}$	Umana J L^{5}	4000	9.90
11Nov92 ^{1}Pha^{3}	Ciel D'Hiver	Lb	5 119	5	12	$9^{\frac{1}{2}}$	$7^{\frac{1}{2}}$	5^{3}	2^{hd}	Arroyo E R	4000	6.90
15Nov92 ^{7}Pha^{1}	Market Quest	L	6 119	9	4	$4^{1\frac{1}{2}}$	$2^{\frac{1}{2}}$	2^{hd}	3^{2}	Reynolds R L	4000	11.30
15Nov92 ^{3}Lrl^{10}	Gee Jamie	L	7 116	2	6	$2^{1\frac{1}{2}}$	1^{1}	1^{2}	$4^{1\frac{3}{4}}$	Jocson G J	4000	1.30
15Nov92 ^{1}Pen^{10}	Bowdoin	Lb	5 119	4	1	$3^{1\frac{1}{2}}$	$4^{\frac{1}{2}}$	4^{hd}	$5^{2\frac{1}{2}}$	Matz N	4000	12.20
1Nov92 ^{6}Pha^{2}	Ruckus	Lb	7 116	8	10	6^{1}	6^{hd}	$6^{\frac{1}{2}}$	$6^{\frac{1}{2}}$	Vigliotti M J	4000	5.60
14Nov92 ^{2}Pha^{9}	B. J.'s Ticket	Lb	5 119	3	8	7^{2}	8^{2}	7^{5}	$7^{3\frac{1}{4}}$	Petersen J L	4000	41.60
9Nov92 ^{3}Pha	St. Peter's Bay	Lb	4 116	1	9	$11^{\frac{1}{2}}$	11^{hd}	11^{5}	8^{nk}	Bisono J	4000	68.80
26Oct92 ^{1}Pha^{8}	Sir Amby Dextris	Lb	5 119	6	2	10^{5}	$10^{1\frac{1}{2}}$	10^{hd}	9^{2}	Pennisi F A	4000	35.40
15Nov92 ^{4}Pha^{4}	Coral Ridge	Lb	7 122	7	3	8^{hd}	9^{6}	8^{1}	10^{3}	Black A S	4000	5.60
11Nov92 ^{1}Pha^{6}	La Bet	Lb	5 119	10	5	1^{hd}	$3^{\frac{1}{2}}$	9^{hd}	11^{nk}	Madrigal R Jr	4000	31.90
22Oct92 ^{3}Pha^{7}	Raindance Harry	L	5 114	11	11	12	12	12	12	Salazar A C^{5}	4000	74.90

OFF AT 12:58 Start good. Won driving. Time, :22^{1}, :45^{3}, 1:12^{3}, 1:27^{1} Track muddy.

$2 Mutuel Prices:

12–MEDIEVAL PROSPECT	....	21.80	9.00	6.20
5–CIEL D'HIVER	....		8.40	5.40
9–MARKET QUEST	....			5.40

$2 EXACTA 12–5 PAID $142.40 $2 TRIFECTA 12–5–9 PAID $1,108

B. g, by Diamond Prospect—Medieval Season, by Medieval Man. Trainer McKee John D. Bred by Parker Roger A (Fla).

MEDIEVAL PROSPECT split rivals when rallying on the turn, engaged for the lead leving furlong grounds, drifted in taking the lead and held sway under pressure. CIEL D'HIVER was slowest from the gate, raced wide throughout and finished fastest. MARKET QUEST split rivals and took up chase on the far turn and finished willingly. GEE JAMIE vied for command inside, opened a clear lead in midstretch and weakened. BOWDOIN saved ground just off the pace and weakened. B.J.'S TICKET saved ground. CORAL RIDGE raced outside. LA BET prompted two wide, bore out and gave way.

Owners— 1, Ward William R Jr; 2, Sandoval Gaston D; 3, Schiano-Dicola Raimondo; 4, Seidman David; 5, Black Robert; 6, Shady Oak Farm; 7, Kentwood Farm; 8, Mayers Angela; 9, Dellapesca Richard; 10, Main Line Stable; 11, Riviello Lawrence R; 12, Kelley Kathleen.

Trainers— 1, McKee John D; 2, Sandoval Gaston D; 3, Shauf Walter J; 4, Desmarais Dennis; 5, Velazquez Alfredo; 6, Smith Ralph R; 7, Busedu Anthony J Jr; 8, Whylie Herold O; 9, Farro Michael; 10, Graci Joseph J III; 11, Iwinski Allen; 12, Smith A Archie Jr.

Corrected weight: Bowdoin 119 pounds.

Scratched—Talented Pirate (17Nov92 3Pha5); Foxy General (11Nov92 1Pha5); Dino Mike (15Nov92 7Pha11); Go Robert Go (11Nov92 1Pha8); Super Bowl Five (1Nov92 2Del3); Johnny Fast (2Nov92 10Suf11).

The DD's paid $139.60 for $2.00. If we had parlayed these horses we would have received $148.24 for our $2.00 investment. In the first race the winner paid $13.60. Since we cannot bet the change amount we add .40 making it $14.00. The parlayed amount then would have been $152.60. For a $20.00 wager, the difference between betting the DD and parlaying would have been $130.00.

FIRST RACE

Phila Park

NOVEMBER 30, 1992

6 FURLONGS. (1.08¹) MAIDEN CLAIMING. Purse $4,500. 2–year–olds. Weight: 121 lbs. Claiming price $8,000; for each $1,000 to $7,000, 2 lbs. (108TH DAY. WEATHER CLEAR. TEMPERATURE 47 DEGREES.)

Value of race $4,500; value to winner $2,700; second $900; third $495; fourth $270; fifth $135. Mutuel pool $21,929. Exacta Pool $24,680 Trifecta Pool $15,678

Last Raced	Horse	M/Eqt.A.Wt	PP St	¼	½	Str	Fin	Jockey	Cl'g Pr	Odds $1
16Nov92 1Pha2	C. C's Mister Ed	2 121	2 4	1hd	1½	12½	12½	Verge M E	8000	1.70
13Nov92 4Pha8	Pappa Pill	b 2 121	10 1	63	4hd	2½	22½	Gomez M A	8000	77.40
16Nov92 1Pha4	Mongo's Game	2 119	11 3	103	93	51	3nk	Taylor K T†	7000	25.50
2Nov92 1Pha	Pen Knife	b 2 121	8 9	92½	8½	7hd	42	Lukas M	8000	100.10
23Nov92 1Pha2	King Kazar	L 2 121	5 10	7½	71	8½	5no	Black A S	8000	4.00
13Nov92 4Pha5	Act Single	b 2 119	12 2	115	102	106	61½	Aristone M	7000	60.60
21Nov92 1Pha6	Quick Nate	2 121	4 12	12	111	91	71	Barbazon D S	8000	17.20
16Nov92 1Pha5	Media Storm	Lb 2 119	3 8	51	51	6hd	8hd	Jocson G J	7000	26.40
21Nov92 1Pha4	Flaming Pleasure	L 2 119	7 5	2hd	2hd	31	9hd	Matz N	7000	1.60
23Nov92 1Pha	Big Play Man	b 2 121	1 7	43	3½	41	1011	Hansby A E	8000	37.30
	Majesty's Knight	b 2 116	6 11	8hd	101	11hd	111½	Umana J L5	8000	15.00
2Nov92 1Pha7	Discovery Mission	Lb 2 112	9 6	3½	61½	12	12	Surrency R S7	7000	125.70

OFF AT 12:32 Start good. Won driving. Time, :23 , :49¹, 1:02², 1:16¹ Track fast.

Official Program Numbers\

$2 Mutuel Prices:

2–C. C'S MISTER ED	....	5.40	3.80	3.20
10–PAPPA PILL	....		38.40	12.00
11–MONGO'S GAME	....			6.80

$2 EXACTA 2–10 PAID $203.40 $2 TRIFECTA 2–10–11 PAID $1,829.00

B. c, (Apr), by Pass The Line—Arrived Late, by Vertex. Trainer Connor James P III. Bred by Appleton Arthur I (Fla).
C. C'S MISTER ED, away in good order to show the way, shook off rivals in upper stretch and won under a drive. PAPPA PILL moved up wide on the turn and finished well. MONGO'S GAME closed between rivals to gain third. PEN KNIFE rallied mildly. KING KAZAR failed to menace. MEDIA STORM was outrun. FLAMING PLEASURE and BIG PLAY MAN forced the pace and tired. DISCOVERY MISSION bore out leaving the turn while giving way.

Owners— 1, Connery Elyse; 2, Kling Cindy; 3, Smith Laurel P; 4, McLaughlin Mary S; 5, Atrium Racing Stable; 6, Aristone Roland; 7, Irwin A T; 8, Porreco Lou; 9, Bryant Daniel F; 10, Joselson Stanley I; 11, Bradan Stable; 12, Stanford Stan.

Trainers— 1, Connor James P III; 2, Kling Cindy; 3, Savidge Robert; 4, McLaughlin Mary S; 5, Marini Thomas; 6, Aristone Philip T; 7, Irwin Alex T; 8, Broome Edwin T; 9, Bryant Daniel F; 10, Decker John B; 11, Jenkins Suzanne H; 12, Lober Steven.

† Apprentice allowance waived: Mongo's Game 5 pounds.

Scratched—Kohinoor's Flyer; In the Clinches (16Nov92 1Pha6); Blue Match (16May92 1Del5); Demon Hooch (12Aug92 11Mth10); Castle Pines (23Oct92 6Pha); September Steal.

SECOND RACE

Phila Park

NOVEMBER 30, 1992

1 MILE 70 YARDS. (1.39) CLAIMING. Purse $5,500 (plus 35% Pa–bred bonus). Fillies and Mares. 3–year–olds and upward which have never won three races. Weights: 3–year–olds, 118 lbs.; Older, 122 lbs. Non–winners of a race since September 30, allowed 3 lbs. A race since August 30, 6 lbs. Claiming price $5,000.

Value of race $5,500; value to winner $3,300; second $1,100; third $605; fourth $330; fifth $165. Mutuel pool $28,685. Exacta Pool $34,058 Trifecta Pool $20,399

Last Raced	Horse	M/Eqt.A.Wt	PP	St	¼	½	¾	Str	Fin	Jockey	Cl'g Pr	Odds $1
22Nov92 8FL4	Bates Stand	b 4 122	12	11	12	11⁴	5½	2ʰᵈ	11½	Coburn L A	5000	6.40
20Nov92 2Pen3	Regal Frisco	Lb 4 109	2	8	3½	3½	2½	3¹	2³	Salazar A C7	5000	45.00
20Nov92 3Pha8	Lawenta	Lb 4 122	7	12	11³½	10²	7½	6²½	3ⁿᵏ	Somsanith N	5000	13.60
16Nov92 2Pha4	Lanie's Luck	4 112	11	5	4½	5⁵	3¹	4¹	4ⁿᵒ	Ortiz R7	5000	11.40
16Nov92 2Pha2	Slugger Blue	Lb 6 119	9	10	10³	8½	8¹	5½	5ⁿᵏ	Villon A J	5000	6.40
24Nov92 7Pha5	Kathie's Sister	Lb 3 107	10	4	2⁵	1¹½	13½	12½	64½	Umana J L5	5000	1.20
16Nov92 2Pha8	Delightful Kris	Lb 3 118	8	9	7½	7½	6¹	7½	7ⁿᵒ	Lopez C C†	5000	26.40
17Nov92 7Pha9	Kane Law	Lb 4 116	3	7	9ʰᵈ	9ʰᵈ	9½	8⁵	8⁶	Verge M E	5000	54.50
20Nov92 2Pha5	Chelsea's Bid	Lb 4 116	5	3	1¹	2⁴	4¹	93½	94½	Santiago C	5000	10.20
11Nov92 2Pha5	Miss Bucou	Lb 3 118	6	6	6²½	6½	10²½	10½	10²	Madrigal RJr†	5000	13.60
16Nov92 2Pha10	Samantha Dancer	L 3 115	4	2	8ʰᵈ	12	12	12	11¹½	Barbazon D S	5000	21.50
16Nov92 2Pha7	Bright Bonnie	L 4 115	1	1	5¹	4ʰᵈ	11³½	112½	12	Surrency R S7	5000	14.80

OFF AT 12:59 Start good, Won driving. Time, :22³, :47³, 1:15⁴, 1:45 , 1:49³ Track fast.

$2 Mutuel Prices:

12–BATES STAND		14.80	6.40	4.80
2–REGAL FRISCO			35.80	13.60
7–LAWENTA				8.60

$2 EXACTA 12–2 PAID $425.60 $2 TRIFECTA 12–2–7 PAID $4,759.60

B. f, by Bates Motel—Stand From Under, by First Albert. Trainer Taylor Robert J. Bred by Rosenberg Louis (Ky).
BATES STAND, allowed to settle early, rallied between rivals leaving the final turn, caught KATHIE'S SISTER in the final furlong and held sway. REGAL FRISCO responded well to close the gap. LAWENTA finished well between rivals to get up for third. LANIE'S LUCK needed a closing bid. SLUGGER BLUE lacked the needed rally. KATHIE'S SISTER faltered in the drive. DELIGHTFUL KRIS was outrun. CHELSEA'S BID disputed the early pace and tired. BRIGHT BONNIE tired.

Owners— 1, Wolf Tina; 2, Collier Reginald B; 3, Two C's Stables; 4, Hammond Wilbur C; 5, Owens Gloria; 6, Braden Stable; 7, Columbus Corp; 8, Hild Sharon; 9, Sala Henry; 10, Longleaf Pine Farm; 11, Dandegian Albert & Maurizio Mario; 12, Riegler Mary P.

Trainers— 1, Taylor Robert J; 2, Betancourt Eli Jr; 3, Correnti Armand W; 4, Hammond Wilbur C; 5, Owens Gloria; 6, Jenkins Suzanne H; 7, Griffith Terry; 8, Hild Glenn L; 9, Digrius Martin W; 10, Houghton Ronald B; 11, Robbins Charles R; 12, Riegler Mary P.

† Apprentice allowance waived: Delightful Kris 5 pounds; Miss Bucou 5. Corrected weight: Bates Stand 122 pounds; Samantha Dancer 112. Overweight: Samantha Dancer 3 pounds.

Courtesy of Daily Racing Form ©

The winner of the first race paid $5.40 and the second race winner paid $14.80. The DD produced a $32.00 payout. If you had parlayed the two you would have received $44.40. Twelve dollars and forty cents may not seem like a lot of money but if you had played a $20 parlay it would be a difference of $124.00.

EIGHTH RACE
Aqueduct
DECEMBER 6, 1992

1 $\frac{1}{16}$ MILES.(InnerDirt). (1.41³) 18th running THE TEMPTED (Grade III). Purse $100,000 added. Fillies, 2-year-olds. By subscription of $200 each which should accompany the nomination. $800 to pass the entry box, $800 to start with $100,000 added. The added money and all fees to be divied 60% to the winner, 22% to second, 12% to third and 6% to fourth. Weight 119 lbs. Winners of a sweepstakes of $50,000 at a mile or over. An additional 2 lbs. Non-winners of a race of $50,000 allowed 3 lbs., of a race of $25,000, 5 lbs., of a race other than Maiden or Claiming 7 lbs. Starters to be named at the closing time of entries. Trophies will be presented to the winning owner, trainer and jockey. Nominations closed Wednesday, November 18, 1992, with 23 nominations.

Value of race $114,200; value to winner $68,520; second $25,124; third $13,704; fourth $6,852. Mutuel pool $181,993. Exacta Pool $333,742

Last Raced	Horse	M/Eqt.A.Wt	PP	St	¼	½	¾	Str	Fin	Jockey	Odds $1
15Nov92 8Aqu2	True Affair	2 121	5	5	3¹	3²	2¹½	1hd	1nk	Bravo J	3.30
21Nov92 10Lrl1	Broad Gains	2 121	2	1	6	6	6	4³	2²	Ladner C J III	4.50
19Nov92 7Aqu1	Touch Of Love	2 114	1	2	2¹½	2½	1hd	2⁵	3³	Smith M E	1.20
19Nov92 7Aqu6	Lady Starlit	2 112	6	4	1½	1hd	3³½	3hd	44	Gryder A T	26.20
14Nov92 2Aqu1	Cercida	b 2 114	3	3	4²	4¹½	4¹	5²½	54	Davis R G	8.20
21Nov92 8CD2	Mollie Creek	2 112	4	6	5³	5⁶	5³	6	6	Bailey J D	3.70

OFF AT 3:44 Start good. Won driving. Time, :24¹, :48², 1:13¹, 1:40 , 1:47² Track fast.

$2 Mutuel Prices:

5-(E)-TRUE AFFAIR	8.60	3.60	3.40
2-(B)-BROAD GAINS		5.80	3.40
1-(A)-TOUCH OF LOVE			2.60

$2 EXACTA 5-2 PAID $49.60

Dk. b. or br. f, (Feb), by Believe It—A Foreign Relation, by Damascus. Trainer Contessa Gary C. Bred by Hilliard–Lyons Thoroughbred Partner (Ky).

TRUE AFFAIR, rated just behind the early leaders while three wide, drew alongside TOUCH OF LOVE to challenge midway on the turn shook off that one leaving the furlong marker then was all out to hold off BROAD GAINS while tiring in the closing strides. BROAD GAINS, raced well back while trailing to the top of the stretch, launched a rally along the inside leaving the quarter pole then closed steadily through the final eighth but could not get up. TOUCH OF LOVE, never far back, angled between horses along the backstretch, surged to the front gaining a narrow lead on the far turn, battled inside the winner into midstretch then weakened in the final furlong. LADY STARLIT set the pace along the inside for five furlongs and gradually tired thereafter. CERCIDA reserved for six furlongs while saving ground, lacked the needed response when called upon. MOLLIE CREEK was never a factor.

Owners— 1, Winbound Farms; 2, Meyerhoff Robert E; 3, Hofmann Georgia E; 4, Pizzitola Joe F; 5, Alecci John; 6, Hermitage Farm.

Trainers— 1, Contessa Gary C; 2, Small Richard W; 3, Thompson J Willard; 4, Jolley Leroy; 5, Meittinis Louis N; 6, Reinstedler Anthony.

NINTH RACE
Aqueduct
DECEMBER 6, 1992

6 FURLONGS.(InnerDirt). (1.08³) CLAIMING. Purse $13,000. 3-year-olds and upward. Weight, 3-year-olds, 120 lbs. Older, 122 lbs. Non-winners of two races since November 15 allowed 3 lbs. Of a race since then, 5 lbs. Claiming price $14,000, for each $1,000 to $12,000, 2 lbs. (Races when entered to be claimed for $10,000 or less not considered.)

Value of race $13,000; value to winner $7,800; second $2,860; third $1,560; fourth $780. Mutuel pool $221,866. Exacta Pool $333,241 Triple Pool $527,008

Last Raced	Horse	M/Eqt.A.Wt	PP	St	¼	½	Str	Fin	Jockey	Cl'g Pr	Odds $1
3Nov92 1Aqu1	Major Mccallum	b 7 112	11	4	6hd	6¹	2¹½	1¹¾	Bisono C V5	14000	13.60
9Mar92 3Aqu1	Crafty Mana	b 6 117	10	3	4¹½	3hd	1¹	2¹¾	Santagata N	14000	5.90
13Nov92 9Aqu3	Tower Of Treasures	b 5 117	8	7	9¹	9²	5hd	3²½	Smith M E	14000	1.20
26Nov92 2Aqu3	Get the Bags	5 117	7	6	8³½	8¹½	6hd	4¹½	Carle J D	14000	14.90
21Nov92 3Aqu10	Secret Alert	5 117	9	2	5½	5½	4½	5½	Bravo J	14000	17.00
27Nov92 4Aqu7	Bet On Bill	b 4 115	4	10	7¹½	7¹½	3½	6¹¼	Carr D	14000	21.50
14Feb92 7Aqu10	I'm A Pickpocket	b 4 117	2	5	2hd	2hd	7hd	7²½	Mojica R Jr	14000	13.00
23Nov92 7Aqu4	The Real Virginian	7 117	1	1	3¹	1hd	8²	8¹	Velez R I	14000	6.70
19Nov92 1Aqu10	Go Beyond	b 3 106	6	9	10	10	10	9²	Frost G C5	12000	39.90
23Nov92 2Aqu7	Calibeau	4 115	3	8	1½	4¹	9½	10	Santiago A	12000	38.60
26Nov92 9Aqu7	Battenburg	b 3 115	5	11	—	—	—	—	Davis R G	13000	6.60

Battenburg, Lost rider.
OFF AT 4:12 Start good for all but BATTENBURG Won driving Time, :22⁴, :46⁴, :59², 1:12 Track fast.

$2 Mutuel Prices:			
11–(O)–MAJOR MCCALLUM	29.20	11.80	3.80
10–(K)–CRAFTY MANA		7.60	3.60
8–(I)–TOWER OF TREASURES			2.60

$2 EXACTA 11–10 PAID $102.20 $2 TRIPLE 11–10–8 PAID $190.00

✧ Ch. h, by Mehmet—My Dream, by Crowned Prince. Trainer Ribaudo Robert. Bred by Stronach Frank (Ont–C).

MAJOR MCCALLUM reserved for a half, launched a rally from outside on turn, then closed steadily to wear down CRAFTY MANA in final sixteenth. CRAFTY MANA never far back, rallied four wide on the turn, opened a clear lead in upper stretch but couldn't match strides with winner in the late stages. TOWER OF TREASURES far back for a half, rallied belatedly in middle of track to gain a share. GET THE BAGS raced just inside winner into upper stretch and failed to threaten while improving his position with a mild late rally. SECRET ALERT raced in close contention between horses into upper stretch and lacked a strong closing bid. BET ON BILL unhurried for a half, made a run to threaten in midstretch and flattened out. I'M A PICKPOCKET was used up dueling between horses. THE REAL VIRGINIAN battled along the rail to the turn and tired. CALIBEAU dueled from outside for a half and gave way. BATTENBURG stumbled at the start unseating his rider in the process. Following a stewards inquiry into the incident at the start, there was no change in the order of finish.

Owners— 1, Sunshine Hill Farm; 2, Cee Pee R Stable; 3, Joques Farm; 4, Greco Emanuel J; 5, Perazzini Robert J; 6, Stripp William H; 7, Camuti T E; 8, Nevino George L; 9, B W Class T Stable; 10, Paton Kenneth H; 11, Finkelstein Morty.

Trainers— 1, Ribaudo Robert; 2, Imperio Joseph; 3, Moschera Gasper S; 4, Greco Emanuel J; 5, Dutrow Richard E; 6, Terrill William V; 7, Ferriola Peter; 8, Streicher Kenneth; 9, Odintz Jeff; 10, Kosiczky Antonia M; 11, Galluscio Dominic G.

Major Mccallum was claimed by Girdner Paul; trainer, Pollard Damon; Tower Of Treasures was claimed by Swarout Peter; trainer, Bolton Amos E.

Scratched—Always Ashley (21Nov92 3Aqu6); Fast Tony (26Nov92 2Aqu4); Affirmative Act (27Nov92 4Aqu8); Racing Splendor (3Dec92 9Aqu3).

Courtesy of Daily Racing Form ©

In this example the DD paid $94.80. If you would have parlayed, you would have received $131.40, a difference of $36.60. Don't let the track rip you off. If you pick the winners you deserve the true payout. This theory also works with other exotics like the Pick-3.

5th—$20,000, 6f., 3YO & up. Off—2:06. Clmg. ($35,000-$30,000), filles & mares. Winner—b f 4, Northern Prospect-Phyllis Weiss by Big Brave. Owner—Joques Farm. Trainer—G. Moschera.

PP Horse & Weight	St.	¼	½	Str.	Fin.	Eq.
1-Boots (113)	5	5:2	5:1	2:hd	1:6	2.60
2-Sharp Image (115)	1	2:½	2:½	1:1	2:½	4.50
6-All Too Well (117)	6	4:1	3:½	3:2	3:1½	20.40
5-Lovely Josephine (115)	4	6	6	6	4:3¼	•1.60
4-Happy Dapple (117)	2	3:½	4:1	5:½	5:15	3.30
3-Flaming Liberal (115)	3	1:½	1:1½	4:½	6	9.10

Time — :23 4/5, :47, :59 3/5, 1:11 3/5.

1-Boots (Smith)	7.20	3.40	3.00
3-Sharp Image (Velasquez)		5.00	5.20
7-All Too Well (Madrid Jr)			5.20

SCRATCHED: Highway Queen.

EXACTA (1-3) PAID $38.80

6th—$27,000, 6f., 3YO & up. Off—2:30. Allowance. Winner—dk b or br c 3, Clever Trick-Face Nord by Northjet. Owner—C'Est Tout Stable. Trainer—M. Daggett.

PP Horse & Weight	St.	¼	½	Str.	Fin.	Eq.
7-Clever Knave (110)	4	4:½	3:hd	2:hd	1:no	4.80
6-Patience Of Jove (117)	1	2:½	2:½	1:hd	2:1½	11.20
2-Freezing Fun (115)	7	7:1½	6:1	6:1	3:1¾	14.60
1-Admiral's Hagley (117)	6	5:1½	4:½	3:1½	4:¾	3.50
8-Sulaco (115)	2	8	8	7:4	5:2¼	*1.10
5-Safe Deposit Box (120)	5	3:hd	5:2½	5:hd	6:1½	14.50
4-Giant Legend (117)	3	1:½	1:½	4:1	7:5½	17.90
3-Cool As Crystal (117)	8	6:1½	7:hd	8	8	11.10

Time — :24, :47 3/5, :59 3/5, 1:11 4/5.

9-Clever Knave (Bisono)	11.60	5.80	3.80
7-Patience Of Jove (Migliore)		9.00	6.60
2-Freezing Fun (Smith)			5.60

SCRATCHED: Revolt, Swayze Power.

EXACTA (9-7) PAID $121.60

7th—$29,000, 1m. & 70 yds., 2YOs. Off—2:55. Allowance. Winner—ch c 2, Deputy Minister-Find Your Way by Buckfinder. Owner—Loblolly Stable. Trainer—T. Bohannan.

PP Horse & Weight	St.	½	¾	Str.	Fin.	Eq.
2-Gulpha Gorge (119)	3	7:2	4:½	1:3	1:4½	12.80
7-Satellite Signal (117)	6	5:½	3:½	2:hd	2:3	3.90
9-Birdies Fly (117)	9	8:3	8:2	4:½	3:hd	7.80
6-Rohwer (117)	4	2:hd	2:hd	3:1½	4:2½	*.80

4-Mango Man (117)	7	6:hd	7:hd	6:1½	5:5¼	53.90
3-Woodman's Joy (117)	5	4:2	6:½	7:1	6:no	20.70
1-Fighting Daddy (117)	1	1:2	1:1	5:1	7:2	8.40
8-Proficient Cadet (117)	8	9	9	9	8:¾	26.40
5-Atlanta Fan (112)	2	3:1½	5:1½	8:1	9	16.00

Time — :23 4/5, :48 1/5, 1:13 4/5, 1:39 4/5, 1:44 1/5.

2-Gulpha Gorge (Smith)	27.60	6.80	5.00
8-Satellite Signal (Davis)		6.00	4.20
10-Birdies Fly (Romero)			4.60

SCRATCHED: Kahleefa.

EXACTA (2-8) PAID $135.40
PICK THREE (1-9-2) PAID $394.00

Courtesy of Daily Racing Form ©

Boots won the fifth, paying $7.20, Clever Knove the sixth, paying $11.60, and Gulpha Gorge the seventh, paying $27.60. The Pick-3 paid $394.00 while parlaying produced a $634.80 payout. That's a difference of a whopping $240.80. The difference can be a day's winnings in itself.

Mike Mercurio has developed another betting method that has been profitable over the years. Its object is to beat the favorite. 33% of the time the post-time favorite wins and 48% of the remaining 66% of the races is won by the second, third, and fourth choices. Mercurio has developed a system based on betting these second, third, and fourth choices. With a bankroll for each race based on nine, you can put Mercurio's system to work for you. We are going to have a per-race bankroll of $90, but you can adjust it as long as it is a multiple of nine (you can bet $9, $18, $27, etc., per race). With our bankroll of $90 per race we put $40 to win on the second choice, $30 on the third choice, and $20 on the fourth choice. Now let's apply this and see our results for a full racing card.

FIRST RACE
Aqueduct
NOVEMBER 18, 1992

1 ⅛ MILES. (1.47) CLAIMING. Purse $25,000. 3-year-olds and upward. Weights: 3-year-olds, 120 lbs.; Older, 122 lbs. Non-winners of two races at a mile or over since October 15 allowed 3 lbs. Of such a race since then, 5 lbs. Claiming price $50,000; for each $2,500 to $45,000, 2 lbs. (Races when entered to be claimed for $40,000 or less not considered.) (25TH DAY. WEATHER CLOUDY. TEMPERATURE 41 DEGREES.)

Value of race $25,000; value to winner $15,000; second $5,500; third $3,000; fourth $1,500. Mutuel pool $159,358. Exacta Pool $305,489

Last Raced	Horse	M/Eqt.	A.Wt	PP	St	¼	½	¾	Str	Fin	Jockey	Cl'g Pr	Odds $1
7Nov92 ^{1}Aqu^{2}	Captive Tune	b	4 113	3	9	8^{6}	7^{2}	7^{8}	$1\frac{1}{2}$	1no	Smith M E	45000	3.70
5Nov92 ^{9}Aqu^{9}	Stately Wager		4 114	5	4	$3\frac{1}{2}$	$3\frac{1}{2}$	3^{2}	2^{1}	2^{3}	Romero R P	45000	a-3.20
22Oct92 ^{8}Med^{3}	Gini McCown	b	5 113	7	5	6^{2}	6^{1}	6^{hd}	5^{4}	$3\frac{3}{4}$	MrquezCHJr	45000	11.50
13Nov92 ^{1}Aqu^{1}	I'll Take a Stand	b	4 113	1	2	2^{2}	2^{1}	1^{hd}	3^{hd}	$4\frac{1}{2}$	Krone J A	45000	a-3.20
6Nov92 ^{8}Aqu^{2}	Two the Twist	b	5 117	4	3	$1\frac{1}{2}$	$1\frac{1}{2}$	$2\frac{1}{2}$	4^{1}	$5^{8\frac{1}{2}}$	Bailey J D	50000	1.10
23Oct92 ^{2}Aqu^{1}	Avasaurus	b	6 117	2	1	5^{2}	$4\frac{1}{2}$	$4\frac{1}{2}$	$6^{1\frac{1}{2}}$	6^{4}	Santagata N	50000	10.40
8Nov92 ^{1}Aqu^{6}	Desert Prospector		3 112	8	6	4^{1}	5^{3}	5^{hd}	7^{4}	$7^{3\frac{1}{4}}$	Davis R G	45000	11.60
23Oct92 ^{2}Aqu^{2}	Flawless Stone	b	6 113	9	7	$7\frac{1}{2}$	8^{10}	8^{14}	8^{20}	8^{18}	Chavez J F	45000	30.90
1Nov92 ^{2}Aqu^{6}	Pride of Summer		4 117	6	8	9	9	9	9	9	McCuleyWH	50000	34.30

a-Coupled: Stately Wager and I'll Take a Stand.

OFF AT 12:30 Start good Won driving Time, :23^{4}, :47^{4}, 1:12^{3}, 1:37^{4}, 1:50^{3} Track fast.

Official Program Numbers↘

$2 Mutuel Prices:				
	3-(C)-CAPTIVE TUNE	9.40	4.20	3.80
	1-(E)-STATELY WAGER (a-entry)		4.20	2.60
	6-(G)-GINI MCCOWN			3.60

$2 EXACTA 3-1 PAID $39.00

B. g, by Fappiano—Captive Spirit, by Affirmed. Trainer Moschera Gasper S. Bred by North Ridge Farm (Ky).

CAPTIVE TUNE, outrun for a half after being pinched a bit at the start, angeld out on the turn, circled four wide rallying into the stretch, accelerated to the front a furlong out then was all out to hold off STATELY WAGER in the closing strides. STATELY WAGER stalked the leaders while three wide to the top of the stretch then battled gamely inside the winner but could not get up. GINI MCCOWN, split horses while rallying on the turn, lacked room while blocked behind the leaders in upper stretch then rallied belatedly from outside to gain a share. I'LL TAKE A STAND forced the pace between horses for five furlongs, surged to the front leaving the far turn, remained a factor into upper stretch then weakened in the final eighth. TO THE TWIST set the pace under pressure while saving ground to the turn then tired from his early efforts. AVASAURUS, checked slightly at the start, raced within striking distance along the inside to the turn, angled out approaching the stretch then lacked a strong closing response. DESERT PROSPECTOR, settled just behind the leaders while four wide for six furlongs then lacked a strong closing response. FLAWLESS STONE was never a factor. PRIDE OF SUMMER was outrun after breaking a step slowly. TWO THE TWIST wore mud caulks.

Owners— 1, Joques Farm; 2, Scuderi Vincent S; 3, Schibell Richard D; 4, Riccio James; 5, Hauman Eugene E; 6, Sommer Viola; 7, Brophy Stable; 8, Cromor Stable; 9, Dutch Acres Farm.

Trainers— 1, Moschera Gasper S; 2, Ferriola Peter; 3, Forbes John H; 4, Ferriola Peter; 5, Hushion Michael E; 6, Martin Frank; 7, Johnson Philip G; 8, Monaci David; 9, Walsh Thomas M.

Overweight: Stately Wager 1 pound; Desert Prospector 1.

Captive Tune was claimed by Steelbinder Arthur; trainer, Toner James J.

SECOND RACE
Aqueduct
NOVEMBER 18, 1992

6 FURLONGS. (1.08) CLAIMING. Purse $20,000. 3-year-olds and upward. Weights: 3-year-olds, 120 lbs.; Older, 122 lbs. Non-winners of two races since October 15, allowed 3 lbs. Of a race since then, 5 lbs. Claiming price $35,000; for each $2,500 to $30,000, 2 lbs. (Races when entered to be claimed for $25,000 or less not considered.)

Value of race $20,000; value to winner $12,000; second $4,400; third $2,400; fourth $1,200. Mutuel pool $132,306. Exacta Pool $229,838 Quinella Pool $60,814

Last Raced	Horse	M/Eqt.	A.Wt	PP	St	¼	½	Str	Fin	Jockey	Cl'g Pr	Odds $1
8Nov92 ^{8}Pha^{4}	Senor Cielo		5 117	4	1	2^{2}	$1\frac{1}{2}$	$1^{1\frac{1}{2}}$	$1^{3\frac{1}{2}}$	Verge M E	35000	2.40
11Nov92 ^{2}Aqu^{3}	Shine Please	b	7 117	5	4	3^{hd}	$3^{1\frac{1}{2}}$	$2^{1\frac{1}{2}}$	$2^{2\frac{3}{4}}$	Velazquez JR	35000	4.00
5Nov92 ^{9}Aqu^{4}	Top The Record	b	4 115	2	5	5	4^{hd}	$4\frac{1}{2}$	3no	Romero R P	32500	7.70
1Nov92 ^{1}Aqu^{1}	Talc's Bid	b	4 117	1	3	$1\frac{1}{2}$	2^{1}	3^{1}	4^{2}	Davis R G	35000	1.70
16Oct92 ^{3}Med^{4}	Brave Adventure	b	6 117	3	2	4^{2}	5	5	5	Lopez C	35000	3.00

OFF AT 12:55 Start good, Won driving. Time, .22^{3}, .46 , .50 , 1.10^{2} Track fast.

$2 Mutuel Prices:				
	5-(E)-SENOR CIELO	6.80	3.60	2.40
	7-(H)-SHINE PLEASE		4.20	2.80
	3-(C)-TOP THE RECORD			3.60

$2 EXACTA 5-7 PAID $27.80 $2 QUINELLA 5-7 PAID $16.20

Ch. g, by Conquistador Cielo—Love Them All, by Drone. Trainer Lehman Edward. Bred by Forster William J (Ky).

SENOR CIELO, away alertly, forced the early pace from outside, took command on the turn, repulsed a bid from SHINE PLEASE in upper stretch then drew off while being kept to the task. SHINE PLEASE, settled just behind the early leaders, made a run three wide to threaten in upper stretch but was no match for the winner while clearly second best. TOP THE RECORD lodged a mild rally from outside on the turn but couldn't sustain his bid. TALC'S BID dueled along the rail for a half then tired form his early efforts. BRAVE ADVANTURE failed to threaten while saving ground.

Owners— 1, Philamount Stable; 2, Scuderi Vincent S; 3, Heatherwood Farm; 4, Joques Farm; 5, Imbesi Joseph M.

Trainers— 1, Lehman Edward; 2, Ferriola Peter; 3, Schosberg Richard; 4, Moschera Gasper S; 5, Imbesi Joseph M.

Scratched—Crafty A!fel (20Oct92 ^{6}Med^{2}); A Corking Limerick (16Oct92 ^{8}Bel^{5}); Northern Teller (13Nov92 ^{1}Aqu^{6}).

THIRD RACE

Aqueduct

NOVEMBER 18, 1992

1 MILE. (1.32^{2}) MAIDEN SPECIAL WEIGHT. Purse $26,000. Fillies. 2-year-olds. Weight: 117 lbs.

Value of race $26,000; value to winner $15,600; second $5,720; third $3,120; fourth $1,560. Mutuel pool $147,751. Exacta Pool $361,541

Last Raced	Horse	M/Eqt.	A.Wt	PP	St	¼	½	¾	Str	Fin	Jockey	Odds $1
24Oct92 ^{6}Aqu^{4}	Missouri Belle		2 117	7	4	$1^{1\frac{1}{2}}$	1^{1}	$1^{1\frac{1}{2}}$	1^{3}	$1^{\frac{3}{4}}$	Romero R P	b-.70
8Oct92 ^{4}Bel^{5}	Defense Spending		2 117	2	8	5^{1}	3^{hd}	2^{hd}	$2^{1\frac{1}{2}}$	$2^{6\frac{1}{2}}$	Smith M E	3.80
29Oct92 ^{4}Aqu^{2}	Cherub		2 117	5	6	$3^{\frac{1}{2}}$	$2^{\frac{1}{2}}$	3^{1}	3^{4}	3^{3}	Samyn J L	b-.70
	Key to the Peace		2 117	6	10	10	10	8^{hd}	$6^{1\frac{1}{2}}$	$4^{3\frac{1}{4}}$	Bailey J D†	9.50
	Topsi Terpsi		2 117	10	3	8^{4}	8^{3}	$4^{\frac{1}{2}}$	4^{1}	$5^{3\frac{1}{4}}$	Velazquez J R	a-6.90
25Oct92 ^{4}Aqu^{6}	Powdrpuf Princes	b	2 117	8	2	7^{2}	5^{1}	$5^{2\frac{1}{2}}$	$5^{\frac{1}{2}}$	6^{6}	Chavez J F	17.90
2Nov92 ^{4}Aqu^{4}	Adventure On		2 117	3	5	2^{hd}	6^{hd}	7^{1}	7^{2}	7^{4}	Krone J A	a-6.90
14Oct92 ^{7}Med^{3}	Cherokee Twiggy	b	2 117	9	1	$4^{\frac{1}{2}}$	$4^{\frac{1}{2}}$	6^{1}	8^{2}	8^{nk}	Nelson D	23.50
8Nov92 ^{4}Aqu^{9}	Runaway Amour	b	2 117	1	9	9^{3}	$9^{3\frac{1}{2}}$	10	9^{4}	9^{15}	Mojica R Jr	109.40
7Nov92 ^{4}Aqu^{4}	Sovereign Queen		2 117	4	7	$6^{\frac{1}{2}}$	$7^{\frac{1}{2}}$	$9^{\frac{1}{2}}$	10	10	Davis R G	9.90

a-Coupled: Topsi Terpsi and Adventure On; b-Missouri Belle and Cherub.

OFF AT 1:22 Start good, Won driving. Time, :23^{1}, :47^{4}, 1:13^{2}, 1:39^{2} Track fast.

$2 Mutuel Prices:

2-(H)-MISSOURI BELLE (b-entry)	3.40	2.20	2.20
4-(B)-DEFENSE SPENDING		3.40	2.80
2-(E)-CHERUB (b-entry)	3.40	2.20	2.20

$2 EXACTA 2-4 PAID $11.20

Gr. f, (May), by Little Missouri—Twisp, by Dancer's Image. Trainer Arnold George R II. Bred by B. G. Hughes & Forest Retreat Farms (Ky).

MISSOURI BELLE outsprinted rivals for the early advantage, widened her margin in upper stretch then was all out to hold off DEFENSE SPENDING in the closing strides. DEFENSE SPENDING settled just behind the winner to the turn, angled out entering the stretch then closed well late but could not get up. CHERUB raced in close contention between horses to the turn and lacked a strong closing response. KEY TO THE PEACE never reached contention after breaking awkwardly. TOP TERPSI made a run four wide to reach contention on the turn and flattened out. POWDRPUF PRINCES raced within striking distance while four wide for six furlongs and lacked a strong closing response. ADVENTURE ON, up close early while saving ground, was finished after going a half. CHEROKEE TWIGGY showed only brief speed. RUNAWAY AMOUR was never close. SOVEREIGN QUEEN was never a factor.

Owners— 1, Asbury Taylor; 2, Janney Stuart S III; 3, Andrews Edwin C; 4, Rokeby Stable; 5, Hickory Tree Stable; 6, Rudina Stable; 7, Brody Jerome; 8, Buckland Farm; 9, Coppola Albert P; 10, Camp Stable.

Trainers— 1, Arnold George R II; 2, McGaughey Claude III; 3, Arnold George R II; 4, Miller Mack; 5, Mott William I; 6, Meyer Jerome C; 7, Mott William I; 8, Cordero Angel Jr; 9, Wood George A G; 10, Carroll Henry L.

† **Apprentice allowance waived:** Key to the Peace 5 pounds.

Scratched—Saffronella (2Nov92 ^{4}Aqu^{6}).

FOURTH RACE

Aqueduct

NOVEMBER 18, 1992

7 FURLONGS. (1.20^{1}) ALLOWANCE. Purse $27,000. 2-year-olds which have never won a race other than maiden or claiming. Weight: 122 lbs. Non-winners of a race other than claiming since November 1, allowed 3 lbs. Of such a race since October 15, 5 lbs.

Value of race $27,000; value to winner $16,200; second $5,940; third $3,240; fourth $1,620. Mutuel pool $168,641. Exacta Pool $332,068 Quinella Pool $85,490

Last Raced	Horse	M/Eqt.	A.Wt	PP	St	¼	½	Str	Fin	Jockey	Odds $1
17Oct92 ^{11}Crc^{5}	Peace Baby	b	2 117	5	1	1^{3}	1^{1}	1^{2}	1^{3}	Davis R G	2.80
30Oct92 ^{6}Aqu^{1}	Colonial Affair		2 119	4	6	$3^{1\frac{1}{2}}$	$3^{2\frac{1}{2}}$	$2^{1\frac{1}{2}}$	2^{2}	Krone J A	1.20
2Oct92 ^{8}Bel^{10}	Virginia Rapids		2 117	1	7	$5^{\frac{1}{2}}$	4^{2}	$3^{1\frac{1}{2}}$	3^{4}	Lidberg D W	12.80
30Jly92 ^{8}Sar^{5}	Hegar	b	2 117	2	8	8	$7^{\frac{1}{2}}$	7^{4}	$4^{1\frac{3}{4}}$	Smith M E	4.80
30Oct92 ^{7}Med^{2}	Coming Fast		2 117	3	5	$4^{2\frac{1}{2}}$	6^{2}	$6^{1\frac{1}{2}}$	5no	Marquez C H Jr	10.40
1Nov92 ^{9}Aqu^{11}	I'm A Big Shot		2 117	8	3	$6^{\frac{1}{2}}$	5^{3}	5^{1}	$6^{2\frac{1}{2}}$	Migliore R	22.30
1Nov92 ^{9}Aqu^{1}	Yeckley	b	2 117	6	4	$2^{\frac{1}{2}}$	2^{hd}	4^{1}	$7^{8\frac{1}{2}}$	Romero R P	8.10
7Nov92 ^{9}Aqu^{1}	Steffie's Pride		2 117	7	2	7^{2}	8	8	8	Meszaros G	37.80

OFF AT 1:50 Start good, for all but HEGAR, Won driving. Time, :22⁴, :45⁴, 1:10⁴, 1:24¹ Track fast.

$2 Mutuel Prices:

5-(E)-PEACE BABY	7.60	3.80	3.60
4-(D)-COLONIAL AFFAIR		2.80	2.60
1-(A)-VIRGINIA RAPIDS			5.20

$2 EXACTA 5-4 PAID $26.40 $2 QUINELLA 4-5 PAID $12.20

Dk. b. or br. c, (Apr), by Hold Your Peace—Cautivante, by Hostage. Trainer Schwartz Scott M. Bred by Equi Frank R (Fla).

PEACE BABY sprinted clear along hte backstretch, was rated on the lead while saving ground into the stretch then edged away under intermittent urging. COLONIAL AFFAIR settled just behind the winner while saving ground to the turn then outfinished VIRGINIA RAPIDS for the place. VIRGINIA RAPID, bumped at the start, was unhurried along the backstretch, angled out on the turn, made a run to threaten at the top of the stretch but couldn't sustain his bid. HEGAR, slipped heels and stumbled while being bumped at the start, then failed to threaten with a late run from outside. COMING FAST, broke inward causing crowing at the start, was never a factor. I'M A BIG SHOT was never a serious threat. YECKLEY stalked the pace while just outside COLONIAL AFFAIR to the top of the stretch then gave way. STEFFIE'S PRIDE was outrun.

Owners— 1, Schwartz Arlene; 2, Centennial Farms; 3, Middletown Stables; 4, Junot James R; 5, Parent Arthur F; 6, Goslow Stable; 7, Zellen Larry; 8, Phipps Stephanie.

Trainers— 1, Schwartz Scott M; 2, Schulhofer Flint S; 3, Jerkens H Allen; 4, Lewis Lisa L; 5, Carlesimo Charles Jr; 6, Hertler John O; 7, Goldberg Alan E; 8, Kopaj Paul.

FIFTH RACE

Aqueduct

NOVEMBER 18, 1992

6 ½ FURLONGS. (1.15) ALLOWANCE. Purse $28,000. 3-year-olds and upward which have never won two races other than Maiden, Claiming or Starter. Weight: 3-year-olds 120 lbs. Older 122 lbs. Non-winners of a race other than Maiden or Claiming since November 1 allowed 3 lbs. Of such a race since October 15, 5 lbs.

Value of race $28,000; value to winner $16,800; second $6,160; third $3,360; fourth $1,680. Mutuel pool $172,403. Exacta Pool $348,582.

Last Raced	Horse	M/Eqt.A.Wt	PP St	¼	½	Str	Fin	Jockey	Odds $1
8Nov92 1Aqu²	Permit	3 115	6 1	3¹½	2¹½	2²½	1¹	Romero R P	6.40
2Nov92 5Aqu¹	Rockford	b 3 115	4 6	1½	1½	1hd	2¹³	Davis R G	4.30
6Nov92 1Aqu⁴	Real Cielo	3 115	7 3	5½	4¹	3¹	3¾	Bailey J D	2.70
23Oct92 8Aqu⁸	Crafty Coventry	3 115	3 4	7	6½	4¹	4¹¹½	Migliore R	5.00
8Nov92 7Aqu⁴	Hope Us	4 117	1 5	6½	7	5hd	5²½	Madrid A Jr	1.60
6Nov92 2Aqu¹	Midnight Sunny	b 4 117	5 2	4½	5½	66	6¹⁵	Corpes M A	26.80
19Aug92 9Sar¹⁰	Uncas Chief	b 3 115	2 7	2¹	3½	7	7	Smith M E	22.20

OFF AT 2:17 Start good for all but UNCAS CHIEF and ROCKFORD, Won driving. Time, :23⁴, :47¹, 1:11³, 1:18¹ Track fast.

$2 Mutuel Prices:

6-(F)-PERMIT	14.80	7.40	4.20
4-(D)-ROCKFORD		6.00	3.80
7-(G)-REAL CIELO			2.80

$2 EXACTA 6-4 PAID $67.80

B. c, (Apr), by Imperial Fling—Logiealmond, by Master Derby. Trainer Galluscio Dominic G. Bred by Shields Joseph V Jr (Fla).

PERMIT, well place early, made a run three wide to challenge on the turn, battled outside ROCKFORD into midstretch then edged clear under brisk urging. ROCKFORD, infractious in the gate prior to the start, broke slowly then stumbled leaving the gate, checked slightly between horses then rushed up to duel for the early advantage; shook off UNCAS CHIEF on the turn, battled gamely inside the winner through the lane then yielded grudgingly. REAL CIELO, reserved early, lodged a mild rally from outside on the turn but couldn't gain on the top two through the lane. CRAFTY COVENTRY, outrun for a half, failed to threaten with a mild late rally from outside. HOPE US saved ground to no avail. MIDNIGHT SUNNY was never a factor. UNCAS CHIEF rushed up along the rail after breaking slowly, dueled along the inside to the turn then gave way. UNCAS CHIEF wore two bar shoes. MIDNIGHT SUNNY raced with an aluminum pad on.

Owners— 1, Shields Joseph V Jr; 2, Kimram Stable; 3, Stephens Lucille E; 4, Edwards James F; 5, Jewel-E Stable; 6, Fabjac Stables; 7, Prew Brian M.

Trainers— 1, Galluscio Dominic G; 2, Toner James J; 3, Stephens Woodford C; 4, Lundy Sarah A; 5, Ferriola Peter; 6, Marti Carlos; 7, Reid Mark J.

SIXTH RACE

Aqueduct

NOVEMBER 18, 1992

7 FURLONGS. (1.20¹) ALLOWANCE. Purse $27,000. 2-year-olds which have never won a race other than maiden or claiming. Weight: 122 lbs. Non-winners of a race other than claiming since November 1, allowed 3 lbs. Of such a race since October 15, 5 lbs.

Value of race $27,000; value to winner $16,200; second $5,940; third $3,240; fourth $1,620. Mutuel pool $196,846. Exacta Pool $433,600.

Last Raced	Horse	M/Eqt.A.Wt	PP St	1/4	1/2	Str	Fin	Jockey	Odds $1
26Oct92 5Aqu1	Apprentice	2 119	4 4	5$\frac{1}{2}$	6hd	2$1\frac{1}{2}$	1no	Perret C	.80
28Oct92 6Aqu3	Slew's Gold	b 2 117	2 5	1$\frac{1}{2}$	11	11	23	Smith M E	6.30
22Oct92 3Aqu1	Itaka	2 119	3 9	61	7$1\frac{1}{2}$	5$1\frac{1}{2}$	3$\frac{1}{2}$	Davis R G	15.70
24Oct92 1Aqu4	Not For Love	2 117	7 6	9	5hd	3$\frac{1}{2}$	4$3\frac{1}{2}$	Bailey J D	8.20
15Oct92 6Bel1	Easy Spender	b 2 117	9 1	31	2$\frac{1}{2}$	4$1\frac{1}{2}$	54	Krone J A	3.90
28Oct92 6Aqu4	Birdie's Fly	2 117	1 8	7$\frac{1}{2}$	8$3\frac{1}{2}$	6$\frac{1}{2}$	62	Romero R P	12.00
24Oct92 1Aqu6	Khaleefa	2 117	5 3	4hd	3$1\frac{1}{2}$	712	710$\frac{1}{4}$	Chavez J F	61.20
24Apr92 3Crc1	Ingot's Medic Man	2 117	8 2	21	4hd	9	82$\frac{3}{4}$	Ferrer J C	19.10
8Nov92 9FL1	Military Friday	2 122	6 7	8hd	9	81	9	Rincon R	99.60

OFF AT 2:44 Start good, for all but EASY SPENDER, Won driving. Time, :23 , :463, 1:114, 1:243 Track fast.

$2 Mutuel Prices:

4-(D)-APPRENTICE		3.60	3.00	2.40
2-(B)-SLEW'S GOLD			4.40	3.80
3-(C)-ITAKA				6.40

$2 EXACTA 4-2 PAID $22.40

Ch. c, (Mar), by Forty Niner—Young Ballerina, by Nijinsky II. Trainer Badgett William Jr. Bred by Whitney Mrs John Hay (Ky).

APPRENTICE, rated just behind the leaders while between horses for a half, launched a rally from outside on the turn then closed steadily to wear down SLEWS GOLD in the final strides. SLEWS GOLD rushed up along the inside dueled inside I'GOT'S MEDIC MAN to the far turn, opened a clear lead on the turn, continued on the fron tinto deep stretch and just failed to last. ITAKA raced just inside the winner while saving ground to the turn then rallied belatedly to gain a share. NOT FOR LOVE, outrun early, steadily gained while five wide to reach contention on the turn butr couldn't sustain his bid. EASY SPENDER stumbled at the start, stalked the pace from outside to the top of the stretch then lacked a furhter response. BIRDIE'S FLY failed to threaten while saving ground. KHALEEFA raced in close contention while four wide to the turn then faded. INGOT'S MEDIC MAN was used up forcing the early pace. MILTARY FRIDAY checked at the start and was never close thereafter.

Owners— 1, Greentree Stable; 2, Campbell Gilbert G; 3, Brophy Stable; 4, Ogden Mills Phipps; 5, Bonita Vista Stable; 6, Cohen Robert B; 7, Hassan Shoaib; 8, Carroll Donald j; 9, Waters Loretta.

Trainers— 1, Badgett William Jr; 2, Allard Edward T; 3, Johnson Philip G; 4, McGaughey Claude III; 5, Mott William I; 6, Shapoff Stanley R; 7, Carroll Del W II; 8, Serpe Philip M; 9, Margaret Annette.

Corrected weight: Military Friday 122 pounds.

SEVENTH RACE

Aqueduct

NOVEMBER 18, 1992

6 FURLONGS. (1.08) ALLOWANCE. Purse $27,000. 3-year-olds and upward which have never won a race other than maiden, claiming or starter. Weights: 3-year-olds, 120 lbs.; Older, 122 lbs. Non-winners of a race other than claiming since November 1, allowed 3 lbs. Of such a race since October 15, 5 lbs.

Value of race $27,000; value to winner $16,200; second $5,940; third $3,240; fourth $1,620. Mutuel pool $173,894. Exacta Pool $428,117.

Last Raced	Horse	M/Eqt.A.Wt	PP St	1/4	1/2	Str	Fin	Jockey	Odds $1
2Nov92 5Aqu3	Ocean Splash	b 3 115	9 6	4$\frac{1}{2}$	41	11$\frac{1}{2}$	12$\frac{1}{2}$	Madrid A Jr	7.00
2May92 8CD17	Snappy Landing	3 115	2 9	9	8$\frac{1}{2}$	4hd	2$\frac{1}{2}$	Davis R G	1.30
2Nov92 5Aqu5	Clever Knave	3 110	3 8	5$\frac{1}{2}$	52$\frac{1}{2}$	2hd	32$\frac{1}{4}$	Bisono C V5	9.40
8Nov92 2Aqu3	Mashriq	b 3 115	1 4	71	6$\frac{1}{2}$	5$\frac{1}{2}$	42	Migliore R	17.40
6Nov92 7Aqu5	Porgy	b 4 117	7 7	8$\frac{1}{2}$	9	81	51$\frac{1}{2}$	Smith M E	16.20
19Jun92 6Bel2	Admirals Hagley	b 4 117	8 3	33$\frac{1}{2}$	1hd	31$\frac{1}{2}$	63$\frac{1}{4}$	Nelson D	3.10
26Oct92 7Aqu4	Sailing On Aprayer	b 3 115	5 5	62	7$\frac{1}{2}$	9	7nk	McCauley W H	7.20
9Oct92 1Bel5	News Editor	3 115	4 1	1hd	3$\frac{1}{2}$	7$\frac{1}{2}$	8nk	Krone J A	37.90
3Nov92 1Aqu2	Patience of Jove	4 117	6 2	2hd	2hd	6$\frac{1}{2}$	9	Santagata N	16.10

OFF AT 3:11 Start good for all but SNAPPY LANDING, Won driving. Time, :223, :46 , :581, 1:103 Track fast.

$2 Mutuel Prices:

9-(I)-OCEAN SPLASH		16.00	5.40	3.20
2-(B)-SNAPPY LANDING			3.20	2.80
3-(C)-CLEVER KNAVE				6.80

$2 EXACTA 9-2 PAID $39.40

Dk. b. or br. c, (May), by Clever Trick—Rain Gauge, by Sauce Boat. Trainer Bond Harold James. Bred by Farish W S (Ky).

OCEAN SPLASH, settled in good position for three furlongs, circled four wide while rapidly gaining on the turn, accelerated to the front in upper stretch then drew off under pressure. SNAPPY LANDING, hit the side of the gate while breaking a step slowly, trailed to the turn, launched a bid four wide while between horses entering the stretch, closed a lengthy gap in midstretch then outfinished CLEVER KNAVE for the place. CLEVER KNAVE, reserved for a half while saving ground, made a run to threaten in midstretch then weakened in the final eighth. MASHRIQ failed to seriously threaten while improving his position a bit through the stretch. PORGY was never a factor while racing wide. ADMIRALS HAGLEY dueled for the lead while three wide to the turn, held a narrow lead advancing into the stretch then tired from his early efforts. SAILING ON APRAYER was never a factor. NEWS EDITOR and PATIENCE OF JOVE were used up dueling for the early lead.

Owners— 1, Rudlein Stable; 2, McNeary Frederick J; 3, C'Est Tout Stable; 4, Davis Barbara J; 5, Paulson Mrs Allen E; 6, Dabru Stables; 7, Bauld James R; 8, Marsh Hazel B; 9, Sommer Viola.

Trainers— 1, Bond Harold James; 2, Manning Dennis J; 3, Daggett Michael H; 4, Moschera Gasper S; 5, Mott William I; 6, Lenzini John J Jr; 7, Klesaris Robert P; 8, Forbes John H; 9, Martin Frank.

EIGHTH RACE
Aqueduct
NOVEMBER 18, 1992

1 1/16 MILES.(Turf). (1.41) ALLOWANCE. Purse $33,000. 3–year–olds and upward which have never won three races other than maiden, claiming or starter. Weights: 3–year–olds, 120 lbs. Older, 122 lbs. Non–winners of two races other than maiden, claiming or starter. Weights 3–year–olds, 120 lbs.; Older, 122 lbs. Non–winners of two races other than maiden or claiming at a mile or over since October 15, allowed 3 lbs. Of such a race since then, 5 lbs.

Value of race $33,000; value to winner $19,800; second $7,260; third $3,960; fourth $1,980. Mutuel pool $119,800. Exacta Pool $296,227

Last Raced	Horse	M/Eqt.	A.	Wt	PP	St	¼	½	¾	Str	Fin	Jockey	Odds $1
9Nov92 8Aqu6	Epaulet	b	3	117	4	4	6 1½	6 2	3 ½	3 1½	1 no	Castaneda K	5.20
11Nov92 8Aqu5	Ebony Magic		5	117	7	5	1 1½	1 ½	1 1	1 1½	2 ¾	Smith M E	1.40
5Nov92 9Med1	Cee Cee Romer		3	117	1	2	3 ½	3 2	4 2	2 hd	3 nk	Thomas D B	13.70
24Oct92 3Med2	Amberfax	b	4	117	6	7	4 ½	4 ½	5 3	5 6	4 5¼	Jocson G J	15.20
15Oct92 9Med1	Koorachee		4	117	3	1	2 2½	2 5	2 1½	4 hd	5 7½	Migliore R	2.70
18Oct92 5Bel5	Lugh	b	3	115	2	3	7	7	7	7	6 nk	Krone J A	3.80
10Oct92 6Lrl8	Tammany		4	117	5	6	5 1½	5 1	6 1	6 1	7	McCauley W H	35.50

OFF AT 3:40 Start good, Won driving. Time, :24 , :491, 1:141, 1:40 , 1:464 Course yielding.

$2 Mutuel Prices:

5–(D)–EPAULET	12.40	4.20	2.80
1–(G)–EBONY MAGIC		2.40	2.20
2–(A)–CEE CEE ROMER			3.80

$2 EXACTA 5–1 PAID $37.80

B. c, (Apr), by Robellino—Hardly Regal, by Majestic Prince. Trainer Scanlan John F. Bred by Strawbridge George Jr (Pa).

EPAULET, unhurried early worked his way forward along the inside on the backstretch, checked briefly on the turn, slipped through along the rail entering the stretch, split horses while rallying in midstretch then nipped EBONY MAGIC in the final strides. EBONY MAGIC sprinted clear in the early stages, set the pace along the inside into the stretch, continued on the front into deep stretch and just failed to last. CEE CEE ROAMER, well placed for five furlongs, made a strong run from outside to threaten in midstretch but couldn't sustain his bid. AMBERFAX reserved for five furlongs, lagged behind on the far turn, then failed to threaten with a mild late rally from outside KOORACHEE prompted the early pace from outside made a run outside EBONY MAGIC to threaten on the far turn then gradually tired thereafter. LUGH never reached contention. TAMMANY, checked between horses on the first turn, was never a factor.

Owners— 1, Fritzpatrick Deborah; 2, Joques Farm; 3, Generazio Patricia; 4, Ardboe Stable; 5, Stonewall Farm; 6, Royal Lines Stable; 7, Robinson J Mack.

Trainers— 1, Scanlan John F; 2, Moschera Gasper S; 3, Generazio Frank Jr; 4, McCarthy William E; 5, Hushion Michael E; 6, Hough Stanley M; 7, Frommer Timothy G.

Scratched—Commissioner Bart (7Nov92 1Aqu3); King's Gent (31Oct92 14Med5); Best Offer (1Nov92 2Aqu3); Pro Serve (18Oct92 5Bel3); Pick Up the Phone (1Nov92 7Aqu7); Applebred (11Nov92 8Aqu4); Traffic Zack (4Oct92 8Pha7); Corrupt Council (8Nov92 1Aqu4).

NINTH RACE
Aqueduct
NOVEMBER 18, 1992

6 FURLONGS. (1.08) MAIDEN CLAIMING. Purse $12,000. 2–year–olds. Weight: 118 lbs. Claiming price $35,000 for each $2,500 to $30,000, 2 lbs.

Value of race $12,000; value to winner $7,200; second $2,640; third $1,440; fourth $720. Mutuel pool $163,008. Exacta Pool $252,075 Trifecta Pool $429,573

Last Raced	Horse	M/Eqt.	A.	Wt	PP	St	¼	½	Str	Fin	Jockey	Cl'g Pr	Odds $1
22Oct92 3Aqu7	Carrnac	b	2	104	1	2	2 ½	2 1	1 hd	1 nk	Grana P10	30000	44.10
22Oct92 5Aqu6	Joe Hartwick	b	2	114	7	1	1 ½	1 hd	2 1½	2 4	Madrid A Jr	30000	9.20
30Oct92 1Med2	Everything's Fine	b	2	118	2	11	3 1	3 2	3 1½	3 1½	Thomas D B	35000	2.20
30Sep92 4Bel7	Eastern Tune	b	2	108	3	3	4 ½	4 ½	4 1	4 ¾	RodriguzRR7	35000	24.60
3Nov92 4Aqu4	Donnacha		2	118	10	7	8 1½	7 ½	7 2½	5 ¾	Bailey J D	35000	2.50
9Nov92 3Aqu6	Pebble Hill	b	2	118	8	5	6 2½	6 1½	5 hd	6 ¾	Santagata N	35000	4.60
1Nov92 4Aqu	Stevie O	b	2	113	9	9	7 ½	8 2	6 ½	7 3	Bisono C V5	35000	39.60
25Oct92 6Aqu11	Enrico Roberto	b	2	118	11	4	5 1½	5 1½	8 1½	8 ½	Montoya R	35000	17.30
	Whisk		2	118	12	8	11 8	11 2	9 1	9 3½	Carr D	35000	6.50
1Nov92 4Aqu11	Shawkonair		2	114	6	6	9 1½	10 1½	10 ½	10 nk	LaboccettFJr	30000	85.50
	Your Lucky Day	b	2	109	4	12	10 hd	9 hd	11 2½	11 3	Frost G C5	30000	25.30
26Aug92 4Sar8	Billy Hunter		2	110	5	10	12	12	12	12	Rosario H D7	30000	56.80

OFF AT 4:06 Start good Won driving Time, :224, :47 , :594, 1:131 Track fast.

$2 Mutuel Prices:

1–(B)–CARRNAC	90.20	55.00	21.60
7–(I)–JOE HARTWICK		8.80	5.80
2–(C)–EVERYTHING'S FINE			3.60

$2 EXACTA 1–7 PAID $1,256.40 $2 TRIFECTA 1–7–2 PAID $4,661.00

B. c, (Apr), by Carr de Naskra—Empire Beauty, by On to Glory. Trainer Kelly Tim D. Bred by BOTO Thoroughbreds Inc (NY).

CARRNAC, angled between horses along the backstretch, forced the pace from outside into the stretch, surged to the front in midstretch then outgamed JOE HARTWICK in a long drive. JOE HARTWICK set the pace along the inside into the stretch then yielded grudgingly. EVERYTHING'S FINE raced in close contention from outside to the stretch and lacked a strong closing bid. EASTERN TUNE raced within striking distance while four wide to the turn and lacked the needed response when called upon. DONNACHA was never a serious threat. PEBBLE HILL went evenly. STEVIE O was never a factor. ENRICO ROBERTO raced wide and tired. WHISK was never close. SHAW-KONAIR was outrun.

Owners— 1, Boto Stable; 2, Jay Cee Jay Stable; 3, Tromby Wayne; 4, Konrad Diana U; 5, Dee John T; 6, Engel Karen K & Richard L; 7, Pascuma Michael J; 8, Perez Robert; 9, Celano Joseph-Martorana Anthony; 10, Anchel Michael; 11, Pond View Stable; 12, McMahon Jay S.

Trainers— 1, Kelly Tim D; 2, DeStefano John M Jr; 3, Dandy Ronald J; 4, Groeschel Arthur; 5, Nash Rita; 6, O'Connell Richard; 7, Pascuma Warren J; 8, Callejas Alfredo; 9, Terrill William V; 10, LaBoccetta Frank; 11, Picone George S; 12, Armstrong Horace W.

Overweight: Billy Hunter 3 pounds.

Scratched—Squirrel Away (5Nov92 5Aqu4); Puma Express (1Nov92 6Aqu9); Bull Mountain (7Nov92 9Aqu8); Best Selection; Customer Account (1Nov92 4Aqu10); Runaway Rocky (21Oct92 5Aqu11); Stoney Que; Gemwood (7Nov92 9Aqu7).

1st Race—The third choice won with a $30 win bet producing a $51.00 profit for that race.

2nd Race—Senior Cielo, the second choice won returning a $46.00 profit.

3rd Race—The favorite won, minus $90.00.

4th Race—The second choice, Peace Baby won by three lengths returning $7.60 and a $62.00 profit.

5th Race—This race was won by Permit and a $58.00 profit was the return.

6th Race—The favorite won, minus $90.00.

7th Race—The third choice was victorious and a $150.00 profit.

8th Race—This turf event returned a profit of $34.00.

9th Race—This race was won by a longshot and that means minus $90.00.

For the day, using Mike Mercurio's system, you would have made a $131.00 profit, not bad for doing no handicapping! Watch this system over a period of time. It will have losing days but the odds are in your favor.

The Wave of the Future is Here Now: Video Replay

CHAPTER 8

Video replay is the way to handicap in the 1990s. By looking at past races we can see many things that are not printed in the Daily Racing Form.

First, we have to wager at a track that offers video retrieval. If the track where you are wagering does not offer this you will have to compile a series of video tapes yourself. You can do this if you have cable television. Most systems have a channel were the previous night's races are shown.

While viewing these previous races, we must make an analysis of each horse's performance. It is important to understand that we do not just look at the winner or the in-the-money finishers. We analyze everyone, applying all of the techniques and angles discussed throughout this book.

One of the most important and often overlooked angles is whether a horse can win if it moves up or down in class. This happens mostly with winners in their next start. Many times the winner of a particular race cannot bounce back and win again. Yet, sometimes that horse steps up and wins against better. How can we predict this? The best way is by video replay. When analyzing the winner of a previous race the main thing to measure is how easily this horse won. Horses that don't bounce back to win usually had everything go their way or had a perfect trip in their last victory. If this occurs, the horse will need all the breaks to repeat. On the other hand, if a particular horse wins impressively, he could consistently compete at that level and may be good enough to move up.

Severe wind conditions favor speed horses or horses that come off the pace. On one mile tracks, winds that blow left to right will favor come-from-behind horses in sprints and routes. Speed is usually nullified and not effective in these conditions. When the wind is blowing with the horses right to left, speed will dominate in sprints and will usually be effective in routes though it is more likely that a horse that stays close to the pace will have an advantage. This angle can only be detected by video replay and can be most effective.

So let's say the wind conditions were blowing left to right and a speed horse led all the way in a sprint and was nailed at the wire in good time. This horse will win the next time it runs in more favorable conditions. In this race the speed horse had to fight the wind the whole six furlongs. With better conditions, he would have an easier time coming home.

On some days it seems that whatever horse gets out in front wins and on some days just the opposite. When reviewing past results on video replay, check the wind conditions occurring on that day and determine if the winning horse was aided by these conditions. Many times when I am at the racetrack I see fellow handicappers using video replay and they only watch the race that the horse they are handicapping is in. This is foolish. Watching more than one race from that day will alert you to any role the wind is playing. Then, when those fellow handicappers wonder why their horse went wire to wire in his previous start and tired in this one, you can tell them why.

The start is the most important part of any race. A bad start can eliminate a horse *immediately*. Also, a bad start by a horse is sometimes over looked by the Daily Racing Form. A handicapper had no way of knowing about a bad start until video replay. A particular horse might need to get the lead to have any chance. If such a horse gets a bad start its race is over. On paper it would appear that he did not even try. Also, jockeys often will not push a horse after a bad start. Video replay will help you detect this.

Trust yourself. It is important to consider how a horse did compared to how you thought he should do. Figure out how and why a horse ran the way he did in his previous start. Perhaps the horse did not run his race and deserves another chance. Do this for each horse, and through video replay see if he had an opportunity to win with a few good breaks on the rail.

OTHER HANDICAPPING
BOOKS FROM BONUS

- ## Overlay, Overlay: How to Bet Horses Like a Pro
  Bill Heller
  Leading trainers and jockeys share hard-hitting, savvy insights that take the edge from the track and give it to the bettor
  Paper, 228 pages, $9.95, ISBN 0-933893-86-8

- ## Harness Overlays: Beat the Favorite
  Bill Heller
  Learn how to handicap for more winners and more fun with this comprehensive plan, based on an innovative analysis of more than 11,000 races at tracks across the country
  Paper, 160 pages, $12.00, ISBN 0-929387-97-X

- ## Woulda, Coulda, Shoulda
  Dave Feldman with Frank Sugano
  Wagering tips in abundance from a columnist who's a racing legend in his own right, in a book *Thoroughbred Times* calls "such delightful reading that it might just be the best introduction to horse racing ever written"
  Paper, 281 pages, $9.95, ISBN 0-933893-02-3

160 East Illinois Street
Chicago, IL 60611
(800) 225-3775